SCHOOL'S OUT

SCHOOL'S OUT

LEWIS J. PERELMAN

AVON BOOKS ◆ NEW YORK

AVON BOOKS
A division of
The Hearst Corporation
1350 Avenue of the Americas
New York, New York 10019

Published in hardcover by William Morrow and Company, Inc.; for information address Permissions Department, William Morrow and Company, Inc., 1350 Avenue of the Americas, New York, New York 10019.

The William Morrow and Company edition contains the following Library of Congress Cataloging in Publication Data:
Perelman, Lewis J.
  School's out: hyperlearning, the new technology, and the end of education/by Lewis J. Perelman.
  p. cm.
Includes bibliographical references and index.
1. Educational technology–United States. 2. Educational change–United States.
I. Title
LB1028.3.P393 1992   92-11361
371.3'078–dc20   CIP

First Avon Books Trade Printing: October 1993

To the memory of Dmitri Komar, Ilya Krichevsky, Vladimir Usov

PREFACE

• • •

This book is not about education. It is about an economic transformation that is being driven by an implacable technological revolution. It is not about saving schools, or improving schools, or reforming schools, or even reinventing schools—it's about removing altogether the increasingly costly barrier schooling poses to economic and social progress.

This book is not written for educators or academicians. Rather, it speaks to the interests of businesspeople, entrepreneurs, investors, workers, political leaders, consumer advocates, scientists, engineers, parents, learners of all ages, and most especially taxpayers—the consumers who pay the bills for services and products that are supposed to nurture learning. And while my own knowledge and experience necessarily give this book a U.S. focus, the trends and issues it describes are global, affecting all other nations, perhaps in different ways, but with no less profound impact.

While the actual writing of this book began in the spring of 1991, the work that went into its creation stretches back over more than twenty years. If there was a starting point for this effort, it probably was sometime during 1968–69 when I was working as a high school physics teacher in my hometown of Mount Vernon, New York. My struggle during that year to serve the needs of young learners while in continual combat with the mind-killing mandates of a corrupt education bureaucracy galvanized my disdain for the academic establishment much as similar experiences did for other apostate teachers and writers such as John Holt, Jonathan Kozol, and Pat Conroy.

Unlike others who channeled their disaffection into calls for "reform," by 1970 I was convinced that the education system could not be amended but needed to be entirely replaced by a new mechanism more attuned to the technology and social fabric of the modern world. This conclusion was nurtured by many sources, but especially influential were the works of B. F. Skinner, George Leonard, and Jay Forrester.

The work of Skinner and his disciples showed that the processes of learning could be analyzed, understood, and organized to serve the *individual* learner's needs in a way that made boredom, frustration, humiliation, and failure unnecessary.

In his 1968 book, *Education and Ecstasy,* Leonard portrayed a vision of high-tech learning that bore no resemblance to traditional schooling. But neither then nor since have Leonard or most other utopian "reinventors" of education understood the basic economic and political forces needed to translate their dreams into reality.

In his 1960s work on industrial dynamics and urban dynamics, as well as later work in the field of "system dynamics" he helped create, Jay Forrester showed that even modestly complex social systems strongly tend to behave in ways he called "counterintuitive," that is, contrary to what common sense presumes is obvious. One result is that most attempts to reform the behavior of social systems turn out to be either impotent or "counterproductive," making worse what they aimed to make better. Thus we have seen welfare programs that have shattered families and inflamed poverty, real estate subsidies that spawned financial collapse, post-Watergate political reforms that have made political corruption epidemic. And nearly half a century of American education reform has yielded an academic establishment as greedily entrenched as ever, but whose obsolescence and sheer irrelevancy have soared along with its skyrocketing cost.

Inspired by such ideas, I returned to Harvard in 1970 and spent the next three years in an intense and largely independent study of most of the key questions that underlie this book: What is learning and how does it work? What technologies can facilitate learning, and how do they work? How does learning fit in with the overall processes of human economy and ecology? And most important, how do you transform or replace established human institutions? Of the several Harvard and MIT faculty who contributed to my exploration of these questions, I particularly benefited from the aid and encouragement of Wassily Leontief, Harvey Liebenstein, Jay Forrester, Ithiel de Sola Pool, B. F. Skinner, and Paul Ylvisaker. After leaving Harvard, I continued my research for another year with the support of a grant from the Rockefeller Brothers Fund and presented the results of the whole five years of study in my first book, *The Global Mind,* published in 1976.

At that point, I decided to stop just thinking and writing about change and to immerse myself in working on it in the real world. A series of subsequent vocational experiences enriched my practical understanding and seasoned my earlier theoretical thinking in ways that profoundly affected the vision and tone of this book.

Over the next several years, positions at the Colorado Highway Department, at the Solar Energy Research Institute, and then at Caltech's Jet Propulsion Laboratory put me into the front lines of work on the most urgent problem of the day: the energy crisis. Among many things, I learned from firsthand experience how dauntingly complex is the task of reinventing and replacing a major chunk of society's technological infrastructure.

Besides acquiring an augmented appreciation for the potency of capitalism and the wisdom of market forces, I gained especially invaluable insights during the period of my involvement in energy and environmental issues from observing at close hand the work of Amory Lovins, one of the most effective change agents I have known. Within the span of a decade or so, Lovins transformed the energy industry's perception of "conservation" from an image of sacrifice and austerity to a pragmatic vision of efficiency and profit. In crafting this book, I have been inspired by Lovins's strategy.

Having wrestled with problems of innovation from the macroeconomic viewpoint, I welcomed the opportunity in 1981 to direct some strategic-planning activities for Holiday Inns, Inc., one of America's biggest service corporations. The continual concern in this book for the challenges and responsibilities of commercial enterprises are derived in important measure from the myriad lessons I learned in Memphis—especially, how utterly crucial is the link between profit and innovation.

ACKNOWLEDGMENTS

Since my move to Washington in 1983, the people and organizations involved in several key projects on which I worked as a consultant and writer laid the foundation for much of the work that ultimately became incorporated in this book. I am indebted for the material and intellectual support I derived from these projects to Jim Souby, Gloria Whitman, and Bert

Wakeley, all formerly of the Council of State Planning Agencies; Jim Mecklenberger, former director of the Institute for the Transfer of Technology to Education at the National School Boards Association; Jim Dezell, general manager of IBM's educational systems division; Paul Cunningham, former director, and Jo Clark of the Western Governors' Association and Bart Alexander, former director of Jobs for Colorado's Future; Beverly Hunter, consultant, and Beverly Sangston, director of computer-related instruction at Montgomery County (Md.) Public Schools; Jack Bowsher, former director of education external programs at IBM; and Bob Martin and Jeff Joseph of the U.S. Chamber of Commerce.

I am particularly grateful to Sue Berryman, director of the Institute for Education and Employment at Columbia University, for allowing me to draw extensively (in Chapter 7) on work she contributed to a report we recently co-authored for the U.S. Department of Labor. That project, managed by Jim Van Erden and Irene Lynn, provided a timely opportunity to sketch out many of the ideas that I developed in detail in this volume.

Project Learning 2001, which I directed at the Hudson Institute from 1989 to 1991, provided me with resources, knowledge, experiences, and personal contacts that vastly enriched this book. For these, I must thank all of the project's donors and sponsors, including Ætna Foundation, Inc., American Express Company, Amoco Foundation, Inc., Arthur Andersen & Co., Carnegie Corporation of New York, General Electric Foundation, GTE Foundation, IBM Corporation, The Charles Stewart Mott Foundation, Frank Strick Foundation, Inc., Tandy Corp., and TRW Inc. I am especially grateful for the personal interest and assistance I received from Alden Dunham of the Carnegie Corporation and Pat Edwards of the Mott Foundation. The Mott Foundation's substantial contribution helped support my work on writing this book in addition to funding the Hudson project in general.

Of the many assets Project Learning 2001 provided to advance the work that went into this book, few were more valuable than the Hudson Forum on Restructuring Education and Training Systems. This intensive workshop we conducted in June 1990 brought together some of the most aggressive and unapologetically radical leaders working on educational change in the United States along with a group of people whose extensive research or personal experience made them authorities on the *processes* of radical change and innovation.

The sparks from the frequently passionate, sometimes chaotic debates in the several sessions at the forum were invaluable in helping me identify the critical, gut issues this book had to address. I am grateful for the diligent efforts of my assistant Ruth Chacon, for the special contributions to the workshop from Unisys Corp. and Synectics, Inc., and for the time and energy invested in the forum by all the participants, including Beverly Anderson, associate director of the Education Commission of the States; Carl Ball, president of George J. Ball, Inc.; Jack Bowsher; Hugh Boyle, president of the San Diego Teachers Association; Joseph Carroll, superintendent of the Masconomet (Mass.) Regional School District; Donald Coffin, National Technological University; Gina Despres, legislative assistant to U.S. Senator Bill Bradley; Jeanie Duck, Boston Consulting Group; James Duffy, president of Project Literacy U.S.; Leonard Duhl, professor of social sciences at the University of California at Berkeley; Pete du Pont; Fritz Edelstein, senior fellow at the National Alliance of Business; Morton Egol, Andersen Consulting; Elizabeth Ehrlich, *Business Week;* Jeff Eisenach, Washington Policy Group; Dan Ellis, director of computer-based education at Queensland University of Technology (Australia); Barbara Farhar, senior scientist at the Solar Energy Research Institute; Robert Foley, senior vice president of human resources of Guest Quarters, Inc.; Jay Forrester, professor emeritus of system dynamics at MIT; Les Franklin, director of the Governor of Colorado's Job Training Office; Dana Friedman, co-president of the Families and Work Institute; Gideon Gartner, CEO of The Gartner Group; Luther Gerlach, professor of anthropology at the University of Minnesota; Sam Ginn, CEO of Pacific Telesis Group; Marshall Goldberg, director of the Alliance for Employee Growth and Development; John Golle, CEO of Education Alternatives, Inc.; Jose Gomez, president of Computer Network Systems, Inc.; the late O. B. Hardison, professor of English at Georgetown University; Jere Jacobs, assistant vice president at Pacific Tele-sis Group; Joseph Kellman, president of Globe Glass and Mirror; Henry Kelly, senior analyst at the Office of Technology Assessment; Ann Lewin, director of the Capital Children's Museum; Lance Marston, U.S. Agency for International Development; John Henry Martin, president of JHM Associates, Inc.; Dorothy Rich, president of the Home and School Institute; Richard Riordan, president of the Riordan Foundation; Everett Rogers, professor of communications at the Annenberg School of Communication, University of Southern California; Phillip Schlechty, president of the Center for Leadership in School Reform; Laurisa Sellers, director of community affairs at Honeywell, Inc.; Bassam Shakhashiri, formerly of the National Science Foundation and now a professor of chemistry at the University of Wisconsin; Albert Shanker, president of the American Federation of Teachers; Douglas Stefanko, director of internal education for Unisys Corp.; Patricia Sturdivant, president of Assured Learning Centers of America; Barbara Taylor, associate director of the National Center for Effective Schools; Thomas Toch, *U.S. News & World Report;* Peter Weddle, president of University Research Corp.; Chris Whittle, chairman of Whittle Communications; and Joyce Winterton, former executive director of the National Council on Vocational Education.

I am grateful to Mitch Daniels and Jay Keyworth for providing me the opportunity to work so productively at the Hudson Institute. Several of my colleagues at Hudson were especially helpful and supportive: Bruce Abell, Bruce Chapman, Bob Collins, Bob Costello, Denis Doyle, Mario Fiori, Mary Fitzgerald, Richard Jackson, Bill Johnston, Dick Judy, Joan Kolias, Mark Lubbers, Adam MacDonald, Bill Odom, Arnie Packer, Neil Pickett, Linda Rusthoven, Chris Smart, and John Tsagronis. I am especially indebted to Bill Pierce, who raised much of the funding and helped lay the groundwork for what became Project Learning 2001.

I appreciate the hospitality and aid provided by the hosts of several site visits that added greatly to my research: Lynn Blakesley at Waubonsee Community College; Roger Schank, Laura Reichert, and the staff of the Institute for the Learning Sciences; Vicki Dobbs, Teri Sturla, and Rachael Fierberg at LucasArts Learning; Lisa Van Cleef at Industrial Light & Magic; Peter Henschel, Susan Stuckey, and other staff at the Institute for Research on Learning; David Boulton and his colleagues at Learning Insights; Captain Ern Lewis, Janet Weisenford, and the staff at the Naval Training Systems Center; Bruce McDonald and Peter Kincaid at the Institute for Simulation and Training, University of Central Florida; Carl Ball, Steve Goldman, and Ann Jeffers at the Ball Foundation. Thanks too to Dennis Meadows for arranging for me to attend the conference of the International Simulation and Gaming Association at the University of New Hampshire, and to Jamie Alexander of Tandy Corp. for helping me to participate in the International Conference on Technology and Education in Brussels.

My research was aided substantially by a series of seminars I attended at the Smithsonian Institution. I am especially grateful to several speakers who spent time with me in personal conversations after their formal presentations: Michael Devitt, University of Maryland; Walter Freeman, University of California at Los Angeles; Ayub Ommaya, Foundation for Fundamental & Applied Neuroscience; Herbert Simon, Carnegie Mellon University; Joseph Weizenbaum, MIT; Red Whittaker, Robotics Institute, Carnegie Mellon University; and Paul Willbust, National Science Foundation.

PREFACE

I am grateful to John Chubb and Tom Mann for arranging for me to have access to the library and research facilities of the Brookings Institution.

Many other people contributed information, ideas, advice, and a variety of other kinds of assistance too extensive to detail here. For all this valuable help, I want to express my appreciation to Edith Ackermann, MIT Media Lab; Jeanne Allen, Heritage Foundation; Steve Arnold, Interactive Home Systems; Lionel Baldwin, National Technological University; Eric Boehm, International School of Information Management; Clint Bolick, Landmark Legal Foundation; Bill Braddick, former director, European Foundation for Management Development; Robert Bransom and David Salisbury, Center for Educational Technology, Florida State University; John Seeley Brown, Xerox Palo Alto Research Center; Anthony Carnevale, American Society for Training and Development; Michael Carter, Apple Computer Corp.; Jean Causey; Rene Champagne, ITT Educational Services, Inc.; Ricardo Charters-D'Azevedo, European Economic Community; Barbara Chriss, Kensington School (Richmond, Calif.); Emily Feistritzer, National Center for Education Information; Richard Freeman, National Bureau of Economic Research; Phyllis Gapen; Beverly Hunter, National Science Foundation; Peggy Hunter, Minnesota Department of Education; Greg Jackson, National Academy of Sciences; Phyllis Kaminer, Instructional Systems, Inc.; Greg Kearsley, George Washington University; Jack Klenk, U.S. Department of Education; Tom Lipscomb, Cryptologics Corp.; Linda Lloyd, Texas Association of School Boards; Jane Lommel, Indianapolis Public Schools; Laura London, Autodesk, Inc.; Harvey Long, IBM Corp.; Steve Moore and David Boaz, Cato Institute; Betty McCormick, IBM Corp.; Bill Moriarty; Judith Pitcher; Stanley Foster Reed; Lauren Resnick, Learning Research and Development Center, University of Pittsburgh; Keith Richardson, European Round Table of Industrialists; Col. Robert Seger, U.S. Army Training & Doctrine Command; Elizabeth Share, Autodesk Foundation; Samantha Solomon, Solomon Associates; Jerry Sroufe, American Educational Research Association; Robert Stoltz, Southern Regional Education Board; Bruce Taylor, Learning Ventures International; Al Thompson and Janice Wood, Periscope Software; Adam Urbanski, American Federation of Teachers; Chris Whittle, Whittle Communications; Frank Withrow, U.S. Department of Education; Scott Woodard, Front Range Community College; Bob Woodson, National Center for Neighborhood Enterprise; and Greg Wurzburg, Organization for Economic Cooperation and Development.

Whatever degree of excellence this volume may have achieved is due in large measure to the generous, detailed, and creative comments and suggestions I received from a group of colleagues and friends who critiqued earlier drafts of the manuscript. For this indispensable assistance, I must give special thanks to John Berenyi, Governmental Advisory Associates; Marsha Davis, formerly with Abacus Software; Jon Garfunkel, White Plains High School; Richard Garfunkel, Amrose Co.; George Gilder; Jacqueline Hess, National Demonstration Laboratory for Interactive Multimedia Technology; Priscilla Hillgren; Sonja Hillgren, *Farm Journal;* Dick Holt, U.S. Department of Energy; Ted Kolderie, Hubert Humphrey Institute, University of Minnesota; Tom Kuehn, Viking Instruments, Inc.; Lew Larsen, Hayes & Griffith; Ern Lewis, Naval Training Systems Center; Myron Lieberman; Andrea Mobilia; Carol Tolbert, Human Affairs Research Center, Battelle Memorial Institute; and Janet Weisenford, Naval Training Systems Center. Another of my readers, Gerald Bracey, formerly with the National Education Association, gave me considerable help in tracking down important information in addition to his many perspicacious comments. And Janet Topolsky gave me the valuable benefit not only of a friendly review but of her consummately professional editorial skills.

Finally, writers find dealing with many editors an ordeal about as gleeful as a visit to a ham-fisted dentist. In producing this book, I have had the rare and delightful experience of working with two extraordinary editors, Robert Mecoy and Adrian Zackheim, who contributed not only their supreme technical skills but genuine moral conviction and outright cheerleading that made my task vastly more rewarding.

My agent, Audrey Adler Wolf, played a role in this project that went well beyond the normal call of duty. This book simply would not have been published without her passionate and stubborn commitment that persisted over a stretch of months in the face of skeptical reactions from a number of editors and publishers less visionary than Bob and Adrian. Moreover, Audrey made valuable intellectual and editorial contributions through every step of the book's creation. The part she has played in this undertaking has been more that of an impresario, coach, and trainer—especially her continual nudging me to keep working and stay on a tight schedule—than a mere delegate. By extension, I must express my gratitude to Tom Lipscomb for introducing me to her.

My acknowledgment of the prolific contributions and aid provided by the many people and organizations I have mentioned should not, of course, be taken to imply any endorsement. Responsibility for the views expressed here and for any errors of fact is entirely mine.

CONTENTS

• • •

SCHOOL'S OUT

I am not an advocate for frequent changes in laws and constitutions, but laws and institutions go hand in hand with the progress of the human mind. As that becomes more developed, more enlightened, as new discoveries are made, new truths discovered and manners and opinions change, with the change of circumstances, institutions must advance also to keep pace with the times. We might as well require a man to wear still the coat which fitted him when a boy as civilized society to remain ever under the regimen of their barbarous ancestors.

Thomas Jefferson

CHAPTER 1

PROLOGUE: LEARNING 2100

• • •

"The wise one knows what time it is," a Zen proverb goes. Maybe the people who have been peddling the hoax of education reform just don't know what time it is. Maybe the folks who have been haranguing us to "save our schools" just don't understand that the classroom and teacher have as much place in tomorrow's learning enterprise as the horse and buggy have in modern transportation. Maybe they don't see that for the twenty-first century and beyond, learning is in and school is out.

Imagine, for instance, that it's near the end of the nineteenth rather than the twentieth century. A national task force on "excellence in horses" has issued a report exclaiming that America is "at risk" because its horse breeding and training are afflicted by a "rising tide of mediocrity." Russian, Japanese, and German horses, the report warns, eat more oats, pull heavier loads, and can run faster and farther than American horses. Since everyone knows that the horse is essential to agriculture, transportation, industry, and the military, it's obvious that an all-out effort is needed to raise the quality of U.S. horseflesh if America hopes to be competitive in the twentieth-century world.

Oh, by the way, the task force suggests, since the "horseless carriage" seems to be becoming pretty popular, all horses and their trainers should take a course in "automobile literacy" so they won't be scared by the noise of these curious contraptions.

Imagine that America's chief executive dubs himself the "equestrian president," and that he gathers all the U.S. governors together to establish a set of national goals aimed at assuring that the "New American Horse" meets "world class standards."

Imagine, too, that top business leaders, instead of investing in Ford and Delco and Goodyear, instead of lobbying for paved roads and traffic lights and parking lots, put millions of dollars into "business-stable partnerships," "wrangler-of-the-year" awards and "break-the-mold" horse breeding demonstrations.

As ridiculously shortsighted as this sounds, it accurately reflects how technologically blind the past decade's costly and futile education "reform" movement will appear to future historians. For a technological revolution is sweeping through the U.S. and world economies that is totally transforming the social role of learning and teaching. This learning revolution already has made the "classroom teacher" as obsolete as the blacksmith shop. In its aftermath, most of what now passes for education "reform" will appear as useful to economic security in the 1990s as the Maginot Line was to military security in the 1940s.

The idea that the evolution of computer and communication technology might spell the end of the industrial era is now over twenty years old—the terms "information age" and "postindustrial society" go back to the sixties. What has been less widely appreciated is that the recent information age has been only a transitional period, a prelude to the new historical epoch that should be more accurately labeled the "knowledge age."

A bevy of technological ripples unleashed during the past few decades is now merging into a tidal wave of new technology. The knowledge age economy it will spawn will be mobilized not merely by automation but by intelligence, and will be filled not just with information but with comprehension.

Because knowledge is the steel of the modern economy—the essential commodity all else depends on—learning has become the strategically central enterprise for national economic strength that steelmaking was in the industrial age. As a result, the nations that stop trying to "reform" their education and training institutions and choose instead to totally replace them with a brand-new, high-tech learning system will be the world's economic powerhouses through the twenty-first century.

Contrary to defeatist rhetoric about America's "lag" in schooling, this is a global race that has not yet begun; a race that is not merely for narrow competitive advantage but for global prosperity and peace. It is a race that

America is better positioned than any other nation to lead. But an array of backward-looking policies—on communications, employment, investment, and technology, as well as education—has squandered the opportunities the learning technology revolution offers, slowing our economy to a drift and threatening to sink it altogether.

Perhaps they will call this "The Great Bamboozlement"—those future historians, looking back on this moment from the prospect of a century or more from now, when they ponder how so many business executives and politicians and just plain people could have been so misled by a cabal of would-be education experts and self-appointed reformers.

The reformers tell us the "future" is the millennial year 2000. And so we get a bevy of America 2000, Omaha 2000, Colorado 2000, and Podunk 2000 projects that aim to get schools ready for a vision of the future that is glued to the rearview mirror. The redoubtable year 2000 was the future in 1950; now it's got about as much futurity to it as last Thursday. The reformers act as if they believe The Future is going to arrive eight years from now, and then change will just stop and society will sit on a plateau of blissful continuity for the next century.

Maybe we're so shaken by the upheavals of the last couple of years that, at heart, we long for a pause, a few tranquil decades to catch our breath. But there's no rational reason to expect that. Dickens described the period of the French Revolution as "the best of times and the worst of times." The same could be said of today, and now as then, that ambivalent intensity of the tidal waves of great revolutions is bound to ripple through the world for at least a century to come.

So if we really want to prepare ourselves and our children for "the future," we need to be thinking about the world of 2030, 2050, and beyond. Does that sound farfetched? You think that's too "futuristic" to have any meaning to you today?

Ponder this. In America today, there are babies alive now, babies bouncing on fathers' knees, babies nestling in mothers' arms, who will be alive in the year 2100. That's not a typo—I mean 2100, not just 2001. And we're not talking about just a handful of babies but thousands. There are several hundred 108-year-olds in the United States today, and with our larger population and further advances in medical science, it's virtually certain that several thousand of today's children will live right on through the next century.

So if you've touched a baby lately, you may well have touched a resident of the twenty-second century. That future is alive now, and it's worth thinking about today.

"War has become too important to be left to the generals," French premier Georges Clemenceau observed. Similarly, learning has become too essential to the modern economy to be left to the schools.

Generally knowing next to nothing about science and technology, most education reform leaders tell us that technology is just a sideshow, that education is an eternal institution, and that reform requires doing more of the same only better.

The reality is that a new generation of technology has blown the social role of learning completely inside out:

- Learning used to be a distinctly human process. Now learning is a transhuman process people share with increasingly powerful artificial networks and brains. Even today, expert systems and neural networks are being "trained" by human knowledge engineers; the machines' automated expertise in turn is providing "just-in-time learning" for car mechanics, power plant operators, and a growing legion of other workers.

- Learning was an activity thought to be confined to the box of a school classroom. Now learning permeates every form of social activity—work, entertainment, home life—outside of school. For what piano lessons would cost, you now can buy an electronic piano that will teach you to play it. Only a quarter of American adults know how to program a VCR; a new model will teach you how in any of six languages. The fastest growing cable TV networks—The Discovery Channel and The Learning Channel—are devoted to learning. Of the more than sixty million Americans who learned how to use personal computers since 1980, most learned from vendors, books, other users, and the computers themselves, not in schools.

- Learning was presented as the result of instruction: a linear, hierarchical process in which an "expert" teacher would pour knowledge into the empty head of an obedient student. With knowledge doubling every year or so, "expertise" now has a shelf life measured in days; everyone must be both learner and teacher; and the sheer challenge of learning can be managed only through a globe-girdling network that links all minds and all knowledge.

- Learning or education was a task of childhood in preparation for entering adult life and work. Now learning is literally the work of the majority of U.S. jobs and will be what virtually all adults —whether employed, unemployed, or "on welfare"—will do for a living by the early years of the twenty-first century.

I call this new wave of technology *hyperlearning,* or just HL for short. It is not a single device or process, but a universe of new technologies that both possess and enhance intelligence. The *hyper* in hyperlearning refers not merely to the extraordinary speed and scope of new information technology, but to an unprecedented degree of connectedness of knowledge, experience, media, and brains—both human and nonhuman. The *learning* in HL refers most literally to the transformation of knowledge and behavior through experience—what learning means in this context goes as far beyond mere education or training as the space shuttle goes beyond the dugout canoe.

These facets of the hyperlearning revolution are not *Star Trek* projections but events happening now. We have the technology today to enable virtually anyone who is not severely handicapped to learn anything, at a "grade A" level, anywhere, anytime.

But this technological revolution inevitably must be matched by a political revolution: The very power of modern technology to liberate learning leaves no role for the sprawling empire of academic bureaucracy but self-serving protectionism.

At its root, this technological revolution puts learning and education on a collision course. The essence of education is *instruction*—something some people do to other people, usually with required "discipline." The word *pedagogy* comes from a Greek verb meaning "to lead," and *education* itself is from the Latin word meaning "to lead forth"—both imply the active leader herding a flock of passive followers. But the essence of the coming integrated, universal, multimedia, digital network is *discovery*—the empowerment of human minds to learn spontaneously, without coercion, both independently and cooperatively. The focus is on learning as an action that is "done by," not "done to," the actor.

Moreover, twenty-first-century technology does not merely permit such an explosion of learning beyond the crypt of the classroom. The whole modern, knowledge-based economy depends on constant, universal learning for its own prosperity and further development.

This reality has been not only ignored but completely convoluted by the backward-looking vision of what passes for education reform.

The reformers have told us that American education is failing, that our schools have fallen behind the schools of other nations, and that the mission of reform is to catch up to their higher standards.

The truth is that, taken as a whole, for the purposes of a pluralistic and egalitarian society, America has the best education system in the world. And even if that assertion is debatable, in any case the issue of whose education system is "best" has become historically irrelevant.

In 1912, Britain's White Star Line boasted the safest, fastest, glitziest, and overall best passenger steamship in the world. And the *Titanic* unquestionably was *the best*—from the day she was launched to the day she sank.

Sometimes being the best isn't good enough.

Even with improvement, the technology the *Titanic* represented had only a limited future. By the time Lindbergh flew from New York to Paris in 1927, it was clear that the transatlantic passenger ship was doomed to eventual extinction no matter what "world-class standards" it might meet.

Marketing guru Theodore Leavitt once noted that people do not buy quarter-inch drills because they want quarter-inch drills—they buy quarter-inch drills because they want quarter-inch *holes*. This simple logic has been aborted by an academic empire that has mystified the public into paying more and more for "the best" bitless drills and forgetting about the holes altogether—at a time when modern technology offers new ways of making holes with lasers or chemicals that require no drills at all.

So contrary to what the reformers have been claiming, the central failure of our education system is not inadequacy but *excess*: Our economy is being crippled by too much spending on too much schooling.

Reform is a hoax. The "new, improved" education it is trying to sell us as an economic savior is really a solid gold life jacket: It glitters for attention. It's outrageously expensive. And the longer we cling to it, the deeper it will sink us.

The principal barrier to economic progress today is a mind-set that seeks to perfect education when it needs only to be abandoned. The prime determinant of not only America's but the world's economic future will be the speed with which hyperlearning is developed and opened up to universal access. Thwarting these advances are tradition-bound educational policies that reinforce monopoly and bureaucracy while stifling competition and innovation.

The hyperlearning revolution demands a political reformation. And that requires completely new thinking about the nature of learning in a radically changed future that now sits on our doorstep.

CHAPTER 2

HYPERLEARNING: A TECHNOLOGICAL REVOLUTION

• • •

Technology is the most purely human of humanity's features, and it is the driving force of human society. The defining benchmarks of the epochs of human history are the dominant technologies: the stone age, the bronze age, the iron age, the industrial age. The rare moments when a society's core technologies for combat, commerce, or communication made a potent breakthrough were days, in historian James Burke's telling phrase, "when the universe changed."

Those "days" of transformation commonly are stretched out over months or years or even decades. The environmental pessimists' oft-repeated parable of the frog—toss a frog into a pan of boiling water and he'll instantly jump out, but place him in a pan of cold water and you can gradually heat it till he boils before realizing what's happened—applies to human progress as well as to our ecological missteps. Few people appreciated the immense social and economic importance of the adoption of the plow, the stirrup, the printing press, or the steam engine at the time these things were happening.

Both survey research and common experience indicate that many people are at best ambivalent about technology, seeing it as much a threat as a blessing, and often preferring to leave it to the "experts" rather than to think too much about science and technology at all.[1] Nevertheless, to echo what Leon Trotsky said of war: You may not be interested in technology, but technology is interested in you.

Albert Einstein said that the atomic bomb changed everything but our thinking. Hyperlearning is going to change everything—*and* our thinking.

To get a glimpse today of the kind of hyperlearning system that will permeate the twenty-first century's economy tomorrow, you can skip the local school or college and look instead for a Buick, Chevrolet, or other GM dealership that has plugged into "CAMS"—General Motors's Computer Aided Maintenance System.

CAMS is a living example of what the computer engineers call an "expert system." At the core of CAMS is a mainframe computer in Flint, Michigan, programmed to know a great deal about how to maintain and repair a GM car. Linked by a telecommunications network to computer terminals right in the repair bay of a dealer's garage, CAMS is constantly available to help the mechanic figure out what's wrong with the customer's car and how to fix it. CAMS can take data directly from electronic testing instruments, ask and answer questions, and prescribe cures for automotive maladies.

Part of the system's intelligence is built into the car itself. Connected to the CAMS workstation in the garage, the car's on-board "driveability" computer chip transmits diagnostic information to the CAMS computer.

"Now we can quickly find the problem and repair it within two hours, on average, where before it could take up to six," says David Beck, service manager at Bob Martin's Chevrolet in Augusta, Maine. "And we fix the right problem the first time."

CAMS, like any good expert system, is not engraved in stone—or even in silicon—but is continually upgraded and improved. In effect, it too is a "learner." Each day, data about hundreds of car repairs are gathered from terminals in garages all over the country and fed back through the communications network to the main CAMS computer to be digested and applied to revising the expert program. CAMS learns to be a better and better expert mechanic.

In a sense, the car is part of the learning loop too. After the car is repaired, the service manager makes sure that the car's chip is replaced with the latest update from GM, which incorporates what's been learned from the experience of the scores of mechanics and garages on the CAMS network.

When GM piloted the CAMS system, mechanics rejected it at first. They felt that the CAMS system, designed to make the processes of diagnosis and repair as automatic as possible, was de-skilling their work and undercutting their aura of expertise. So the CAMS program managers went back to the drawing board and added a "manual" mode to the system, giving technicians control over the computer. The change made a big difference.

"When the system was first installed, I'll admit I was skeptical," says Beck, "but this is the answer. Most of the guys are really receptive and eager."

Beck's experience reflects the trend GM managers subsequently noted in their follow-up studies of the revised system. Most new CAMS users relied on the automatic mode for just a few weeks, then gradually shifted to the manual mode as their experience grew. In other words, the mechanics *learned* from the computer expert, and became more expert and effective themselves. So CAMS turned out, completely inadvertently, to be a highly effective, automatic training system, a *teacher* in its own right.[2]

Mr. Goodwrench actually has more to tell us about the future of education than Mr. Chips ever imagined. While CAMS is only a few years old, the technology it incorporates already is closer to the trailing edge than the leading edge. But in its overall design CAMS is a harbinger of a new kind of learning system that will comprise the brains and nerves of the entire twenty-first-century's economy: Vast volumes of data accumulated, digested into knowledge, and infiltrated into work. Intelligence distributed beyond the boundaries of space or time.

Most significantly, "teaching" and "learning" are fused and transformed into hyperlearning: machines helping humans to learn. Humans helping machines to learn. Nobody calls it or thinks of it as "education" or "training." There is no "school."

Hyperlearning is a categorical step—the proverbial "quantum leap"—beyond "artificial intelligence," beyond broadband telecommunications, beyond information processing, beyond biotechnology. Rather, hyperlearning represents the fusion of these technological threads. HL is weaving them into the fabric of a new industrial base for a new kind of world economy.

To understand the fabric of what is truly a "new world order"—and its implications for your business, your family, and your own place and prospects in it—you first need some substantive understanding of its four key technological threads:

- The first thread is the "smart" environment, where every artifact you touch or are touched by—cars, houses, toilets, clothes, tools, toys, whatever—is endowed with intelligence. The special significance of that intelligence is that it increasingly includes the ability not only to aid humans to learn but to participate in learning itself.

- The second is a "telecosm" communication infrastructure that makes all knowledge accessible to anyone, anywhere, anytime. The telecosm takes the most powerful knowledge, intelligence, and learning capacity of an environment that otherwise would be only local, and makes it global. For both human and nonhuman learning, the telecosm makes the "best and brightest" located anywhere available everywhere.

- The third thread is a kit of "hypermedia" tools that you will need to navigate through a knowledge-dense universe. Hypermedia is to multimedia roughly what an index is to a book. Only there's an unlimited number of simultaneous indexes and they are built into the text or other material—you don't have to go to the "back of the book" to get a reference. The vital role of hypermedia in hyperlearning is to provide the technical bridge between informing and understanding.

- As the fourth and last thread in the matrix of HL technology, brain technology—a broad category representing the application of biological and other sciences to thinking and sensing systems—has a special role. Brain tech is, in a sense, the "wild card" in the HL deck. It is contributing much of the basic science and technical tools that underlie the other three areas of hyperlearning technology: the smart environment, the telecosm, and hypermedia. But it also offers a growing potential for biotechnology that can alter the learning process from the inside out.

THE SMART ENVIRONMENT

At the heart of the smart environment is the economics of what author George Gilder calls the microcosm: the exploding capacity to create, transmit, and transform information with technologies that become exponentially smaller and smaller, faster and faster, cheaper and cheaper, and ever more prolific and universal.[3] A key to the microcosm's economic power is the ability to represent all kinds of knowledge in *digital* form, as numbers, making all knowledge combinable, transformable, and communicable in ways previously unimaginable.

By the year 2030, compact, PC-like machines will be able to reason, perceive, and act upon their environment with full "human equivalence," forecasts Hans Moravec, director of the Mobile Robot Laboratory at Carnegie Mellon University. He anticipates big supercomputers with humanlike power by 2010.[4]

Machine intelligence has remained clearly "artificial" so far because, even with ever more powerful computers, it has been largely limited to manipulating propositions and facts about the real world reported to it by humans. For this reason, such technology might more accurately be labeled "applied intelligence" than "artificial intelligence."[5]

To march up the "android curve" toward something like "human equivalence"—beyond Arthur Clarke's HAL 9000 from *2001* if somewhat short of Commander Data of *Star Trek: The Next Generation*—certain key technical advances are required. Humanish androids need to be able to *see* and *feel* their environment, as well as to be able to move around in it and manipulate things, as robots can do. Then they need to be able to think not only with great computational power but with at least the crucial animallike ability to *learn* from their experience of the world. Finally, to have some android sociability, advanced machines should be able to communicate in a natural way with humans, in *conversation*. In reality, progress in all these key areas is coming rapidly.

The humanlike level of performance will require only that computer power continue to advance at the same rate over the next few decades as it has over the past half century. So there is little doubt that the necessary technology will be achieved within the foreseeable future. A milestone was reached in a recent exercise based on a test proposed in 1950 by British computer pioneer Alan Turing to see whether people could tell whether they were conversing (in writing) with a computer or another human: At least one of the latest computer systems competing for a $100,000 prize was able to fool half of a panel of ten judges into thinking they were having a conversation with a real person.[6]

What has gotten Moravec in trouble with many scientists is not his technology forecast. Even such Moravec critics as Joseph Weizenbaum of the Massachusetts Institute of Technology and Herbert Simon of Carnegie Mellon concede that the technical capabilities probably will arrive sometime before the middle of the twenty-first century.[7] What really bothers scientists and philosophers is Moravec's term "human equivalence."

But it's not necessary to settle the deep philosophical questions about whether a machine could ever be "equivalent" to a human being to recognize that, for *economic* purposes, ever-smarter machines already do and increasingly will perform roles that once only could be performed by a human.[8]

What ultimately may prove more significant about smart technology is that it can and will do things that humans never would or could do. About a decade ago someone figured out that it would take five *trillion* human clerks to perform the calculations being done by the world's then-current population of computers. With the great expansion in the power and numbers of computers employed now, the number of clerks would be thousands of times greater still. But the point is that computers did not eliminate five trillion jobs—a thousand times the earth's human population.

Philosophical debates over the meaning of "intelligence" and "human" are causing no discernible delay in the rapid improvement and spread of automated expert technology. Paradoxically, while today's computerized experts are stymied by tasks that any human three-year-old finds a breeze, like learning that a string is meant to be pulled not pushed, they are impressive at duplicating the esoteric skills of a psychiatrist, an accountant, or a computer-systems designer.

Specialists at a California electric utility spent a few years and several hundred thousand dollars to automate the amazingly elaborate expertise of a retiring engineer who, for thirty years or so, had been responsible for maintaining the large earthen dam of a hydroelectric station. The considerable cost and effort of building the computerized system still was an attractive investment compared to the cost, and risk, of the years or even decades of trial-and-error experience a replacement engineer would require to attain the same expertise.

Broad swipes at "dehumanizing" technology tend to obscure the tangible human benefits of such expert tools. For example, Merced County, California, employs a computer expert named Magic in its Human Services Agency that has cut the time required to figure out whether an applicant is qualified for welfare benefits from as long as three months down to just three days—a real blessing to the disadvantaged people the agency is supposed to serve. And machines do not discriminate. True, the 28 percent staff reduction Magic will permit may seem a threat to paper-shuffling bureaucrats. But the $400 million the state could save by adopting Magic statewide might be viewed as a humane benefit by California's overburdened taxpayers.[9]

Rather than merely replacing human roles, smart technology for the most part has created and will continue to create new possibilities, new opportunities, and ultimately an entirely new environment for working and living. And the on-rush of smart technology is not limited to the ethereal universe of intangible data. In the form of robotics, it is equally destined to transform manual and mechanical work.

Robots are especially attractive for doing work that humans cannot or will not do. "Anywhere there are protective suits is a market for robots," argues William "Red" Whittaker, director of the Field Robotics Center at Carnegie Mellon University. Robots played an indispensible role in cleaning up the aftermath of the nuclear reactor accident at Three Mile Island and in entombing the nuclear reactor that exploded at Chernobyl, Whittaker points out. Ever more advanced robots will be wanted to cope with the dangers of undersea mining, hazardous-waste management, space exploration, and the battlefield.[10]

Whatever others may do, Japan is determined to lead the charge toward a robot workforce. Because of a baby bust that makes America's look tame, and cultural barriers to immigration and female employment, Japan faces a worsening labor shortage—there are now 145 job openings for every hundred people looking for work.

Scarce Japanese workers, who often complained about being treated like robots, now are being replaced by robots performing work once thought to require human labor: In a department store food section, a robot carefully molds rice balls and pieces of raw fish into servings of sushi. Robot anglers crew Japanese fishing boats, casting lines and reeling in fish—each "robofisher" costs less than a human fisherman's annual salary.[11]

Nor is the future of robotics limited to human-scale machines like C3PO and R2D2. The applications of microscopic robots will range from performing repairs inside unmanned satellites in deep space to performing incision-free surgery in the crannies of the human body.

Another important step on the path to smarter technology that can adapt itself to the real world is fuzzy logic, an important mathematical invention first published in 1965 by Lofti Zadeh, a Russian-born American mathematician at the University of California at Berkeley, and now being translated into a mushrooming array of practical consumer products by Japanese manufacturers. Unlike the conventional logic of most computer programs that can cope with only "true" or "false," the mathematics of fuzzy logic can handle ideas like "sort of," "mostly," or "sometimes."

Built into computer chips, fuzzy logic provides automated control systems for all sorts of products that are faster, more accurate, and more adaptable in adjusting to special conditions. One example is the new Minolta Maxxum 7xi—which one magazine touted as "the closest thing yet to a 'thinking' camera" that is "so smart it actually anticipates the shutterbug's desires."[12]

Japanese consumers are reportedly obsessed with having "fuzzy" (which in Japanese pronunciation comes out sounding like "fahdgy") in everything from washing machines—that automatically figure out the right cycle, temperature, amount of detergent, bleach, softener, and so forth needed for the particular fabrics and degree and sort of soil in each wash load—to camcorders, air conditioners, elevators, subway trains, automatic transmissions and antilock braking systems for cars, or just about anything that runs on electricity.[13] The rapid and widespread consumer acceptance of the new fuzzy logic wave is a sign that even more advanced forms of smart technology are destined to quickly permeate the living environment.

Fuzzy logic chips are a step toward learning machines in that they are highly self-adaptive to external conditions. However, being hard-wired for a particular application, they do not really "learn" as such.

But "neural networks" do. Growing knowledge of the brain's mechanics is being applied to the construction of these "thinking" machines that mimic in silicon and wire the simplest brain's architecture of nerve connections. While the thinking mechanisms of real brains involve complex chemistry as well as the structure of "wires" and "switches" formed by neurons and synapses, even relatively simple nervelike webs of computer parts can produce some remarkably intelligent behavior.

For example, scientists at Johns Hopkins University built a neural network machine that learned to read English—that is, it learned how to decode the stream of printed symbols into words and sentences. The computer was not *programmed* to read, it was *trained,* learning the skill through practice and feedback in much the same way as a human child. This need for training is typical of neural net systems, and is symptomatic of the new HL environment where learning and teaching are processes that are shared by human and nonhuman participants.

This technology is not "pie in the sky"—it's here now. In fact, you can buy software today that will simulate a simple neural network on a standard PC; California Scientific Software's Brainmaker costs less than $200.[14] Shearson Lehman uses neural nets that read financial data and predict stock and bond performance. And oil companies such as Arco and Texaco employ neural networks to sift through geological data and help find oil and gas deposits.[15]

Neural networks promise to further increase the power of computers to recognize visual, sound, and other complex *patterns* in the way that living sensory organs—like eyes and ears—do. Ultimately they may prove less significant as stand-alone synthetic "brains" than as smart interfaces for robots and other kinds of computers.

The performance of some of the newest neural net chips is not only at the level of some costly supercomputers, but is comparable to the data-processing power of the human eye. This is the kind of "artificial intelligence" needed to construct computers and robotic devices with the sharp eye of the eagle, the sensitive hearing of the elephant's ear, the smell-detecting power of the bloodhound's nose, or the discriminating touch of the human fingertip.

These advances in computer power are bringing machines that not only can sense the world around them, but can *learn* about it without the aid of programmers. The latest generation of Japanese consumer products feature "fuzzy net" chips that combine the abilities of both fuzzy logic and neural nets in one device that not only is quick at recognizing patterns, but that learns to do a better job as it gains experience.

The "learning" of a fuzzy net device is still limited in range to the kind of job it was designed for. But a programming technology, developed by a team led by Allen Newell of Carnegie Mellon University, called "SOAR" (an acronym for the program's three main operations) may be bringing more broadly intelligent computers within reach. SOAR, both a theory about thinking and a thinking computer program, is basically designed to solve problems—but any kind of problem. So SOAR is able to *learn* from its own experience in attacking a wide variety of tasks.[16]

The last key goal on the road to quasi-human smart technology is to develop machines that can handle the complexities of human speech. Synthesized speech is here: Computers no longer are limited to tinny, monotone voices that simply ... announce ... one ... word ... at ... a ... time. The best systems now can speak in male or female voices whose tone and inflection are virtually indistinguishable from a real person's.

The big problem has been to get computers to recognize and understand what five billion different human voices are saying. After four decades of research, useful solutions are starting to arrive and the pace of technical progress is accelerating. Using software-hardware packages now marketed by Dragon Systems, a Massachusetts company, ranging in price from about $3,000 to $9,000, PCs can understand up to thirty thousand spoken words and can take down more than forty words a minute in dictation.[17]

The potential of advanced technology such as fuzzy logic and neural nets to crack the translation problem has barely been tapped yet. For instance, Toshiba has started experimenting with using neural nets to distinguish homonyms—different words that sound the same. NEC aims to produce a voice-recognizing translator by 2000 that can instantly translate telephone conversations.[18]

THE TELECOSM

A related and complementary thrust of technology destined to transform both work and learning is in the communications domain George Gilder calls the "telecosm," where information flies as light, through space or along wires—once metal, now evermore glass. The central challenge of this fast-evolving arena, as Gilder puts it, is "how to move the entire realm of telecommunications to an integrated digital environment, both wired and wireless, suitable for the computer age."[19] *Digital* again is a key word in this diagnosis, because the ability to represent information in the numerical language of computation is crucial to the ability to combine and communicate what's now called "multimedia" information—pictures, sound, words, data—in an environment that takes full advantage of what smart technology can do with it.

The essential solution to this problem will turn the existing communications infrastructure upside down. "Bandwidth"—the range of radiation frequencies available to carry information—lies at the heart of a set of critical technical and economic issues.

Today's system has the "airwaves" heavily absorbed by bandwidth-hungry television transmission—severely limiting the growth of popular new technologies like cellular telephones—while wires and cables are mostly devoted to voice communications, which need only narrow bandwidth. In other words, the signals that need the most frequency space now go over the "air"—the medium with the least space—while the signals that need only a little space are sent through wires and cables, the medium with the greatest space. As confusing as this technical glitch may sound, it stands as a major impediment to the HL revolution, and therefore (as we'll see in a later chapter) to development of the modern economy.

Tomorrow, HL will be unleashed when high-resolution digital multimedia images will travel through the nearly unlimited bandwidth capacity of glass wire, while the scarce electromagnetic spectrum will be devoted to communicating many channels of relatively narrow-band voice, data, and low-resolution graphic information.

Breaking the bandwidth barricade will accelerate the spread of HL tools into popular gadgets. The portable, personal _telecomputer_ will combine and succeed the palmtop computer and the cellular telephone. And the home TV and PC will be replaced by a multimedia computer terminal—a step beyond what's now called "high-definition television"—offering a crystal-clear window on the sights and sounds of both real and artificial worlds.

The telecomputer is getting closer to reality. The Federal Communications Commission recently approved applications from three cable TV companies to try out wireless personal communication networks. Motorola has introduced a wireless local area network (LAN) called Altair that allows laptop or other portable computers to be moved around freely within an office, building, or factory while sharing information on the network.[20] Portable computers with cellular telephones built in are on their way to the market.[21] And Hewlett-Packard's new palmtop 95LX computer can exchange information with other 95LX units by infrared beam, and is designed to be able to work with cellular phones or other wireless networks. With the computerized digital telecosm network in place, you will be able to keep just one telephone number for life, and use it for any communication carrier, anywhere you happen to be.[22]

Even with their limitations, existing media offer tantalizing hints of the digital multimedia revolution that is around the HL corner. At the root of this revolution is the rapid convergence of what used to be different information forms and businesses: movies, TV, music, radio, telephone, mail, computing, libraries, and so forth.

For example, as a result of the accelerating spread of voice mail, voice response, audiotex, voice recognition, and other advanced technology, you can communicate with computers by phone to "find out when your CD will mature, order tulips, reserve an airline seat, broadcast a voice message to your sales force, or have your e-mail read to you in a robotic monotone," reports *Business Week*.[23] With new, digital "video-on-demand" systems, educational or other special-interest videos that are not economical to store in cassettes on a video store's shelf could be archived in compressed digital form in large, centralized libraries and delivered by wire where and when wanted.[24] An advanced technology being developed by ACTV for its "do-it-yourself TV," now being tested in Springfield, Massachusetts, allows viewers to actually alter what they are watching: choosing tailored exercise workouts, picking joke topics on a comedy show, getting personalized counseling from family advisers, or creating their own music videos.[25]

It might seem that hyperlearning is going to be so globally distributed and networked and coordinated that it threatens to leave no room for the individual, learning person. But the smart environment and the telecosm network that puts all the world's knowledge on-line are not just utilities that you will have to go somewhere to plug into.

Galloping miniaturization means that copious knowledge bases and powerful smart tools already are portable enough to carry around with you, even to wear like articles of clothing. Today's leading-edge semiconductor technology can squeeze millions of transistors onto a single, fingernail-sized chip. Within a decade, the number will grow to billions, bringing supercomputer power to items the size of a belt buckle.[26]

The number of knowledge-dense gadgets you can tote in a briefcase or purse already is pretty awesome. The hot items three years ago were electronic dictionaries the size of a paperback book that could check spellings, definitions, synonyms, or translate between languages—unlike a paper book, the smart dictionaries let you guess at spelling, then they figure out what word you are looking for.[27] By a year ago, you could buy a similar-sized device that contained an electronic version of the single-volume *Concise Columbia Encyclopedia,* an impressive increase in useful knowledge-per-ounce.[28]

Now this year, for the same money you can get Sony's new Data Discman, which puts large books on two-inch mini compact discs in a player that can fit in a briefcase or a large coat pocket, with a viewing screen about the size of an index card.

The growing horde of porta-gadgets is full of smarts as well as knowledge. If you're more the lyrical than the literary type, you might like Yamaha's Music Sequencer, a device the size of a VHS videocassette that enables you to compose your own music in any of seventy-six styles, ranging from jazz to hard rock to country and western, even if you can't read a note of music. Then, when you invite your friends over to party to your handmade tunes, you can plop Konica's Kanpai camera on a convenient table or shelf and go join the crowd—the camera will automatically swivel on its built-in tripod to take snapshots wherever it "hears" a burst of sound like laughter or cheers.[29]

These exciting porta-tools are still puny compared to the power of what's coming in just a few years. What may be at least as profound in its impact as the ever shrinking and more potent telecomputer is the video microcamera. A prototype camera-on-a-chip, with a lens the size of the capital letter at the beginning of this sentence, already has been developed at the University of Edinburgh in Scotland. Beyond near-term applications—such as unobtrusive security cameras for houses, automatic teller machines, and eventually automobiles—this microvideo technology promises Dick Tracy–style videophones in a wristwatch.

Combined with tinier data discs and improved solid-state "flash" memory chips, microcameras will permit video camcorders to shrink to the size of a pocket calculator or even a credit card—the price will shrink that much as well. Considering the impact the purse-size camcorder already has had on law enforcement, journalism, entertainment, and military intelligence, the societal implications of virtually invisible, cheap, all-seeing "eyes" easily could fill another book.

A key contribution of the telecosm thread of technology to the hyperlearning revolution will be what Bruce R. Schatz, a scientist at Bellcore, the regional phone companies' research center, calls "telesophy"—the potential ability to make all knowledge available to anyone, anywhere, anytime. "It's actually going to be possible to have all the world's information at your fingertips," says Schatz.[30] Those with the greatest ability to pay will still get greater access to the most valuable knowledge. But the cost of access will be so greatly reduced that vastly more knowledge will be available to everyone.

If you can't imagine that the advent of telesophy within a generation or two would transform the social and economic role of learning beyond all precedent or recognition, consider the following, ultimate benchmark of portable knowledge: Within the first quarter of the twenty-first century, information storage will be so compact that *all* the information a well-informed person could consume in a whole lifetime—all the books, manuals, magazine and newspaper articles, letters, memos, reports, greeting cards, notebooks, diaries, ledgers, bills, pamphlets, brochures, photographs, paintings, posters, movies, TV shows, videos, radio programs, audio records, concerts, lectures, phone calls, whatever—will be able to be stored in an easily portable object, no bigger than a book and potentially as small as a fat fountain pen.

HYPERMEDIA

For the past ten years, the evolution of the computer industry has been dominated by the desktop computer—PCs and workstations. The next phase of technology will step beyond data crunching, word processing, and drafting to integrate in digital form on a single platform every medium of information: high-resolution full-motion video, high-fidelity multi-channel sound, pictures, words, numbers, charts, graphs, whatever. The key to the impact of these new multimedia systems is that they will be *interactive*—the user does not merely observe or absorb information, but gets unprecedented power to create and act upon it.

The personal computer revolution was unleashed a decade ago when the International Business Machines Corporation decided to establish the PC standard—Microsoft DOS operating systems and Intel "x86" computer chips—as an "open system," that is, a design that other firms could freely copy and sell. This led to the explosion of "clone" manufacturers and a cornucopia of software that could run on tens of millions of "IBM compatible" machines.

A fervent scramble now is on to establish multimedia standards as broad-based and productive—and therefore as lucrative—as the PC. Computer hardware and operating systems need to be adapted to handle and combine the variety of different information forms—an example is Apple Computer's new QuickTime, an extension to its System 7 operating system for the Macintosh that allows video and audio to be added to conventional documents. The creation of high-resolution multimedia display systems—the successors to TV sets—offers American and European firms a chance to recapture crucial chunks of the consumer electronics market lost to Japanese dominance. Communication networks, both local and long-distance, need compatible formats to enable multimedia information to be shared. Alliances of the most powerful companies in the information industry—IBM, Apple, Compaq, Digital, Sun, AT&T, Intel, Microsoft, Motorola, Next, Sony, Tandy, Philips, Commodore, Hewlett-Packard—are forming and reforming, jockeying for position in a race for leadership.

The stakes could not be higher: The establishment of multimedia will have as profound an impact on all future communications as the invention of writing had on human language.

But as the exploding power of information technology itself adds to the mushrooming problem of data overload, it becomes ever more difficult to discern the shape of the forest made up of the spreading horde of twigs and leaves. The problem in most technical fields now is not a shortage of data, but making sense of the flood of data pouring in—which, as the saying goes, is like "trying to drink from a fire hose."

The good news is that the same technology that's creating the problem of information overload offers the solution—in fact, what probably is the only solution. Properly designed, assembled, and applied, the tools of multimedia can create *hypermedia* that help the user find the needles of knowledge in sprawling hayfields of data.

The key may be visualization. The old saying that a picture is worth a thousand words actually understates neurological reality: The human eye-brain system can perceive images about a million times more efficiently than it can decode lines of words or numbers. Actually, as much as 60 percent of the brain may be involved in seeing. As a result, the ability to present information in *visual* form is becoming ever more crucial not only to basic science and engineering but to a growing range of work, from market research to military combat. A major (perhaps *the* major) impetus behind the obsession with ever faster and more powerful "supercomputers" is the need for tools that can translate a roaring cacophony of data into the visual (and sometimes even aural as well) music of understandable knowledge.

Where is the leading edge of visualization technology to be found? Hollywood has been driving the development of three-dimensional interactive advanced graphics more than industrial or military engineering, according to Bud Enright, president of Wavefront Technologies in Santa Barbara, California.[31] For instance, Pixar Inc.—a spin-off of *Star Wars* creator George Lucas's film company that was taken over by computer tycoon Steve Jobs and Pixar's employees in 1986—has been a leader in providing advanced imaging technology for medical and other applications. By translating the two-dimensional pictures from CAT or MRI scans of the human body into 3-D images, doctors can see, from any angle, what's going on inside body parts, changing the way, and even whether, surgery is done. Dr. Elliot Fishman at Johns Hopkins University Hospital says that most surgeons there "wouldn't dare operate" without using Pixar as well as X-ray images.[32]

Such improved imagery will amplify the already potent power of "virtual reality" (VR) systems. Behind this oxymoronic and somewhat misleading label is a new thrust in visualization technology that is truly mind-blowing. Much like Alice going through the looking glass into a fantastic other world of talking flowers and poetic walruses, VR technology allows the user to transcend the barrier of keyboard and screen and enter the synthetic universe *inside* the computer.

To use Autodesk's experimental "Cyberspace" VR system, you don a bulky but lightweight pair of stereo display goggles—each eye gets its own little color TV—and slip on an elastic, sensor-crammed glove. Zip! You're standing in a 3-D "Toon" world, not unlike Roger Rabbit's hometown. You might find yourself in a room in a simulated building, full of computer-generated objects: a table, a lamp, a chair, books on a bookshelf, and so forth. Look up and you see the ceiling; look down at the floor. Turn around and there are the walls and other objects "behind" you. Point the finger of your gloved hand and you glide in whatever direction you are pointing. Want to fly? Point up and you take off, down and you descend. Hold the gloved hand in front of your face and you see a cartoon hand floating in space. Reach toward the shelf and the sim-hand gropes for a book. Close your fingers and you can grasp the book and move it or carry it around. Fling it and the imaginary book goes sailing across the artificial room, bounces off the simulated wall, and plops to the make-believe floor.

VR technology almost certainly will force a recantation of a key theorem of today's leading-edge research on workplace skill requirements: Namely, that high-tech production demands that worker expertise be grounded in "abstract reasoning"—because workers can no longer see and feel how complex tools work. VR soon will bring the "high touch" back to high tech, but in a vastly more powerful way. A mechanic no longer will have to break down an engine to see and manipulate the parts in his hands, or puzzle out the abstract meaning of gauges and computer charts. He will be able to "go inside" the engine and watch the parts move as the engine runs, speeding up or slowing down the motion as needed, turning a setscrew by "hand" while looking to see how it affects valve motion from inside the cylinder.

VR seemed like exotic technology just a year ago; by the time you read this it may be closer to commonplace. "Virtuality," a VR game developed by a joint venture of W Industries, Spectrum Holobyte, and Horizon Entertainment, already has debuted in shopping mall video arcades around the United States. And Hollywood giant MCA Inc. is exploring a new kind of VR "voomie" theater to complement or even replace the now-fading traditional movie theater.[33]

That kind of powerful VR visualization is a leading-edge element of the broad domain of simulation technology. Computers have been used almost from the outset to answer the question: What if . . . ? But the exploding power and ever-diminishing cost of computers and related information technology has vastly expanded our ability to simulate (mimic) or synthesize (make up) sights, sounds, and experiences of stunning richness and complexity.

Simulation has been at the heart of a multibillion-dollar computer and video game business that has grown steadily for the last half decade. More elaborate games are starting to converge with the universe of training simulators. A California entrepreneur developed the Stimulator by taking the kind of cockpit on a large centrifuge long used for pilot training and combining it with a remote-controlled half-scale racing car. A video camera transmits the car's view of the road to the screen serving as the cockpit "windshield." The Stimulator provides the look, sound, and feel of actually driving a race car at high speed, without the hazard of being injured in crashes.[34]

Tamer but still intriguing computer games are having an increasing impact on learning and instruction. *Where in the World Is Carmen San-diego?*, a computer game that involves chasing a spy all over the map, produced such noticeable albeit unintended gains in geographic knowledge that teachers started bootlegging it into schools. The game now has spun off a public TV show. *SimCity,* a simulation game in which the player gets to design an entire working metropolis—with consequences that may range from benign to disastrous—was such a hit with teachers of everything from grad school urban design courses to grade school special ed classes that it spawned an even grander sequel: *SimEarth,* an environmental simulation that lets the user play creator with an entire planet.

Such visualization, VR, and other simulation techniques can help condense mountains of boring info-bits into exquisite sandcastles of insight. But these vessels are not sufficient to keep up with the gathering storm of information overload. Actually, the growing power of ever cheaper, more portable multimedia tools and the expanding bandwidth of modern telecosm networks may simply be making complex imagery a denser part of the deluge, like hailstones in a thundershower.

We're already starting to be blinded by this blizzard of multiplying messages. The problem isn't just a matter of finding the proverbial needle in a haystack (a magnet can solve that easily)—it's finding the *right* needle in a silo full of needles and pins, tacks, staples, and nails.

Like Cinderella's fairy godmother, Dorothy's witch friend Glenda, Pinocchio's Jimminy Cricket—or Bob Hope's pal Swifty Lazar—"agents" are what we all need to help us find what we're looking for in the a-*maze*-ing worlds of the knowledge age. Fortunately, technology in fact is sending the agents we need to rescue us from the quagmire that technology has plunged us into.

Information scientists actually are developing the two kinds of agents needed to cope with the information flood: one kind to help us find the knowledge gems we're searching for and another to filter out the junk from the jewels.

People-based services to read and condense information are at least as old as *Reader's Digest.* For years, business services like John Naisbitt's have prospered by tracking and clipping huge volumes of periodicals and distilling them into brief newsletters and breezy books like *Megatrends.* Now these services are quickly being amplified or replaced by automation. Several companies, including Desktop Data Corp., Individual Inc., and Dow Jones, now offer computer-based services that automatically track news wires and other voluminous sources, identify key items of interest to the subscriber, and deliver the filtered results almost instantly to the user by e-mail or fax. A major function of Lotus Notes and specialized software products such as BeyondMail is to automatically categorize and sort electronic mail by user-established priorities.[35]

A key step toward finder agents—which is also an essential strand in this whole thread of HL technology—is the general category of software called "hypermedia."[36] An early version, "hypertext," provided the ability for multidimensional (hence, "hyper") cross-referencing and indexing of word-based information libraries. Add multimedia pictures, movies, sounds of speech, music, and so forth to the library and hypertext becomes hypermedia. "Hypercard," developed by Apple computer whiz Bill Atkinson, is widely considered the breakthrough hypermedia program which gave computer users unprecedented power to organize and manage information without having to master the cryptic syntax of a computer-programming language. Other important hypermedia products for the MS-DOS world include Hyperpad, Guide, and Toolbook.

Here's a glimpse of how hypermedia tools work: Eleven-year-old Jessie is sitting at a multimedia computer and reading some text about the Civil War in an encyclopedia program. She comes to a mention of General Burnside. Curious to know who he was, she points at his name on the screen with the mouse and clicks. The "button" zips the screen instantly to another file—represented as a card in a stack of index cards, or as a page in a book—with biographical information about Burnside. Among other things, Jessie learns that "sideburns" were named after the way he wore his whiskers, and that he composed the bugle call, "Taps." She might point and click on the word "Taps" and hear a recording of the tune. Or, clicking on a mention of the Battle of Fredericksburg, she might view a sequence from a movie about the battle.

For HL's more demanding objectives, filters and finders have to be much smarter. So the quest for hyperlearning agents inevitably takes us back full circle to the AI tools of the smart environment.

Douglas Lenat, a leading research scientist at the Microelectronics and Computer Technology Corp. (MCC) in Austin, Texas, is working on a product called "CYC"—as in "cyclopedia"—that represents one revolutionary approach to creating an intelligent agent. Expected on the market by the end of the decade, CYC is a kind of superencyclopedia, containing three or four million facts, all boiled down to a single, fingernail-sized electronic chip that would fit in something the size of a fat wristwatch. Unlike many AI applications, CYC aims not to codify expertise on a narrow subject, but to build "common sense" into a computer.[37]

CYC is not the only approach to the creation of smart agents to help us learn what we want from an information-impregnated environment.

Roger Schank and his colleagues at the Institute for the Learning Sciences at Northwestern University emphasize a tack that uses on-line agents as storytellers.

A "Silicon Valley" company, Learning Insights Inc. (LII), may be reaching even closer to a general HL agent. LII president David Boulton is developing a common user interface that could overlay almost any kind of knowledge base or instructional program, and that could work on nearly any computer "platform," from a large corporate network to a portable unit like Sony's Data Discman. Boulton's interface, or agent, goes beyond other hypermedia tools by being designed especially to facilitate learning, not just information retrieval. His agent is even adjustable by the user to adapt to different individual learning "styles."

Put one or another of these commonsensical HL agents into a portable telecomputer only slightly more developed than Hewlett-Packard's 95LX, use a simulation program to give the agent a human (or Vulcan or Muppet) face and synthesized voice, and you have what Apple fellow Alan Kay dubbed the "Knowledge Navigator"—everyone's pocket Aristotle, a Walkman window on all the world's knowledge, expertise, teaching. The development of a commercially feasible form of such a system is no more than a decade or so away.

In just a few years, our young friend Jessie won't be bound to a desktop to use powerful multimedia tools to nurture her curiosity about General Burnside and the Civil War. On vacation with her family in Fredericksburg, Virginia, she could carry a Discman-sized knowledge box that would answer her questions about "Taps" and the general's whiskers while she tours the battlefield.

A decade or so into the future, she wouldn't have to tote a bulky box. Even more powerful knowledge technology will fit in a wristwatch or, better, a pair of smart eyeglasses that respond to voice requests, and that could project holographic images of maps or simulated troop movements over the vista of the real battleground before her—somewhat like today's military "heads up" displays—while she listens to a narrative or music of the period.

BRAIN TECHNOLOGY

Biochemical technology is having at least as dramatic an impact on learning processes as are electronic and optical tools for processing and transmitting information. Biotech is developing probes to illuminate more precisely how the cells and structures of living brains do the work of thinking. The resulting insights are adding to the accelerating advances of cognitive and molecular psychology—the sciences that reveal the fundamental mechanisms that enable the living brain to produce a thinking mind. Within these broad areas, neuroscience is exploring the function of nervous systems, both organic and artificial. And genetic science is illuminating the ways genetic programs govern how cells work, leading to technology that can repair defects or even add new capabilities to living tissue, including the brain and nervous systems.

The application of these sciences is now permitting the engineering not only of machines that think, but of the human mind itself. The outcomes include both new computer technology that mixes organic and inorganic elements as well as drugs and other techniques to improve the thinking and learning capabilities of the human mind.

One of the most important impacts of this research is the development of probes that reveal how nerves and brains actually function. These probes include microscopic needles that can touch and tune in to the electrochemical activity of a cluster of nerves or even an individual nerve cell; electroencephalograph (EEG) and magnetoencephalograph (MEG) sensors that are applied to the surface of the head and can observe the electromagnetic waves of brain activity; and CAT, MRI, and PET scanners that use, respectively, X rays, radio waves, and radioactive emissions to produce 3-D pictures of the brain's structure and behavior.

Of the many dramatic results from this fast-evolving field of science and technology, a few are particularly noteworthy. One is that brain tech tools have allowed the once separate fields of computer science and animal (including human) psychology—including related elements of genetics and physiology—to converge in the young but increasingly powerful discipline of cognitive science. Cognitive science has become a taproot for the technical development of the high-powered smart tools, communications systems, and hypermedia of the HL universe. At least equally important is cognitive science's application to the crucial "human factors engineering" needed to match human and machine performance in highly complex systems such as air traffic control systems, military combat information centers, modern automated manufacturing complexes, or electric power operations centers—all of which are increasingly organized around the kind of hyperlearning loops demonstrated by CAMS and other examples I noted earlier.

Another important outcome of brain tech research is the discovery that the limbic system, which is the center of *emotion* in the brain, plays an absolutely central role in the phenomenon we recognize as purposeful, conscious, "intelligent" thought.[38] Science now knows that emotion is a necessary feature of high-order, conscious intelligence. The neuroengineering program directed by Paul Willbust at the National Science Foundation has developed computer simulation models of neural networks enhanced with an "adaptive critic" that mimics the emotional "hopes and fears" of the mammalian brain's limbic system. The design now is being implemented in a number of practical applications, from robotics to "smart" structures to prosthetic devices for the disabled.[39] So the intelligence of the coming smart environment might turn out to be less artificial, maybe even more sympathetic, than some of us have imagined.

But what may turn out to be the most significant outcome of brain tech research is the recognition that the brain is far more a chemical than an electrical computer. Focusing attention on the chemistry of thinking, this all leads toward the possibility of technologies that work *on* the brain, rather than just *like* the brain.

The main focus of research in what's called "molecular psychology" now is on curing diseases such as schizophrenia, depression, and Alzheimer's.[40] Scientists at the National Institute of Mental Health already have demonstrated drugs that significantly improve the memories of Alzheimer victims. Similar compounds could enhance learning by slow and even normal children or adults.

A problem with all brain drugs is the blood-brain barrier that nature built in to keep alien chemicals out of the brain. But overcoming that obstacle is one of the prime objectives of the hundreds of millions of dollars pharmaceutical companies are investing in R&D to develop new brain drugs.[41]

Leading researchers in the field of neurobiology expect a revolution in pharmacology by the turn of the century that will produce drugs that do for the brain what steroids do for muscles.[42] Jon Franklin, author of the Pulitzer Prize–winning book *Molecules of the Mind,* anticipates drugs in a few years that will increase intelligence and creativity.

A practical concern surrounding the issue of performance-improving drugs is that many drugs have undesirable, even dangerous side effects. An even more fundamental practical problem with using drugs to hypercharge brain power is that the brain has a strong tendency to adapt itself to drugs—so the effect wears off with extended use.

But biotechnology is fast developing the means to permanently alter the functions of body organs, including the brain. Johns Hopkins University scientists have found a way to grow human brain cells outside the body. Researchers at Nova Pharmaceutical Corp. in Baltimore are working on splicing in genes to make the Hopkins cells produce dopamine, the neurotransmitter that is depleted in Parkinson's disease—then these cells could be injected into the brain to alleviate the illness.[43]

Similar gene therapies eventually will be developed to attack other brain disorders: perhaps Alzheimer's, schizophrenia, Down's syndrome, fetal alcohol syndrome, epilepsy, or others. Not so far in the future, microbots the size of a pinpoint will be able to swim through the bloodstream and insert individual cells, or genetic material, or quasi-biological artificial devices at strategic locations in the brain inaccessible to normal surgery. To the victims of these devastating illnesses and their families, these therapies will come as an immeasurable blessing.

THE HL REVOLUTION

Each of the four threads of HL technology—the smart environment, the broadband telecosm, hypermedia, and brain tech—obviously promises great economic and social impacts by itself. But the real power of HL is growing from the progressive synthesis of this series of fast-advancing technologies.

Taken one at a time, each of the developments of smart technology may seem exotic yet narrow in its impact. But the handful of examples of smart tools I have cited is only a sample of hundreds of applications—soon to be thousands, and eventually millions. The intelligence they display perhaps still may seem crude but it is growing ever brighter.

As these devices rapidly advance in sophistication, grow, spread, and interlock, they are quickly defining a new, smart human environment that can observe, think, make decisions, work, converse, and *learn* with us. And the smart environment is no *Star Trek* fantasy of the fourth millennium—it is the imminent future world our children will inhabit and our grandchildren will inherit.

The telecosm thread of HL will tie human "smarts" together in a way that's essential to keep people in charge of their own smart world. The immense power of telecomputers and knowledge-packed porta-tools spells a new age of personal learning "on-demand," "just-in-time," wherever and however the opportunity is wanted. Even with today's Data Discman technology, there's no need to construct a room full of bookshelves for your scholarly child—all the books needed for twelve or sixteen or twenty years of schooling (which, we'll see, she won't really need), when squeezed onto tiny laser mini-discs could be carried around in a backpack.

The data storage technology of the next century will put a lifetime of information in the palm of your hand. Long before that, however, the measure of human competence in the HL world will be not what you can remember, but what you can understand.

At the heart of the HL revolution is a vital human challenge: We risk being suffocated in an avalanche of data—the more extravagantly we are informed about everything, the more difficult it becomes to *know* anything. But the coming efflorescence of ever more powerful, ever cheaper technology for producing and transmitting multimedia messages is going to pour even more volatile fuel on what already seems a daunting information "explosion."

Hypermedia so far has been concerned with easing information retrieval. The "hyper" literally refers to many-dimensional connections, but the key idea is the connectedness: the ability to link hordes of data bits into patterns or structures the human mind can grasp. Hyperlearning needs to push this technology a quantum jump further than just grasping information: to make the higher level connections needed to extract knowledge, insight, understanding, and skill from a maze of information and experiences.

The "skill" factor is crucial. The mission of hyperlearning is not only vision but action. HL's purpose is to enhance the human user's ability to direct the potent technology of the smart environment, lest the human be reduced to technology's object. The job of hypermedia alone is to inform; its job as part of the fabric of hyperlearning is to empower.

The hypermedia tools that will enable a child to explore her world with the unlimited companionship of a universal tutor that can serve her curiosity with visions and sounds and words and sensation, and that can seamlessly merge knowledge and experience, will be equally common features of her parents' world of work and play and homelife. Hypermedia will put the immense power of the smart environment and the telecosm at the constant service of learning knowledge and skill in every facet of economic activity. While many features of this hyperlearning world can be seen in place today, the wellspring of science from which it flows promises only to accelerate the HL revolution in the immediate future.

The human brain is designed to be adept at learning from experience. But simulation vastly expands the richness, complexity, and value of the experiences available for learning—another key plank in the bridge to hyperlearning. As a result, the rapid advance of simulation technology has ignited an evolutionary process that is progressively blurring the boundaries between entertainment, instruction, work, and learning in general.

The potential impact of advanced simulation and visualization technology on hyperlearning has not yet even been scratched. Einstein developed the special theory of relativity by "riding" a light beam in his mind's eye—those with less vivid imaginations could share Einstein's "thought experiments" through VR imagery. The possibilities exceed imagination (at least most adults'). Kids hundreds or thousands of miles apart could act out *Macbeth* with computer-generated costumes—or even simulated adult bodies and voices—in a camera-captured and video-re-created scene that duplicates the actual Birnham Wood or Dunsinane castle.

Powerful teaching capabilities even now are not limited merely to expressly instructional systems but are built in to a wide range of home and workplace tools from office photocopying machines to highly complex military combat control systems. In fact, such "embedded training" is becoming so commonplace that the term, coined by instructional designers, seems to be fading from use, according to Greg Kearsley of George Washington University, who has worked extensively on the development of such systems. "Building help and tutorial and practice capabilities into software has become so obvious and normal that many people don't even think of it as a separate task anymore," says Kearsley.[44] And, as CAMS and other expert systems show, teaching and learning are ever more unintended but inherent features of advanced HL technology whose design automatically includes powerful visualization and simulation capabilities.

The final thread, the advancing "brain technology," drives the spinning of the other threads that fill the world outside the human skull with growing intelligence. At the same time, it holds the potential to transform the mind inside the skull as well.

The significance this advent of new technology has for society can hardly be overstated. The hyperlearning revolution represents nothing less than an evolutionary watershed in the history for our species and, in fact, our planet.

The HL revolution that is already unfolding and accelerating before our eyes above all poses political challenges that can no longer be ignored, and that completely overwhelm the trivialities that pass for education or training "reform." Because of the pervasive and potent impact of HL technology, we now are experiencing the turbulent advent of an economic and social transformation more profound than the industrial revolution.

The same technology that is transforming work offers the new learning systems to solve the problems it creates. In the wake of the HL revolution, the technology called "school" and the social institution commonly thought of as "education" will be as obsolete and ultimately extinct as the dinosaurs.

CHAPTER 3

LIFE WITHOUT SCHOOL: LEARNING IN THE HL WORLD

• • •

In the beginning, human learning was limited to what could be accumulated in a single human brain in one lifetime. The invention of spoken language, then written language, then printing, and later, electronic communications media, incrementally expanded the human ability to accumulate and share knowledge among people and across generations. But all those innovations simply expanded the *storage of information* outside the human head; the basic processes of thinking, deciding, and learning still were mainly confined within the skull.

Technology now is extending the *learning process* outside the human brain and into the environment. Tomorrow's technology is quickly transforming the role of learning not only in human labor but in the economy as a whole.

Vocabulary tends to lag behind such massive shifts. In the lead of the dynamic charge that achieved the liberation of Kuwait was the U.S. Army's First Cavalry—deriving its name from the Latin for "horse"—whose armored and other motorized vehicles still were nominally driven by "horsepower."

So some people may still speak in the twenty-first century about "schools" and "colleges" and "students" and "teachers." But the hyperlearning systems of the imminent future in reality will bear less resemblance to old-fashioned classrooms than the M1A1 Abrams tank bears to a Roman chariot.

What will life be like in a society without schools, without what we would recognize as an institution of education? The cultural details of that coming society are as unpredictable as fuzzy dice, tail fins, low-riders, drive-in movies, Levittown, and a host of other features of automotive culture would have been in the 1890s. But some of the key social impacts of the HL revolution can be seen today.

IMPACT 1: LEARNING IS IN EVERYTHING, EVERYWHERE

CAMS, cited above, is just one example of many existing technological systems in which learning occurs not only among the human participants but within nonhuman elements and throughout the system as a whole. The technological developments of the next several years will vastly accelerate and expand this phenomenon, producing orders-of-magnitude gains in extrahuman or artificial intelligence within the next generation. And the impact will not be seen just in large-scale corporate systems; it will ripple through the most prosaic facets of everyday life.

In the smart environment, the learning made possible by advanced visualization and VR technology is likely to be worth more than millions of textbook pages or hours of classroom lectures. In fact, old-fashioned teaching methods will be unable to challenge, much less match it. This kind of hyperlearning, unattainable by any traditional means, will become crucial both to performance in the high-tech workplace and to everyday living.

The world's population of smart tools and gadgets, with built-in computational control and information-processing capabilities, is exploding: telephones, cars, washing machines, stoves, dishwashers, camcorders, weapons, credit cards, houses, whole office buildings. As this higher order intelligence permeates mundane products and systems, hyperlearning will become an inherent part of working, of living, of our *total* environment.

Surveys indicate that despite the fact that about 75 percent of American households own a VCR, only about a quarter of Americans know how to program one. How much more daunting still must it be for the typical U.S. consumer to exploit a fraction of the potential of the fully equipped home entertainment center: stereo TV/monitor, digital VCR, multiformat laserdisc player, cable TV tuner (possibly "interactive"), Nintendo game unit, and hi-band hi-fi stereo camcorder, hooked up to the Pro-logic Surround Sound, true five-speaker, audio-video system with its programmable CD changer, programmable seven-band active equalizer, and new digital tape recorder, which may also be plugged into the home security system. All this while trying to figure out how to cancel call forwarding on the touch-tone telephone and remember the right code for speed dialing to call back the friend whose office number was seventh on the caller ID box but whose home phone was disconnected in the message on the digital answering machine that ran out of RAM and either cut off or switched over to the fax machine.

If you think this list of gadgets is made up just to *sound* confusing, let me mention that I own most of this stuff, and the remaining couple of items are on my shopping list. In my living room I have one of those "universal" remote controllers with a slew of buttons that you can program to direct all the functions of the panoply of entertainment components. It took me three days after I acquired my bevy of new toys to read all the manuals, figure out what those functions are, program or set up each device, and then program the controller to operate the whole shebang. Getting the fax machine and the answering machine and the telephone to switch automatically from one to another as needed was another epic adventure. Don't even ask about all my computer doodads. So I speak of "daunting" from experience. On the other hand, the demands these tools make are more than compensated, I think, by the wonderfully powerful services and amenities they offer.

All this increasingly intelligent technology both overwhelms and enhances human abilities. The intelligent technology of today's business tools and consumer products already illustrates that learning is built in somewhere along a continuous spectrum that runs between the human user and the nonhuman operating system. In other words, there is a trade-off between the intelligence and learning demanded from the humans who use low-cost but enormously powerful equipment on the one hand, and the intelligence and learning that must be built into the equipment to make it "user friendly" on the other.

This leads to a range of design options more diverse than simply choosing whether to train smarter people or build more intelligence into the tools they use. To continue to sell increasingly sophisticated products, vendors are compelled somehow to accommodate the learning curve; and they are starting to use intelligent technology itself to do so. In the case of the now commonplace VCR, most manufacturers first offered on-screen programming, using menus and the remote control device to make the task more understandable. A new version provides programming guidance in several languages. Some brands offer TV guides printed with bar codes to accompany bar-code-reading remote control devices so that multiple instructions can be input with a simple wave of the user's hand. An even newer "Plus" system builds more intelligence into the VCR controller so that entering a digital code from the TV listings will program the VCR to record a show.

Many emerging products similarly adapt themselves to a variety of conditions or user preferences. Soon cars not only will "learn" the preferred seat, steering wheel, and mirror adjustments of a particular driver, but will adjust engine, transmission, and suspension performance to fit a specific driver's "style" as well as varying road conditions.

Ko-Pilot, a software add-in to a word processing program, shows how intelligent technology can provide a virtually infinite variety of ways to manage the learning curve. At the simplest level, Ko-Pilot offers the usual on-line "help" screens that answer the user's questions. Or, instead of simply telling the user how to perform a function, like cutting and moving a paragraph from one document to another, Ko-Pilot can show the user how to do it, step by step, with a tutorial and practice exercises. Or the user who just wants to get the job done quickly rather than learn a new skill can simply ask Ko-Pilot to carry out the desired task automatically.

So the tangible expression of hyperlearning in everyday life is that it makes the smart environment intrinsically a learning environment. And the learning is multidimensional (hence "hyper"): The smart environment challenges us to continually learn new things just to be able to use the tools and resources it offers. At the same time it includes teaching, training, informing, and other kinds of "help" systems to make the user's learning easier. Or it incorporates greater intelligence into the tools themselves to reduce the amount and difficulty of learning the user needs to do. With higher-order intelligence built in, the tools of the smart environment "learn" to adapt themselves to our demands.

And all these dimensions of learning coexist, overlap, and interact. So learning in the HL world is "in the air, everywhere."

IMPACT 2: SCHOOL BUILDINGS ARE REPLACED BY HYPERLEARNING CHANNELS

If learning is in everything, everywhere, how do we confine learning to the box of a classroom? We can't. Then what's the point of having schools at all? There isn't any.

The design of existing school and college systems in the U.S. and most of the rest of the world has been virtually unchanged since the nineteenth century. Now, the same technological revolution that has disconnected the environment of the traditional classroom from the experience of the modern workplace and home also offers the systems to replace conventional schools with effective, relevant learning media. While these new delivery systems may continue to be called "school" or "college" or "university"—until language habits catch up with technological realities—their form and operation will differ vastly from traditional academic institutions.

The two most notable things about the impact of the ongoing communications revolution on education are (1) how little has changed and (2) how much has changed. At the dawn of the television age a half century ago, David Sarnoff and other TV pioneers dreamed that television would totally transform education. It didn't. And more than a century after the debut of the telephone industry, hardly any classrooms in America have telephones. A decade and a half into the age of the personal computer, the use of PCs in most schools and colleges remains trivial.

Yet, while not much has changed technologically in the mainstream of education for a century (or two or five or ten), at the edges of this huge enterprise modern media have had important effects, and rapid, even revolutionary changes are happening. Under the deceptively benign label of "distance learning," the swift technological eddies of the telecosm are eroding the foundation of academic bureaucracies in much the same way they are toppling the established institutional structures of the telephone, broadcast television, and financial services industries.

"Telecourses"—the interactive form of distance learning that puts faraway teachers and students into two-way communication—are spreading rapidly. An Office of Technology Assessment study found that distance learning programs had spread from only ten states in 1987 to "virtually all" fifty states by 1989. The impetus for the growth of telelearning is productivity; but telecourses seem to make productivity attractive to institutions that may not believe or realize they are concerned about cost-effectiveness. The "effectiveness" lure of telecourses is that they offer instructional services whose content and/or quality simply would not otherwise be available locally. Moreover, research shows that distance learning is at least as effective as regular classroom teaching, and may even be more effective, regardless of subject. The cost of distance learning is steadily declining; when transportation and other costs including student time are properly accounted, the cost of telecourses may be less than conventional classroom services.[45] The following examples provide hints of the transformation of learning the coming broadband, digital, multimedia networks of the knowledge age will bring:

- National Technological University, an electronic graduate engineering school with no campus and no full-time faculty, beams its 12,000 hours of courses by satellite from its Fort Collins, Colorado, headquarters to over 5,000 engineers in video classrooms at worksites of scores of subscribing organizations scattered all over the United States. Leading faculty at over forty participating universities nationwide provide NTU's telecourses.
  Students—generally, employed engineers pursuing continuing education and professional development—can attend courses either in real time at the workplace or by tape delay. They communicate with professors by telephone or electronic mail. With new digital signal-compression technology, NTU now can deliver courses anywhere a satellite dish can be put up at one quarter the cost of a typical college class, according to NTU's president, Lionel Baldwin.

- In contrast to austerity measures, networks increase teaching productivity. The Broward County, Florida, school district—eighth biggest in the U.S.—has linked all 180 of its schools in a comprehensive computer network. "We can see how we could expand curriculum offerings without having to find stand-alone teachers [for each classroom]," said school superintendent Virgil Morgan.[46]

- The AT&T Long Distance Learning Network is designed around clusters of eight or nine classrooms located throughout the U.S. and other countries organized for cooperative learning on interdisciplinary projects. The groups, called "learning circles," were developed to assure a rich level of two-way communication, and were conceived with the requirements of work-connected learning in mind. "Increasingly, we all depend on and work with people who are not in the same room," explains Margaret Riel, AT&T education program manager. "Cooperative groups via telecommunications teach students ways to interact over the network."[47]

Distance learning is an intermediate step toward a telelearning environment where distance, location, and attendance become arbitrary and largely irrelevant factors in learning. Basically, schools will be transformed from a centralized architectural and bureaucratic *structure* to a dispersed information and service *channel*. Technological opportunity and economic necessity will give the individual learner of any age at least as many choices of "schools" as the television audience now has of cable TV channels. For most adults and many youth, school will not be identified with any distinct building or location, but rather with a brand or franchise of media through which services are accessed. Home technology—video, audio, computer, telephone—is far more adroit at meeting diverse life cycle needs for entertainment, information, work, and learning than is the technology of conventional academic structures. And telelearning technology can help conserve the modern family's scarcest resource, time.

Even to the extent younger children require custodial care in some central facility, those buildings no longer will contain simply a collection of classrooms. Rather, they will house a diversity of alternative services and programs, somewhat analogous to today's shopping mall "food court" which provides, under one roof, a wide choice of menus and vendors to serve individual preferences and needs.

On one hand, schools are going to work. In Florida today, public schools have established "satellite classrooms" at major employers' worksites to enable parents to commute and spend more time with their children. Distance learning networks could enable such classrooms to offer the full spectrum of educational subject matter for children of all ages, not just the elementary level. The same network can serve the parent's need for on-the-job education and training. Parents and kids could even share common learning experiences, such as for health or drug education. The benefits to employers: reduced employee stress and fatigue, reduced absenteeism, increased worker productivity, enhanced recruiting, reduced employee turnover, and an inherently closer school-work connection.[48]

Pacific Bell is an $8.7 billion company with 65,000 employees. In 1985, it launched a pilot program with 100 employees to determine the benefits of telecommuting. The project was so successful that the company decided to offer the program on a continuing basis. Today nearly 2,000 employees across California—ranging from financial management staff to engineering and planning personnel—spend between 20% and 100% of their workweek at home.

—Edward Segal

"How to Commute in Your Bathrobe," *The Wall Street Journal* (July 1, 1991)

On the other hand, work is coming back home (where it used to be centered, before the industrial revolution). A survey for the Electronic Industries Association found that one-third of all U.S. households have a home office or workspace.[49] A 1989 *Washington Post* survey found that 62 percent of working mothers in the Washington region would, if they could, work at home to be closer to their children. Spending more time with the family was the fourth favorite reason (named by 30 percent) for working at home, a *Home Office Computing* magazine survey found, after changing life (31 percent), making more money (42 percent), and being your own boss (51 percent).

For these and other reasons, studies by Link Resources, a market research firm, find that the number of Americans working at least partly at home—already over a fifth of the workforce—is zooming upward. The number of people doing money-making work at home was 34.8 million in 1990, a 30-percent increase over the previous year, and up 10 million from two years earlier—some 5.5 million, about one in six, are telecommuters, working at home for an employer. Since 1990, the number of self-employed people working at home increased 5.4 percent to 11.8 million. Projections indicate that there may be 40 million U.S. home workers by 1992 and more than 50 million by 1994. Another survey by a California consulting firm, JALA Associates, concluded that only 20 to 30 percent of today's jobs could *not* be done by workers telecommuting from home.[50]

The same communications and computer technology enabling more and more workers to stay home at least part-time with their children while telecommuting to work can provide educational, health care, and other services at home for both parent and child. Looked at the other way around, such HL technology can permit educators to telecommute to the consumers of their services, without the encumbrance of a school building or classroom. This is another way of creating a more intimate link between work and learning for the whole family.

IMPACT 3: EXPERTISE IS MORE IN THE NETWORK, LESS IN THE PERSON

HL technology also makes the very status of the individual expert obsolete. Scientists now know that the "expert" professor pouring knowledge into the empty mind of a passive student is a counterproductive model of effective learning.[51] But it's true for a reason that goes beyond method. Because of new technology, expertise itself is rapidly becoming less an attribute of individual persons and more a property of *systems* and *networks*. The latter have become the key location of valuable expertise in the modern economy—not only in science and engineering, but in finance, retailing, entertainment, arts, and just about every other kind of business.

Why? For one thing, the capacity of a single human brain to absorb—much less interpret—all the significant knowledge in an important subject area is limited. But the sheer volume of available information being generated by the new technologies is exploding. Analysts estimate that the total volume of encoded information doubles at least every decade; in fast-paced fields, available information doubles every few years—or even months. One study cited by George Gilder even indicated that stored data would *double nineteen times* (in other words, would be over half a million times greater) by the year 2000.[52] Indeed, rapid advances in science and technology have reduced the "half-life" of valid knowledge in many areas to as little as eighteen months.

Besides the rapid obsolescence of almost every expert's knowledge base, personalized expertise is fading because of the inherent limits of applying it to the myriad of decisions that need to be made in the highly complex, far-flung operating systems of modern businesses. An example of the value of integrated and networked expertise, similar to CAMS, is Moca, another expert system developed by American Airlines to handle the mind-boggling problem of routing and maintaining 622 aircraft. A team of three knowledge engineers spent a year building the combined knowledge of thirty of America's best experts on airplane routing into Moca, which runs on a network of Macintosh computers. Moca now saves the airline half a million dollars a year by scheduling maintenance more efficiently than any one or even all of the company's human experts could do.[53]

It's important to understand that Moca has neither abolished expertise nor obviated the human role in problem solving. Rather, it has diffused expertise from an individual possession to a team creation, integrated and encoded in an automated system that makes that expertise far more accessible and useful to those who need it.

Such expert systems illustrate only the most concrete way that expertise is becoming progressively more a property of networks and less of persons. Groupware such as Lotus's Notes or IBM's new TeamFocus is a major step toward making the shared expertise of teamwork the standard for almost every type of business and organization.

Visit an engineering or design meeting at Boeing today and you are unlikely to see people clustered around a table shouting at each other for attention, or passively sitting with hands raised waiting to be called on while one person holds court standing at a blackboard. Rather you will see people sitting at personal computers typing their thoughts into a networked "meeting" via software that keeps tabs on every person's input and makes it instantly available to everyone else. Using the TeamFocus groupware, Boeing has cut the time needed to complete all sorts of team projects to *one-tenth* of what it used to take.[54]

Given that 30 to 70 percent of American managers' time typically is spent in meetings, the economic value of such savings looms large. In fact, as the spread of participatory and collaborative management practices engages workers, suppliers, and customers in a growing cascade of meetings to identify needs, set goals, and solve problems, management by groupware is likely to become irresistible. But that points again toward the end of the academic notion of expertise.

Whether based in special computerized meeting rooms where all participants gather at once, or dispersed over national or even global communications networks, teamwork via computer-mediated groupware is obliterating the elite role of the personal expert. Among the keys to the time- and money-saving power of decision-targeted systems such as Team-Focus is anonymity. Participants are free to contribute at any time, as much as they want, without risk of being shouted down or being judged for saying something silly or wild or impolitic. Ideas are judged on their merit, not on the status or credentials—or race, gender, creed, national origin, etc.—of the contributor.

This is clearly a far more truly democratic work environment. For the same reason, though, it reduces if not erases any justification for the status symbols and bureaucratic perks normally conferred on individual experts.

Even in systems in which anonymity is not a factor, such as Notes, the openness of the network itself tends to flatten hierarchy—any message from anyone is a message to everyone. The substantive content and value of what a person actually knows and can contribute quickly outshine credentials or other superficial trappings of "expert" status.

A hint of the kind of brain power groupware may be leading to is in the latest approach to designing supercomputers. Instead of trying to make one or a few processors crunch scads of numbers at a furious pace, builders of new "connection" machines connect hundreds or even thousands of relatively cheap computer-on-a-chip microprocessors of the sort you would find in an ordinary desktop computer. Having many connections for sharing information, these machines let the many not-so-smart processors divide up a big problem into small parts that each works on simultaneously. The resulting efficiency enables the machines, sometimes called "hypercubes," to solve many problems with the speed of multimillion-dollar supercomputers, at a small fraction of the cost.

If connection in hypernetworks can enable fairly dumb computer chips to perform at a relatively "genius" level, the same kind of amplification of the far more powerful human brain may occur when groupware and large capacity telecosm networks link people together in a similar way. The resulting superexpertise of "human hypercubes" may be the key to keeping human power in the lead and in control of systems marching steadily toward "human equivalence."

IMPACT 4: LEARNING SPANS THE HUMAN LIFE CYCLE

A recent report from the Committee on Economic Development calls for new kinds of education and training services to address the needs of the entire human life cycle.[55] But there is more to a true life-cycle learning system than just a collection of discrete programs targeted on preschool children, youth, workforce adults, and retirees. The new hyperlearning enterprise not only cuts across age groups but joins people of diverse ages in shared or collaborative learning activities.

As school buildings are replaced by channels on telelearning networks, the age and other social characteristics of participating learners become irrelevant, sometimes even invisible. A special class I observed in the fall of 1990 on the distance learning network at Waubonsee Community College, located in the suburbs west of Chicago, featured actor Laurence Luckinbill showing excerpts from his one-man show about Lyndon Johnson, giving a lecture on the actor's research and preparation for the role, and then engaging in give-and-take discussion with the students. The students, located at a half dozen locations—including Waubonsee, other colleges, a high school, and a grade school, all linked to Luckinbill's downtown studio by two-way video and audio channels—included young and middle-aged college students, high school students, fifth graders, and a number of local residents of various ages who just dropped in to share a rewarding experience.

Joining children and adults—especially parents and their offspring—in cooperative learning experiences is not only more efficient but more powerful and productive for both. Instructional Systems Inc. is currently using established technology—laptop computers connected by telephone to an integrated learning system running on larger computers in the company's Hackensack, New Jersey, offices—to deliver at-home basic skills instruction to 1,800 welfare mothers and their children in New York City. As the mothers work toward attaining their GEDs, their relationships to their children as role models, tutors, and peers are all strengthened.

Life-cycle integration is more complex than just passing through successive stages of "lifelong" learning—it means people of various ages "recycling" learning at any or all levels (basic, intermediate, advanced), depending on individual needs and circumstances. Career switching and job obsolescence mean going back to "square one" occasionally, at any age. Technological diffusion of expertise means that anyone may serve as someone else's expert, tutor, or mentor regardless of either's age or social condition. Working and learning via groupware on networks, combined with telecommuting, make it not only unnecessary to discriminate a worker's age but maybe impossible. And not only do home-based workers get more opportunity to provide parental nurturing, their kids also get the opportunity at an early age to participate in work-based learning by helping out with Dad's job or Mom's business, traditional notions of "child labor" notwithstanding.

THE END OF "EDUCATION"

This imminent hyperlearning world, where learning and expertise are diffused everyplace and where people of any age and status may be engaged in learning anytime, makes the infrastructure of "schooling" irrelevant and even obstructive. Yet, as I noted at the beginning of this chapter, the inertia of language may lag for a while behind the sweeping reality of this technological transformation.

In the seventies it was trendy to define schools, colleges, or universities "without walls" to suggest a variant academic institution that was open to the real world. Like "distance learning" or "distance education"—which imply that the telecosm is a mere adjunct to academia rather than a time bomb destined to blow it up—other mongrel platitudes will burden us for a while with a vocabulary contrived to portray revolution as mere evolution: electronic classroom, embedded training, campus free college, and a term I find particularly idiotic, "technology-based" teaching (as if talk and chalk, books and pencils and such are not technology). Bolder editorialists may begin to speak of classrooms without teachers, schools without classrooms, or ultimately even education without schools. But eventually it will become clear that the system break I identify with hyperlearning represents not merely a new form of "education" freed of this or that encumbrance, but a world freed of the encumbrance of education altogether.

While it may seem difficult to believe at the moment that "hyperlearning" or some other terminology will simply replace tweaked variations on the vocabulary of "education" by the early years of the twenty-first century, a precedent can be found in the automotive revolution at the beginning of the twentieth century.

In 1895, ten years after the invention of the increasingly popular "horseless carriage," a Chicago newspaper offered a $500 prize (serious money) for a new name to indicate what the technology was, rather than what it was not. Suggestions ranged from "autowain" to "petrocar," and the prize-winner was "motocycle."

But by the turn of the century, it was the French term "automobile" which started to catch on, to the great consternation of the perspicacious *New York Times,* which condemned both the machine and its name in a January 3, 1899 editorial:

There is something uncanny about these newfangled vehicles. They are all unutterably ugly and never a one of them has been provided with a good or even an endurable name. The French, who are usually orthodox in their etymology if in nothing else, have evolved "automobile," which being half Greek and half Latin is so near to indecent that we print it with hesitation; while speakers of English have been fatally attracted by the irrelevant word "horseless."

All this angst was to no avail. A year later the *Times* acceded to the people's choice and changed its index to cite horseless vehicles thenceforth as automobiles.[56]

However quaint it may seem in hindsight, there was and is nothing trivial about this kind of semantic struggle. In the case of the automotive revolution, the economic—and hence political—stakes could not have been greater. At the end of the last century, farmers represented over 40 percent of the U.S. workforce, and a majority of Americans lived on farms or in rural towns. The farmers themselves owned eighteen million horses and mules, and millions more such animals were used in transportation, the Army, mining, and other fields. Altogether there was at least one horse or mule for every four or even three people in the U.S. The horse and its offspring ate like, well, horses—at least a quarter of the country's cropland was used to provide them with fodder.

Over half of the American workforce at the time had a stake in the horse economy. So every time an automobile or truck or tractor replaced a horse or mule, it cost the farmer a consumer of two cash crops as well as some of the market for the animals he raised, and it threatened the livelihood of a host of blacksmiths, mule skinners, saddle and bridle makers, liverymen, veterinarians, and such. Not surprisingly, Farmers' Anti-Automobile Leagues were among the political coalitions that formed to combat the dangerous machine.

So the ferment to replace "horseless carriage"—implying an incomplete or deficient technology—with "automobile"—a term almost synonymous with "independence"—was charged with political importance. As sociologist David Riesman once observed, words are not merely transitory objects, "they change us, they socialize or unsocialize us."

"Hyperlearning" may not be the ultimate people's choice to label the fabric of new technology that is making teachers and classrooms as archaic as buggywhips and horsecollars. After all, as the *Times'* current linguistic tribune, William Safire, may point out, the term obnoxiously commingles Greek and Old English etymology. Maybe "autowain" deserves a second look.

Whatever the words, it is inevitable that, as the HL revolution unfolds, a sufficiently potent public before long will seize on some term to package its recognition that learning has been liberated from the thrall of academia. Soon thereafter "school" truly will be out and "education" will be kaput.

The practical question this startling thought no doubt raises is: How are we going to work and make a living in an economy in which no one goes to school? Stay tuned.

CHAPTER 4

MINDCRAFT: WORKING IN THE KNOWLEDGE AGE

• • •

Automation was something a lot of people worried about in the early 1950s. The memory of the Great Depression was still fresh as the United States wondered whether the demobilization of the wartime economy might throw millions of workers back into unemployment. Anxiety over economic conversion was heightened by popular suspicion that the torrent of advanced technology unleashed by the war would eradicate jobs in wholesale numbers. These fears were crystallized in Kurt Vonnegut's 1952 novel, *Player Piano,* which satirically traced the gloomy vision of a soon-to-be America where computers wound up taking over all but the most skilled jobs. In Vonnegut's dystopian economy, everyone other than an elite cadre of engineers and managers was on the dole, either in the army or doing WPA-style makework like sweeping streets.

Despite some industrial upheavals, things haven't turned out the way Vonnegut portrayed. But with the world today again in the midst of sweeping structural changes, and with the United States once more facing the challenge of military conversion, the even more daunting power of today's "smart" technology raises similar fears of "de-skilling" and "downscaling" and "displacement" of jobs. And the greatest technological revolutions still lie ahead.

The kind of vast technological revolution the rise of the knowledge age economy represents has occurred only rarely in human history. As Alvin

Toffler has explained, this is only the third such "wave" of transformation—the first being the shift from tribal hunting and gathering to agricultural civilization, and the second being the overthrow of agrarian society by the industrial revolution. These waves of climactic change always have included massive shifts in the distribution of employment and the nature of work:

- Agriculture, which employed over a quarter of American workers as recently as 1920, provided only 4 percent of the U.S. jobs in the 1980s, and will account for only about 2.5 percent of the workforce of the 1990s.
- Manufacturing, which provided one of every four American jobs in 1960, accounted for only one of every five jobs in 1980 and will represent fewer than one job in six during this decade. Fewer than 10 percent of today's U.S. workers actually make a product, and the number may be down to only 5 percent by the end of the 1990s.
- From 1940 to 1990, service industries' share of total U.S. employment went from 45 percent to over 70 percent.

The small amount of employment in mining (less than 1 percent) and the less than 7 percent of the U.S. workforce employed in construction can be lumped with the larger share of "making" jobs in manufacturing to simplify matters and make the general trend clear: Jobs that involve growing things and making things are fast disappearing, leaving the large majority of workers—soon, nearly all—engaged in doing things for other people.[57]

The broad trend of the past seems to counter the Luddite anxiety that advanced technology and automation reduce employment. As a recent econometric analysis by Michael Boskin and Lawrence Lau concludes: "[T]echnical progress is capital-saving rather than labor-saving. . . . [I]t is not likely to be a prime cause of unemployment for the aggregate economy."[58]

When mechanization swept the agricultural sector, a growing industrial sector was able to absorb the displaced farmers and field hands. When automation took off in manufacturing, an expanding services sector provided new job opportunities. Even as a newfound zeal for quality and competitiveness led to rapid growth in U.S. manufacturing productivity during the past ten years, millions of new jobs still were created in the American economy as a whole, and nearly all "displaced" industrial workers eventually were reemployed in service jobs, if not other manufacturing work.

But now we face a dilemma—the old cycle of job replacement and recreation may not work anymore. The spurt of labor force growth that occurred when the baby boom generation was pouring into it and female participation was increasing rapidly kept the American economy as a whole growing during the period after 1970 when U.S. productivity growth became anemic compared to earlier times. Because of the baby bust that followed the baby boom, the U.S. workforce now is growing only about half as fast—fewer new producers means less new production, unless each worker's output can be significantly increased.

The country's key economic problem is centered on the productivity of the services sector—where the great majority of workers now are employed. Part of the problem is that official statistics that measure service productivity are thin, antiquated, and probably distorted—most notably by having a hard time gauging improvements in the *quality* of services delivered.[59] But many economists believe that even improved services data would show that both the level and growth of productivity in the services sector as a whole are significantly lower than in the producing sectors.

Whatever the statisticians may decide, it's clear at present that the U.S., in the midst of a real recession, is not producing sufficient income to meet its needs, pay its debts, and take care of its global strategic interests and obligations. In the absence of major expansion of the workforce, the only way to increase the nation's income is through far more rapid total productivity growth than has been common for two decades. Given that most employment is in the services sector, that is where a substantial increase in productivity must occur.

Market forces must agree, because in the latest recession the most turbulent structural dislocations and the sharpest unemployment peaks have been in services, notably in the key "FIRE" segment—finance (S&Ls, brokers, banks), insurance, and real estate. The embedded services within the producing sectors also are shedding jobs by the millions, in pursuit of efficiency and competitiveness.

This is an ironic flaw in Vonnegut's early vision that has just dawned on many people in the recent U.S. recession: Modern automation is no less likely to displace the elite managers and experts and "professionals" than the proletariat of the factory floor. The new unemployed are not just field hands or blue-collar steelworkers and auto assemblers—they are well-to highly-educated white-collar office workers, middle managers, professionals, and bureaucrats, now being joined by several hundred thousand engineers, technicians, officers, and other skilled people displaced by cutbacks in the defense sector. In the last recession, in late 1981, only one in eight persons collecting unemployment payments was a white-collar worker; in mid-1991 white-collar workers represented one of every five people collecting jobless pay.[60]

And the gross statistics understate white-collar and professional unemployment and underemployment, because these people tend not to declare themselves "unemployed"—instead, they become "early retirees" and self-employed "consultants."

The apparently inescapable need to use new technology and organizational restructuring to raise productivity growth in services to the same high levels as in agriculture and manufacturing raises profoundly interesting questions: Where are the displaced workers going to go? Where are the new job opportunities going to be found?

The problem is: *We seem to have run out of sectors.* The previous technological revolutions shifted jobs, first from farming to industry, then from industry to services. There seems to be nowhere but unemployment and welfare to put the surplus service workers. Is there?

Maybe. The same HL technology that is transforming the role of learning in human society, making education obsolete, is also restructuring the global economy in a way that offers unprecedented opportunities for economic freedom and prosperity. While the economic transformation is inevitable, and its major impacts are now visible, how broadly the benefits it offers will be distributed depends greatly on the political choices made by the U.S. and other nations in the near future.

IMPACT 5: LEARNING AND WORK MERGE IN THE "FOURTH SECTOR"

The first hopeful answer to the dilemma of the sectoral squeeze on employment lies in the growth of the "knowledge sector" as a unique, fourth sector of the modern economy. Work and businesses based on information have a special, pleasant advantage: Information is the closest thing we will ever have to an inexhaustible resource. Unlike energy and materials, information is practically boundless. So, in theory, the knowledge sector need never run into "limits to growth."

. . . I have worked with a plant manager in a very advanced manufacturing operation who was toying with the idea of calling the plant a college. More and more of what they were doing from day to day was some form of learning, based on their engagement with abstract information and figuring out new courses of action based on what they've learned. Work and learning had become increasingly interconnected, and the organization had to become a learning environment if the work was to be carried out optimally.

—Shoshana Zuboff

"Smart Machines and Learning People," *Harvard Magazine* (Nov.–Dec. 1988)

The good news in the expansion of the knowledge sector is that "mindcraft" is fast replacing "handicraft" as the major form of human work. Government data indicate that about 60 percent of U.S. workers today hold jobs that mainly entail handling information; a more accurate assessment of job performance would probably show that an even larger number are doing a substantial amount of "knowledge work." In an increasingly "smart" HL environment, that knowledge work means not just crunching and shuffling data but *learning* in elaborate systems combining human teams and intelligent machines. With the number of hands-on production jobs fast approaching zero, the remaining mindcraft work is in a sector that is theoretically limitless.

There is, of course, as much room to slip between theory and practice as between the proverbial cup and lip. The knowledge sector is not the same thing as other sectors. But, because knowledge content is ever more crucial to the value of production in nearly every business, the knowledge sector tends to overlap other fields, rather than being a distinctly independent domain.

Moreover, information has special characteristics that distinguish it from all other economic entities. Most notable may be that information can be taken without being lost. By the same token, information may be licensed or leased to a large number of people at the same time without being divided or diminished. This makes intellectual property, or more simply "software," extremely profitable to own—and therefore very attractive to steal. So information's special nature also makes property law far more critical to information-based businesses, even as it makes enforcement of that law more complicated.

As I mentioned, who realizes the benefits that mindcraft work and the knowledge sector offer, and to what extent, depends greatly on public policies. Ironically, one of the most important issues of the day—securing the global protection for intellectual property sought through the latest, so-called Uruguay round of international trade negotiations, which have been stymied by France's stubborn refusal to reduce its agricultural subsidies—has gone virtually unmentioned in the recent U.S. political campaign. This is the sort of multinational political myopia that threatens to squander the greatest opportunity for economic prosperity the world has ever known.

Taking full advantage of the opportunities the knowledge age economy offers, and avoiding the painful chaos and social friction technological revolutions usually bring cannot be attained through incremental adjustments and "more of the same" strategies. Realizing the most hopeful promises of the technological and social trends of the HL revolution will require abandoning outworn assumptions, policies, and institutions.

As knowledge converges with capital to become the prime source of economic value, the "learning enterprise"—the business of research and learning that creates and transmits knowledge—already has become the crucial source of capital formation. But the knowledge age learning enterprise must and will resemble the little red schoolhouse as little as future transportation systems will resemble the horse and buggy.

The real "school-to-work transition" has been largely misunderstood by the "competitiveness" doctors—it is not a mere adolescent stepping-stone from childhood studies to adult labor. Now it means a collective economic transformation from a vanishing age where "school" could exist as a masonry cloister separated from the worlds of living and working to a new knowledge age where active learning impregnates all work and social life.

The extinction of academic education that HL technology makes inevitable is not merely a tolerable impact of hyperlearning. It actually turns out to be *essential* to removing one of the key barriers to the opportunity mindcraft work offers: Credentialism.

At the heart of the connection between school, learning, and work is employers' need to be assured that workers will have the essential competencies when they *begin* employment, and will continue to adapt and expand their productive capabilities throughout a working lifetime. Increasingly, traditional academic credentials—diplomas—do not provide this assurance.

The teaching model of traditional education consciously serves the needs of a machine age, industrial economy. In practice, it maximizes failure. Its criteria for academic performance are based on finding a "norm" to measure against; it grades "on the curve." Time is structured, scheduled, and fixed uniformly to meet the requirements of the school. Students are forced to compete to achieve as much as they can within the periods of time allotted for each activity: so many minutes per period, so many periods per day, so many days per semester/quarter/session, so many sessions per year. This design requires that most students fail or do less well most of the time so that a minority of them can be labeled "excellent." The system sorts students into *A, B, C, D,* and *F* much like a machine that sorts eggs into jumbo, extra large, large, medium, and small. Thus, the main functional focus of the system is not *learning,* it is *screening out.*

In the mindcraft economy, educational credentials that represent the residue after screening out failure have as little place as the obsolete industrial age practice of inspecting products for defects at the *end* of the assembly line. In the new environment of what's sometimes called Total Quality Management, increasingly canny hyperlearning systems will pursue the goal of zero failure by using statistical assessments, expert systems, teamwork, and so forth to assure that every step of production is done right—the first time. And the very nature of both HL technology and mindcraft work demands that the "production" of learning, including its human and nonhuman elements, be as nearly defect-free as possible.

Just as HL dissolves other conventional academic notions, modern learning technology now makes the distinction between teaching and testing irrelevant. Automated instructional systems build real-time, continuous assessment and feedback into the teaching and learning processes that are ever more embedded in the many tools of the smart environment.

Intelligent tutoring systems create and use minute-to-minute measures of the learner's performance. Because such technology enables virtually every learner to achieve "grade A" competency in every module of every course of every subject, the idea of "failure" is obsolete and irrelevant.[61]

The diffusion of expertise through networks erodes the status of personal expertise academic credentials are supposed to mark. The common practice of mindcraft work in teams linked through groupware eliminates most if not all the functional distinction and rewards such credentials are now expected to confer.

Policies that force the imposition of degrees and diplomas against this technological tide simply work to corrupt and sabotage the most essential production systems of a knowledge age economy. Such credentials can only thwart access to mindcraft work and subvert productivity.

The mindcraft economy will replace degrees and diplomas with precise instruments that *certify* attainment of *competency*. Groupware-based teams will give little or no premium to what you did in school fifteen years ago but will be quite interested in what knowledge, skills, and talents you can bring to solving this problem right now. Competency-certifying instruments are not uncommon even today—we have bar examinations, medical board certification exams, and basic driver's license tests—but competency-based learning and certification will become virtually universal for mindcraft workers. And, instead of being used to screen people out of employment opportunities, the new, high-tech processes of certification will focus on *screening in*—identifying the nature and degree of specific shortcomings and leading directly to the most efficient learning resources needed to close the gaps and qualify people to perform the work they desire. HL technology now makes such procedures feasible—and virtually unavoidable.

IMPACT 6: OWNERSHIP OF CAPITAL PROGRESSIVELY REPLACES LABOR

The steady, rapid advance of HL technology is leading inexorably toward economically "human equivalent" automation by sometime in the first third or so of the next century. The philosophical meaning and timing of this development are less important than the watershed this implies in the history of work and society:

Within the lifetimes of people alive today—certainly including America's youth—it will become cheaper to employ robotic systems to perform a growing number of jobs, both skilled and unskilled, than to hire humans at the lowest minimal subsistence wage of the poorest Third World country.

At least by that point—and probably much sooner in the U.S. and many other countries and regions—the "choice" proffered by *America's Choice,* the report of the Commission on the Skills of the American Workforce,[62] will be obsolete: No longer "high skills or low wages," it will be something closer to high skills *and* low wages *or* low skills and no wages. Already today, workers at high-tech, state-of-the-art automobile engine factories in Mexico have attained U.S. levels of productivity and quality at wages of about $3.00 an hour.[63]

More precisely, ownership of capital from now onward will be progressively more important to personal and family income than performance of "labor" as it traditionally has been envisioned, even for those with nominally "high" skills. The reason: Knowledge age technology makes the value of physical goods as well as services depend increasingly on their knowledge content.

"Capital" and "intellectual capital" become ever more the same thing. For example, when the 386 microprocessor chip was Intel's top-of-the-line product a couple of years ago, the company was earning over 80 percent of its profit from a button-size device that represented only 5 percent of its manufacturing volume, as measured in numbers or kilograms of chips and circuit boards. The economic value in what Intel sells is in the knowledge that went into the design, not in the physical mass of materials, which is ever shrinking.

Nevertheless, the importance of intellectual capital to the modern economy tends to be understated because of accounting practices left over from an earlier era. Amazingly, the thousands of patents and copyrights owned by companies like IBM, or Merck & Co., or Texas Instruments do not appear on the corporate balance sheets as "assets," even though the companies are being paid millions of dollars in license fees for the rights to use that intellectual property. Under established U.S. accounting rules, a patent a company buys can be reported as an asset; but the zillions of dollars that companies put into their own R&D have to be counted as an expenditure, not as an investment.[64]

Again, the critical issues in the increasingly dominant knowledge sector of the economy are (1) owning intellectual property and (2) protecting it from being taken. Today, the most efficient way to transfer a few hundred million dollars across a border, whether in the form of trade or theft, is not in a sackful of diamonds but in a prototype computer chip that could be hidden comfortably under a postage stamp. Effective establishment and protection of intellectual property rights is crucial to the entire global, knowledge age economy because the profitability of either making or taking software is so enormous: A bootleg copy of the $95 million hit movie *Terminator 2* can be and certainly has been pirated in countries with lax or negligible copyright laws on a videocassette that cost only pennies to make from nine ounces of common plastic and maybe a gram of high-tech rust.

Even as the dollar value of world trade climbs, the material mass and labor content of what is exchanged steadily fall. Japan has gotten rich making and selling consumer electronic gadgets that get smaller and lighter and cheaper to build with each passing day. The money is not in the size or weight of the product but in the "smarts" not only expressed in the product's design but increasingly built into the product itself. About thirty times more money flows around the world for financial transactions—as data, in the form of massless electromagnetic impulses—than is used to pay for international purchases of goods.[65]

The personal ownership of knowledge as capital begins with the common endowment of brainpower each adequately healthy human is born with. This birthright of human capital is protected by the constitutional prohibition of slavery—ownership by the individual is guaranteed. But as intellectual capital is increasingly not only stored but generated in intelligent systems outside the skin boundary of human capital—data networks and artificial "brains"—participation in not only the use but in the ownership of these tools will be essential to economic democracy.

Fortunately, it appears that the very nature of knowledge age technology makes economic democracy essential to economic development and "competitiveness." The whole thrust of the development of both computer and communications technology now is toward openness and connectedness—if only because of the primal fact that the value of information grows the more it can be connected to other information. As the dramatic events of the past few years have demonstrated, Soviet and other authoritarian or bureaucratic regimes that depend on the suppression and control of information cannot effectively compete against the knowledge-intensive capital—whether military or commercial—that thrives in democratic environments. An information-repressing organization cannot effectively employ information-exploding technology.

At the same time, ever smaller, cheaper, and more agile information technology already has become almost impossible to repress even by regimes that want to do so. Portable video cameras and umbrella-size satellite dishes now bring global eyewitnesses to the scenes of freedom-hungry protesters standing unarmed in front of tanks in Tiananmen Square, Stealth fighters bombing Baghdad, and out-of-control cops beating up Rodney King on a night-shrouded L.A. street.

The accelerating trend of information-based technology is clearly toward more power, faster, smaller, and cheaper. More open and more competitive markets enhance this trend. Cheaper, more portable, more universal technology offers the best hope to the poor and disadvantaged to share in the income-producing ownership of knowledge capital.

The movement toward democratic knowledge technology, and economic democracy, may be thwarted by the backlash of obsolescent but still-potent bureaucracies seeking to defend their threatened privileges and authority—as we saw in the Soviet Union, as well as in giant corporations or public agencies in their own throes of "restructuring." It also could be distorted or obstructed by the inertia of outworn rules, policies, institutions—or simply what the struggling democrats of the FSU (former Soviet Union) decry as "old thinking."

There is a real hazard that backward-looking policies could deny some people access to knowledge-generating, wealth-producing tools even as the onward sweep of technology is erasing the industrial age "jobs" they still depend on for income. Epochal economic transformations like the agricultural and industrial revolutions of the past often have been marked by turbulent and even violent social upheaval.

The Luddite rebellions against the technological revolution in textile manufacturing dragged on for over five bloody years in England during the same period as the War of 1812. While the Luddites are now recalled derisively as enemies of progress, it's hard not to sympathize with the displaced cottage workers who were saddled with the losses of economic restructuring while being denied, in the short run, opportunity to share in the gains. The Luddite rebellion petered out as industrialization began to create more and better jobs than the ones that had been deposed. But the flood tide of the industrial revolution in the late nineteenth and early twentieth centuries was continually punctuated by similar violent conflicts, such as the Haymarket Square riot in Chicago in 1886.

Trend does not have to be destiny, as the historian Lewis Mumford pointed out, and there is no reason that the structural upheavals of a new economic revolution cannot be handled more wisely and peacefully than in the past. But precedent shows that the cost of short-sighted, reactionary policies can be painful.

As management consultant Charles Handy accurately portrays it, the workforce of the immediate future will be divided into three folds, like the leaves of a shamrock: (1) The *core* of highly proficient technical and managerial talent that most larger organizations will want to employ as intensively and permanently as possible. (2) A cadre of skilled *contractors* and consultants who work only temporarily for a given organization, but full time for themselves as entrepreneurs. (3) A substantial mass of *part-timers* who may work nominally either as contractors or employees, including: women (and some men) wanting to devote much but not all of their time to child-rearing; nominal "retirees" who neither want nor can afford (or be afforded by society) to stop working entirely; and youth or people of any age who need part-time income while they devote the rest of their time to "recapitalizing" themselves either through reeducation and retraining or entrepreneurship.[66]

The realistic set of economic roles Handy surveys—widely visible even now—may not even constitute a "workforce" in the traditional sense. Virtually all the economic players Handy charts are more aptly seen as "human capitalists" than as "workers." Obviously two-thirds of the working people described above—the consultants and the part-timers—are proprietors of businesses that market services "à la carte" to one or several customers.

But look today at the workers in Handy's "core" group—the supposedly invaluable full-time "employees"—and what you will find mostly are "free agents" (in the sports business sense) working formally or informally under contract, always with an eye toward their personal value and opportunities in the marketplace. "Lifetime employment" is vanishing even in Japan (where it never applied to more than a minority of the workforce anyway), as a more ambitious generation of youth in a labor-short economy accurately perceive greater rewards from strategic job-shifting than from patient plodding for an industrial *daimyo*. The same precious personal assets that make the core workers seem too valuable to lose also make them too valuable not to try to shanghai or reduce away from a competitor.

Nearly all the people in Handy's shamrock economy gain income not by selling their labor but by renting their human capital. While for a small and dwindling group—perhaps ultimately limited to dancers and athletes—their human capital includes a major share of physical, bodily prowess, for most people their human capital is intellectual capital: knowledge and skill. And, for a large and growing number of telecommuters and home-workers, that capital base of brain-stored know-what and know-how can be (and probably must be) enhanced by an array of external information assets: computers, fax machines, cameras and other recording devices, databases and libraries of print, sound, and image information, and so forth.

Cel-Sci Corp., a biotechnology firm based in Alexandria, Virginia, is one of a growing number of examples of the minimal-employment organization of the coming mindcraft economy. The company contracts with about forty technical specialists to work on developing a chemical called interleukin-2 into a possible cure for cancer. "Employees are not what we call our people," says Geert Kersten, the firm's chief financial officer and one of its four full-time staff. "We call them the greater family of Cel-Sci, which includes the scientists, consultants, and advisers who have worked on this project over the past eight years."[67]

The workforce-less knowledge age economy of human capitalism can be viewed today in America's most advanced and successful industry, "Hollywood," a short-hand label for the diverse businesses of entertainment products and services, including sports. Underneath the rhetorical residue of the archaic notions of "owner" and "employee" or "management" and "union" is the visible reality of rampant participatory intellectual capitalism at work.

Everyone who works in the movie industry constantly seeks compensation not in wages or salaries but in "points"—a percentage share of *ownership* of the equity produced by creative effort. The end of every movie includes a long "crawl" listing the names of every person who worked on the project, from the assistant director to the gofer who brought in doughnuts during coffee breaks. The acknowledgments are not a sentimental gesture: The order, position, and size of print of each name is the result of a negotiated contract.

A milestone in the professional athlete's quest for the free agent's liberty to sell the use of his human capital in a competitive market was rookie football star Raghib "Rocket" Ismail's contract, which included a substantial equity share in the Toronto team that employed his services. A similar landmark: Capitalists called "producers" and "artists" in the music recording industry recently consummated a long-sought deal with the manufacturers of new digital recording products that requires a royalty to be paid to the software creators from the sale of each machine and storage unit (tape cassette or disc)—compensation for their intellectual *property* lost to copying.

Musicians are not the only "performers" who are in a race with technology. Movie actors who, a half century ago, were employed for wages or scale salaries, now make megabucks as owners of intellectual property—how much longer they will be able to do so is an open question.

The kind of powerful simulation technology that is displacing many musical performer jobs eventually will have the same effect on the silver screen. A 1987 video, *Rendezvous à Montréal,* featured performances by computer-generated recreations of actors Humphrey Bogart and Marilyn Monroe. "Tomorrow, more advanced technology will be able to replace actors with 'fresher faces,' or alter dialog and change the movement of actors' lips to match," producer/director George Lucas speculated in a 1988 interview. One of the new "synthespians," Billy, the computer-synthesized baby and star of *Tin Toy,* helped the short film's producer, Pixar, win an Oscar in 1989.[68] Lucas's forecast has come closer to reality with the villain of *Terminator 2,* a "liquid metal" killer robot created on Industrial Light & Magic computers that merges seamlessly with a human actor.

Computer-created movies reduce requirements not only for human actors but for production staff as well: "The total number of people required to produce a feature film will be substantially less," says Steven Jobs, co-owner of Pixar.[69] But that also means technology will enable more people to be producers and owners of movies, not just hired staff.

This sort of human capitalism, based on owning and leasing knowledge, may make sense for writers or artists or inventors. But how are regular working people going to create and own intellectual property?

The following example hints at the answer: Carnegie Group Inc., a Pittsburgh-based firm specializing in expert system software, has been working since 1988 with five major U.S. corporations in an alliance called the Initiative for Managing Knowledge Assets. The project is aimed at developing "knowledge processing" systems to capture the virtuoso know-how of highly skilled and experienced employees in such areas as design, engineering, financial analysis, markets, and corporate culture—making personal know-how a corporate asset.[70]

It might seem replacing skilled workers by auto-experts might fulfill Vonnegut's grim *Player Piano* scenario of mass unemployment. But the actual trend is likely to alter the economics of employment in a way that enriches both the worker and the workplace. Here's how:

As economist Anthony Carnevale has reported extensively, American employers tend to underinvest in educating and training their employees.[71] A major reason is that, in a nation whose constitution prohibits indentured servitude and slavery, employers face the genuine risk of getting less or no return on investments in worker development if the employee leaves. The economic loss is compounded if the employee goes to work for a competitor.

But the knowledge systems Carnegie Group and its partners are creating, and similar expert system projects such as American Airlines's Moca, will, by design, have the effect of allowing those firms (or other companies) to retain a substantial share of the *intellectual capital* their investments in employee training and development helped create. Moreover, as the CAMS example suggests, expert systems properly implemented in total learning systems become de facto trainers, passing their expertise on to new workers.

When the economics are thought through, this kind of HL technology could do more to ignite a major effective expansion of human capital investment in the workplace than "jawboning" exhortations to management or even government regulation. Expert and knowledge systems/networks could create positive growth spirals for both employers and workers.

These systems give the employer a means both to retain a major share of intellectual capital and to productively upgrade the value of its human resources through "embedded" learning. The employees who benefit from such learning in turn add their growing expertise to the employer's stock of intellectual capital assets. The employee comes out ahead by getting more and better investment from the employer in personal intellectual/ human capital, becoming a more productive worker as a result, and thus having the basis for greater income gains. Moreover, workers whose knowledge and skill is subject to capture by expert systems will want to bargain to secure their property rights in the resulting software, just as musicians, photographers, and other creative artists are becoming necessarily more protective of their intellectual property's use in digital, multi-media systems.

These examples symbolize the imminent transformation of "work" from an expression of labor to an instrument of capital. People will still continue to perform work in the sense of expending effort to achieve economic gain. But increasingly the gain will be measured and rewarded not by the intensity or duration of the effort but by the value of its product. Because knowledge-based products can continue to generate income for an indefinite period, most workers will want to own a share of the product, and will not be content to sell it for wages.

IMPACT 7: "HANDICAP" IS REDEFINED

A book called *A Brief History of Time* dominated the best-seller lists for week after week during 1988. A photograph on its night-blue cover showed the forty-six-year-old author, Stephen W. Hawking, holder of Isaac Newton's faculty chair at Cambridge University and the world's foremost thinker on the origin of the universe, seated before a black sky speckled with the glowing dots of stars and galaxies—slumped in a chrome wheelchair that holds the shriveled dreg of a body wasted by Lou Gehrig's disease.

Trapped in a body that can barely move or speak, much less write, one of a generation's greatest minds continues to work and communicate with the aid of ingenious computer technology. Hawking looks at a screen displaying letters, numbers, and common words. A sensor that tracks Hawking's eye movements knows exactly what he's looking at—a blink registers an item with the same effect of a finger pressing a key on a keyboard. Stare by stare, blink by blink, sentences are composed. Another blink hits a switch that commands a computer-synthesized voice to speak the words. Printing them on a page is even faster and simpler. And so the teacher goes on lecturing, the author keeps on writing, the father continues to chat with his children, even as the body withers away.

While Hawking's condition may not be enviable, no longer is it the pitiable tragedy it would have been in an earlier age. His example stands in joyful contradiction to common qualms about "dehumanizing" technology. Nor is his case unique. The ability of HL technology to pierce the bounds of once-imprisoning handicaps is not limited to academic super-stars. A computer system similar to Hawking's is being used today in a Tampa, Florida, high school to enable the still-fertile mind of a teenage boy severely impaired by the trauma of an automobile accident to continue to learn and grow.

As HL technology gets steadily more powerful, cheaper, and more accessible, the barriers of more and more "disabilities" are being breached. Some of the technological fixes to disabilities now available or forthcoming include:

- TDD or TTY machines, now available, enable the deaf to use telephones. Today's smart hearing aids have microprocessors that selectively amplify frequencies to overcome hearing impairments. Microsurgery now cures diseases that once led to total deafness. Computer programs now teach sign language to deaf or hearing students. Other programs generate colorful graphic screen images that enable deaf people to learn to speak by matching their voice patterns to normal speech patterns. Artificial ears eventually will overcome some kinds of deafness.

- Synthetic eyes that can transmit rough but usable images to the blind person's brain are in development.[72] Computer guru Raymond Kurzweil, working closely with musician Stevie Wonder, has developed computer tools for the blind that can speak, read printed text, and print out braille. Sonar and infrared sensors exceed the probing capabilities of the wooden cane.

- With a puff of breath or even, as in Hawking's case, a simple eye movement, quadriplegics or persons with even more severe physical impairments can write, speak, and operate a wheelchair or other computer-smart machines. Smarter robots promise ever more capable aids and extensions for people who are movement-impaired. Robotic limbs for amputees increasingly can take directions through sensors that detect nerve impulses. Eventually, synthetic nerves will enable smart prosthetic devices to transmit pressure, heat, and other feelings to the user.

- Advances in biotechnology offer even more miraculous reversals of disability, particularly for those with mental impairments. Today, drugs enable persons with diabetes, epilepsy, some mental disorders, and other diseases to be autonomous, productive economic actors. Existing and experimental drugs already have shown some benefit in improving the memories and motor functions of victims of Alzheimer's and Parkinson's diseases. Better drugs and even genetic surgery may, and probably will, alleviate and perhaps reverse the mental or other handicaps caused by birth defects such as fetal alcohol syndrome, Down's syndrome, or fragile X syndrome. Progress is being made in reconnecting or regrowing spinal nerves severed by trauma, offering the hope of eventually reversing the causes of paralysis and other neurological disabilities. And, while automation is sometimes sneered at for "dumbing down" work, that technological option has the collateral benefit of expanding employment opportunities for mentally handicapped persons—who, the recent experience of McDonald's and other employers shows, turn out to be extraordinarily productive workers.

HL technology is redefining "handicap." And in a manner that cuts two ways. It's not just that people once categorized as disabled can become equally or even more productive workers than "normal" people—certainly a welcome development.

What may be more daunting about the technological transformation of work and the workplace is the reverse possibility: Like the squeaky-voiced silent movie star who suddenly is asked to speak lines in a "talking picture," persons who seemed normally competent, challenged by a new set of performance requirements, will discover that they have limitations or even impairments of once-unneeded but now-demanded abilities.

The skilled machinist who now is required to program computer-controlled tools may find that he did not acquire all the needed skills in school because he suffered from a disability such as dyslexia or dysgraphia. An architect who is a virtuoso when it comes to drawing sketches or blueprints with pen and paper is not quite so adroit at computer-aided design; when she's asked to use a virtual-reality system, the vertigo or claustrophobia that never had affected her work suddenly could become a genuine handicap. Or people with tin ears or tunnel vision who were wizard workers in the age of print might find themselves seeming not so gifted in the world of multimedia.

FROM MUSIC TO MINDCRAFT

To get a sense of what it will be like to live and work in the kind of mindcraft economy HL is bringing, a good place to look is today's music industry. In few other businesses has knowledge age technology demonstrated as dramatic a transforming effect. Since Edison's invention of the phonograph, the music world has been obsessed with ever more sophisticated sound technology—today it is quickly seizing the possibilities HL offers.

In the old days—a year ago—Los Angeles guitarist Peter James wrote songs for his rock band in his head: this meant sometimes spending hours trying to translate his inner vision to fellow band members.

These days Mr. James takes a quicker, high-tech route. He goes to practice with his songs already recorded on a regular audio cassette. He plays and records all the parts himself at home using equipment—including a portable "multitrack" tape recorder, a drum synthesizer and a so-called signal processor capable of producing album-quality sound effects—compact enough to fit inside a briefcase. Better still, Mr. James's investment in his mini-studio is only about $1,500, less than a fifth of what comparable equipment would have cost five years ago, assuming it could even have been found.

—"Homemade Music Is Going High Tech at a Low Price," *The Wall Street Journal* (Feb. 15, 1989)

The accelerating, revolutionary impact of HL technology on music-making clearly has been to elevate the power of the composer, and progressively to replace the recording engineer, the instrument, and the performer—a clear example of the coming shift from labor to human capitalism. The trend toward economic democracy also is evident: For what a decent home stereo system costs, any of the twenty-eight million amateur and pro musicians in the U.S. can acquire a home music studio that enables them to compose on a computer using a program like Coda Music Software's Finale, which does for musicians what word processors do for writers. They then can "perform" their compositions on a virtually unlimited array of both real and synthetic instruments—Korg's $2,600 M1 synthesizer can recreate the sounds of up to 150 different instruments playing in harmony, giving any budding Beethoven or Beatle (of any age) a "basement philharmonic" to work with. Finally, with inexpensive, portable multitrack recorders, the garage Gershwins can make broadcast- or theater-quality recordings of their music.

Access to the growing power of high-tech music making requires neither academic credentials nor bureaucratic status. And those who may be physically handicapped, or simply lack dexterity, still can create virtuoso performances.[73]

People who don't yet know how to write music, or maybe even read it, can learn from computer-based tutors: A hot item during last year's Christmas season was The Miracle, a product from Software Toolworks that combines an electronic piano keyboard, a computer interface, and software that will teach you to play the piano on your PC or Nintendo game system. For a suggested price of $400, the product is a steal compared to the cost of buying some kind of piano plus lessons, and further promises your money back if you, or your kid, do not learn to play real music within thirty days.

Talk about teamwork and groupware: Most records no longer are mere transcriptions of a group of people in a room playing together. Now recordings are assembled from component parts created all over the world: Tracks are laid down by a lead guitarist in London, a drummer in New Orleans, a keyboard player in Tokyo, a singer in Toronto, and maybe even some riffs by a South African jive chorus and a Czech chamber orchestra. The pieces might be put together anywhere from a Hollywood studio to a barn in the Berkshires.

No technological advance is an unmixed blessing, and some purists lament a trend that they see as "dehumanizing" music. "Another electronic sound machine has come along to transform pop music from an art born of craft into a science born of technology," groaned one critic in a recent column. And: "The result is music that has more in common with a $40,000 Japanese car than an object of popular art."[74] (Of course, most Americans would deny that cars and objects of popular art are supposed to be separate categories.)

At worst, synthesis and simulation have the potential to descend into kitsch and even fraud. The case of Milli Vanilli, the pair of mannequins posing as rock singers, offends any standard of artistry. But an irreducible element of vulgarity is part of the price of economic or any other kind of democracy.

Nevertheless, serious musicians exult in the power of modern technology to liberate the creative process. "I use computers for everything," says Iris Gillon, a Juilliard-trained concert pianist and composer whose Manhattan apartment is crammed with electronic keyboards, synthesizers, sequencers, a drum machine, and a Macintosh computer, alongside her Steinway grand piano. Instead of taking weeks to compose a full orchestral score, the $6,500 worth of smart tools enable her to spin one out in a few hours. Even better, her synthesizers allow her to hear and polish her compositions immediately, saving the delay and cost of revising after a live orchestra has been assembled.[75]

And, despite the regrets of traditionalists, the fact remains that new HL technology is expanding the opportunity to participate in creating music, not just auditing it, to millions of people who previously were excluded by lack of time, money, teachers, or physical gifts. "The new technology has put everything on a level playing field," says Michael Levine, another professional musician who creates commercial jingles in the high-tech basement studio of his three-story loft in midtown Manhattan. "Now you just have to be good."[76]

CHAPTER 5

OVEREDUCATION: THE SOLID GOLD LIFE JACKET

• • •

If there is an iron law of economics it is that nature extracts a price for self-deception. In the recession of 1990–92 (ongoing at this writing), America got a cold shower of comeuppance for at least three costly delusions: (1) You can borrow prosperity without paying for it. (2) You can always make money in real estate. (3) You can never spend too much on education. The roles of the first two errors in the latest downturn were fairly quick to be recognized. The impact of the third delusion has been more widely felt at the grass roots than publicly grasped by the economic experts and political pundits.

The recent decline was a structural recession, not just a normal business cycle dip. And the inherent bankruptcy of the education industry played a key part.

THE RUDE AWAKENING

The education bubble began to burst when the recession began with a sharp increase of unemployment and decrease in income among the most-schooled members of the workforce: white-collar, managerial, and professional workers. Richard Belous, senior economist at the National Planning

Association, observed that "the current recession has become much more a white-collar experience than any recession since the Great Depression."[77] From 1989 to 1990, the real incomes of college-educated men fell by 4 percent, and white-collar pay in general was down 2 percent. While neo–New Dealers were prattling about the rich getting richer, families in the top 5 percent of income saw their incomes decline over two-and-a-half times faster than middle-income families and nearly five times faster than families in the bottom fifth.[78]

In the last quarter of 1991 alone, a slew of job cuts were announced by major U.S. employers: 6,000 by McDonnell Douglas, 10,000 by TRW, 14,000 by GTE, 20,000 by IBM, and a whopping 74,000 by General Motors. Only 30 percent of the jobs being cut were those of traditional production workers, according to Dan Lacey, editor of the newsletter *Workplace Trends,* who noted, "By and large, these are managerial, administrative, and technical people." About two million middle management positions were eliminated in the United States between the mid-eighties and the early nineties. While middle managers make up less than 7 percent of the U.S. workforce, nearly 17 percent of corporate layoffs since 1989 came from their ranks. Moreover, unlike in past recessions, in which industrial workers were *temporarily* laid off until business picked up again, most of the recent workforce reductions reflected *permanent* restructuring to improve productivity and competitiveness. While 90 percent of the white-collar workers laid off in the early 1980s fairly quickly found similar jobs in big companies at comparable pay, only 25 percent were able to do so in the early 1990s, and the number was still declining.[79]

A key scenario of the "American dream" suddenly seemed to lead to a rude awakening: The "professional" diplomas and credentials churned out by colleges were not the surefire passports to secure middle-class and upper-middle-class prosperity that a couple of post–World War II generations had been promised. Yet the cost of those credentials continued to rise several times faster than both inflation and most families' income.

The unsettling but largely unspoken truth is that America has a surplus of overschooled "professionals." Forced by the combined pressure of competition and suffocating debt to restructure, top-heavy corporations, banks, brokers, and gutted savings and loans shed thousands of master's- and other college-degreed managers, consultants, analysts, and bureaucrats—while U.S. universities continued to crank out seventy thousand new MBAs a year. Harvard business school professor Robert Hayes has argued that there is no evidence that the growing amount of money spent on business schools (now $3 billion a year) has served America well during the last twenty-five years. As Lester Thurow, dean of MIT's Sloan School of Management, put it: "If our business schools are doing so well, why are our American companies doing so badly?"[80]

Few would question that the United States has too many lawyers. Yet law school enrollment recently hit a record 150,000 even as America's most prestigious law firms were dismissing not only associates but full partners, and compensation for lawyers at major firms was declining.[81] Even while academics and politicians were publicly worrying about a supposed U.S. shortage of engineers and scientists, thousands were being dumped in New England, southern California, and Silicon Valley by the stumbling giants of the computer industry and by weapons makers reaping the first installment of the post–Cold War "peace dividend."

During the 1980s, half the U.S. physicians in private practice didn't have enough work to fill their calendars; meanwhile, a glut of empty beds has been driving many hospitals into bankruptcy. The surplus of dentists has led some notable universities such as Georgetown to shut down their dental schools.

Esteemed economists such as Alan Greenspan, chairman of the Federal Reserve, confessed to being perplexed by the severe decline in confidence—hitting a seventeen-year low in February 1992—in a recession that appeared "milder" than the one in the early 1980s when measured by such macroeconomic statistics as total unemployment and sales. In reality, the economic zapping of America's overschooled white-collar middle class, while evidently not planned for, was not only understandable but predictable.

The freewheeling Young Upwardly mobile (or Urban) Professionals, or Yuppies, who sparked and rode the eighties' boom, were destined by demography and the top-heavy structure of a bloated economy to be replaced, when the inevitable bust came, by a gloomy mass of MADMUPs—a label for Middle-Aged Downwardly Mobile Underemployed (or Unemployed) Professionals I coined in an early-1986 article. "The disappointment and frustration of this group of overeducated, overqualified, and underemployed workers will affect other strata of society besides their own," I wrote in that forecast, and concluded: "Their failure at upward mobility threatens faith in an 'American dream' subscribed to by their parents, by their children, and by a host of other working people. . . ."[82]

What number-crunching economists had a hard time grasping was that the progressive downfall of the diploma-endowed "professional" class was bound to have an emotional and cultural impact out of proportion to its numbers alone. Not that the numbers were trivial: White-collar and service employment had grown right through previous recessions but declined in the latest one—the difference by the end of 1991 was over a million-and-a-half jobs.[83]

When these high-paid workers went down they not only took a big chunk of so-called discretionary income (meaning spending money) with them, but torpedoed consumer confidence (another name for spending) more broadly when their affluent peers among coworkers, friends, relatives, and neighbors got scared that *they* might get hit next.[84] The spending drought in turn spawned the broad decline that eventually took the jobs of millions of front-line service and manufacturing workers. The recession's fiscal pinch provoked layoffs of government workers, who also tend to have more and higher academic credentials than average, further feeding the cycle of "academic deflation."

The special malaise of this recession was crystallized in a widely noted January 1992 TV news report that showed thousands of Chicagoans lined up in the snow to apply for five hundred entry-level jobs in a new Sheraton hotel. Interviewers found that many in the queue were managers, professionals, consultants, and university graduates who had been fruitlessly seeking work for months, or a year or two years, and were desperate for the chance to work as a cook or waiter or maid. One woman, tastefully dressed in the for-success mode despite the cold, vented her exasperation to a reporter: "I got my degree after five years at the university and can't find a job. What a waste!"

Economist Robert Reich attributed the industrial hollowness of the eighties' boom to what he labeled "paper entrepreneurialism," referring to the arcane gimmickry of debt-financed stock raids and leveraged buy-outs. But Reich and his ilk, usually vested in the academy themselves, gave less attention to the "paper entrepreneurialism" of the academic credential mills, which have made diplomas the "junk bonds" of the human capital economy.

The solons of "competitiveness" may only have added to the malaise with their common advice to the MADMUPs and others of the new class of "overqualified" dislocated workers to: stay in school, go back to school, get more education. Small comfort to the former airline marketing director who is now an entry-level sales agent at the Sheraton in Chicago, feeling relieved to be among the "Fortunate 500" hired out of eight thousand applicants.

The "more school" prescription has an ever more hollow—and maddening—ring to the middle-class family just starting to assemble a retirement nest egg after paying the equivalent of another house mortgage to send their kids to a hoity-toity college, only to see their brilliant twenty-five- or thirty-year-old unemployed offspring "boomerang" back to the family nest after five or ten years in graduate school. That kind of academic prolongation of adolescent dependency is becoming epidemic in America. One out of every nine U.S. twenty-five- to thirty-four-year-old *adults* were living in their parents' home in 1990. A 1988 survey revealed that nearly 40 percent of U.S. men between the ages of twenty-nine and thirty-one had held their current job for less than one year.[85]

In the United States of a generation ago, virtually any investment in more education offered an attractive rate of return—the cost of education was more than paid back by the greater incomes commanded by college graduates and those with advanced degrees. But the return on investment in generic education has become increasingly dubious for all concerned.

America now has the most-schooled workforce in its history. From 1970 to 1989 the fraction of the U.S. workforce with at least four years of high school grew from 31.1 percent to 38.5 percent and the portion with four years or more of college nearly doubled from 10.7 percent to 21.1 percent. Yet even as its schooling burgeoned, the growth of productivity, and thus income, of that workforce became historically anemic. Productivity of U.S. businesses outside farming grew at a healthy 2 percent annually during most of this century, surging to nearly 3 percent a year during the two decades after World War II. But since 1970, while the workforce's schooling zoomed, U.S. productivity growth has hovered around only 1 percent a year.[86]

In the 1970s, the difference in lifetime income between U.S. high school graduates and college graduates became so narrow that some economists estimated that the return on investment in formal higher education might even be negative.[87] By the late 1980s, the gap between the incomes and employment rates of college and high school graduates had widened dramatically, making higher education appear to be not only an attractive but perhaps essential investment. During that decade, the real median income of men with four years of high school declined by over 15 percent while men with four years of college realized a modest gain of 1.6 percent in real median income.[88] Between 1978 and 1988, the ratio of the wages of the college men to those of the high school men rose from 1.31 to 1.61. (Note that these kinds of statistics almost always reflect years of schooling, not graduation or diplomas.) Such data led many economists to the plausible, but ultimately erroneous, conclusion that going to college had become "an extraordinarily attractive investment."[89]

These gross measures of the value of postsecondary education in the American economy are misleading, however. The growing division between the economic status of college and high school graduates has occurred not because the demand for more-educated workers has increased but because the employment opportunities traditionally available to individuals with no more than a high school education—mainly in manufacturing or agriculture—have been rapidly vanishing.[90]

The apparent demand for "more educated" workers actually is a kind of inflation phenomenon. While the basic skill requirements for entry-level work have been somewhat increased by technological and organizational change, the U.S. economy's demand for highly schooled "professional" workers is largely oversupplied. More college graduates will enter the U.S. workforce and be seeking work during the 1990s than will be needed for the 15 to 23 percent of U.S. jobs projected to call for college diplomas. A. Gary Shilling, head of an economic and investment advisory firm in Springfield, New Jersey, projects 10 percent unemployment for college graduates at the end of this decade.[91]

And the official labor statistics on which most forecasts of educational "needs" are based overestimate the real workforce demand for college degrees. A major source of this costly confusion is that reports and studies of job "requirements" often do not distinguish between the educational qualifications employers *ask for* in their job requisitions or ads and the specific knowledge and skills needed to perform the work. In practice, employers commonly ask for more academic credentials than are needed, in an attempt to reduce the number of underqualified applicants.

Because jobs *requesting* no more than high school credentials are disappearing much faster than jobs asking for college degrees, it appears that the educational requirements of employment are increasing. But the numbers of jobs whose content genuinely requires college or postgraduate training are neither large enough nor growing rapidly enough—if they are even growing at all—to make up for the number of low-skilled jobs being structurally displaced.

The coming of age of the U.S. baby bust generation implied a shortage of entry-level workers in the 1990s, but that expected shortage may be offset in some areas by immigration resulting from the possible U.S.-Mexico free trade agreement as well as possible immigration increases from other areas. Similarly the "skill gap" forecast by the U.S. Labor Department's 1987 *Workforce 2000* study may be diluted or erased by the increase in older, overeducated, or overskilled MADMUPs. Increased investment in automation and other structural changes aimed at improving productivity are likely to further work against either kind of workforce shortage.[92]

Workforce 2000, more recent Labor Department forecasts, and other studies find that the most acute human capital need in the modern economy is for skilled technicians.[93] As the analysis of international competition by Michael Porter of the Harvard Business School concludes: "[America particularly needs] a new national effort to upgrade technical and vocational schools. . . . What is required for competitive advantage is specialized skills tailored to particular industries."[94] Such needs for specialized skills are a function of relevant technical training and experience, and have little or no correlation with either years of schooling or academic diplomas.

Workforce 2000, America's Choice, and a number of other major reports that defined much of the conventional wisdom about U.S. workforce, competitiveness, and education and training issues between the early 1980s and 1991 were somewhat suspect because they missed, to varying degrees, the effects of overeducation and diploma devaluation that were bound to be exposed in the next recession, which is now under way. But their expectations and recommendations, which still color most of today's political discourse on these issues, may have been aborted by the wild-card event none of them anticipated or could have accounted for: the collapse of the Soviet Union.

Of the many complex and still uncertain impacts of the sudden dissolution of the Soviet Union between the middle and end of 1991, the most likely and germane here is what the media eventually will trumpet under the headline, "The Brain Glut." Specifically, that epochal event is almost certain to greatly add to the problem of a MADMUP, overskilled, overqualified, overeducated workforce in the United States (and other countries as well). Dismantling America's Cold War defense establishment is now expected to unemploy from 1.5 million to 2 million U.S. military personnel,

Defense Department civilian employees, and defense contractor workers between 1992 and 1995.[95] The sheer numbers alone are likely to attenuate any economic recovery if not actually prolong or renew the recession. More significantly, the people involved are among the most schooled, skilled, educated, and trained of the whole U.S. economy—their flood into the job market is bound to add to the image of an "overqualified" workforce.

What may turn out to be an even heavier blow from the Soviet-collapse wild card was exemplified in one news item: In March 1992, Sun Microsystems, a major Silicon Valley producer of computer workstations, announced an agreement to employ Boris Babayan, Russia's top computer scientist, and his entire fifty-person team of programmers, considered among the best supercomputer software specialists in the world. Sun did not substantially dispute reports that the Russian scientists, who would work for Sun in Moscow, would be paid an average salary of *fifty U.S. dollars a month*.[96] (AT&T and Corning Glass later announced similar deals.) This is considered good money in the shattered FSU; it's more than former Soviet President Gorbachev's pension and several times more than the current salary of the president of the Russian Academy of Sciences.

The desperate condition of hundreds of thousands of highly educated, highly trained, highly skilled ex-Soviet scientists, engineers, physicians, and technicians promises a deflation of academic credentials and technical skills on a global scale. Those who do not emigrate outright when Russia and other FSU republics issue passports in the next year are bound to seek and get Babayan-type deals to work for foreign employers and investors. If the U.S. government yields to pressure from its own un- or underemployed intelligentsia to block ex-Soviet immigrants, the work and money will simply go elsewhere. The American government actually is committed to do everything it can to secure employment for the FSU's technical elite because it rightly fears the prospect of the former Soviet weapons makers selling themselves and/or their technology to Third World countries like Iraq and Libya.

So the most *hopeful* scenarios of the peaceful and democratic reconstruction of the former Soviet empire entail at least several years if not a decade or even two of academic deflation. And if that's not enough to make a MADMUP's eyes water, consider that India—with little American media fanfare—is following a path similar to Russia's toward replacing socialism with an open, competitive market. With a total population of

850 million, India has more scientists and engineers than any nation other than the U.S., and graduates a new crop of 400,000 engineers a year, more than any other English-speaking country.[97]

So even when/if Russia and other FSU republics stabilize their currencies and economies, and their technical personnel are able to increase their incomes toward more normal levels, the overall deflation of the most educated workforce talent still will be deep and long. In Israel, where the flood of overeducated Soviet immigrants started years sooner, the $1,500-a-month average salary a company like Decision Systems Israel is paying to new FSU immigrant scientists is still 25 to 50 percent less than what similarly qualified Israeli scientists have been paid; with unemployment among the Israeli immigrants running over 30 percent, it's likely many would work for less if jobs were offered.[98]

All things considered, the popular advice to heal family and national economic woes with more education is expensively wrong on three major counts. First, the confluence of trends I've just described all indicate that the apparent economic benefit of further schooling beyond high school, especially of four years and more of college education, is likely once again to diminish through the 1990s.

Second, even while a statistical gap between the wages of high-school- and college-educated workers persists, it is an almost shamefully erroneous basis for advising individuals and families that college and graduate education is, on average, "an extraordinarily attractive investment." Such advice rests on the fallacious thinking of the man standing with one foot in ice and the other in boiling oil who claimed to be, on average, comfortable.

A sensible, just plain sane, strategy for any kind of investment requires knowledge not only of potential rewards but of *risk*. Behind the festering fury of the growing legion of MADMUPs is the painful discovery that college sheepskins turned out to be as much a "can't lose" investment as Sun Belt condominiums, WPPSS bonds, and Michael Milken's junk. American families in the last two years have gained a growing, overdue awareness that the average gains promised by a college degree that now may cost $100,000 and up also include a significant degree of *insecurity*, as well as a real risk of outright *loss*. If higher education really is such a golden, can't-lose investment, why do U.S. banks demand that virtually every student loan be guaranteed by the federal government? If the payback is so lucrative, why does the federal government have to subsidize the education loan interest payments for students from half of all U.S. households?

Excessive schooling not only entails a growing risk of wasting family and community resources, but actually may leave overschooled workers worse off in the job market: One study found that overeducated workers actually get paid *less* than undereducated workers to do the same job.[99]

Third, the most costly misunderstanding of the "wage gap" data may be the popular belief that if the U.S. workers who do not now attend or graduate college would just "stay in school" or "go back to school" and get those diplomas their incomes would match the median income of current college graduates. But the hard truth is that, with workforce demands for college graduates both oversupplied and overstated, if everyone in the U.S. who lacks a college degree got one in the next couple of years, the inevitable result would be to *reduce* the median income of college graduates toward the level of today's high school graduates. In short, the floor would not rise, the ceiling would fall, and the whole U.S. economy would move a giant step closer to bankruptcy.

What about the plight of the "undereducated," then? It's been estimated that twenty to forty million U.S. workforce adults are hampered by some deficiencies in basic skills. But so little is really known about the actual knowledge and skill requirements of the modern economy that most of the "facts" purporting to demonstrate an epidemic skill shortage turn out, on closer inspection, to be little more than folklore. For reasons I'll discuss later, most of the academic tests that are used to label people incompetent are actually irrelevant or contrary to what the workplace requires.

There's little doubt that a turgid, self-serving academic establishment has shortchanged millions of Americans' opportunities for economic independence. But a thoroughly restructured national learning enterprise has the technical means to meet all those neglected human development needs far more effectively, and at far less cost in time and money than the lethal medicine of "more school." In an economy in which work and learning are ever more convergent, the greatest threat to those at the bottom of the ladder comes from academic credential barriers that arbitrarily block access to the learning-by-working that is truly critical to economic development.

At the heart of all these dilemmas is the crucial—but commonly overlooked—difference between learning and schooling. The same technology of the knowledge age economy that has made learning an ever more essential feature of working and living has made the process and culture of traditional schooling obsolescent. With the "specialized skills" Michael Porter mentions becoming obsolete every few years, the prerequisite skill for a growing majority of occupations is "learning to learn."

More specifically, a major cause of America's economic malaise is that the country's current education and training system largely neglects this need for flexible, "on-demand," "just-in-time" learning in favor of a spurious and wasteful chase for hollow diplomas.

THE PRODUCTIVITY CRISIS

The ongoing economic deflation of academic credentials has not yet reversed an explosive inflation of education costs and spending. America spends as much as or more than any other major nation on educating each of its students. Spending on schools in real dollars, discounting inflation, grew by nearly a third from 1980 to 1990; the federal Education Department projects another 26 percent increase during this decade. College costs grew even faster, about 50 percent in real dollars during the last decade.

With interest rates on secure savings accounts such as certificates of deposit currently below 6 percent and college costs continuing to grow by at least 8 percent annually, it's becoming ever more difficult for families to save or pay for the spiraling cost of higher education—especially as more families feel compelled to purchase private day care and private schools for their children to get the quality of services the public schools they've already paid taxes for cannot or will not provide. The tactic of shifting attendance from pricey private colleges to tax-subsidized public institutions is also running out of steam as financially strapped state governments cut higher education budgets, forcing public colleges and universities to raise tuition at rates of 10 to 20 percent or more a year now in some states, even as they reduce services.[100]

U.S. education and formal training expenditures are now over $400 billion a year—over $215 billion for K–12, over $143 billion for colleges and universities, and at least $50 billion for employer-provided education and training. This does not include the $200–300 billion economists estimate as the cost of on-the-job training, which would bring the total to over $600 billion annually, roughly tying the education sector with health care as the biggest industry in the U.S. economy.

What I dubbed the "learning enterprise" in a 1985 publication[101] is even larger than just the education sector. It includes further billions of dollars' worth of investments in learning that may not expressly be called "education" or "training." For instance, the horde of meetings, seminars, and conventions hosted in hotels and conference centers are rarely counted as part of the national "education" system, even though they involve annually about as many people as colleges do and the more than $70 billion of annual spending they represent is in the same ballpark as the total revenues of four-year colleges. Psychological counseling, psychotherapy, and even much of the nonpsychological business of health care involve helping people to learn things. Advertising, television, radio, periodicals, and book publishing are some of the other large businesses that engage millions of people and billions of dollars in segments of the learning enterprise that rarely are recognized or accounted for as "education."

This "hidden matter" of the learning enterprise, which gets little attention or study, is where the prospects for innovation and efficiency increasingly will be found. The formal, institutional "education" sector, which represents perhaps two-thirds or less of the overall enterprise of learning, is where the malignancy of waste, bureaucracy, and technological backwardness festers most acutely, and where major surgery is most needed.

The central failure of the formal education and training sector is poor and declining *productivity*. Understand that "productivity" is more than just efficiency. A prerequisite to any kind of productivity is relevance. An organization can be highly efficient in producing a product or service that is not what the consumer wants or needs—that's not being "productive." So the first failure of productivity in education generally is that it focuses resources and attention on institutions and goals that are irrelevant to the needs of the knowledge age economy.

Moreover, viewed as an industry or economic sector, the inherent organization and technology of "education"—including the schools and colleges and formal training programs, but not necessarily the more implicit and hidden parts of the rest of the overall learning enterprise—are also disastrously inefficient in delivering learning of any kind. While the definition of educational productivity can become almost theologically esoteric, even the simplest comparisons of effectiveness and cost show a severe decline in education's productivity. While the costs of schooling have grown about five times in the last four decades, neither test scores nor any other chosen measure of the results of education shows anything near a five-fold increase. Rather, critics point to declines in some measures of academic performance, while education advocates claim that the system is working as well as ever, or even a few percent better by some measures. No one really denies that costs have grown far out of proportion to education's results or benefits. *By definition,* that means productivity has been going down.

When compared with other economic sectors, education actually has the worst productivity record of any major U.S. industry. An essential measure of productivity is labor productivity: how much human work it takes to produce whatever is produced. This is the basic standard of economic development or progress—people create more wealth or income with less effort. One way to measure labor productivity is to compare labor costs to the value of the output, whether a product or service, as indicated by the revenues the output returns to the producer. For commercial organizations the revenues come from sales and include a margin for profit. For nonprofit or government agencies, like most educational institutions, some or all of the revenues may come from grants or appropriations, but overall revenues generally equal total costs.

Education is our most labor-intensive industry; at 93 percent of output (or total costs), education's labor costs are nearly double those of the average U.S. business and more than twice those of such high-tech information industries as telecommunications. In 1956, education's labor costs were 85 percent of total costs—three-and-a half decades of "reform" left education even less productive than it was before Sputnik.[102] One reason for education's poor efficiency is easy to discern by anyone who visits a typical school or college classroom. In the midst of a world-shaking hyperlearning revolution, the archaic technology of classroom teaching's productivity simply as a medium for communicating knowledge is actually declining, as labor costs rise, while the efficiency of all other media for communicating and processing information is zooming upward.[103]

This trend needs to be reversed. Education must be shifted to the ramp of "total quality," "continuous improvement," and "just-in-time" delivery aimed at steadily decreasing the cost of learning, even as we seek to make learning more relevant and useful.

WHY PRODUCTIVITY MATTERS

Productivity is crucial to any economy because it is the essential source of wealth and progress. "The only meaningful concept of competitiveness at the national level is *productivity*," says Michael Porter of the Harvard Business School.[104] The recession in the U.S. and other economies, capital shortages, financial instabilities, and a host of other current economic problems all hinge on the need for growing productivity. In particular, there are at least three reasons why education's disastrous lack of productivity is an acute problem for American business:

First, the sheer size of the education sector makes it a drag on the economy—when a nation's second or biggest industry has the worst and most consistently declining productivity, the numbers alone must reduce the average performance of the economy as a whole. Moreover, the services sector—representing about half the U.S. gross national product—is where lack of productivity growth seems to be mainly centered. For the U.S. to have a healthy 2 percent rate of overall productivity growth during the 1990s, services productivity would have to grow at about 1.5 percent a year, assuming that manufacturing resumes the 3 percent growth rate it realized during the 1980s recovery. The problem is that services productivity barely grew at a fraction of that rate during the eighties boom, and even declined in some years when the economy as a whole grew.[105] So considering that education represents an even larger share of the services sector, about a fifth, than of the total economy, the education industry's poor productivity looms even larger as an economic handicap.

Second, education is not just a big industry—in a knowledge age economy, where knowledge really is the key factor of production, the learning enterprise is strategically crucial. Learning is as essential to capital formation in the knowledge age—when intellectual capital is the primary source of wealth—as steelmaking was in the industrial age. Declining productivity in the industry that is critical to productivity growth in all other businesses is a serious brake on the economy as a whole.

A third reason educational productivity is critical is related both to social equity and overall economic efficiency. When we view the distribution of national investments in all kinds of education, training, and related activities, it's clear that the nation's "portfolio" is grossly imbalanced. The great majority of America's "workforce 2000" are now adults. Perhaps 50 percent or more of U.S. adults have largely unmet needs for reeducation and retraining to be fully employable and productive. That includes the often overlooked group of the workforce—perhaps 15 percent—who are overeducated or overqualified, in the sense that their considerable knowledge or skills no longer fit what the economy demands.

Yet for every dollar the U.S. spends on schooling children, the country invests less than a penny for adult basic education. Furthermore, the adults who are most in need of effective learning opportunities are the parents of the fifth to a quarter of the nation's children who are labeled "poor" and "at risk." Of the resources spent on adult education and training, the most educated and most skilled get the greatest investment; government programs target the few percent of workers who form the hard core of the poorest and most disadvantaged, leaving the mainstream of workforce adults with a general shortage of instructional investment.[106] The imbalance affects the earliest as well as the middle years of life—only pennies of public funds are invested in the development of children younger than five years old for every dollar expended on the education of "school age" children.

There are only three ways the imbalances and inequities in America's human investment portfolio can be redressed—and two of the three are clearly impossible. One is to more than double the current $400-billion-plus education budget and limit the increase to fund only those persons and services that now are underfunded. That is impossible because the money simply does not exist: The federal deficit is $400 billion and growing; at least thirty of the fifty states began the 1992 fiscal year in the red; many local governments are in equal if not greater financial distress. Americans are now paying the greatest share of their income for taxes in the nation's history—over 35 percent—and have shown no enthusiasm for an even greater burden. Education now claims roughly half or more of state and local taxes in most of the country; neither increasing education's share to 100 percent nor doubling the total tax burden is a realistic solution.

A second way to correct the investment imbalance would be to take away half the funds now allocated to K–12 schools and colleges to support now underfunded services for adults, the poor, disadvantaged, preschool children, and so forth. In the absence of major productivity gains, this approach would entail reducing services popular with the middle class to expand services needed mainly by the poor and working classes. This "Robin Hood" strategy plays better in the movies than in legislatures. It won't work.

The third and only realistic way to create a sensibly balanced national plan of human capital investment is to greatly increase the productivity of education and training in general. By providing much more effective service to the learning consumer at much lower cost, the surplus of existing education budgets can be reallocated to underserved and unmet needs without diminishing benefits to those now being served. By doubling the productivity of educational services—which we have the technology to do not only once but several times over—we can free up $200 billion and more a year to meet human needs that now are served little or not at all.

Is this a serious possibility? Absolutely. Computer-based, multimedia, and telelearning systems are getting steadily more cost-effective than conventional classroom instruction. In fact, vastly more efficient alternatives to eleventh-century classroom technology have been around for quite a while.

Despite its shortcomings, the power of even regular broadcast or cable TV to educate is prodigious. An example is 1990's much-lauded *The Civil War* series. Producer/director Ken Burns's documentary essay on the most critical event in American history, hauntingly told in an eleven-hour montage of pictures, music, letters, conversation, and narration, cost about $3 million to create, and was seen originally by thirty-eight million viewers—a cost for each viewer/learner of about one cent per hour or less than ten cents for the entire "course." Had Burns wanted to convey the same subject matter to the same number of people through the hoary technology of the college lecture hall, the project would have cost something over $6 billion and would have required the full-time classroom efforts of all the college history professors in America for at least a year or two. Since the broadcast, Time Warner has sold over $20 million worth of the videocassette version of the program—showing the potential of this kind of educational program to actually pay for itself. And an interactive, multimedia version of the program is now being produced.

Productivity is measured by the ratio of the effects of an investment to its cost. Two ways *not* to improve educational productivity are (1) try to purchase better instruction by spending more money, and (2) try to save money by cutting services that produce useful results. The only way to be sure of increasing productivity is to demand *both* lower costs and better results.

HL technology will bring results that are better not only by conventional standards but especially in their relevance to the real-world experience of working and living in the knowledge age. So replacing the academic blob with a productive, modern learning enterprise demands a strategic focus, first and foremost, on cutting the cost of the education monster.

CUTTING COSTS

The whole U.S. effort to "restructure" education has been stymied for over a decade by the failure to come to terms with the central issue of *money*. The first mistake made during most of the 1980s was the attempt to reform education by measures that demanded increased spending.

An exhaustive review of two decades of educational research by Eric Hanushek of the University of Rochester yielded the "startlingly consistent" result that there is no systematic relationship between variations in school expenditures and variations in school performance. Moreover, Hanushek found little or no evidence of improved student learning resulting from the ways increased K–12 funding typically has been spent in pursuit of "excellence": smaller classes, higher teacher pay, more teacher training, bigger and better school buildings, and so forth.[107]

A study by Deborah Inman at New York University showed that while total state spending on K–12 education grew by about a third from 1983 to 1987, less than 2 percent of that sum was allocated to any kind of "reform."[108] Her study further indicated that the majority of these limited "reform" investments—which still totaled some $6 billion—went to the more-of-the-same kinds of measures Hanushek's research found fruitless, rather than to any genuinely new, innovative, or more productive approach to meeting America's educational needs. In fact, the $40 billion the United States added to its annual K–12 expenditures during the 1980s resulted in only minor academic improvement, as measured by the usual tests.

Throwing more money accomplishes little more than feeding the blob of stifling administrative overhead in the public education bureaucracy. One study of New York City's public school system found that some 70 percent of the $6,107 spent per student in 1988–89 was eaten up by nonclassroom overhead—nearly half the total spending never got out of the board of education's headquarters.[109] With an organization chart that is eighty-seven pages long, the board has a lot of mouths to feed.

The public school district of Portland, Oregon, has one central office bureaucrat for every ninety-two students, while Portland's Catholic archdiocese runs the largest private school system in the state with one central office employee for every twenty-three hundred students.[110] Similarly, the District of Columbia runs an eighty-one-thousand-student public school district with a headquarters staff estimated at fifteen hundred bureaucrats;

IMPACT OF EDUCATION INPUTS ON STUDENT PERFORMANCE (HANUSHEK)

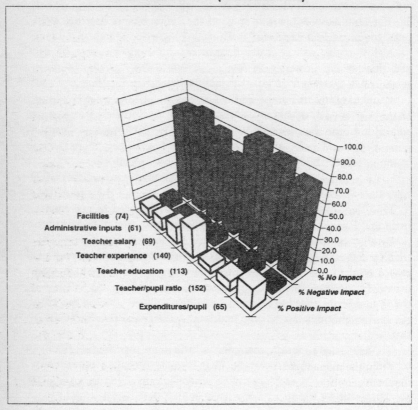

the Catholic schools of the archdiocese of Washington serve fifty thousand students with a central administrative staff of seventeen people.[111] Over two years ago, two commissions representing a cross section of Washington's business and civic leadership demanded that the D.C. public schools cut out hundreds of superfluous administrative positions. But two years later, the number of paychecks had increased, even while the overall budget had been cut, and the beleaguered new superintendent confessed publicly that he was unable to say how many people were actually employed by the school system.

If anything, the net result of the spend-more-on-education "reforms" of the last decade was to make the future lives of America's children poorer. For every dollar added to public spending for education "reform" in the 1980s, unrestrained government deficits swelled the U.S. public debt by roughly $100. The interest payment on the debt that will burden America's children for the remainder of their working lives is now a budget item nearly ten times the budget of the federal Education Department and is almost equal to the total amount spent on K–12 education by federal, state, and local governments.

By the end of the eighties, politicians besieged by restive taxpayers tried to deflect demands for more education spending with calls for improved results in test scores, dropout rates, and such—while still dodging the need for cutting costs by improving efficiency. But the lame tactic of trying to reframe the reform issue as one of "results not resources"—as the Bush administration, many of the governors and other politicians of both major parties, as well as a number of business organizations and leaders have tried to do—has been a total flop.

From the moment it was unveiled with much fanfare on April 18, 1991, the Bush administration's "bold" and "ambitious" *America 2000* plan failed to redirect the national education debate from resources to innovation, despite its feeble assertions that so-called New American Schools would cost no more than conventional schools and that "ingenuity, commitment and accountability matter more than money."

NBC News's coverage of the announcement that evening was typical of the media reaction: NBC opened the segment by reporting that twenty-one thousand teachers had gone on strike for more money in Washington State on the same day the "education president" announced a plan that offered little money to fix the nation's education deficits. The segment went on to cover the White House ceremony and review the outline of the

America 2000 strategy. For reaction, the report cut to the president of the Los Angeles teachers' union, who proclaimed that new visions could not be achieved while local school budgets were being cut 7 percent in the name of austerity. Back to an administration adviser who pointed out that education spending grew substantially in the 1980s while test scores did not improve. The report ended back in Washington State with the unanswered question of how schools could be improved in the face of declining tax revenues and relentless demands for more funding.

The same message was echoed over and over in every report in every news medium. Every effort to promote the president's plan and the education goals he contrived with the nation's governors provoked the same persistent concerns about money.[112]

No one should be surprised that a recent poll found that three-quarters of the American public says that more federal money is needed to reform and improve the education system, and that two out of three voters claim that they would be willing to pay more taxes to improve schools in their own communities.[113] Parenthetical slogans and off-the-cuff comments to the effect that "more money is not the answer" to our education problems are simply drowned out in the constant din of education establishment lobbying and propaganda aimed at perpetuating the popular belief that more money is always an essential part of the solution to any educational problem. Teacher unions and associations representing principals, superintendents, college presidents, and a host of other education bureaucrats spend millions of dollars annually to keep selling the myth that teachers are underpaid and education is underfunded in America.

The simple truth is that education in America *costs too much.*

To fully appreciate how affluent the socialist state of American academia really is, imagine that it were a separate country—call it "Academica"—that had the same kind of monopoly of school and college services that South Africa has in diamonds. In other words, suppose that everyone in the U.S. who now enrolls in a school or college had to purchase that service by importing it from Academica, which might be located on a mythical island off the U.S. Pacific coast. And suppose that all the employees of American schools and colleges were citizens of that scholastic republic.

Would Academica's endless pleas of poverty be justified? Hardly. If Academica were an independent nation, in 1990 it would have had the ninth largest gross national product in the world, barely trailing the USSR. With the dissolution and economic tailspin of the former Soviet Union, by the end of 1991 Academica would have passed whatever replaced the USSR as the number eight national economy. Moreover, with a population smaller than South Korea's, Academica would be among the highest per capita income countries in the world. And Academica would now be the largest, and possibly last, socialist economy on earth. By the way, the "socialist" label applies quite literally: American academia is about 90 percent owned, operated, and/or financed by government; and most of the remainder is government-regulated.

Despite these facts, the U.S. education lobby continues to put out phony statistics claiming to show that America "lags" behind other nations in spending on education. A favorite trick is to chart education spending as a share of national income—an absolutely meaningless statistic—which makes America look like a piker compared to other countries. By the same flawed logic, Americans should be starving while Indians should be signing up for Weight Watchers, since the U.S. spends a far smaller share of its income on food than India (or any other country) does.[114]

Besides being untrue, this propaganda line promotes the belief that the U.S. should *want* to lead the world in education spending. But you don't get to be a competitive leader in any industry by being the world's highest-cost producer—you want to aim to be the producer with the highest quality and the lowest cost.

As in the fable of the emperor's new clothes, many more people know that education is a costly scam than are willing to say so publicly. The opinion surveys that conclude that a large majority of the public is willing to pay more for education are misleading. In the polls that count, when people have to vote for bond issues or for politicians aiming to throw more money at education, American voters more often than not have been saying no. In the face of the constant drumbeat of the education lobby's cries of poverty, many people evidently fear that their resistance to having their pockets picked will be attacked as selfish, antisocial, even un-American. So they pay lip service to the myth that education is underfunded, even while they deny it with their votes.

America's effort to deal with the very real problems of education, training, and workforce competency so far has failed to break out of the fruitless boom-and-bust cycle of "reformism" that has gone on for half a century or more. The cycle follows the same old pattern: (1) The call to alarm about the "crisis." (2) A flurry of new policies, programs, projects, and appropriations aimed at "radical" innovation. (3) Rhetorical praise for reformers, pleas for patience, the inevitable demands for increased funding, and molasseslike inertia from the education establishment. (4) Progressive loss of momentum, boredom, disillusionment, frustration, cynicism, and distraction by other crises. (5) The abandonment and reversal of reforms and innovations in the name of fiscal austerity—"back to basics"—during the next economic downturn.[115]

The latest of these dead-end cycles began in the early 1980s with several state reform initiatives, but was symbolized by the 1983 publication of A Nation at Risk, the report of a White House commission. The America 2000 plan comes in the midst of that cycle's terminal phase. Even as the education president and his allies proclaim bold new ventures, the economic recession and federal, state, and local government deficits are combining to unravel the superficial education reforms of the last decade.

The biggest state tax increases in a generation—totaling over $15 billion so far this fiscal year and potentially over $18 billion before the year is over—have not been sufficient to eliminate the further need for austerity cuts in programs, staff, and budgets, according to reports from the National Conference of State Legislatures and other analysts. None of this has stopped the overall growth of state budgets, spurred by endless spending demands for Medicaid and corrections (partly stoked by federal mandates), which increased 23 percent and 17 percent respectively in the last fiscal year.

The apparently irresistible federal mandate for state Medicaid appropriations, and the public passion for building more prisons, have started to bite into education's huge share of the state revenue pie: State K–12 education spending grew by only 3 percent during the last fiscal year—less than inflation—and state spending on higher education actually declined about 1 percent. Nor does economic recovery offer any prospect of restoring fiscal health to state and local governments anytime soon. Even Texas, whose economy has been in recovery for some time, and which expects a $2 billion increase in tax revenues by 1993, has had to confront a $4.7 billion shortfall in its 1992–93 budget.[116]

The typical response of education bureaucracies to these inevitable financial limits is what inside-the-Beltway types call "selling the Washington Monument." Whatever is new, productive, innovative, or just popular is sacrificed first to preserve whatever and whoever is most tenured. The accounting of education reform has been and remains LIFO—last in, first out.

"At a time when many states had expected recent school-improvement experiments to flourish, they instead face a new budget year colored by widespread reports of larger classes, reduced honors and remedial programs, and growing local cynicism about policymakers' commitment to costly school reforms," proclaimed an *Education Week* article under the headline "States Slashing Reform Programs As Funding Basics Becomes Harder."[117] No one should be surprised—this is part of the persistent strategy schools and colleges have used to prevent change with near-perfect success for decades.

The key words in that report are "experiments" and "costly." As long as reforms are instituted as experiments, demonstrations, pilots, or otherwise provisional activities, and as long as they are presumed to add to total costs, they are doomed to be jettisoned at the first hint of fiscal austerity. The widely touted and much overrated "radical" experiment in which Boston University contracted to administer the downtrodden Chelsea, Massachusetts, public schools has been aborted by deep budget cuts the city had "promised" not to make.[118] The Richmond, California, school district was driven to the brink of bankruptcy in 1991 by an ill-conceived and costly "school choice" experiment, and had to sue the state government to bail it out. And so it goes.

Businesses other than education understand that the message of recessions is to cut the fat and get leaner and meaner. Even other sectors of government seem to be able to figure this out. In the spring of 1991 Defense Secretary Richard Cheney announced plans to save $70 billion from his department's budget over the next five years by cutting "wasteful duplication and red tape" and excess personnel while improving military effectiveness (there's no option to stand still in the competitive business of warfare).[119] No comparable strategy to cut waste from America's bloated education bill has been offered by Education Secretary Lamar Alexander or any other national education or business leader. But there is no less potential or need to cut waste, reduce costs, and improve productivity in education than there is in defense or any other service business.

In fact, it is the misunderstanding and misdirection of the business community role that has been at the root of the perennial failure of educational reformism, and that is now hampering the development of the kind of learning enterprise a knowledge age economy requires. Business in general has the most immediate and tangible need as a *consumer* of the human and intellectual capital that HL generates and education increasingly undermines. Business also is explicitly sensitive to the tax and other cost burdens imposed by a swollen, greedy academic bureaucracy, and conversely to the savings offered by a productive, HL-based learning enterprise. And business has organizational and financial resources that could vastly amplify the political clout of the millions of families and workers who are the most vulnerable consumers, and most aggrieved victims of a self-serving education establishment.

A different but no less compelling business interest is in producing the HL systems that are needed to infuse learning into the entire twenty-first-century economy, and in the process replace education altogether. As the numbers cited earlier indicate, replacing academic classrooms with hyperlearning technology offers a *potential* commercial market opportunity worth a few hundred billion dollars a year in the U.S. alone—and several times more in the rest of the global economy. This is the greatest business opportunity since Rockefeller found oil. Yet it is being thwarted by a thicket of legal and regulatory barriers, and vested interests, that can only be cleared by forceful, cunning attack by unapologetically ambitious, entrepreneurial business leaders. *Enlightened* self-interest, after all, is supposed to be the fuel of free enterprise capitalism.

In contrast to what's needed, U.S. business efforts to promote a much-needed revolution in education and training systems have been hamstrung by an inherently contradictory and self-defeating strategy. Or maybe "nonstrategy" would be more apt.

This Great Bamboozlement could be ended by a clear message not only from the president's "bully pulpit" but from national and local business leaders that cost reduction is an essential goal of education reform. Instead, we have the kind of unhelpful performances seen at a 1991 National Alliance of Business conference where, as *Education Week* reported, Paul O'Neill, Alcoa CEO and chairman of the President's Education Policy Advisory Committee, stated that "business leaders should push to raise local taxes to pay for early-childhood and other education efforts if money cannot be found in other public programs"; and where Robert Kennedy, CEO of Union Carbide, weakly countered the National Education Association's demands for more money by suggesting that "while . . . more funds for education will be necessary . . . educators must first produce results with what they have, and then show how more funding can further their cause."[120]

Business has left itself wide open to the criticism made by Harvard's Robert Reich and other commentators that its alleged concern about education reform is hollow hypocrisy. "The suggestion that the private sector is taking—or will take—substantial responsibility for investing in America's work force is seriously misleading," Reich charges.

The key conflict: Top business executives present speeches and legislative testimony calling for "full funding" of reform projects or pet programs like Head Start. Or they publicly concede that education reform will cost more money while meekly demanding that substantial improvements be demonstrated before further funding is granted. Meanwhile their companies strive assiduously to *avoid the taxes* needed to pay for the existing public education system, much less an improved one.

Reich points out that General Motors' public relations touting of its generosity to public education is contradicted by the corporation's tax policies. "GM's successful effort to cut by over $1 million its annual taxes in Tarrytown, N.Y., forced the town to lay off dozens of teachers and administrators, eliminate new library books and school supplies, and postpone routine school repairs. . . . And as a condition for locating its new Saturn factory in Tennessee, it got the local government to waive all property taxes until 1995."[121]

There is nothing unique about GM's behavior. Overhyped PR gimmicks can no longer mask the reality that business is taking more away from U.S. education and training than it is putting in. Here are a few more of countless examples:

- In the same year it got about $250,000 in business donations, the Corpus Christi, Texas, public schools lost $900,000 because of business tax exemptions.

- Local businesses in Wichita, Kansas, made $1.1 million in donations; then took back $1.6 million in school tax concessions.

- Florida's public education system lost some $500 million from tax breaks to business, while business gave back $32 million in charitable contributions to schools.[122]

While top business executives "talk a good game," says Reich, they are putting their money somewhere other than where their mouths are: Most corporate employee education expenditures are lavished on senior managers, not on the mainstream of workers, and least of all to tune up deficient basic skills.[123] Another Reich complaint: The rate of corporate donations to education slowed steadily even as the U.S. economy boomed during the 1980s and reform rhetoric inflated. While corporate grants to support public schools did increase from 6 percent of corporate education giving in 1987 to 11 percent in 1991, most corporate philanthropy for education still goes to colleges.[124] Furthermore, Reich charges that shipping jobs to literate but cheaper workers in foreign countries removes much incentive for companies to invest in upgrading the skills of the U.S. workforce.

The result of these blatant contradictions is that the political credibility of business leaders in education reform is sinking like a rock. The clear impression they are communicating, as Michael Apple, an education finance expert at the University of Wisconsin, puts it, is that "they want more spent on education but preferring [sic] that it not come out of their own pockets."[125]

The dilemma here stems from a basic failure of business strategy. The CEO and other top executives of any business wear several hats—administrator, leader, preacher, fiduciary, advocate, role model, worker, adviser, builder, inventor, citizen, sometimes owner, and so forth. But all these roles are parts of just one job, to grow a particular business in an ethically and socially responsible way. Effective business strategy requires aligning the actions taken under all the manager's hats to pursue a coherent direction. When business leaders advocate policies under the umbrella of social service that contradict the policies they practice in the domains of financial management or political lobbying, they undermine the firm's capacity both to do well and to do good.

Management needs a consistent strategy for pursuing several legitimate business interests: (1) Minimizing undue tax burdens. (2) Reducing operating costs. (3) Securing a competent and productive workforce. (4) Promoting the growth of its customers' income, so that they will be able to buy more of what the firm sells.

A sensible business *learning policy* must serve all these objectives. And it can. But a prerequisite is for business leadership to actively oppose increased taxing and spending for education and instead to advocate cost reduction through efficiency. Cost reduction through efficiency is the opposite of a budget-cutting, "austerity" exercise—it means implementing new technologies and complementary organizational designs to achieve given results at ever-declining cost.

RESTRUCTURE BUDGETS

Spending more has utterly failed as a strategy of education reform. Now America's dire fiscal condition makes increasing education budgets impossible, as well as fruitless. The productive restructuring—and eventual replacement—of educational systems that advancing technology makes ever more feasible will reduce costs while increasing the quality and effectiveness of learning. Investment capital needed to reinvent learning delivery systems and to retrain staff must come from economies in the existing system budgets.

There is some irony in the difference of approach the U.S. government has taken to the restructuring of the erstwhile Soviet Union, on the one hand, and of the sovereign-acting "republic" within America's borders I called "Academica" above, on the other. The Bush administration, with the sympathy of much of the U.S. business community and the public as a whole, took an appropriately tough stand on aid to the Soviet republics. When Soviet President Gorbachev beseeched the Group of Seven leaders for a commitment of at least five years of economic aid estimated at up to $30 billion a year, the American president insisted, and the other G-7 members generally concurred, that substantive commitment to a free, democratic, market economy would have to be demonstrated first.

Yet, for all the rhetoric about "a nation at risk," "radical reform," "systemic restructuring," and lately even "revolution" in American education over the past decade, the U.S. has meekly added some $90 billion a year to its total school and college spending without demanding or exacting any significant structural change in Academica, the world's biggest socialist economy.

It may be hard to understand at first how the same government can be so strong-willed in standing up for America's strategic interests in one case, and so weak in the other. But Academica, unlike the late Soviet Union, employs several million U.S. voters. Still, there are twenty voters employed outside the education bureaucracy for every one employed in it.

And more politicians have been dumped by irate, overburdened taxpayers than by dissatisfied educrats.

America's leaders resisted throwing money at the Soviets because they knew that, in the absence of true free-market reform, the money would just go into the rathole of the bureaucracy that caused the communist disaster in the first place. The same no-nonsense discipline is long overdue in U.S. education politics. It's time to tear up the blank check. The time has come to insist on the real free enterprise restructuring of the education sector that will deliver lots more bang for lots fewer bucks.

CHAPTER 6

TECHNO-POLITICS: THE NEW REFORMATION

• • •

When Johann Gutenberg produced the first printed Bible in 1456, he unleashed a technological revolution that doomed the religious and political establishment of his time. Printing permitted the mass production of knowledge, rendering obsolete the basic function of a hierarchical priesthood of "experts."

It took about a half century after Gutenberg's Bible for the Roman Catholic Church to perceive the threat to the ecclesiastic monopoly posed by a technology that could give each person direct access to the words of Holy Scripture. The priesthood's protective reaction was to make translating the Bible into any language other than Latin a crime of heresy.

Sixty-one years after Gutenberg's Bible, Martin Luther nailed his Ninety-five Theses to the door of the Wittenberg castle church to protest the corruption spawned by the Church's self-serving monopoly. The power of the press quickly transformed protest into Protestantism, and the Reformation was under way. Four years later, in 1521, Luther was condemned as a criminal by an edict of the Diet of Worms, but set about translating the Bible under the protection of Frederick the Wise of Saxony. Five years later in Worms, a young clergyman and admirer of Luther, William Tyndale, secretly published his English translation of the New Testament. Ten years after that, Church authorities finally hunted down Tyndale in Belgium, where he was convicted of heresy and executed by strangling and burning at the stake. But Tyndale's work could not be extinguished—over four-fifths of the King James Bible, published in 1611, used Tyndale's translation.

Another great reformation is now unfolding. We are about a half century past the introduction of the core technologies of multimedia communication—the computer and television. These, and an associated skein of other technologies that make up the new global nervous system of the knowledge age, are destined to have the same cultural impact of liberating personal access to knowledge that the printing press did—only magnified a million-fold.

The priesthood of academia is no more inclined or even capable of coexisting with the intellectual democracy driven by HL technology than an earlier, medieval church was able to tolerate the theological democracy made both possible and inevitable by the technology of mass literacy. In a feckless spasm of self-preservation, the National Education Association proclaims the use of information technology for learning, without a teacher, as a heresy. NEA aims to legally prohibit the implementation of distance learning or computer-based instruction without a featherbedded union teacher present and in control.[126]

Academia's universally recognized and much lamented resistance to change cannot endure much longer. The reformation is now under way and out of control. The academic empire is less likely to gradually fade away than to reach a critical point at which it suddenly implodes and is overturned in a fairly short period of time.

The salient illustration of what to expect and what needs to be done can be seen in the swift decline and fall of the Soviet empire. The collapse of communism is arguably the most dramatic expression of the ongoing reformation driven by knowledge age technology, but it's only the first. At the heart of that collapse was the inherent inability of an autocratic, hierarchic bureaucratic state to compete with the power and pace of technology spawned by free economies. The exotic technology promised by the Strategic Defense Initiative, or "Star Wars," threatened to emasculate the sprawling military-industrial complex that dominated and expropriated the lion's share of the whole Soviet economy.

But SDI posed only the last nail in a coffin that had been made and mostly sealed by the unstoppable power of modern information technology—notably the cheap, compact video recorder and portable satellite transponders—to puncture the police state's cloak of secrecy and imposed ignorance.

The toppling of the Soviet empire was not merely the end of communism but one of the extreme expressions of the imminent end of *bureaucracy* as an economically viable form of social organization. Unlike theoretical Marxism, which imagined a "withering away" of central control, communism as defined by Lenin and Stalin made bureaucracy into a state religion. One comprehensive bureaucracy, unified and controlled by a single "Party," would organize, regulate, control, and monopolize every facet of economic and cultural life.

While bureaucracy has by now earned a bad name, nineteenth-century reformers greeted bureaucracy as a wondrous social advance. Max Weber, the German sociologist who is well known for lionizing the Protestant ethic of profitable labor, also celebrated bureaucracy as a democratic replacement for aristocracy that would distribute authority and rewards based on personal merit rather than birth or title.

Bureaucracy was a social design that actually fit the massive mechanical technology of the industrial age to a T. The high-mass, high-energy tools of the economy of "steel" (aptly the literal meaning of Stalin's name) were subject to inherent "economies of scale"—meaning bigger factories, bigger power plants, bigger railroads and such were more efficient than smaller ones. Bureaucracy is an efficient way of organizing and controlling big structures for mass-producing lots of standardized stuff. The main contradiction between conservative capitalists and communists, or state socialists, soon focused not on the organization of industry but on the ownership and distribution of its products. In fact, bureaucracy suited the socialist notion of how the fruits of industrial production would best be distributed as well as generated.

"The exercise of control on the basis of knowledge"—this was what Weber rightly recognized as the defining characteristic of any bureaucracy. Any bureaucracy must seek to absorb and sequester information in order to maintain control. Every bit of information in a bureaucracy, regardless of the degree of formal secrecy with which it is "classified," must be authorized. Data must flow up and down the pyramid through "channels." Every act of communication requires a decision about "need to know."

The meritocracy Weber found such an admirable trait of bureaucratic management also depends on a scarcity of knowledge. Employment and the assignment of status by merit depends on the extent to which the candidate for any position knows more than others. What a meritocracy employs is "experts," no matter how mundane or exalted the job.

The decontrol of knowledge therefore inevitably must drain the life-blood from bureaucracy. Information technology that diffuses and disperses the creation and communication of knowledge assaults the genetic program, the very DNA of bureaucracy, in a way that is ultimately indefensible. Unless the bureaucracy can suppress or control the technology globally—which none has ever been able to do—its very attempts to insulate itself from information technology become suicidal.

Cut off from the knowledge flowing around it, the bureaucracy sinks ever deeper into obsolescence, atrophy, and gangrene. Alternatively, the more an organization or institution attempts to join the information revolution, the more the technology itself will break down the internal bureaucracy until the organization either becomes ungovernable, and breaks apart, or flips into a new, viable, but nonbureaucratic form of governance. That "flipping" process often is called "restructuring," and the new form of governance, to the extent it works, gets a trendy label like "zero defect management," "concurrent engineering," or "flexible production," and may become a standard feature of whatever is emerging as the new way to get things done in the knowledge age economy.

So the information technology that overthrew the Soviet empire is having a similarly terminal effect on other not-quite-so-huge but sprawling and turgid bureaucratic institutions, including all state-owned industries as well as corporate behemoths like IBM or General Motors.

Education and schooling as mass institutions—touching the way of life of the majority of national populations—are actually a fairly recent invention, despite the popular sense that they are ancient. Formal schooling was part of the lives of only a small elite in most societies until the industrial revolution. The popular and particularly the public academic institutions most people equate with education today are products of the industrial society they were formed to serve. Schools were designed as factories to mass-produce the workforce for mass production industries. Successful modern colleges and universities are far more industrial age than Renaissance institutions. They sprang from a pragmatic, research-focused design pioneered by Wilhelm von Humboldt in Berlin in 1809 that was widely copied in Germany and America. And the universities realized their full economic role with the development after 1862 of the U.S. "land grant" institutions devoted to advancing the agricultural and mechanical or industrial "arts."

Education developed in scale and bureaucratic density to mimic the industrial bureaucracy it was styled to serve. Education in its less than two-century-old modern form is an institution of bureaucracy, by bureaucracy, for bureaucracy. Educational institutions are more remarkable for their similarities than their differences across industrial nations, East or West, conservative or socialist. Curricula, language, and tactics may vary, but technologically, institutionally, and administratively schools and education systems are virtually interchangeable throughout the industrial world. In the more "undeveloped" or preindustrial societies on earth, schooling is not more preindustrial—it is more nearly nonexistent.

The decline and ultimate extinction of bureaucracy with the dawn of the knowledge age is an inherent outcome of the democratic character of the new technology itself—quite the opposite of what George Orwell envisaged, even by 1984. Therefore, the disappearance of education is inevitable, not only because education itself has become a huge socialist bureaucracy, but because it is a bureaucracy designed for a bureaucratic society.

Reformers who aim to free schooling from bureaucracy are trying to free an aircraft from air. An aircraft for airless transport is, in fact, a spacecraft—not a "reformed" aircraft but a whole different thing.

The lesson to be taken from both the Protestant Reformation and Soviet *perestroika* is that, while the process of schism and reconstruction driven by information technology is inevitable, the path along which it unfolds is not. *How* the reformation proceeds, and the specific social policies chosen to cope with it, matter greatly to the costs and ultimate success of the transition.

The earlier Reformation unleashed a violent, bloody, protracted conflict that still festers half a millennium later in Northern Ireland. The collapse of the Soviet empire has been swift, sudden, and absolute, at a cost that is at least disastrous, and that may yet prove catastrophic. Much of the current economic malaise in the West reflects the more tempered but still strenuous and often painful costs of "restructuring" entrenched, brittle bureaucracies.

The lesson from all these examples is that delay and denial of the inevitable outcome only magnify the ultimate costs and risks of the reformation. "For a long time I really did think that the [Communist Party of the Soviet Union] could be reformed," Mikhail Gorbachev wrote in his memoirs. "But the August coup destroyed those hopes."[127] Gorbachev stands as a monument to Douglas MacArthur's dictum that the essence of all human tragedy can be summarized in two words: "Too late."

So policies that speak of reform, or restructuring, or radical change, or even revolution and "breaking the mold" of education, that do not begin with the aim of *replacing* a technologically and economically obsolete institution serve no more useful purpose than the glib utterances of *perestroika* by the likes of such "reformers" as Ligachev, Rhyzhkov, Kryushkov, or even Gorbachev himself, who squandered precious time and resources on the doomed quest for a "new" socialism.

In tackling the reformation of learning that must replace schools with a whole new kind of HL enterprise, the stakes are at least as high. Within America, continuance of business-as-usual education reformism promises only to magnify the polarization of haves and have-nots. The well-off will gain rapidly expanding access to the tools and media of hyperlearning no matter what public education policies the country pursues. Those with the right jobs in the right communities will soon get the technologies to liberate them from the thrall of schooling.

More-of-the-same reform means that public schools and colleges will continue to devolve into an intellectual ghetto for the poor, minorities, and disadvantaged—a kind of brown Brigadoon that makes only one day of progress for every century that passes in the real world outside. Social inequality and resulting conflict will grow. Progress toward a bright new economic future will be retarded by a population divided and handicapped by a surplus of schooling and a deficit of learning.

The global stakes are even higher. The learning reformation is a worldwide, not just domestic, imperative. Europe, which has been wracked by nationalist civil wars for centuries, is groping toward integration in the West even as ancient ethnic hatreds are being unleashed by schism of the East. Some 400 million people in the remnants of the Soviet empire who have been isolated from capitalism for two or three generations must learn the skills and culture of a market society overnight. India's recent turn away from socialism creates a similar need among a population of 850 million. China may be at the verge of exhausting the possibilities for incremental reform without the final abdication of communist rule—that would add another billion-plus converts needing to learn a new economic and political way of life in a hurry. South Africa, Ethiopia, Argentina, Brazil—the new world order is no empty slogan but an imperative for learning on a scale and at a pace unprecedented in human history. To believe that this massive task can be accomplished with teachers and textbooks and classrooms is to believe that pixie dust holds the key to human flight.

THE RIGHT LEADERSHIP

Before even considering the political and other actions needed to accelerate the reformation of learning, we need to be clear about the responsibilities for leadership of the effort. In general, the most important leadership must come from the business community, in alliance with employees and families—the consumers of learning services. If business won't lead the formation of a profitable learning industry, who will? As I noted earlier, business has the organization, resources, and political clout to overcome the resistance of the education establishment lobbyists. The other key reason for a central role for business leadership: The new hyperlearning enterprise needed for the twenty-first-century economy must be run *as*, not simply *like*, a major business. In the U.S. setting, the reformation effort will have to be focused mostly at the state and local levels. And the leadership of this reformation movement also must include far more people with solid experience in science and technology than has been typical of education reform.

A political coalition is needed to represent learning consumers. "Learning consumers" includes employers, families and children, and other individuals who seek the benefits learning opportunities can provide. In the politics that govern our current national education and training system, the voice of the consumer is almost completely unheard. The practices of conventional schooling are designed to instill the notion of the student as servant—or at least passive object—of the educational provider, rather than the normal economic relationship of the service vendor as servant of the consumer. As a result, students and their employers are the most passive and least organized class of consumers in our economy.

"Partnerships" and "consensus" settings that put business leaders, parents, and other consumers into interdependent roles with education/training producers can be useful under the right circumstances. But such arrangements are counterproductive substitutes for independent coalitions empowered to enforce the political and economic interests of the consumer. The only forums where consumer demands can be assured of parity with vendor self-interests are open markets and honest legislatures or courts.

Consumer empowerment is a necessary condition for the growth of hyperlearning technology markets. Even if consumers become far more widely aware than they are now of the prolific power of modern technology to serve their needs, vendors will find little increase in effective demand for their products as long as the learning consumer remains politically and economically disabled.

In America, the major focus of the new reformation has to aim at the state and local rather than federal levels. Historically and constitutionally, education has been primarily a state government responsibility. The federal government provides less than 10 percent of the overall funding for elementary, secondary, and higher education, and there is no serious prospect of that changing in the foreseeable future. The state governments now provide, on average, about half the total funding for K–12 schools and pay more than half the bill for postsecondary education. This is not to say that the federal government is irrelevant—the federal role can be highly influential in forging a new national learning enterprise. But the nitty-gritty work of replacing education with new institutions and enterprises will be mostly local. Even in other countries where the central government can form and implement national policies, the necessarily decentralized nature of the new free enterprise of learning the knowledge age demands will require a lot of local entrepreneurship.

The progress of the HL reformation demands leadership that is scientifically and technologically astute. Science and technology leaders need to be much more concerned about the organization and process of the learning enterprise, and much less about curriculum. The science and engineering communities in the United States, including corporate leaders in high-tech fields, have taken an unduly narrow role in the education reform movement, focusing their efforts almost entirely on revising science and math curricula, while being virtually absent from the broader political effort to restructure entire education and training systems. Because education reform has been led by people whose scientific and technological "literacy" mostly ranges from sparse to phobic, reform program predominantly have ignored the potential of fast-evolving science and technology to radically change the processes of teaching and learning.

At the same time, the much-needed improvements in the quality and accessibility of science, math, and technical learning have faltered for lack of connection to system-wide restructuring. A clogged and severed pipeline will fail to deliver the goods—regardless of whether the input is champagne or sewage.

Scientists and engineers need to take a more central role in the leadership of education restructuring as a whole. Their focus needs to be less on learning *about* science and technology, and more on the science and technology *of* learning.

One barrier to this needed refocusing of attention is a ridiculous but real political "turf" problem. The members and staff of the congressional science and technology committees have a good appreciation of the need to advance the science and technology *of* learning. But these committees' jurisdiction in education and training matters is limited to education *about* science and math and engineering. The committees concerned with education and labor, on the other hand, have little expertise or apparent interest in the technological opportunities and issues raised in this book.

The perverse result of this turf conflict is that what little investment the federal government is making in civilian science and technology *of* learning is rationalized as being for the improvement of teaching *about* math and science and technology. So the $15 million the National Science Foundation is investing in the development of truly innovative learning technology—focused on computer-based instruction and distance learning—is authorized under the "Excellence in Mathematics, Science and Engineering Act." Similarly, the strategically important and malnourished federal "Star Schools" program—which funds development of distance learning networks—is limited to applying a revolutionary technology to the narrow purpose of expanding instruction only in subjects where qualified teachers are acknowledged to be in short supply, which generally means math, science, and some foreign languages.

Meanwhile the overwhelming majority of not only federal but national U.S. investment in advanced learning science and technology continues to be made by the Defense Department, to the tune of about $300 million in 1991. As noted earlier, most of the specialized products of this investment—such as combat simulation trainers—are not immediately transferable to civilian use. But the underlying science and technology, design and validation methods, and highly skilled and experienced staff in both military and contractor organizations are all highly transferable to civilian application.

This absolutely crucial national technology asset is now at risk of being seriously diminished by the coming cuts in defense personnel and budgets. The U.S. science and technology community should be screaming about the importance of sustaining, complementing, and extending this precious R&D base that is critical for the civilian economy as well as national security. But America's scientists and engineers so far have been as silent and passive as jellyfish in responding to these issues.

One of the costliest consequences of the shortage of scientific and technological proficiency in political leadership is that the public has been left largely in the dark about crucial discoveries already made by the scientists who are studying how learning works in the classroom and in the real world of working and living outside of school. In fact, key scientific findings now expose many of the most popular beliefs about the value and effectiveness of schooling as hollow myths.

CHAPTER 7

SCIENCE LESSONS: BEYOND THE "EFFECTIVE SCHOOL" MYTHS

● ● ●

Going to school is clearly one of the most broadly shared of American social experiences. It powerfully frames the public's idea of what learning environments should look like—whether in a seventh-grade classroom, a college lecture hall, an adult literacy course, or a corporate training seminar. As a result, the design and practices of our childhood schoolrooms tend to be reproduced in most education and training settings, even those that aspire to be nontraditional or "radically" innovative. Despite decades of experience with models, demonstrations, and experimental programs, the "New American School" persistently gravitates back to our familiar models of school, classroom, and teaching.

In reality, these widely shared stereotypes of effective schools routinely and profoundly violate what scientists have come to know about how people learn most effectively, and the conditions under which people apply their knowledge best in new situations. A powerful knowledge base called "cognitive science" provides the evidence. "Cognitive" refers to perceiving and knowing, and cognitive scientists work to understand how we think, remember, understand, and learn. Their research is very diverse. They observe children learning mathematics or experienced workers handling on-the-job knowledge and judgment demands. They program computers to do complex problem solving or to simulate intelligent behavior. They analyze the very nature of meaning.

> Because of . . . pervasive constraints on human learning and a parallel set of constraints operating on community institutions, it is difficult to mount an effective school and even more difficult to demonstrate that it has been effective. We run the risk of investing incalculable resources in institutions that do not operate very well and that may never approach the effectiveness that their supporters—and, for that matter their detractors—would desire. Moreover, it is my own belief that until now, we have not fully appreciated just how difficult it is for schools to succeed in their chosen (or appointed) task. . . . [W]e have not been cognizant of ways in which basic inclinations of human learning turn out to be ill-matched to the agenda of the modern secular school.
>
> —Howard Gardner
>
> *The Unschooled Mind* (New York: Basic Books, 1991)

In recent years, cognitive research findings have challenged much of the conventional wisdom about how teaching and learning work. Distilled, this research contradicts a number of popular myths that, at great cost, continue to shape the bulk of education and training efforts not only in America but around the world.

MYTH 1: PEOPLE LEARN BEST IN SCHOOL

In reality, the vast majority and most productive share of human learning takes place in real-world settings outside of schools. Moreover the traditional design and practices of even "excellent" schools are either divorced from or contradictory to the natural learning abilities most people are born with.

Cognitive research shows that learning *in context* is essential to acquiring knowledge and skills that are truly useful to working and living. Context turns out to be critical for understanding, and thus, for learning. The importance of context lies in the *meaning* that it gives to learning through the workings of the human's natural learning system. Human beings —even the small child—are quintessentially sense-making, problem-solving animals. As a species, we wonder, we are curious, we want to understand.[128]

Both children and adults acquire knowledge from active participation in holistic, complex, meaningful environments organized around long-term goals. Fractionated instruction maximizes forgetting, inattention, and passivity. Today's school programs could hardly have been better designed to prevent a child's natural learning system from operating.

—Sylvia Farnham-Diggory

Schooling (Cambridge, Mass.: Harvard University Press, 1990)

Context is evidently critical in using and understanding language. Most of us readily can recognize that words have meaning in relation to the context in which they are appear. Consider, for instance, the use of the word *saw* in "Jim *saw* the wood" and "*Saw* the wood, Jim."

Cognitive scientists believe that all knowledge, like language, is inseparably linked to its context. Ideas, concepts, or skills are tools whose meaning can be understood only in relation to the circumstances in which they are used.[129] If you are from an isolated society that has no experience with a "cork" or a "bottle" (much less wine), you probably won't know how to use a corkscrew, or even what it is. In the context of Chinese culture, nitrate explosives were prized as entertaining "fireworks"—in the European context the same technology was appreciated more as "gunpowder."

The human brain is designed and developed to learn through experience. And experience has no meaning except in relation to some context. For instance, we are taught in driving school that a red light means "stop." After years of driving experience, stopping when you see a red light becomes a reflexive habit. But we go about our business every day surrounded by all kinds of red lights—in a store window, on a Christmas tree, in a TV picture, on a toaster, and so forth—without suddenly stopping dead in our tracks. We've learned to stop at a red light only in the proper context: driving a car down the street, facing a special kind of red light in a device like a traffic light or taillight that is designed to be a signal.

This learning in context doesn't take any great genius. A pigeon or even a roundworm—whose whole nervous system has just a couple of hundred cells—learns the same way. That's what learning is.

The inventions of spoken language to represent experience and then of abstract, written symbols to represent words and numbers enabled humans to learn from experiences that were remote in space or time. The impact of these innovations on human society of course was explosive. But learning through the transmission of abstract, printed symbols works in direct proportion to the degree that the symbolic representations hook up to real human experience. The more disconnected symbolic communication becomes from the context of authentic, *personal* human experience—your own experience, not someone else's long ago and far away that you've never seen or felt—then the more meager learning becomes until it degrades to no more than mere memorization or, at worst, total confusion.

Yet education generally just wants us to be "right." Typically, academia evaluates the success of school learning by counting the number of correct responses on tests. The public has been misled to believe that answering a predetermined number of questions correctly is the scientific way to measure learning achievement. In fact, an entire industry is now in the business of making these tests more sophisticated and "elegant."

Unfortunately, as long as learning continues to be mismeasured by tests that mandate "right" and "wrong" facts for answers, educators are prompted—almost forced—to break complex tasks and ideas out of the productive context in which those elements are applied. The seamless fabric of knowledge instead is shredded into school subjects that can be "taught" and "learned" separately. But cognitive science knows that people who are forced to learn disconnected subroutines, items, and subskills wind up losing comprehension of the bigger picture, the natural context that gives their actions meaning.[130]

Real-life experiences, and therefore knowledge, do not come chopped up in discrete subjects but are invariably "interdisciplinary." Disciplines such as chemistry, economics, calculus, finance, Spanish literature, fine arts, and American history are arbitrary domains defined for the convenience of researchers, academic administrators, or would-be specialists. Dennis Meadows, head of the Institute for Policy Studies at the University of New Hampshire, has pointed out that we would think it bizarre for a geographer to specialize in knowing everything about the surface of the earth between eight hundred and nine hundred feet above sea level and nothing else—but that's pretty much the way the academy attempts to organize and transmit knowledge.

This is not to deny that learners must perform simple "subtask" operations from time to time in school and in life. Indeed, studies of apprentices show that novices start with simple tasks. Nonetheless, they perform these simple tasks *in context.* By observing how the master executes different but related subskills to achieve the end process or product, apprentices develop a conceptual map of the target task, an advanced "organizer" that helps when they first attempt to execute the complex skill themselves.[131]

For instance, Zinacanteco Indian girls in Mexico are introduced to weaving at an early age by first simply observing their mothers, then later helping with basic tasks such as boiling yarn and dyeing wool. With considerable maternal guidance, the girls begin to do their own weaving around age eight, and within three or four years they develop enough skill to be able to weave almost independently.[132]

Context-connected learning should not be confused with simple notions of practical or applied instruction as in the idea of "vocational" education. A relevant context for learning *comes out of* specific, real-life situations of the learner; vocational curricula often fall short by attempting to transmit skills *for use in* specific situations which may or may not be relevant to the learner's real-life experience.

There are examples of educational institutions that have adapted their practices to the necessity of learning in context. At McMaster University School of Medicine in Ontario, students start their medical studies immediately with clinical problems, meeting regularly with each other and a resource person in tutorial groups. Tutorials are organized around major biomedical problems that cannot be solved unless students understand physical, biological, and behavioral principles and know how to collect data and evaluate evidence. The students bear the responsibility to determine, with faculty help, what they need to know and then to learn it.

The medical school in Maastricht, in the Netherlands—where the government assigns students to medical school by lottery—uses a similar approach. Despite having had no formal instruction, Maastricht students on average score higher on tests of anatomy than do residents trained in the Netherlands' traditional lecture-approach medical schools. After seven years in school, 88 percent of the Maastricht school's 1974 class had received diplomas, versus 21 percent of students in other schools.[133]

These examples also suggest, however, the limitation of conventional schools and colleges to adopt authentic-context learning as their standard practice. Medical and other vocational schools have a specific, real-world context of professional practice to which they can justifiably connect the total learning experience they offer.

But general education institutions serving general populations face the daunting mission of connecting learning to virtually the total spectrum of human motives, experiences, and real-life contexts. That can be done only by customizing instructional services to the needs and goals of each individual learner. HL technology now can provide that degree of fine-tuning, and can bring the sight, sound, and even physical experience of real-world contexts to the learner. The traditional academic technology of classroom, textbook, and teacher cannot.

MYTH 2: SCHOOL IS PREPARATION FOR WORKING IN THE REAL WORLD

The point of going to school, we have been told, is to prepare students for effective and responsible functioning outside of school, especially in the workplace. We assume that students will automatically transfer and apply the concepts, skills, and knowledge they acquire in the classroom to other life and work situations.

Cognitive researchers, however, have found that the conditions in which knowledge transfers are neither obvious nor common. Researchers do know that people routinely apply *basic* skills—the "three R's"—to new situations with some success. But extensive cognitive research, spanning decades, keeps finding circumstances in which people don't predictably apply knowledge learned in one situation to another. Three situations where it seems knowledge should transfer—but doesn't—stand out.

From school to life. Educators and reformers routinely praise our traditional school curriculum because the knowledge and concepts it teaches are *general.* In their view, general concepts and knowledge are valuable because students can use them in a wide variety of situations beyond the classroom. But are the knowledge, skills, and strategies acquired in formal education in fact being used appropriately in everyday practice?

The answer, according to the best research addressing this question, is *no.* For instance, researchers have found that when college students who have mastered solving "book" problems in physics courses are asked to analyze ordinary phenomena, the students revert to intuitive explanations that violate Newton's laws. In one study, 70 percent of the engineering students who had taken a mechanics course incorrectly claimed that a coin, after being flipped up in the air, was still acted on by some "upward force"—in fact, only the force of gravity affects the coin after it is released. Another study found that nearly half the students who studied physics argued that an object expelled from a curved tube would continue moving in a curved path—rather than in a straight line, as Newton's law of inertia dictates. Significantly, the students in these studies get high scores on standardized tests and honor grades in physics courses. They simply have not made much connection between academic knowledge and the real world.[134]

Likewise, studies of expert radiologists, electronic troubleshooters, and lawyers all reveal a surprising lack of transfer of theoretical principles, processes, or skills learned in school to professional practice.[135] Ask your own physician or attorney whether the courses they took in medical or law school have much use in the work they do every day and the chances are very high they will tell you: not much.

From life to school. Psychologists have recognized for a long time that intelligence is built out of interaction with the environment. Indeed, all human waking experience (and maybe even some part of sleeping experience) is directly connected to the natural process of learning. Experience from which a person learns or remembers nothing arguably can be said not to be "experienced" at all.

People learn outside of school all the time, but once they walk in the school doors, what do people do with what they learn in life outside the classroom? Does sound, everyday practice get applied to school learning?

Once again, scientific research tells us *no.* In a well-known research study, a middle school teacher working with students who had failed in mainstream classrooms discovered that one of his students had a regular job scoring for a bowling league. The work demanded fast, accurate, complicated arithmetic. Other students had similar arithmetic success calculating their paper route change or shopping mall purchases.

But after lecturing the students on how smart they were in practice, and devising problem sets from which the students could choose bowling score, paper route, or shoe purchase problems to solve, the teacher reported a startling result: The students seemed incapable of arriving at correct answers when their real-world expertise was tested through classroom paper exercises. "Kids immediately rushed me yelling 'Is this right?' 'I don't know how to do it!' 'What's the answer?' 'This ain't right, is it?' and 'What's my grade?'" teacher James Herndon reported. "The brilliant league scorer couldn't decide whether two strikes and a third frame of eight amounted to eighteen or twenty-eight or whether it was one hundred and eight and a half."[136]

From school subject to school subject. Do the skills, strategies, concepts, and other knowledge learned in one school subject at least transfer across the traditional curriculum into other school learning?

Yet again, researchers conclude with a *no*. Not so long ago, it was still common practice for students to study Latin and mathematics not only for the subjects' utility, but for the "mental discipline" and logical constructs that were presumed to be useful in learning other things. Yet at the turn of the century psychologist Edward Thorndike conducted many studies of the transfer of such learning from one school subject to another, and his "negative findings . . . devastated the discipline hypothesis," as Roy Pea recalls.[137] More recent research shows that teaching children to use general thinking and learning strategies produces no clear benefits outside the specific subject areas in which they are taught.[138]

The fact that knowledge does not transfer in these situations means that simply increasing the amount of knowledge relayed in our schools will not enhance students' ability to apply knowledge beneficially in real-life situations. While more needs to be learned about how knowledge and skill can be transferred to practice, the surest way to achieve that objective is to reduce the need for "transfer" by bringing learning as close to the real context of practice as possible.

Indeed, "embedded training" and the developing designs for "just-in-time" (JIT) learning are using advanced HL technologies such as simulation and virtual reality to erase the boundary between learning and doing altogether.

The irresistible allure of simulations for learning lies in their ability to provide experiences that would be too dangerous, costly, or just plain impossible to get any other way. For example, at the Federal Aviation Administration Academy in Oklahoma City, student airport tower controllers are learning their jobs in a Logicon Tower Operator Training System (TOTS) simulator whose advanced computer graphics and voice recognition and response make it almost indistinguishable from reality. The $10 million system's graphics are so precise that the simulated aircraft the student operator sees on the twenty-three-foot screen outside the TOTS window look real even when viewed through binoculars. A disaster in early 1991 at Los Angeles International Airport—where thirty-three people died when a USAir 737 struck a commuter plane a controller had cleared onto the wrong runway—shows the incomparable value of this kind of simulation training: Students can learn from their mistakes before anyone gets hurt.

Simulation training systems like TOTS mimic the context of real work closely, but are still separate from it. As the CAMS story suggests, training and learning more and more are becoming embedded in the smart systems used to perform the work itself (and even those used for entertainment, housekeeping, and other social functions).

The military, as is often the case, has been in the lead in using advanced simulation methods to embed more training and learning into operating systems. One obvious advantage is saving the cost of dedicated training systems (such as TOTS) as well as the considerable cost of personnel leaving their workplaces to go somewhere to get trained. And training embedded in the real work setting necessarily means more and better hands-on learning.[140]

An outstanding example of this kind of HL technology is the U.S. Navy's Aegis Combat Training System. ACTS is a training and learning capability that was built into the billion-dollar Aegis combat radar and weapons control system of the Navy's most advanced class of guided missile cruisers.

Because the Aegis Combat Information Center demands that an entire team of more than a dozen people perform flawlessly under extreme pressure, continual training and honing of skills is essential. The very nature of shipboard service requires that the learning be done in the same place the work is to be performed.

. . . I spent some time directing aircraft into and out of Academy Airport. At one point, I had a United DC-10 waiting for takeoff as an American 727 approached on short final, already cleared to land.

I turned to Logicon's Herb Noll, who was serving as my instructor. "What would happen if I cleared United onto the runway right now?" I asked.

"Go ahead," he says. "Try it."

I keyed my mike. "United 433. Taxi into position. Cleared for takeoff."

"United 433 . . ."

I watched the DC-10 begin to move, turning onto the runway directly in front of the rapidly approaching 727. As the aircraft merged, a huge orange fireball erupted on the screen. When it faded away, the planes were gone.

"We didn't program it for debris," Noll says. "The message is clear enough."

—Jim Schefter, "Air Traffic Training Gets Real," *Popular Science* (July 1991)

ACTS uses the same displays and consoles of the CIC to run authentic combat simulation scenarios lasting anywhere from a brisk half hour to a grueling five hours. ACTS can allow the combat teams on several ships to work on the same exercise at the same time—an even closer and more valuable simulation of real conflict conditions.

The same kind of embedded learning is needed and being designed into a wide range of civilian work environments. Like the Aegis CIC, more and more high-tech workplaces demand high levels of human skill to be exercised in relatively infrequent crisis situations. A modern airliner, for instance, is quite capable of taking off, flying, and landing itself—except when something goes wrong. Studies by the commission on the Three Mile Island nuclear power station accident in 1979 found a problem common to many modern industrial operation control centers: Most of the work, most of the time is routine, constant, and boring. The operator's key job is to solve unusual and thus unpredictable problems, and to manage the rare but critical disaster. The commission concluded that operators needed not only better designed operating displays, but continual practice with simulators to hone crisis-management skills. Similar needs exist in complex air traffic control, electric and gas and telecommunications grid management, and chemical and other industrial operations systems.

One implication of the increasingly JIT learning environment of work is that Nintendo and similar "game" products are doing more to cultivate the skills needed in the mindcraft workplace than most schools or colleges are. As the above examples suggest, the human role in a growing number of work environments is ever more focused on three functions: creativity, crisis management, and continual learning in a real or closely simulated work context. To be effective in these settings, workers need not only the skills developed by a particular simulation "game" but what we might call "metagame skills"—reflecting the higher order skills needed to master new games from scratch. That *new games* ability is crucial to working in environments that require anticipating a virtually infinite number of crisis scenarios and that present continually upgraded operating technology.

Learning to play one particular game well is not enough to acquire those metaskills, just as mastering a single song on the piano is not enough to qualify you as a "musician." Rather, you develop the gaming metaskills by "learning to learn" to play a substantial number and variety of games, including play that requires both individual skill and teamwork. That depth and diversity of virtuoso competence is built up from being an active consumer of many products in the game market, whether at home, in the mall arcade, or walking around with a device like the Nintendo Game Boy or Atari Lynx.

MYTH 3: THE TEACHER IS THE FOUNTAIN; THE LEARNER IS THE BOWL

There may be no more common and erroneous stereotype than the image of instruction as injecting knowledge into an empty head. Whether in a typical schoolroom, or a congressional hearing, or a corporate training session, the same one-way process is acted out. In each, the teacher or expert faces the learners, taking on the critical role of "fountain of knowledge." The learner plays the "receiver of wisdom," passively accepting the intelligence being dispensed, like an empty bowl into which water is poured. Education, in this view, is merely a conveyance of what experts already know to be true; it is not a process of inquiry, discovery, and wonder. The image of teaching as knowledge-injection emanates from an implicit assumption that education's basic purpose is to transmit a society's culture from one generation to the next.[141]

But this model of instructional practice, often called *passive learning,* contradicts what cognitive science researchers now know about how people learn most effectively. Chief among the objections to passive learning methods are four significant research findings.

Passive learning reduces or removes chances for exploration, discovery, and invention. As noted earlier, students today typically study by subject in fragmented and highly delineated studies that leave virtually no room for the learner to explore, invent, and construct ideas in the natural way any normally curious small child constantly employs. Consequently, students come to regard learning as a thing, not a process; something received, not discovered; part of a body of knowledge, rather than a form of activity, argumentation, and social discourse. To learn effectively, students need chances to engage in choice, judgment, control processes, and problem formulation. They need the chance to be discoverers, not just sponges.

Passive learning creates a lopsided learning dependency that impedes skill development. Passive learning encourages learners to become dependent on teachers for guidance and feedback, undercutting the students' trust in their own abilities to make sense of what they observe and experience. People can experience the world in two ways, as subjects and as objects. Outside of school in their recreational and daily living, free people can be in control of their activities, able to seize opportunities, explore their own interests, and generate solutions to the problems that concern them. As researcher Jean Lave points out, school creates "contexts in which [students] . . . experience themselves as objects, with no control over problems or choice about problem-solving processes."[142] Because of this, passive learning undercuts the development of the "higher order" skills of creativity, problem solving, and initiative that are increasingly being demanded of all workers in the mindcraft economy.[143]

Passive learning reduces learning motivation, creating "crowd control" problems. Teachers commonly complain about certain student behaviors that frustrate both the teacher's ability to teach and the students' ability to learn. A leading culprit is the bored student who "spaces out" during a teacher's presentation. Authors of comic strips like "Calvin and Hobbes," "Shoe," and "Peanuts" have a virtual annuity in the inexhaustible subject of the bored and fractious student. Outside the funny papers, students of different ages and from different countries go into the same "waiting it out" and other self-defense behaviors during a standard lecture—a situation that typifies passive learning.[144] And unfortunately, as teachers know so well, motivation problems turn into crowd-control problems when non-involved students band together to act out their frustration. Research indicates that students become deeply engaged, more motivated, and less a discipline problem when their learning tasks are organized as collaborative *discovery* projects.[145]

Passive learning encourages the veneer rather than the reality of accomplishment. Passive learning places a premium on the ability of the learner to reproduce the learned *word.* This translates into sounding and testing "right" within the school system, often without the achievement of effective, useful learning—the ability to apply concepts and skills in new situations. Anyone who has crammed arduously to prepare for pivotal multiple-choice qualifying exams like the SAT or GRE, only to forget the thousands of key "learned" facts short weeks after taking it, will recognize this phenomenon. In the case of American students, this has been called the "veneer of accomplishment": Students *look like* they grasp what teachers and schools want them to learn, but in reality they do not.[146]

Typical curriculum design is based on a conceptual analysis of the subject matter that ignores—or assumes—what is already in the learner's head. But learners rarely come new and empty to what is being taught. Research on students learning science offers many examples of how the learner's prior knowledge and concepts affect new learning. As researcher Senta Raizen points out, both younger and older students bring to the learning of science their own concepts of natural phenomena like light, heat and temperature, electricity, or physical and chemical transformations. These ideas may be personal, constructed out of the person's own interpretations of experience, and coherent in their own terms. Or the ideas may come from partially understood or inappropriately applied previous school learning.[147]

Unfortunately, the limited time devoted to specific lessons in the typical classroom, coupled with the passive nature of classroom learning, hardly suffices to disclose, let alone change, the ideas and assumptions that individuals bring to the lesson. The result? Students make mistakes that arise from undetected ideas they bring into the classroom. Or they play back newly memorized "knowledge" and concepts, but return to their own ideas when confronted with unfamiliar questions or nonroutine problems. In short, the challenge of teaching and learning is to confirm, disconfirm, modify, replace, and add to what is already written on a student's slate—and that requires the *active* participation of the student in the process.

MYTH 4: MORE OR LESS ACADEMIC ACHIEVEMENT MEANS MORE OR LESS LEARNING

In reality, the human brain is genetically programmed and born to learn—constantly, from experience. The design of the brain predates the introduction of academic institutions by several million years. Everything that humans learned to make the birth of civilization possible was learned before and without schools, and many civilizations grew and thrived without significant participation in schooling.

Over 99 percent of what the average American will learn in the course of a lifetime will not be learned in a classroom. In fact, most situations of "spectacular learning"—in which the individual picks up knowledge and skills rapidly and with little apparent effort—occur out of school. Chief among these situations is the first five years of life when, as children, we acquire concepts, language, motor, spatial, and social skills through normal interaction with parents and other people, but with little or no classroom instruction.

Researchers Roy Pea and J. D. Bransford and their colleagues analyzed the conditions in which a young child learns "spectacularly," to provide three reinforcing clues for designing more effective learning opportunities:

When Western-style school tasks—the kind that appear on standardized tests—are administered to both populations, schooled children typically perform much better. . . .

But when unschooled children are given materials from their own environment with which to work, when they have become familiar with the circumstances of the testing, or when their own behaviors are examined for evidence of the sought-after capacities . . . , the apparent differences across schooled and unschooled populations either disappear altogether or are radically reduced.

—Howard Gardner

The Unschooled Mind (New York: Basic Books, 1991)

Spectacular learning takes place in context. Children learn during the first five years in the midst of culturally meaningful or practical ongoing activities, and they receive continual feedback on the results of their actions.

It is often effectively mediated. Parents, friends, and peers not only serve as models for imitative learning, but help the children learn by providing structure to and connections between the children's experiences. They highlight information in the situation that will particularly help the child carry out a task. They let them take on "part" activities in completing a whole task, such as measuring out sugar, flour, and other ingredients in the process of making a cake.

The learning is functional. Context and mediation help children understand how information is used to solve problems. Children acquire concepts and skills as *tools* that can be used for many different purposes. The functions of new knowledge—and new learning—are not only shown, but often are explicitly stated.[148]

Of course, what children learn is not always positive. Children exposed to abuse and dysfunctional families are spectacular learners too, and what they learn—lack of self-esteem, for example—often winds up haunting them to the grave.

MYTH 5: YOU HAVE TO LEARN TO WALK BEFORE YOU CAN LEARN TO RUN

It has become commonplace in speaking and writing about the workplace demands of a high-tech economy to talk about "basic" skills and "higher order" thinking, as if to imply one must (chrono)logically come before the other. But, in truth, the type of skill or knowledge being acquired does not dictate the order in which it should be learned.

There are three distinct reasons for this. The first rises from common

---

The most important single message of modern research on the nature of thinking is that the kinds of activities traditionally associated with thinking are not limited to advanced levels of development. . . . In fact, the term "higher order" skills is probably itself fundamentally misleading, for it suggests that another set of skills, presumably called "lower order," needs to come first. This assumption—that there is a sequence from lower level activities that do not require much independent thinking or judgment to higher level ones that do—colors much educational theory and practice. Implicitly at least, it justifies long years of drill on the "basics" before thinking and problem solving are demanded. Cognitive research on the nature of basic skills such as reading and mathematics provides a fundamental challenge to this assumption. Indeed, research suggests that failure to cultivate aspects of thinking such as . . . higher order skills may be the source of major difficulties even in elementary school.

—Lauren B. Resnick

Education and Learning to Think (Washington, D.C.: National Academy Press, 1987)

---

sense about context: Real-world situations require people to use and learn different kinds of skills all at the same time. Children do not learn first to walk and then to communicate—they pursue the motor and mental abilities at the same time. Likewise, a baseball player does not need to master bunting before hitting, and then baserunning before throwing, and that before catching. None of these skills is more "basic" to playing baseball than others, and, except for American League pitchers and designated hitters, players need to develop and practice all the skills simultaneously.

Second, modern research on the nature of thinking concludes that people at "advanced" levels of development are not the only ones who engage in the activities associated with higher order thinking—that is, making judgments, attaching meaning to things, finding multiple solutions, or sorting through conflicting information. Advanced thinking is an intimate part of learning at any level from elementary school to postretirement.

Finally, simply because each human being is truly unique, how learning happens—and *what* learning happens *when*—is different for different people. People learn by experience, but no two people share the same experience. As anthropologist Gregory Bateson observed, each learner is inherently free to "punctuate" in his own way the stream of experienced events into the elements of stimulus, response, and reinforcement that comprise the most fundamental learning processes.[149] The practical implication is that there is no way to separate learning from what may be called personality, or attitude, or simply emotion. It is no more possible to define a certain behavior conclusively as either a "basic" or "advanced" skill than it is to settle once and for all the question of whether a glass is half empty or half full.

The "walk before run" metaphor actually says more about the peculiarities of the human body than it does about the learning process. Humans happen to be born top-heavy—a human baby's head is too big and heavy for its undeveloped body and limbs to support either walking or running. Four-legged animals with small brains, like gazelle or wildebeest, are able to run within minutes after birth—any of their ancestors who couldn't do that became instant lion snacks.

School curricula reinforce the impression that logical subjects like math and science require starting with basics and progressively adding more sophisticated conclusions and applications. But the very nature of logical laws makes it equally feasible to work backward from conclusions, or observations, to hypotheses. Deduction and induction are entirely complementary.

In reality, scientists and mathematicians do not *do* their crafts in the linear, progressive way their subjects are usually taught. Practitioners commonly start with a flash of insight (the stereotypical light bulb lighting), a hunch, a dream, a guess, an elaborate hypothesis or postulate, and then work backward, forward, and around it to try to make it fit with established knowledge. Physicists or engineers commonly try using complex mathematical gadgets to solve the problems that interest them without knowing or caring how the math was logically derived. Experimenters tinker in laboratories and make surprising discoveries that theoreticians then labor to try to explain logically. Alternatively, theorists like Einstein come up with wild new theories like relativity that experimenters may have to struggle for decades to find a way to test and prove. Scientific knowledge does not grow incrementally down a predictable track. Rather it grows volcanolike, sometimes oozing in patient rivulets, sometimes erupting in fiery ferment, and occasionally exploding, blowing away the rock of established truth.[150]

Pedantic, linear teaching rarely conveys the true drama and mystery of the human quest for knowledge. School plods where human imagination naturally leaps.

MYTH 6: EDUCATION IS DIFFERENT FROM TRAINING

The scientists who study learning increasingly recognize that *apprenticeship* is a powerful way of organizing learning-in-context for any purpose. In contrast to the traditional view of academic learning as different from or even superior to vocational learning, scientists now speak of "cognitive apprenticeship" as the key to acquiring the higher-order thinking skills that, in turn, are increasingly needed for working and living in the knowledge age.

So any kind of learning that aims to be relevant to the real world can benefit from the following characteristics that Jean Lave, Brigitte Jordan, and other researchers have observed in traditional apprenticeships.

Apprenticeship learning focuses on doing rather than just talking. Apprenticeship is concerned with the *ability to do* rather than the *ability to talk about doing* something. The apprenticing process arranges opportunities *for* practice, whereas school curricula—where the focus is typically on verbal and abstract information—tend to be a specification *of* practice. Apprenticeship learning comes through the practice of skills. The master is less likely to talk than to guide by modeling, assigning tasks, overseeing, and critiquing. Indeed, it may be quite difficult to get craft masters and apprentices to articulate what it is they know how to do. The division between academics and apprentices goes back to the classical age of ancient Greece, when the "liberal arts" curriculum was originally designed as vocational education for politics. The first and foremost goal of such instruction was apprenticeship in the skills of *rhetoric,* in preparation for the craft of political argumentation. So in early academia the ability to do and the ability to talk about were the same thing. But with the vast expansion of academic institutions since the early nineteenth century, rhetoric as an *end* became mistaken for a *means* of teaching. As a result, the rhetorical methods of academic vocationalism have been increasingly misapplied to a wide range of nonpolitical crafts and skills which, to be learned effectively, need doing and talking about to be separated.

Apprenticeship is a way of life. Apprenticeship happens in the course of daily life. In fact, apprentices seldom sense any separation between activities of daily living and learning of "professional" skills. Rather, the apprentice is exposed to a certain environment, is socially engaged with a community that shares some common interest, participates in sets of activities, handles (plays with) certain tools, and is trained in the sphere of specialist work the same way a child is in the home environment.

Work is the driving force. Masters and apprentices engage in activities that are driven by the requirements of the work to be accomplished: Pots must be fired, a shawl woven, trousers manufactured. Whatever teaching or learning may happen is coincidental to the overriding concern of the work to be done. Consequently, the apprentice values progressive mastery of tasks not so much as a step toward a distant, symbolic goal (like a diploma), but for its immediate benefit. Apprentices are not practicing for the real thing—they are doing it.

Apprentices acquire skills in a meaningful order. While on the surface apprenticeship may seem to impose a "walk before run" orderliness, in effective apprenticing the order derives from the organic structure of the work and its real context, rather than from an artificial model of cognitive difficulty. Apprentices commonly are directed to start with skills that are relatively easy, where mistakes are least costly. For example, young tailor apprentices, rather than constructing a garment from start to finish, first experiment with parts of the production process that are least costly in terms of wasted materials, like sewing garments from pieces someone else has cut. Working from the "sidelines" of a complex task toward its center stands in contrast to the ways that knowledge is usually transferred in formal schooling. In a formal classroom, things are usually learned in chronological or some other arbitrary order divorced from learning in context. The components are treated as equally important, and it is assumed that they must be acquired in a linear way—one after another. But apprentices acquire skills in bunches or bundles that fit together to solve a practical problem. Much of the learning is "just in time"—immediately connected to a problem that has to be solved now for the work to proceed.

Performance and competence evaluations are implicit, embedded in the work environment.   For an apprentice, expert execution of a task is obvious and easily observable—in the master's performance. Judgment about the apprentice's competence is likewise obvious and needs no commentary: It emerges naturally and continuously as work is accomplished, rather than occurring as a specially marked event, like a test. In fact, to a great extent, the person who judges the apprentice's performance *is* the apprentice. Having observed the work sequence many times, the apprentice knows what remains to be learned. Moving on to acquire the next skill is largely up to the apprentice, rather than under the master's control. Apprenticeship is inherently individualized. The master promotes and assigns apprentices as their talents and limitations are demonstrated in practice.

Teachers and teaching are largely invisible.   In apprenticeship learning—as well as informal on-the-job training in modern workplaces—it may look as if very little teaching is occurring. Whatever instruction the apprentice receives originates not from a "teacher" who is doing teaching but from another worker doing his or her work, which the apprentice observes.[151]

In apprenticeship learning, the apprentice is being inducted into a *community of expert practice.* The community is not limited to the local "studio" but extends across space and time, joined by a variety of professional associations and by the formal history and informal folklore of the craft. Apprenticeship learning illustrates the distinction between doing and waiting it out, between an active and a passive environment.

Moreover, contrary to what may appear at first glance as an orthodox ritual, apprenticeship learning is neither static nor simply concerned with the one-way transmission of tried-and-true practices from masters to novices. In effective apprenticing there is a healthy, dynamic friction between preservation and renovation of expertise. "Change is a fundamental property of communities-of-practice and their activities," Jean Lave and Etienne Wenger observe. And they note that "inexperience is an asset to be exploited," not just a vacuum to be filled. Precocious and irreverent apprentices challenge and inspire masters as well as follow them. Members of a community of practice all learn from each other.[152]

Only a fraction of a percent of U.S. workers—mostly in construction trades—are trained through the traditional, formal kinds of apprenticeship programs that are common in other countries, and that are especially widespread in Germany.[153] But apprentice learning is becoming such an inherent feature of the mindcraft economy that more formal programs may not be needed.

With expertise ever more embedded in networks and smart tools, rather than personal "masters," the features of apprentice learning are becoming almost universal in the HL environment. Most apprenticing now is going on almost invisibly through the use of expert systems like CAMS, Magic, and others mentioned earlier, through simulation and embedded training systems, and through the collaborative relationships forged through communication network utilities such as groupware, electronic mail, and bulletin board systems (BBS).

For instance, here's another example of how video games may be more relevant to the needs of a mindcraft economy than classrooms are: There hardly could be a more graphic and energetic example of a "community of expert practice" in action than the community of video and computer game players, whose numbers in the U.S. alone may represent a fifth or more of the national population.

At Nintendo's U.S. headquarters in Redmond, Washington, a "faculty" of five hundred game masters takes one hundred fifty thousand telephone calls a week from apprentice gamers seeking guidance to hone their playing skills.[154] The game community is further linked by a host of magazines, books, newsletters, clubs, meetings, and tournaments. Visit any shopping mall game arcade and you will see self-organized apprenticeship in action: Clusters of players of diverse age, gender, race, creed, color, and national origin arc around the player currently engaged with a machine, observing play and exchanging comments and tips on tactics and strategy. Mastery is relative to the composition of the ad hoc group and the particular game—the master-apprentice roles continually shift among the members of the community.

This kind of self-organizing HL community of practice is as typical of the mindcraft workplace as of the world of knowledge age entertainment. The same kind of collaborative user groups and telecommunicated help and guidance have enabled over sixty million Americans to become handy with personal computers—the great majority without attending any school or classes. With four out of ten U.S. workers now using computers at work,[155] individual ability to join and work with a self-created apprenticing community is becoming ever more crucial to organizational performance and national productivity.

And this "Nintendo-izing" of work-connected learning is not limited just to the white-collar office, as an anecdote from a *Fortune* magazine story of a few years ago illustrates. Computer experts who were starting to teach a steelworker to program a new inventory control system at an American Steel & Wire mill in Cleveland ran out of time and decided to postpone the training to the next day. "That night, the worker went home, sat down with his kids at a computer, and figured the program out," the magazine reported. "The next morning he went in and taught it to other workers. By the time the computer experts came back to complete the training, the guys in the mill already had the system up and running."[156]

MYTH 7: SOME PEOPLE ARE SMARTER THAN OTHERS

The rigid, uniform, lockstep pattern of instruction followed in most schools and colleges nurtures the popular illusion that there is a one-dimensional spectrum of human intelligence that ranges from dumb to smart. The common experience of schooling has convinced most people that students who get higher grades and test scores are "better" students because they are "smarter," and have a higher "IQ." Americans are more prone to this belief than Asians such as the Japanese, who are more likely to attribute superior academic achievement to greater effort and discipline than to natural talent. Still there is a broad tendency to believe that people who have accomplished more academically are more capable *in general.*

But scientists know that human performance is far more diverse and complex than the linear sorting that arises from a schooling process designed for standardization. First, it is well established that learners have as many as a dozen different "styles" of learning. That is, some people learn best by reading words, others by seeing pictures, listening to sounds, touching things, or moving around—or by particular combinations of these various modes of sensing and doing.[157]

HOWARD GARDNER'S SEVEN HUMAN INTELLIGENCES

- language
- logical-mathematical analysis
- spatial representation
- musical thinking
- use of the body to solve problems or to make things
- understanding of other individuals
- understanding of ourselves

Thanks in important measure to over two decades of study of human ability by Howard Gardner of Harvard University, we know that human talents are more diverse, focused, and variable than a single lump-sum measure like IQ can capture. Gardner's interest in the nature of human talent began when, as a young researcher at Harvard Medical School, he was struck by the diverse effects of brain damage—victims might lose only a very specific skill, such as the ability to match words and pictures, or alternatively might demonstrate extraordinary skill in a specific task such as performing complex arithmetic calculations despite severe disabilities of other brain functions. Gardner's years of subsequent study of these and related phenomena, reported in six books and numerous other publications, probably has done more than the work of any other researcher to dispel the notion of a single, simple measure of human competence. In particular, Gardner has identified seven different areas of mental ability or "intelligence," each of which is endowed or developed more or less independently of the others. Different people have their own combinations of strengths and weaknesses in each of these areas. The several intelligences contribute in all sorts of ways to the great variety of human achievement that extends far beyond the range of mere scholastic standards: People can be "geniuses" in many ways other than those normally credited by schools.

And, while the pioneering studies by Swiss psychologist Jean Piaget suggested that children's brains tend to develop certain abilities in progressive stages at about the same ages, researchers now observe wide individual variations around these average generalizations for the population as a whole. Particular children may be years apart in their "readiness" to take on certain mental tasks successfully. And Gardner concludes that Piaget's findings, at least after age six or seven, are the result of cultural influences—schooling in particular—not inherent stages of brain development. Moreover, even if some abilities, like learning language, are easier to acquire during childhood, that doesn't mean those abilities can't still be developed, perhaps with more time and effort, in later life.

In short, what science knows is that human abilities are diverse in their form, range, and development and are intensely individual—they do not match the mass-production "standards" of schooling.

The insistence on smart-dumb standards inevitably requires reliance on standardized testing and grading practices. But testing acts as a double-edged sword against learning in context.

Besides its tendency to encourage teaching and learning topics outside their natural applications, testing in and of itself is out of context: It does not reflect how problems are solved and success is gauged in the workplace or any other real-life environment. Researcher Jean Lave observes, "Classroom tests . . . serve as the measure of . . . 'out of context' success, for the test taker must rely on memory alone and may not use books, classmates, or other resources for information."[158] As the twenty-first-century workplace and technology increasingly employ teamwork and complex problem-solving processes that no longer produce right or wrong answers—just worse or better thinking—the results of rote testing will be less and less able to signify a well-prepared learner, a person capable of working, managing, and building successfully.

The reverse cut of testing's two-edged sword is that academic testing demonstrates not only phony competence but *false incompetence* as well. In particular the flurry of national tests and surveys that claim to show that frighteningly large portions of the American population are illiterate, ignorant, and incompetent should be viewed, to put it mildly, as suspect.

For instance, social scientists who observed young street vendors in Brazil doing their business in the real world found that these little-schooled, wayward children had informally developed their own calculating techniques well enough that the children could successfully solve 98 percent of marketplace math problems—such as figuring total costs or making change. But when the children were presented with the same kinds of calculating tasks in the form of arithmetic problems stated verbally with only a symbolic description of the context of the problem, the children solved only 74 percent of the problems successfully. And when the problems were presented purely as mathematical operations with no descriptive context, the children's success rate fell to 37 percent.[159]

These results are not unusual. In another study, scientists found that minimum-wage workers employed on the loading dock of a dairy who showed almost flawless math skills in dealing with often complex work tasks, such as filling orders and making out bills, nevertheless scored poorly on academic math tests with problems equivalent to those they were successfully solving on the job. Moreover, the dairy workers showed greater flexibility in adapting their calculating strategies to real problems than did math students in school.[160]

So what science reveals about all this out-of-context academic teaching and testing confirms what many of us suspected all along: The "best and the brightest" aren't really so smart. And the "least and the dullest" aren't really so dumb.

MYTH 8: FACTS ARE MORE IMPORTANT THAN SKILLS

Whatever the public as a whole may feel, it is an article of faith among many would-be education experts concerned with "cultural literacy" that the recent presumed failure of American schools can be blamed on a movement in teaching to emphasize higher-order thinking skills over the memorization of a "canon" of facts that "everybody should know." The argument, in its simplest form, goes that you can't be a good thinker if you don't know anything.

There is, in fact, an element of scientific validity to that argument. But that element is only part of what science knows about effective thinking and learning, and taken by itself it leads to erroneous conclusions about what constitutes useful instruction.

Cognitive scientists recognize that intelligent behavior—whether of a computer or a human or other brain—requires knowledge. After all, intelligent thinking requires thinking about something. And at least some of the key strategies being pursued by researchers in artificial or applied intelligence presume that the functional "intelligence" of AI systems depends directly on the amount of knowledge they can encode and manage.[161]

But the status of "facts" as elements of knowledge has a different meaning in the world of cognitive and computer sciences than in the academic vision of effective schooling as an exhaustive game of Trivial Pursuit. In the perspective of science, data are not "knowledge" nor do they become knowledge simply by being stored and retrieved to and from memory.

As the anthropologist Gregory Bateson explained, data are messages, recorded as bits in some medium, whether a stone tablet or a magnetic disc. Information, in Bateson's elegantly simple definition, is a message that *makes a difference*—that is, it is perceived in a way that has an impact on whoever or whatever receives it. Knowledge, then, is information that makes a difference in meaning, that is, in the way other information is perceived. The difference between information and knowledge is the difference between perceiving and understanding.[162]

To illustrate these distinctions: Slapping a dog on the rump with a rolled newspaper sends a message. If the dog is awake, the message will be received and become information by making some difference in the dog's brain that is likely to be observable in the dog's physical reaction. But if the dog is under anesthesia, the message of the blow won't convey any information to the dog's brain; it just won't make any difference. On the other hand, if you transmit the spank to an awake dog in the context of rubbing his nose in the wet spot he left on the carpet, a reasonably intelligent animal ought to acquire some knowledge about the rules of housebreaking.

In short, data become information and information becomes knowledge through the *processes* of communicating, thinking, and learning. In research on the phenomena of intelligence in both artificial and living brains, the "facts" of interest are not mere data points but propositions—basically, facts about facts.

If anything simple can be said about the awesome complexity of intelligence it may be that intelligence lies in *connecting*—not only connecting information to information to weave the elemental fabric of knowledge, but connecting knowledge to action and to experience.

For instance, here's what E. D. Hirsch, Jr., author of *Cultural Literacy* and other tomes of triviaphilia, thinks is "what every American should know" about a common academic test item, the Battle of Hastings: "A battle in southwest ENGLAND in 1066. Invaders from the French province of Normandy, led by WILLIAM THE CONQUEROR, defeated English forces under King Harold. William declared himself king, thus bringing about the NORMAN CONQUEST of England."[163] This is an epitome of the kind of feckless factoid the cognitive scientists call "decontextualized"—scientific jargon for *borrrrrrring*. It is about as interesting to an AI programmer, or even his computer, as it is to you, me, or the average high school student.

There's no obvious reason why "every American" should know anything about the Battle of Hastings. But there is something quite interesting, even memorable, about the battle that is unmentioned by (perhaps unknown to) Hirsch and his associates.

What's really important about the Battle of Hastings, as James Burke reveals in his book with the not-coincidental title *Connections*, is that it was a milestone in the power of technology to transform society. Burke uses a picture from the Bayeux Tapestry, which recorded the battle eleven years later, to expose the decisive technology, a simple device that gave England to the Normans and changed the shape of history:

> The device itself is hard to see on the tapestry, but its presence is apparent from something else that can only be there because of it: the kite-shaped shield carried by a rider whose right arm is occupied holding a lance, and who is therefore too busy to protect his vulnerable left leg. The fact that the shield is long enough to protect the entire length of the body reveals the extent to which the right arm is busy, and the only thing that would keep it so busy is a lance. And the lance is there only because of the device in question: the stirrup.[164]

You still may not know why Hastings is a big deal, or why you should care, but odds are that Burke has made you a lot more curious than Hirsch has. Even in these few sentences, he shows the power of connections made by truly intelligent thinking, in contrast to Hirsch's row of Teflon trivialities that offer nothing to stick to each other or to comprehension.

Assuming that all knowledge is human knowledge—and so far we have no evidence of other beings that think consciously—it follows that all knowledge is connected to all other knowledge. This is not to say that each human knows everything but that humanity as a whole knows all that is known. Or to put it another way that sounds almost trivial: There is no unknown knowledge—because data become knowledge through the processes of knowing, thinking, learning. Much of the history and cultural legacy of ancient Egypt was recorded as data but was *unknown* until someone found the Rosetta stone, which permitted the information encoded in hieroglyphics to be connected to the knowledge of living people.

So the proper "map" of the universe of all knowledge would be something like the surface of a sphere (actually a hypersphere), one that is also expanding, like a balloon. Every "fact" is a point that is connected to every other point.

The key thing is that there is no center on that sort of map. In point of fact, any fact or group of facts claiming to be the center or source of all other knowledge would be, well, pointless. Cambridge has as much claim to being the center of knowledge as to being the center of the earth or the whole universe for that matter. It can believe that if it wants, and maybe even convince others to agree, but can't find support for such a claim in science.

The conclusion from all this is that there is no universal canon of facts whose memorization is prerequisite to advanced skills of thinking or know-how. Intelligence does need to think about something. But intelligence creates knowledge from data. Data don't create anything but the costs of storage. Actually, one of the most essential skills of intelligent thinking is learning what to think about.

Take the Battle of Hastings. I wouldn't be surprised if you've not been too tuned in to my profound explanation of the meaning of knowledge because what you really wanted to know is: What was so important about that darned stirrup?

Okay. The stirrup had trickled into Europe from somewhere in Asia, but Hastings was its first really important implementation in battle. William became "The Conqueror" because the French had figured out before

... [T]he problem of how we teach, how education is delivered, becomes far more important than one might initially imagine. Actual content may not be the issue at all, since we are really trying to impart the idea that one can deal with new arenas of knowledge if one knows how to learn, how to find out about what is known, and how to abandon old ideas when they are worn out. This means teaching ways of developing good questions rather than memorizing known answers, an idea that traditional school systems simply don't cotton to at all, and that traditional testing methods are unprepared to handle.

—Roger Schank

The Connoisseur's Guide to the Mind (New York: Summit Books, 1991)

the English that the stirrup allowed cavalry to be used as a shock-troop to break the lines of the opponent's infantry: The Bayeux Tapestry shows the Norman knights charging the English lines at full gallop with lances held *horizontally*, a maneuver that's feasible only if you have stirrups to keep you from getting knocked off your horse. The effect of a spearpoint propelled with the momentum of about a ton of horse and rider behind it turned out to be profoundly disheartening to foot soldiers.

With the stirrup, the ever more heavily armored knight dominated the battlefield with as devastating effect as his lineal descendant, the main battle tank of today. No monarch can afford to let his adversaries get that kind of competitive advantage, as hapless Harold demonstrated.

So Hastings unleashed an arms race that changed the shape of European society, and ultimately therefore the world. Knights were essential to national security, but very expensive. Armor and weapons got bigger and heavier and more costly. More, bigger, and stronger horses were needed. Each knight required an entourage of staff for maintenance and repair, and a baggage train of supplies, extra weapons, spare parts, and such.

Kings met the knights' need for wealth with grants of large estates. To protect the estates from attack by other knights, expensive fortresses and then castles were needed, which required even more land and peasants to support them. To try to keep the potent knights in line, kings promoted codes of chivalry (another name for *cavalry*). Nevertheless, the English barons got particularly uppity one night in 1215 and forced King John at swordpoint to sign a document called the Magna Carta—basically a promise to say "May I?" a lot.

So the whole structure of European feudalism, and then aristocracy, flowed directly from the simple stirrup. And the eventual toppling of that social structure began three-and-a-half centuries after the Battle of Hastings when another dominant technology, the Welsh longbow, was employed by a small army commanded by the English king Henry V to virtually eradicate the French aristocracy at the Battle of Agincourt, returning William's favor by conquering France. But that's another story.

Unless you are a jockey or fox hunter or mounted police officer (or Prince Charles), you still may not see any particular connection between the Battle of Hastings and anything that's important in your life. If you are deeply concerned with linguistics or English literature, the Norman Conquest may be notable because its infusion of French speakers to England transformed the old English language to something close to its modern form. But actually, there may be no reason why you "should" know anything about the Battle of Hastings. On the other hand, the next time you see a stirrup or even just someone stepping onto a horse, you may have a hard time *not* remembering Hastings.

The point of all this is: Knowing what data are worth thinking about, like the effectiveness of thinking and learning themselves, depends on the *context.* If the context is scoring points on an academic exam, the braindead "facts" about Hastings that Hirsch and his ilk peddle may be worth memorizing for about two weeks, and then forgetting once the test is over—exactly what most students wisely learn from that kind of artificial context. If you're interested in warfare, horseback riding, language, or especially the impact of technology on culture, the Battle of Hastings acquires a more potent and durable meaning in any of those contexts, and a somewhat different meaning in each.

Still, it might seem that at least within the framework of a given academic subject, say physics, there certainly would be a canon of crucial facts or knowledge that must be mastered. But I can tell you from personal experience that "knowing physics" in the context of a standardized test involves a very different mass of knowledge and skill from what's required in the context of doing research in a laboratory, designing an electric generator, fixing the busted whoozits on your VCR, or playing racquetball.

It has taken our nation's school establishment about two decades to figure out the obvious: It doesn't make sense to spend weeks of class time forcing students to memorize multiplication tables or interpolate logarithms in a world where electronic calculators come built into rulers, pens, watches, and key rings. Schooling is simply too inert to adapt to an imminent HL world where an unlimited supply of "facts" is available instantly, anytime, anywhere—and where, within a generation or so, you will be able to carry around an entire lifetime's supply of information in an object that will fit in the palm of your hand.

In the context of a knowledge age society where humongous volumes of data can be generated, stored, and communicated with lightning speed to just about anyone, anywhere, anytime, know-how clearly has become more important than know-what. But what that requires in practice is learning how to combine knowledge with skills to achieve your goals in a real-life context.

When you consider the almost stifling cornucopia of sources and media of knowledge that confronts us, the several kinds of intelligence or skill all humans have in varying measure, the richness of human aspirations, and the immense diversity of real-life situations people care about, it's clear that nurturing the hunger for know-how is no mean task. In fact, it's a task that cannot possibly be mastered in childhood—it must be a lifelong occupation.

MYTH 9: LEARNING IS SOLITAIRE

In America at least, schools are designed on the model of the learner as a strictly independent operator, and learning as an entirely private action. Academia's way of accounting focuses on tests of individual performance in strict, austere isolation from cooperation with others or use of resources or tools outside the learner's head. The role of collaboration or technology in learning is placed in the category of cheating.

This mythical and misguided vision is, fortunately, being eroded by a mass of social and cognitive science findings that there are limits to what can be learned alone, and that the most effective and useful learning is a shared enterprise. Over eighty studies by brothers David Johnson and Roger Johnson of the University of Minnesota show that students not only master subject matter better in cooperative settings than they do working in isolation, but they develop better social skills and self-esteem.[165]

Contrary to the popular vision of the isolated "hacker," HL technology only reinforces the imperative for cooperative learning. As noted earlier, with information mushrooming beyond the capacity of any one human mind, expertise being absorbed into networks, and productivity in most economic arenas increasingly dependent on teamwork, the necessity or even possibility of isolated learning is rapidly diminishing in the mindcraft economy.

The technologies of individualized instruction and cooperative learning are not contradictory or mutually exclusive. Intelligent tutors and other automated teaching systems are about as cost-effective as the cooperative practice called "peer tutoring"—peers teaching one another.[166] The practices are complementary and tend to occur naturally in HL environments like video game arcades and high-tech workplaces where, as mentioned before, apprenticing seems to be almost self-generated. Many successful applications of automated instruction group students in clusters of two, three, or four sharing a tool such as a computer. Computers and other smart tools joined in networks, especially when enhanced by groupware, inherently draw the individual user through gateways to collaboration.

Whether the inherent sociology of academic institutions will allow would-be educational innovators to succeed in displacing the traditional divide-and-conquer ethos of schooling with cooperative learning in practice is another matter entirely.

Engineering students at MIT were recently caught in this whipsaw. The students were urged to work on a term project in teams—the idea, appropriately, was to cultivate the teamwork skills increasingly required in a Total Quality Management industry environment. But the same students then were sanctioned for cheating when the project reports turned in by each of the members of the same team were, unsurprisingly, virtual verbatim clones of each other.[167]

MYTH 10: SCHOOLING IS GOOD FOR SOCIALIZATION

While many of the audiences and friends with whom I've discussed these myths of schooling over the last several years are willing to recognize the many paradoxes if not hypocrisies of what passes for academic teaching, they often still cling tenaciously to the faith that school as an institution is needed for what they've been told is "socialization." People generally are far more willing to discuss reforming schools than to seriously ponder the reality that school is an obsolete institution whose time has come and gone, and that is ready for extinction and replacement.

One of the greatest errors in education is to assume that the larger social context of the school is irrelevant or even secondary to learning. . . . The social structure of the school is not simply the context of learning; it is part of what is learned. What a student learns in the classroom is indeed a very small other part. . . . What the Burnouts learn in school is how to be marginalized. . . . High school, therefore, is not simply a bad experience for these students—it teaches them lessons that threaten to limit them for the rest of their lives.

—Penelope Eckert

Jocks & Burnouts (New York: Teachers College Press, 1989)

This nostalgia for schooling as cultural ritual, as a rite of passage, as a way of life, is as understandable as it is costly. Many of us justly have rich memories of school as a positive force for our development, maturity, and fulfillment—shared experiences with lifelong friends, the exhilaration and hoopla of athletic triumphs, dating rituals and first-time benchmarks in sexual coming of age, and even the occasional special teacher or coach who befriended us and piloted us past the reefs of adolescence toward a voyage of achievement.

But what we commonly overlook or misremember is what *Star Wars* guru Obiwan Kenobi called "the dark side of The Force." Every yin has its yang. If we look honestly at what scientific study reveals about the dark side of schooling's "socialization," we should conclude that the benefits can be obtained in other ways that are far less costly.

One of the keenest yet often unappreciated insights of modern thinking was Marshall McLuhan's maxim that "the medium is the message." No mere slogan, McLuhan's observation expresses the key finding of cognitive science: Learning is empowered by its context. One grave flaw of schooling, noted already, is that, by design, it disconnects learning from the real-life contexts that give learning meaning and value.

But it's a mistake to assume that school simply deprives learning of *any* context. Rather schooling replaces the contexts of real life with the context of school life. Learners do not simply stop learning in an artificial context—they proceed to learn artificial lessons taught *by* the context in which they find themselves. To clarify McLuhan's warning, the message and the medium are always learned together; they can't be separated. In practice, school creates a context that often makes learning not just sterile but hazardous.

For instance, whatever it has done for test scores, academic education following the European "liberal arts" tradition also has served to reinforce feudal class structures and ethnic/national division in Europe and the Orient. In America, the same academic conceit has bred what the late Herman Kahn labeled a "New Class" of credentialed experts infected with "educated incapacity." The cultural bias of "liberal" academia against manual labor, commerce, and even capitalism has contributed to Europe's festering unemployment and to America's flagging industrial competitiveness.

And if academia has been a mixed blessing to human development in Europe and America, in the Third World the disdain for work and productivity bred into the European-style schools inherited from colonial masters has been an economic and social catastrophe. In countries such as Zimbabwe and Sri Lanka, the overdose of academic education has bred a socially disruptive class of overeducated unemployed. Charting the same phenomenon in Indonesia, Nathan Keyfitz concluded: "To sell education to the public as a means to upward mobility ultimately risks disillusionment."[168]

One of the major hazards is social polarization. Penelope Eckert, an anthropologist at the Institute for Research on Learning, has found in her studies that a major social impact produced by the normal schooling context, culminating in high school, is to divide youth into lifelong cultures of winners and losers. "While curricular tracking has come and gone in the American public schools, adolescent social categories remain as an enduring and uncontrolled social tracking system," Eckert observes. "It is largely as a result of the polarization between the Jocks and the Burnouts

Then the island blew up. . . . A numbing cycle of violent reprisals, carried out mainly by educated, unemployed and well-armed youths, began to escalate. . . . "With liberalization, you gave these Sinhalese and Tamil students the impression that they could gain not only an education, but could achieve upward mobility. This turned out not to be true," said . . . a Harvard-trained attorney and Tamil activist. . . . The economy changed during the 1980s but the school system didn't. Sri Lanka's highly regarded British-style schools were designed to churn out qualified civil servants. . . . Classrooms emphasized literacy and the liberal arts, not science or vocational training, meaning that few graduates were prepared for the kinds of jobs available in a dynamic economy. . . . Said [the assistant director of] Sri Lanka's leading private think tank: "The problem is people coming out of the universities, saying, 'I'm ready,' and the country says, 'For what?'"

—"Sri Lanka's 'Model' Economy in Ruins," *The Washington Post* (Oct. 10, 1989)

that people are thrown into a choice between two set patterns of behavior on the basis of a variety of unrelated interests and needs. . . ."[169]

Moreover, this pernicious form of socialization is the result not of school quality or administration or location but of the inherent structure of the institution itself. In particular, Eckert finds that "the segregation of adolescents in an age-graded institution, isolated from the surrounding community, focuses their attention on the population, the activities and the roles that are available within the school," instead of those of what we commonly call *the real world*.

Eckert saw that the effect was particularly destructive to the losers or "Burnouts," who both value and need communal ties to a social network for their human and economic development. Schools not only ignore but actively oppose the Burnouts' ties to poor, lower class, or minority communities that academia treats as inferior to the culture of school itself.

An academic culture that makes college and even graduate credentials the ultimate measure of social value and success creates far more losers than winners. In the American education system, the most democratically open and progressive in the world, 75 to 85 percent of students will not enter the Valhalla of what academia considers "educated" persons. Without a breakthrough of consciousness, the academic underclass will bear the undeserved burden of wounded self-esteem and social and economic inferiority for the duration of their lives.

The polarization inherent in schooling increasingly is harmful to the Jocks as well as the Burnouts. Even most of the winners will wind up feeling like losers when they fail to be anointed or treated like the "best and brightest" of their class. School handicaps the Jocks with a delusion of superiority that has little tangible basis in the real world. There never has been any significant association of academic success with success in working and living in the real world outside the ivory tower. As a number of education critics have accurately observed, school is vocational education for the job of college professor. The recent disillusion of the MADMUPs and the rejected "overqualified" reflects the growing disutility of academic success to the real economic opportunities offered by a mindcraft economy.

The persistence of the polarizing effect of scholastic socialization is almost stunning. When I attended my twenty-fifth high school reunion a few years ago, I was struck by the ironic contrast between the actual life achievements of the members of my class and the attitudes of social status that were reenacted at the gathering. When we were students, academic and vocational "tracking" was still a common practice. But the U.S. economy is truly more concerned with effort, ambition, enterprise, and a big dose of luck than about such scholastic distinctions. So among the participants at our reunion I found "voc ed" students who had risen to high executive positions in major corporations as well as former academic "stars" who, at the age of forty-something, were back in graduate school, still struggling to "find themselves." Nevertheless, you could still see and hear the vice president of one of the country's biggest communications companies, a successful husband, father, and pillar of his prosperous suburban community, acting deferential to his penurious, Ivy League, bohemian intellectual classmate, who had yet to partner, parent, pillar, or produce much. There they were still playing the game of Jock and Burnout, "college-bound" and "work-bound," smart and dumb, winner and loser a quarter century after what should have been the final gun.

Polarization is just one of numerous subversive messages buried in the medium of school culture. Some of them are recalled by an incident from my experience as a young physics teacher in the same high school I had graduated from five years earlier.

One of my unorthodox practices was to have my students present each of their homework problems on the blackboard in front of the class. My motive was partly laziness—correcting homework is no fun. But my whole approach to teaching (based on zero time in ed school but twenty years as a student) was to give my students maximum responsibility for teaching themselves, and minimum dependence on me for anything but encouragement, pacing, and refereeing. The whole point of this and everything else I did was to overcome that lethal fear of failure that now as then has young Americans dropping out of math and science in droves. Doing homework on the board was practice in teamwork, helping each other, being active learners, and most important recognizing that mistakes are not failures but just stepping-stones toward the truth.

Anyway, one of my students was a black girl—a precious resource not often found in physics classes then or now—who had a particularly hard time with this exercise. Whenever it was her turn to do a homework problem for the class, her immediate reaction was to protest, "I can't Mr. Perelman, I'm not good at math." And I would have to goad her, step by step, to pick up her textbook, come to the front of the room, open the book, and, finally, start by reading the problem to the class. All the while her broken record is clicking, "I can't, I'm not good at math."

Okay, write the first step of the solution on the board. (By now you can guess her response.)

Now I'm playing cheerleader and coach: Don't worry. Just write something. It doesn't matter whether it's right or wrong. There's no grade on this. You can do it. Just write anything at all.

So she writes some math stuff on the board and, the class all agrees, it's right. That's fine, I say. Now let's see the next step.

"Ican'tI'mnotgoodatmath" became a kind of mantra, like "Amen" in church except a denial instead of an affirmation of faith. And so it would go, step by step, each punctuated by her inverted prayer for failure, always unanswered because *she always got everything exactly right.*

That, sadly, is not the end of the story. After a few months, she suddenly dropped the course. She was an excellent student, not just in the win-lose accounting of grades (I had an even more unorthodox policy on that) but absolutely: She was mastering physics, as nearly all of my students were—I believed then as now that everyone is supposed to get an A, and if they didn't that meant I wasn't doing my job well enough.

I guess I didn't do it well enough for her. I was shocked and perplexed. Twenty-plus years later, I'm still furious about what I learned from that experience. Why would someone run from success toward failure? It punctured a number of our—my—schooling myths, especially the ones about smart being better than dumb, winner better than loser.

With time, reflection, and insights from my students, I think I figured it out, at least partly. That girl learned, through the *context* of seventeen years of life and schooling, that blacks, females, and therefore especially black females are not, cannot, and must not be "good at math." There were much higher stakes in her vulnerable adolescent heart than just another grade on a transcript. Unwittingly and with the best intentions, I had thrown her into what was virtually a life-and-death struggle.

Adolescence is more than anything a quest for identity: What am I going to be when I grow up? is really *Who* am I going to be when I grow up? This talented girl had been told all her life by teachers, friends, family, and maybe the whole country who and what she was, and whatever that might be, it had to include "not good at math." And there I was, eager beaver young Harvard brain-jock, proving beyond a shadow of a doubt to her, her friends, her family, and the whole world that that was a *lie.*

It didn't take me too long to figure out what a heavy message that was: Her friends, her parents were finding out that she was not the person they thought she was. She was at real risk of having some costly social stigmas stuck on her: uppity, acting white, nerd, unfeminine. Would they still love her? Would they even accept her? If not, what other community would embrace her? Eventually I suppose she decided the price of that academic success was too high, too scary. It probably would have helped open economic as well as intellectual opportunities for her, but quite possibly at the cost of great loneliness.

I wasn't wrong to try to help my students fulfill their abilities. I can't say she was wrong to react the way she did. We were caught in cultural rituals imposed by a larger system, like two enslaved gladiators who were forced to combat in an ancient Roman circus that cared nothing about what either of them wanted, needed, or felt.

There's nothing unique about her story. It's happened millions of times before and since, and is still going on today. I've been through similar rituals with friends' daughters in recent years who are still being brainwashed by schools and parents not only to doubt but to suppress their talents.

These experiences are echoes of a growing body of research showing that girls in all-female schools maintain high levels of self-esteem and accomplishment in all fields including math and science, while the confidence and performance of girls in coed schools take a steep and steady nosedive after about grade seven or eight. Detailed analyses of video records of classroom behavior show that teachers or professors, both male and female, persistently call on, praise, and encourage males several times more frequently than they do females. The teachers rarely realize they are being biased; they are reflexively acting out rituals deeply embedded in the culture of schooling.[170]

The medium of schooling delivers similarly subversive lessons to various minorities in America. Some minority cultures, some blacks and some Hispanics, seem more vulnerable to these assaults than others—notably Asians, particularly from societies with Confucian traditions.

Just because some groups and individuals have endured and overcome these insults does not mean that the insults should be tolerated, and the victims blamed. It also does not mean that the victimization should be perpetuated by telling the victims of school-manufactured failure that they have accomplished what they have not, that they know what they do not, and that they have been released from the responsibility for learning—which is foremost a responsibility to themselves.

In reality, the people who "flunk" academic tests or "drop out" of school do not stop learning—they just learn other, generally undocumented and uncredited, but often sophisticated, things. Prisons provide exemplary models of spectacular learning where novice lawbreakers learn the art and culture of crime.

These are just a few facets of the dark side of the force that school passes off as socialization. "[B]y the time students reach high school," Eckert observes, "the Jocks and the Burnouts are all too generally perceived as representing good and bad, cooperation and rebelliousness, success and failure, intelligence and stupidity." For the losers, the lessons of socialization become articles of surrender—Eckert finds that "[r]ather than asking themselves how they can succeed in spite of the school, Burnouts discard goals along with the means to achieve them."[171]

The myth of the decline of schooling is that our students are failing to learn. The real outrage of schooling is that our students are learning to fail.

A corollary to the myth of school as a constructive medium of socialization is the myth that "technology"—computers and other modern multimedia—is a negative influence on socialization. For instance, there is a craving (popular even among some educational researchers) to believe that Nintendo and other video games promote antisocial, even violent behavior.

While game and computer markets are now so huge and fast-changing that they defy the capacity of social science to track accurately, virtually all the available evidence indicates that the effects of these tools on social behavior range from harmless to highly positive. While some observers worried about the violent content and male gender bias of an earlier generation of games, no tangible harm was scientifically demonstrated. Today's popular games—such as *SimCity,* the *Carmen Sandiego* series, geometric puzzles like *Tetris,* graphically stunning computerized versions of various card and board games, and even *Super Mario Brothers*—are far more intellectually diverse and challenging, and more likely to appeal to female as well as male interests.

As I noted earlier, simulation games generally cultivate both individual and team skills that are far more relevant to the mindcraft workplace than the behaviors demanded by traditional classrooms. Rather than isolation, games and computers inherently tend to encourage self-organizing communities of practice, as observed by psychologist Robert Kubey of Rutgers University. Memphis psychiatrist Joseph Cassius believes games can boost children's self-esteem by encouraging "a sense of proficiency without fear of conflict." As for game playing being a waste of time, studies by Gary Creasey of Illinois State University found that children's involvement with video games increased at the expense of time taken from only one other activity, watching television.[172]

Modern communications technology further is expanding opportunities for students to develop and practice social skills in realistic contexts, getting timely feedback and intrinsic rewards—shown by research noted earlier to be essential characteristics for productive learning. Steven Pinney, a seventh-grade writing teacher in California, developed Kids 2 Kids, a learning program carried on both state and national electronic mail networks. Rooted in the notion that students best develop skills that are useful to them, Kids 2 Kids pairs students with distant writing partners for several writing projects, each of which requires both an anthology and a newsletter written and produced by students. Al Rogers, executive director of the FrEd Mail Foundation, suggests that e-mail may be the most practical context for learning writing skills since, he believes, "electronic text may be the last frontier for written discourse in the age of information."

Similarly, John Wollstein, a former foreign language specialist for the Hawaii Department of Education, wondered, "How motivated are students to know that ten years from now they're going to use their French in a French restaurant?" Realizing that using foreign language skills in a realistic context immediately would be far more motivating, Wollstein started a program that now has equipped every one of the 250 schools in the state with a "Luma Phone"—a speaker phone that also can send and receive still video pictures of the speakers. After using this "Teleclass" setup to converse with kids in Japan, students in high school teacher June Kuwubara's Japanese classes show the gains Wollstein aimed for: "A high school student's greatest fear in class is to make a mistake in front of his peers," she says. "But I've noticed that students who do the Teleclass exchanges no longer have this fear."[173]

While these examples of socialization by way of telelearning come out of current classroom experiences, there's nothing about these technological opportunities that requires the mediation or even existence of a school. Rather, they represent intermediate steps toward the dissolution of school-as-box altogether. The point is that learning through such HL media is not merely compatible with the goal of socialization—rather, institutions that deny or obstruct access to such media create a context for socializing that is downright contrary to the mores and competencies of a knowledge age society.

Still, many parents and others will ask, as a friend of mine did: How can HL technology replace the function of schools to teach children the basics of living values: work, ethics, morality, wisdom, character, strength, courage, civics, sacrifice, self-control, self-reliance, love, life, and so forth?

The answer is that the young will learn such virtues and behaviors the same way they always have: from observing and adapting to the normal behaviors of their parents and the other adults who make up the society they grow into. The question itself is rooted in the myth that schools are engines of culture. What social science knows is that schools are no more than expressions of culture. When communities of families are free to choose or control the schools that serve their children, the school staff are likely to demonstrate and encourage behaviors that are consistent with the community standards.[174] Schools *reflecting* cultural norms are a far cry from schools *producing* values and virtues.

The impotence of schools as culture factories is glaringly demonstrated by the experience of the defunct Soviet empire. A public education system backed by a cloak of censorship and the sinister threats of the secret police, gulags, and "psychiatric" institutions of a ruthlessly totalitarian regime worked for half to three quarters of a century to manufacture a population imbued with a dogmatically definite set of socialist virtues, including atheism, internationalism, socialist realism, and disdain for material acquisitiveness. The effort failed utterly: Within days or even hours of the release from state repression, churches were filled, national banners were unfurled, "modern" artists burst from the woodwork, and the unvarnished greed of the Communist *nomenklatura* was exposed to public display.

What schooling cannot depose it cannot impose either. Cultures, values, ethics, and mores are created and renewed by communities of people, not by schools. Socialization is a function of societies, not of classrooms.

BEYOND MYTHOLOGY

Considering the incorrect assumptions we bring to teaching and learning and the new realities science has uncovered about the mismatch between traditional school instruction and the requirements for effective learning, it's no wonder that the learning environment still found most frequently in today's classrooms—where teachers largely dictate abstracted knowledge to students only passively involved in the learning process—has produced results that are disappointing to policymakers, parents, students, teachers, employers, and society at large.

The reality behind the myths is that "school"—as a technology, as an institution, as a process—simply does not work as a way to organize learning for living in the real world. Schooling and learning are at odds—more of one means less of the other.

Science reveals that schooling is disconnected from the needs of working and living—and HL technology is rapidly widening that disconnection to an unbridgeable chasm. That disconnection of school from real life is a matter of inherently inappropriate system design, not of curriculum or training or equipment.

More schooling—longer days, more days, more years—cannot be a solution to the conflict between school teaching and real learning, and promises only to make all the problems of that conflict worse. Similarly, reforms pursuing academic "excellence"—trying to impose the myths of effective schooling with even greater rigor—are doomed to be counterproductive exercises in "suboptimization," a term economist Kenneth Boulding once defined as "trying to do well what should not be done at all."

The good news is that science shows the way—and HL technology now provides the means—to empower every learner to learn whatever is needed to realize that person's real-life goals, and to do so with passion and confidence instead of drudgery and fear. But the ecology of the new hyperlearning enterprise that is needed—and is already emerging—to replace the outworn infrastructure of schooling will bear little resemblance to what most people conventionally think of as "education."

In the new, posteducation learning enterprise, learning is not only *for* the real world, it is *of* the real world. Not sequestered in the box of a classroom, learning takes place as close as possible to the real-life contexts in which people want learning to be useful. The hyperlearning enterprise is a wide-open community of practice, where learning is by doing, the roles of apprentice and expert are continually shifting with the demands of the problem at hand, learning is self-paced and custom styled by the individual learner, and passionate—sometimes "spectacular"—learning is motivated by the natural drive of the human brain freed of the fear of failure.

Even as a highly cooperative community of practice, the new hyperlearning enterprise does not exclude the reality and importance of competition. As in most sports, cooperation and teamwork are means to competitiveness. HL provides opportunities for both group and individual competition. Competitive activities give learners the chance to identify strengths and weaknesses, and, more specifically, to spot errors and improve performance.

But competition in the new learning enterprise is not in the contrived academic framework of tests and grades. Instead, learning to meet the demands of real-life competition and performance takes place in real-life contexts. For instance, one of Eckert's key recommendations is that so-called extracurricular activities such as sports should be anchored in real, nonacademic community organizations rather than bound to the pseudo-community of the school campus. Students will be better prepared for the rough-and-tumble of business competition by participating in an organization like Junior Achievement—which engages young students in actually planning, creating, and operating a real business—or developing their basic and "higher order" skills through telecourses while working in a real workplace, than they will by competing for grades on a paper-and-pencil economics test in a classroom.

The gathering momentum of hyperlearning technology, guided by the revealed truth of the science of learning, spells the inevitable extinction of schooling and the turgid bureaucracy of education. But *how* this transformation is achieved will make a great difference in its ultimate cost and value to current generations of students, families, employers, and taxpayers.

Technology is power and power means politics. The education establishment is fighting to preserve the status quo. Most education "reformers" are working to reinforce academia, not to retire it. The new learning enterprise demands a new politics of learning.[175]

CHAPTER 8

MBFC: BEYOND THE "EDUCATIONAL GOALS" FIASCO

• • •

Productivity is more than just efficiency—it also accounts for the relevance and value of the output to the consumer. Again, being efficient in doing the wrong thing or what should not be done at all is not being productive. While the exorbitant cost of education needs to be drastically cut, spending only half as much on a schooling process that is irrelevant and even damaging to human development would still be a bad bargain.

The other half of the productivity equation is achieving effective results or benefits. At least since 1986, when the National Governors' Association proclaimed in a wide-ranging task force report that it was "Time for Results," there has been growing talk about the need to focus on the outcomes of educational investments. Unfortunately, there has been more talk than substance to this effort; and what substance there is mostly is misguided.

Most of the recent talk about the results of education has focused on a set of national education goals contrived in the wake of an education "summit" meeting of President Bush and the nation's governors in the fall of 1989. Former Education Secretary William Bennett dismissed the product of that conference, with more accuracy than tact, as "pap and a lot of stuff that rhymes with pap." But the summit deserves credit for its one substantial accomplishment: For the first time in memory, the nation's chief governmental executives acknowledged that the vast treasure poured into education ought be expected to yield some demonstrable benefit.

Unfortunately, the six education goals the governors and president proceeded to define over the following half year, and to trumpet since then—and which have been echoed and endorsed by other politicians of both major parties as well as many business and other civic leaders—were ill advised and misconceived. The goals define objectives to be achieved by the year 2000 that are either unnecessary, undesirable, or unattainable:

1. All children in America will start school ready to learn.

Healthy humans are born ready to learn—humans are genetically programmed learning machines.[176] But many American children are exposed to toxic assaults in the womb by their mothers' lack of proper medical attention, poor nutrition, venereal diseases such as herpes or AIDS, or exposure to dangerous drugs ranging from alcohol to tobacco smoke to cocaine or narcotics. After birth, an even larger number of poor and disadvantaged children are plunged into environments that range from unnurturing to hazardous, and that undermine not only the children's native learning potential but often their very prospects for survival.

That these threats to children should be remedied is indisputable. Starting school ready to learn is the most trivial and backward statement of the needed mission—it reinforces the perverse but common notion that children exist to serve schools, rather than the other way around, as well as the nonsensical assumption that learning does not begin until age five or six.

This would-be goal is a thinly veiled pitch for one of the most sacred cows sanctified by the current crop of education reformers: to "fully fund" the federal Head Start preschool program. Overlooked is the inconvenient fact that the benefits of Head Start have been widely overestimated: The "Head Start Evaluation, Synthesis and Utilization Project," contracted by the federal Department of Health and Human Services in 1985, concluded that any educational and social benefits realized by children participating in Head Start vanish within two years, beyond which "no educationally meaningful differences" were found between children who participated in Head Start and children who did not.[177] The narrowly focused design of Head Start is far less responsive to the full range of unmet development needs of the country's genuinely "at risk" children than approaches that engage the entire family and serve the literacy, employment, and other needs of parents as well as children. A good example is the less-noticed federal Even Start program, which is funded at about one hundredth the level of Head Start.

"Full funding" of any program is a lethal stratagem that surrenders from the outset any effort or prospect for providing more, better, and faster services at lower cost. Applied to Head Start, it serves only to divert resources from Even Start and other activities that promise greater effectiveness. It also overlooks technological opportunities to provide benefits to more people at significantly less cost. For instance, the TV program *Sesame Street*, which now reaches over eleven million U.S. households and is seen in more than eighty countries, has been enriching the early development of children for over twenty years at a cost of about one cent an hour per viewer.

The statement of this goal is like saying that all adults should enter the workforce ready for retirement. Without an explicit commitment to seeking lower cost and more effective services that address all the needs of all the humans that make up whole families, this goal stands as a benign but hollow wish.

2. The high school graduation rate will increase to at least 90 percent.

This goal, for what it's worth, has already been achieved—U.S. Department of Education data show that by 1986, 91 percent of the class of 1980 had obtained a high school diploma. The goal attempts to attack a "dropout" problem that is widely misunderstood and that may not even exist. America's high school completion rate actually has increased steadily through this century, and is greater today than it has ever been. The proportion of the seventeen-year-old population completing high school grew from 10 percent in 1910 to the roughly 75 percent level it has been at since 1965. When General Equivalency Diplomas are counted, the rate is 83 percent.[178]

There are numerous things wrong with setting goals for graduation or dropout rates. One is that dropout data are so poor that no one really knows what the dropout rate in America is—many students counted as "dropouts" have moved to another public or private school or continued their education in community college or other settings; some have died; the large number who drop back in after a pause are rarely subtracted from the dropout number.

The key defect with this goal, as it is for most of the others, is that it confuses means with ends. Learning is what people need to do, not only in youth but through a lifetime. Staying in school is not necessary for learning, and many schools provide many people with negative incentives for learning. Not attending school, on the other hand, presents no inherent barrier to learning and personal advancement for those who are motivated.

3. American students will leave grades four, eight, and twelve having demonstrated competence in challenging subject matter including English, mathematics, science, history, and geography; and every school in America will ensure that all students learn to use their minds well, so they may be prepared for responsible citizenship, further learning, and productive employment in our modern economy.

This goal is comprehensively misdirected, counterproductive, and unattainable. Its sheer complexity makes the proverbial motherhood, apple pie, and the flag sound like trivial pursuits. While it has many times less chance of being achieved than universal compliance with the Ten Commandments, much precious time and treasure could be squandered on its pursuit.

The first of the many things wrong with this goal is that it has unleashed a passionate political drive for an orgy of national standardized testing on the wrong subjects at the wrong time using archaic and erroneous measurement technology. Cognitive researchers know that student learning requires feedback and reinforcement properly scheduled over periods from days to every few minutes or even seconds—modern instructional technology provides that. Automated instructional delivery systems produce a continual stream of data so that student performance can, if necessary, be monitored day by day or even minute by minute. Standardized tests every four years do nothing to help students and are designed only to provide fodder for political witch hunts.

The expressed first objective of the advocates of national testing is to expose school failure. But the success or failure of schools again confuses means and ends—it's the success or failure of individual persons to learn that should be the concern of education policy. Because modern instructional technology makes failure to learn any subject virtually unnecessary for any modestly healthy person, the obsessive quest to demonstrate failure only ensures the continued production of failure—tests that do not show most people are failing will be condemned as guilty of "Lake Wobegon" bias (where all the children are "above average"). Blame and shame remain the name of the game.

The other objective of the national testing advocates is to install a standardized national curriculum. There is a legitimate argument that all Americans should be assured the opportunity to acquire the essential cognitive tools to be able to participate in the modern economy. The Commission on the Skills of the American Workforce (CSAW) made the eminently practical recommendation that a certificate of initial mastery be established as a standard of minimal competency, and that its attainment be a prerequisite for teenage employment. The (Labor) Secretary's Commission on Achieving Necessary Skills (SCANS) made important strides in 1991 in defining more specifically what the essential employability skills are and how they should be measured. The clear and proper aim of these efforts is to define real competencies required by real employers for real workplaces in real businesses—they deserve aggressive support.

But this third of the official "National Education Goals" is aimed at serving the interests of academic bureaucracy, not economic democracy. The result of this goal can be and already has been only to further politicize a public education system that already suffers from a lethal overdose of politics.

Failure to understand these political dynamics leads to continual misunderstanding of public sentiment and effective policy. For instance, a recent Gallup poll found that 81 percent of those Americans surveyed supported national achievement standards and 77 percent were in favor of standardized national achievement tests.[179] Goal number three would seem to have enthusiastic political backing. But there is a world of difference between endorsing the *idea* of national standards and tests in theory and providing the votes needed to implement *specific* standards and tests in practice. It is the proven impossibility of forming an effective national political consensus on particular educational objectives and "fair" testing mechanisms that makes such opinions politically hollow.

In practice the entire "Goals" effort, especially number three, is intended to be run by politicians, who have appointed themselves to various committees charged with deciding for the rest of the population what is "demonstrated competency" and "challenging subject matter," as well as the meaning of "use their minds well," "responsible citizenship," "further learning," and "productive employment." This presumes an ability to form a national consensus on all these topics when a consensus on any one of them has virtually never been achieved within any of America's 15,400 local school districts.

4. U.S. students will be first in the world in science and mathematics achievement.

Take your pick: This goal is (A) meaningless; (B) unnecessary; (C) unachievable; or (D) all of the above. The correct answer is (D).

The goal is meaningless at least because the existing instruments used to compare student competency in science and mathematics are so poorly designed that we do not currently have any reliable basis to know how U.S. students stand in comparison with those of other countries. The kinds of tests used are more likely to reflect drill and memorization than real competency in these subjects, and they are given to student populations in different countries that are as comparable as apples and oranges.

Moreover, the tests target youth, usually thirteen years old. Given that American kids spend less time in grade school than those in most other countries and do not have to worry about the feudalistic entrance exams other nations use to filter out their elite at an early age—which motivates a frenzy of test cramming in countries like Japan—it should be unsurprising that American youth came out with somewhat lower scores on these tests.[180]

Considering that the valid public policy worry behind this goal focuses on the competency of the U.S. workforce, the capabilities of young adults would be a more relevant subject for evaluation. Few examinations are made of the knowledge of adult populations, but one that did compare the science knowledge of U.S. and Japanese adults found that the two populations came out about equal in scientific knowledge and the Americans actually scored higher on some questions about technology.[181]

The goal is unnecessary if its aim is to strengthen U.S. international competitiveness in science and technology. There is no evidence that the U.S. lacks sufficient science and engineering talent to meet its economic and other competitive objectives. A frequently cited National Science Foundation study from the late 1980s that claimed to project a shortage of scientists and engineers was recently exposed as fatally flawed, and perhaps willfully deceptive. Not only did the forecast shortage never materialize, analysts told a congressional subcommittee, but the early 1992 unemployment rates in some fields were above the overall national unemployment rate. Starting salaries for PhDs in many fields, the subcommittee was told, typically range from $18,000 to $25,000.[182] And the full flood of the "brain glut" from the collapse of the Soviet Union and from military cutbacks is yet to come.

The fact that the majority of PhD students in many technical fields in U.S. universities are foreigners only bears witness to the competitive advantage of being a nation of immigrants. The size and quality of the U.S. science enterprise still leads the world by a substantial margin. The problems in U.S. science stem mainly from budget priorities distorted by the burden of defense and by costly pork barrel projects such as the space station and the superconducting supercollider (SSC). The U.S. has lost its dominant position in several key technologies to Japan, but that is mainly the result of the managerial ineptitude of American companies in translating scientific advances into competitive commercial products, not a shortage of technical talent.

While the country as a whole can meet its scientific and engineering workforce needs through immigration, it's also true that large numbers of females and minorities are being discouraged from pursuing the more lucrative career opportunities found in technical fields. But those people are being filtered out intentionally by the *culture* of science and engineering even more than by shortcomings in K–12 teacher qualifications or curricular designs.

Up to 60 percent of college students who *choose* science, math, or engineering majors—and presumably were qualified to be admitted to those programs—drop out, according to National Science Foundation data. While faculty are prone to blame the inadequacies of the students who switch out of these technical disciplines, an important recent study by University of Colorado sociologists Nancy Hewitt and Elaine Seymour shows that the main difference between the switchers and the survivors is not talent but the ability to tolerate and cope with an abusive environment.

America's native talent pool is being drained away from science, math, and engineering not only by instructional ineptitude but by critical demographic and culture gaps. Some 85 percent of America's current scientists and engineers are white males—the majority of the new generation of students and workers are not and will not be. The resulting conflicts of

[Hewitt and Seymour] found that "the switchers and nonswitchers [among college science and engineering majors] are essentially not two different kinds of people. . . ."

What all share are problems with the science faculty at their schools. . . . The chief complaints were poor teaching and unapproachability on the part of faculty members. . . . The switchers didn't find any way to cope with these difficulties; the persistent nonswitchers did. Yet even among those who stuck it out, a telling 40% reported being "turned off" to science by the experiences they had as undergraduates.

A quarter of the nonswitchers . . . had come to believe . . . that other majors were intrinsically more interesting than science and engineering. And a slightly smaller but significant percentage cited an aversion to the lifestyle associated with careers in science and engineering. . . .

As to complaints about lack of faculty support, the Colorado sociologists posit that many science departments intentionally scrimp on the kind of course and career advising that helps students survive because of a "weed-out" mentality that assumes attrition is a good thing, because it leaves them the best and most dedicated students. That outlook, the authors note, is mistaken.

—"They'd Rather Switch Than Fight," *Science* (Oct. 18, 1991)

social values and work styles are compounded by the tendency of the traditional social Darwinist culture of scientific professions—which views failure as a necessary means to "improve the breed"—to turn away talented youth in droves. As one faculty member Hewitt and Seymour interviewed put it, "We're not just weeding people out, we're ripping out half the garden."[183]

The defoliation of technical talent continues well after even successful students graduate and go to work. By 1991 only 66 percent of the students from the high school class of 1980 who had completed degrees in natural science and engineering were full-time employees. And only about one half of that 66 percent were in traditional, readily recognizable natural science and engineering jobs.[184]

Finally, for what it's worth, the achievement of this national education goal by the year 2000 is utterly impossible, no matter what education policies the U.S. embraces. It is now evident that the country that is destined to be number one in the world in its endowment of science and math talent is . . . Israel. This is the direct result not of U.S. education policy but of American foreign policy, which has willfully diverted the flood of Soviet (and now ex-Soviet) Jewish emigrants—the great majority of whom would prefer to come to the United States—to Israel.

"This huge pool of migrants is one of the most talent-rich ever to pour into Israel, or any other country, at one time, top heavy with scientists, engineers and doctors drawn from the professional elite of Soviet society," *The Washington Post* reports. Of the quarter million Soviet Jews who have immigrated to Israel since late 1989, the overall proportion of scientists, engineers, and doctors is five to seven times that of the general population of Israel or of other developed Western countries such as the U.S. And, because the Israeli economy is too small to absorb the flood of scientific talent in industry or government work, the surplus mathematicians, physicists, and biologists are being retrained at universities to become teachers in community colleges, high schools, and teachers colleges.[185]

Similarly, the federal government has kept the U.S. immigration door mostly closed to the gush of smart, diligent Hong Kong Chinese seeking refuge from the Communist takeover scheduled for 1997—Canada, with a tenth the population of the U.S., has been taking in twice as many Hong Kong immigrants.[186] Given the disproportionately high level of science and mathematics achievement of such Asian, especially immigrant, students, this policy provides backup assurance against American achievement of academic leadership in these fields. What little the Education Department giveth, the State Department taketh more away.

5. Every adult American will be literate and will possess the knowledge and skill necessary to compete in a global economy and exercise the rights and responsibilities of citizenship.

Some 99 percent of U.S. adults already are classified "literate" on international surveys. English literacy and "functional" literacy are other matters, not mentioned in this goal. Universal English literacy is a desirable but somewhat controversial objective which the "goals" coalition has not explicitly addressed, although English is one of the core subjects (for youth) for which the National Education Goals Panel is supposed to establish some kind of "world" standard.

It is the "functional" literacy of the U.S. workforce that has prompted outcries of concern. From 20 to 40 percent of American adults are claimed to have deficiencies in the traditional basic skills of reading, writing, and calculating that make them uncompetitive or unemployable workers. Unfortunately, the data on which these claims rest are extremely poor.

A 1986 survey of the literacy skills of U.S. young adults by the National Assessment of Educational Progress indicated that 93 to 97 percent of twenty-one- to twenty-five-year-old high school graduates had at least basically useful skills; dropouts tended to score worse.[187] Since cognitive science knows that most people are more skilled in the context of real work than in taking these kinds of tests, it's likely that skills in practice are probably better than what these data indicate. Whether the level of skills of the workforce as a whole are inadequate, and how, are far from clear. Contrary to popular impressions conveyed by media reports, most U.S. employers complain little about shortcomings of their employees' functional skills or academic achievements—rather, managers' main gripes are about workers' attitudes, work habits, and social behaviors.[188]

The Education Department has been working for several years to carry out a thorough national survey of adult literacy, but the results have not yet been produced. While there is certainly some number of adults, including a substantial number of recent immigrants, who need to improve their basic skills, the real scope and nature of the adult literacy problem is largely and unfortunately unknown.

One thing that is certain is that no committee of politicians and politically anointed "experts" could possibly define what knowledge and skill is "necessary to compete in a global economy," much less what are the "rights and responsibilities of citizenship." If academic standards are *necessary* to effective economic competition, how to explain the phenomenal business success of a host of dropouts from Wendy's founder R. David Thomas to auto maker Soichiro Honda? Do the rights and responsibilities of female citizens include abortion rights and combat duties? Will a national education committee truly resolve these and a host of other contentious questions about the nature of citizenship?

As in goal number three, these high-sounding phrases are trapdoors that lead straight to an endless quagmire of political quibbling. The Goals Panel has as much prospect of defining and implementing the conditions of economic competition and "politically correct" citizenship as the Soviet Politburo had in nearly three-quarters of a century of trying to do the same thing.

6. Every school in America will be free of drugs and violence and will offer a disciplined environment conducive to learning.

While this seems like a benign and eminently desirable goal, its focus may be misplaced—the grim problem of violence afflicting America's youth, especially minorities, is not centered mainly in schools.

The gravity of the crisis certainly should not be underestimated. A recent study by the Centers for Disease Control reported that firearms have been carried by one of every five U.S. high school students, including almost one of three male students. Shockingly, the survey found that nearly 40 percent of black male students reported carrying some kind of weapon—more than half of those were firearms.[189]

But the danger of mayhem facing many—far too many—of America's kids should not be confused as a problem mainly centered in schools. The Center to Prevent Handgun Violence estimates that 135,000 students may have carried weapons on to school property—a number that is intolerably large, but still small compared to the more than 45 million students in schools.[190] The several dozen incidents of shootings on school grounds reported in the last year, while deeply troubling, still need to be viewed as rare in relation to the huge population of schools and students. Nor is this problem one whose solution is likely to be found in schools. As George Butterfield, deputy director of the National School Safety Center in Westlake Village, California, told a reporter, "A whole community has to be mobilized to deal with the problem—it's not just a school problem."[191]

While a study by the University of Michigan for the National Education Goals Panel claimed around a fifth of high school students reported being victims of some kind of violence, a recent survey by the U.S. Justice Department indicated that only about 2 percent of students age twelve to nineteen claimed to be victims of violent attacks. And the Justice Department study found that most of these violent crimes were simple assaults, without weapons, probably resulting in only minor injuries.[192] As for drugs, studies of twelfth graders show that use declined substantially from 1980 to 1990, with alcohol use going down by 21 percent and illicit drug use declining by 54 percent, including marijuana use down by 59 percent and cocaine use down by 60 percent.[193] A more recent survey showed these trends generally continuing, although there was a slight increase in daily marijuana use, and a more notable increase in alcohol "binges" and LSD use.[194]

Violence and drugs are a real and intolerable threat to too many of America's young. But this doesn't mean schools are the major site of violent attacks or drug abuse. A study a couple of years ago of the New York City public schools found that the large majority of schools in that city already were mostly free of drug use and violence—the streets surrounding them may not be, but most school buildings themselves were fairly safe.

Dangerous schools obviously should be cleaned up. But that is almost entirely a matter of local initiative. Any local community that currently tolerates the existence of such a corrupted school is unlikely to become motivated to fix it as a result of a "goal" proclaimed from the White House lawn.

The reality is that in the ghettoes where violence is epidemic, the school most often is the one safe haven children have from the bedlam that surrounds them. Protecting that haven is important. But if education goal number six is a pitch to see that laws are enforced more rigorously in school than elsewhere, it begs the question of why it should be more tolerable for children to be exposed to mayhem during the 91 percent of their time they spend outside than the 9 percent they spend inside schools. Saving children from assault and murder is not an education goal—it's a fundamental social obligation that needs to be far more vigorously enforced.

A further weakness in the sixth goal is that there is little or no consensus about what a "disciplined" school environment looks like. Also, there is considerable theory and research evidence that some kinds of "disciplined environments" are hostile to learning—or, more accurately, they are unconducive to learning that builds self-esteem, self-reliance, or social responsibility. On the other hand, science reveals that many of the environments most conducive to learning appear "undisciplined" or even chaotic to some people.

THE MBFC SOLUTION

Altogether the National Education Goals don't make much sense. Worse, their unfortunate effect has been to divert attention and energy from more worthy objectives.

The fundamental error in the well-meaning but inept "national education goals" effort is not in the misconceived goals that have been proposed but in the exercise of goal-setting itself. W. Edwards Deming, the dean of modern quality management, urges his clients to avoid setting these kinds of "target" goals because at best they will become *limits to performance*. Simply put, goals that are intended to be floors wind up becoming ceilings. The essential credos of "Deming's Way" are continuous improvement (what the Japanese called *kaizen*), and Total Quality Management—constantly seeking to eliminate errors, faults, and failures in every aspect of a production process.

Deming's advice is reinforced by the outcome of an exhaustive, more than year-long study of Best Practices undertaken by General Electric in a quest to discover the secrets of competitive success of the leading companies in a wide range of businesses. The "earthshaking" conclusion of this study, as *Fortune* magazine reported, was that GE had been measuring and therefore managing the wrong things: "The company was setting goals and keeping score; instead, says business development manager George Zippel, 'we should have focused more on *how* things got done than on *what* got done.'"[195]

In fact, the experience of education reform in the 1980s bears out Deming's warning. The establishment and enforcement of minimum standards for high school graduation seems to have had the effect of encouraging better performance from those at the bottom of the academic curve. In particular, the one accomplishment of 1980s school reform was a narrowing of the gap in some of the standardized test scores of black and white students. But overall system performance did not improve, and productivity declined as costs continued to grow.

The kinds of education "goals" that would be compatible with Deming's Way and the discipline of quality management are directions rather than destinations. In a sense, instead of "targets" the learning enterprise needs "arrows" that point in the direction of ever-increasing productivity. The goals needed to direct a steady march toward a more productive learning enterprise are simple and do not require national tests or centralized political commissariats to be pursued effectively. The right learning goals can be summed up in four words:

MORE
BETTER
FASTER
CHEAPER

This is what the urgently needed commitment to ever more productive learning comes down to: Not only America but the whole world, and each of us, needs to learn more about anything and everything; needs to learn all of it better, in terms of quality, relevance, and value; needs to learn it faster, with less waste of precious time; and needs products, services, and methods for learning whose cost is continuously declining. The power to pursue those kinds of goals successfully can be found only in the creative engine of the competitive marketplace.

CHAPTER 9

MICROCHOICE: BEYOND THE "SCHOOL CHOICE" DIVERSION

• • •

The lethargic swamp of school reform got churned into white water in the spring of 1990 by the publication of a book called *Politics, Markets & America's Schools*. Because the Washington-based think tank that published the book, the Brookings Institution, was popularly viewed as a bastion of liberalism, the book shook up press and politicians with its unorthodox message: U.S. public education suffers from an overdose of democratic meddling, and needs the tonic of capitalist competition, even privatization. In particular, authors John Chubb, a Brookings fellow, and Terry Moe, a political scientist at Stanford University, argued from their wide-ranging analysis of research on "effective schools" that families should be allowed to use public education funds to enroll their children at any *public or private* school they choose. Chubb and Moe's most famous, or notorious, finding was that school choice is not just a needed treatment of, but a "panacea" for, the malignancy of the public education system.

The Brookings book became a virtual New Testament to the ongoing campaign for school choice that had been embraced by the Bush administration as the centerpiece of its America 2000 strategy, as well as by a number of business-led state and national initiatives. The book has become so influential that it was cited by the majority in the four-to-three decision of the Wisconsin state supreme court upholding the constitutionality of the law permitting poor black children in Milwaukee to use state education funds to enroll in private schools.

But Chubb and Moe's analysis, while useful in provoking serious consideration of market alternatives to education's socialist establishment, still fell short. The underlying technological and economic illiteracy of the school choice strategy has destined it to fail.

Chubb and Moe and other restructuring advocates in business, government, and education who rightly see "choice" as a key to educational *perestroika* for the most part do not realize that technology is essential to the success of such a policy. On the other hand, many business and other leaders who are eager to see education embrace leading-edge technology often have been unwilling to recognize that, in the absence of wide-open choice and competition, the school-of-the-future, the classroom-of-tomorrow, or the "New Generation of American Schools" will continue to be the meretricious hoaxes they always have been.

For the learning enterprise to be the increasingly productive industry the knowledge age economy requires, the agendas of technology and choice need to be melded into a single platform for change. So far, no national or state policy initiative—including the America 2000 strategy—has done this.

"CHOICE" IS ESSENTIAL

"Choice" as a synonym for free markets—where consumers are free to choose and vendors are free to create and sell a variety of products and services—is undeniably essential to cure education's morbid productivity and festering irrelevance. Replacing the government-owned and -commanded economy of schooling with competitive markets for learning is a prerequisite to truly productive change.

However, the need not merely for "choice" but for *commercialization* of education has been overlooked by most would-be reformers.[196] We need commercial choice and competition in education first to goad technical innovation—the profit motive is essential to reward the creation and provision of productive technologies. Reviewing the long march of prolific innovation that has flourished in Western society since the beginning of the Industrial Revolution, economists Nathan Rosenberg and L. E. Birdzell, Jr., conclude: "The success of Western economies in assimilating Western technology *is not a consequence of unregulated markets alone* but of markets in which there are productive firms that can gain much by commercializing new ideas more quickly than their rivals can."[197]

Profit-motivated competition also is necessary to provide quality control. Only markets can create the information needed to determine "what works" economically. The competitive market is the only solution to the "one best system" fallacy that has yielded, among other disasters, the dumbing down of the school textbook to perfect idiocy—the result of a book oligopoly selling products by political lobbying of a handful of state bureaucrats instead of directly to millions of consumers in a truly competitive market.

U.S. public schools and colleges are technologically stuck in the Middle Ages for the same reason Soviet collective farms were: a complete lack of accountability to the consumer and total insulation from competitive, market forces. Central, bureaucratic, "command" management provides no incentive—and a thicket of discouragements—for productivity, and hence for innovation. Russian groceries were not barren because Soviet farmers were ignorant of the potential of hybrid seed, fertilizers, and so forth to increase food production. It just didn't pay any better for the collective farmer to grow corn than just to grow old.

American teachers and schools are trapped in the same political quagmire. An entrepreneurial friend of mine who developed a marvelous interactive video system for building the basic skills of subliterate adults went broke trying to market it in public education's command economy. When he tried to sell the program to the adult education division of a major urban public school district, he presented the results of government-sponsored trials to show that the system would virtually pay for itself by increasing productivity at least 30 percent—students could get through the curriculum with better achievement about a third faster. "You don't understand," the division director explained, "the district pays us for attendance, not achievement. There's no reward for getting students through here faster; if anything, my ADA [Average Daily Attendance] might go down and my budget could get cut."

Similarly, when I did a study a couple of years ago for one of the country's most affluent school districts to find out why the vast majority of teachers had shown no interest in participating in a multimillion-dollar program aimed at expanding computer-based instruction, one teacher I interviewed could have spoken for thousands when she said, "Why should

I do anything different next year from what I did last year? Who cares?" Changing to new ways of teaching takes time, effort, risk, and money. The bureaucracy was offering nothing even to cover these costs to her, much less any reward for success.

Only when educators have to earn their income in the marketplace by competing to serve consumers who are free to choose where to take their business (and money) will schools, teachers, and other vendors have the incentive to adopt productive technologies. And only when government-owned and -regulated schools are replaced by autonomous, profit-making enterprises will educators have the opportunity to use their own resources to acquire and offer the technologies they judge to work best.

SCHOOL CHOICE: THE INADEQUATE PANACEA

"School choice" is the wrong kind of choice needed to reverse educational waste and obsolescence. While choice and competition are prerequisites to the market systems needed to replace unproductive education systems, school choice does not provide real consumer choice and does not lead to genuine competitive markets for learning.

Elasticity is the key. This somewhat arcane economist's term identifies the foremost in a list of reasons why school choice has not and cannot lead to true restructuring and improved productivity in education.

School choice seems reasonable—in fact, to *deny* families the right to choose what schools their children will attend is eminently unreasonable, as Education Secretary Lamar Alexander often points out. But rights and reason are not the same as competition and efficiency. Those who expect school choice to unleash "market forces" that lead to better, more efficient education face inevitable disappointment.

Efficiency in markets depends directly on the "elasticity" of supply and demand—that is, the ease with which supply stretches and shrinks to match changing demands, and vice versa. "Inelastic" supply or demand tends to get stubbornly stuck, and inefficiently out of sync with the other.

School choice has not and will not lead to more productive education because the obsolete technology called "school" is inherently *inelastic*—it cannot significantly respond to changes in the size or direction of demand. As long as "school" refers to the traditional structure of buildings and

In East Harlem in New York, Susan Winston, a teacher-director of a new alternative middle school on 113th Street, has 80 minority students in writing and publishing school. . . . Her students are "societally abused children. . . ."

She said they are eager to come to school, and engaged in their work as they might not have been with a bigger, impersonal, assembly-line type of middle school.

Testimony like Winston's gives encouragement to those favoring parental choice because it introduces pride, accountability and innovation. [Richard] Kruse [executive director of the National Association of Secondary School Principals] concedes that East Harlem's plan works, but adds that it does not answer a key question: Alternative schools can't take all students. He worries about those left. Indeed, Winston's school has a limit of 90 students this year, but she says the school works better when there are only 80.

"I get calls every day," she said. "Now we've got a reputation in the community, and the community is wonderfully happy about finally having some quality schools up here on 110th Street. It's very hard to turn people down. But our problem is that you can't get too big. Then you're unable to do what you want to do."

—"Critics Say Bush Proposal Would Politicize Learning," *Chicago Tribune* (Sept. 16, 1991)

grounds with services delivered in boxes called classrooms to which customers must be transported by car or bus, "school choice" will be unable to meaningfully alter the quality or efficiency of education.

So-called "good schools," whether public or private, have not and will not expand or relocate to satisfy all the demand for their services. And "bad schools," especially public but often even private ones, are difficult to shrink or shut down, much less move, when demand falls or disappears. This genetic inelasticity of schools-as-buildings lies at the heart of many of the objections to and problems with school choice.

The root of this crippling inelasticity is not in the human brain or in the technology of learning—it is in the outworn technology of schooling. The acute lack of knowledge of HL technology on the part of the architects and advocates of school choice is the source of the strategy's undoing.

If choice in television worked the way "school choice" is conceived, switching channels from HBO to CNN would require putting your TV set in the back of the minivan, driving back to the store to exchange it for a new model, and then moving to a new house. In reality, video choice requires nothing more complicated or costly than pushing a button. Obviously, modern information technology is far more flexible, more adaptable, more universally accessible, and overall more *elastic* in its ability to respond to consumer demands than technology bound by real estate, geography, and transportation.

In fact, instructional and knowledge resources provided by today's and tomorrow's multimedia technology can give every individual learner even more choices of "schools" than of cable TV channels, as long as "school" stops referring to buildings and classrooms. The salient fact overlooked by the whole misguided school choice movement is that we have the technology to enable virtually anyone to learn anything, anywhere, anytime, any way that yields "grade A" results for that individual.

The choice that really matters is not a family's annual choice among a few school buildings but the individual learner's minute-to-minute choice among a wide array of specific media, programs, services, products, and sources of knowledge available to nurture the learner's brain—whether the individual makes that choice alone or in cooperation with other members of a team. That's the "point of sale" that the true market for learning rotates around. And school choice does almost nothing to alter the efficiency of that transaction compared to the status quo.

What Difference Does It Make?

Chubb and Moe and their sympathizers make much of the association of "effective" schools with some kind of "choice." But the body of relevant research shows that the difference between so-called "effective" schools and merely average schools or even poor schools is relatively minor. The choice of schools just doesn't make very much difference.

In fact, the differences in average academic performance among most schools are small compared to the wide variation in performance of indi-

vidual students. Chubb and Moe's own data show that the gains in standardized academic test scores are equivalent to 3.11 years for high schools
in the top quartile and 0.83 years for high schools in the bottom quartile—this means that after three years in high school, the student population in the best-scoring schools gained a little over three years' worth of
improvement while the student body in the worst-scoring schools showed
somewhat less than one year's worth of improvement. But the gain in
scores of individual students on the same standardized tests ranged from
5.46 years for the highest quartile to −1.40 for the lowest quartile of
students. So, in the figures used by Chubb and Moe, the range in individual test performance was three times wider than the range in test scores
among schools.[198]

In the middle of their book, Chubb and Moe note that, in looking for
what accounts for variations in student academic achievement, "student
ability is the most influential independent variable, followed by family SES
[socioeconomic status] and school organization . . . and school SES. . . ."
Much of the rest of the book goes on to demonstrate "not only that a well-
organized school can make a meaningful difference for student achievement, regardless of the ability and background of its students, but that
the influence of the school, through its organization, is comparable in size
to the influence of each student's own family." And they conclude, "All
things being equal, then, it appears that students can really gain a great
deal from attending an effectively organized school."

If this all sounds a bit academic, its political and economic impacts
certainly are not. To summarize the rest of Chubb and Moe's argument:
After factoring out the influence of "tracking" students into non-academic
vocational programs—which necessarily hurt school-wide academic test
scores—they find that the really important thing about school organization is "autonomy" from bureaucratic control. In short, effective schools
are autonomous; except for public schools in a few snooty suburbs, autonomous schools are private; so families have to be free to send their kids
to privatized public schools as well as traditionally private schools if most
schools are to be effective. And, by the way, attending an effective school
is worth a third to a half of a year gain in test scores—this is the measure
of the "panacea" a couple dozen states, a growing number of local communities, many business leaders, and the White House are pushing at no
small cost.

STUDENT BODY HOUSEHOLDS AND SCHOOL PERFORMANCE (CHUBB AND MOE)

Characteristic	Low performance schools	High performance schools
Two parents in home	74.4	83.1
Mother working while student in high school	67.5	69.1
Number of home learning tools, above average	**34.6**	**76.4**
Father closely monitors school work	64.7	71.7
Mother closely monitors school work	84.9	84.8
Student expected to attend college		
By father	65.3	76.4
By mother	67.8	79.4

SOURCE: *Politics, Markets & America's Schools,* Table 4-5 (emphasis added)

Ironically, buried in the statistical forest of Chubb and Moe's dense analysis is the key to far greater and more valuable gains in student learning. Yet it has been almost totally overlooked by Chubb and Moe, their fans, and even their critics.

Not only did Chubb and Moe recognize that family status was at least as potent in influencing student achievement as school organization, they listed the contribution of specific household characteristics to the achievement differences of "low performance" and "high performance" schools. What leaps out of this list is a factor they called "number of home learning tools, above average"—it clearly shows a far greater difference between high and low performance schools than any other family factor. It is also a much greater difference than seen in most of the organizational factors Chubb and Moe used to compare ineffective and effective schools.[199]

What are these "home learning tools"? The High School and Beyond (HSB) survey that provided the data Chubb and Moe used in their analysis asked about the availability at home of such things as "a typewriter, a calculator, a set of encyclopedias, and more than fifty books" among others. That's the sort of technology behind the impressive difference in low and high performance school scores that even prompted Chubb and Moe to comment, "Clearly, the homes of the best schools are better equipped for learning."

But wait a minute: The HSB survey data go back to 1980–81. In 1981 there were only 750,000 personal computers in U.S. homes—today some thirty million American homes have PCs! And available computing power has multiplied over two hundred times since then. If the kludgy "learning tools" of over a decade ago could make such a notable difference in school performance then, the mind boggles to imagine the difference made by the high-powered home technology of today, much less tomorrow.

But neither the Brookings crew nor any of the major analysts and advocates of school choice policies have given more than the slightest thought to the importance of technology in learning and markets. When I asked John Chubb why he had passed over the glaring message in his own data, he explained that he and Moe had dismissed the significance of "home learning tools" because it was highly correlated (about 0.8) with family SES.[200] He and Terry Moe, among others, thereby missed the point—actually several points—rather grievously.

One is that learning tools are not just a coincidence of family status—they are tools that help produce more learning. If you are looking for "what works" to get people to learn more, better, faster, and cheaper, that's a point to hold on to, not to gloss over. That the kids of well-off families have more access to effective learning tools than the kids of less-well-off families do is at least as notable as the issue of access to supposedly "effective" schools. Actually the point of this whole book is that tools are far more important than schools.

There is, in fact, an important issue in the equity of distribution of learning tools between rich and poor families. U.S. Education Department data indicate that over 53 percent of high school students use computers at home in households with annual incomes of $75,000 or more, while only 6.5 percent of students do in homes with incomes between $10,000 and $15,000.[201]

A key part of the solution to that problem is falling prices—the consumer's best friend. To buy technology equivalent to the IBM PC and printer I paid over $6,000 for in 1982 would cost less than $500 today. And instead of hogging a whole desk, the tools could fit in a briefcase or backpack, and would work a lot better to boot. The computer system I'm writing this book on cost half what the system I had a decade ago did and not only has hundreds of times more raw power, but qualitative capabilities for desktop publishing, multimedia, and so forth that simply could not be had at all when the HSB survey was being conducted.

The technological advance spawned by intense commercial competition has made TV sets so cheap that virtually every household in America, including nearly all the poor homes, has at least one. It took an average of four days of work to pay for a TV set in 1950; by 1986 it cost only four hours of work to pay for a technically far superior TV set.[202] Similarly, over 93 percent of U.S. households have telephones. And videocassette recorders have gotten so inexpensive that nearly a third of all homes with incomes below $10,000 have them. Computers and other ever-more-powerful information tools are now as affordable as TVs and telephones and VCRs.

So whatever the association may be between socioeconomic status and access to learning tools, and increasingly to hyperlearning tools, rapidly declining costs mean that the reasons for inequality are steadily becoming less economic, and hence more social—and political. The causes and cures of the threat of technological apartheid are explored throughout this book. But it should be evident here that school choice has almost no bearing on them.

The simple data above actually understate the far greater importance of access to tools compared with choices of schools. The best advanced instructional technology today offers more rapid and cost-effective gains in the kinds of standardized test scores Chubb and Moe claim as the benefits of school choice. But, as discussed at length elsewhere in this book, such test measures range from meaningless to downright harmful.

None of this is to deny the legitimacy of the demands of community leaders such as legislator Polly Williams in Milwaukee to free black and other minority children from being pawns in desegregation games, and to give poor and minority families the same freedom to send their children to neighborhood or private schools that the better-off enjoy. But what serves the cause of equity may not—and in the case of school choice will not—serve the needs of economy.

The Unwanted Panacea

Demand for better schools, as opposed to demand for more productive learning, is the wrong focus for another reason: There isn't much of any.

"School choice" is a solution in search of a problem that mostly does not exist.

The same recent Gallup poll noted earlier found that 62 percent of the public supports parental choice. These and similar survey results allow the school choice advocates to argue that the public agrees with their aim.

But while the public as a whole thinks that school choice is a reasonable idea, there is very little demand among families with children for schools that are notably different from or better than what they are now provided. One reason is that the existing system already offers school choice—through the choice of residential location or through the private school option. Department of Education survey data show that half of families with children in school chose their residences based on the local schools available to them. Another 10 percent or so of families choose private schools. So at least 60 percent of families already have chosen their schools.

Not surprisingly then, a number of surveys, including a Roper poll sponsored by the U.S. Chamber of Commerce, find that while a large majority of the public thinks American education generally is falling short, from two-thirds to three-quarters of respondents say that their own kids' schools and teachers are just fine. With six out of ten families having already chosen the schools they want, it is hardly startling that another 5 to 10 percent are content with the school that the public education system happened to provide.

Moreover, an extensive survey by School Match, a private consulting service based in Westerville, Ohio, found that the large majority of parents do not want "excellence" in their children's schools but only a high standard of mediocrity—over 70 percent say they seek schools whose student test scores are only average to above average. In short, "parents are more interested in their child being successful than in finding the schools with the highest marks."[203] A more blunt but accurate way of saying the same thing is that parents are more concerned about their children being *labeled* "successful" than about the kids actually learning anything.

While righteous reformers condemn the bad attitudes of American parents, most fathers and mothers are only acting upon the main lesson they acquired from their own years of compulsory education: that schooling is a game whose principal objectives include not learning but enduring threats, preserving normality, forming social alliances, and scoring points. In Eckert's terminology, parents know that it's better for their kids to be "Jocks" in a mediocre school than "Burnouts" in an excellent one.

In Minnesota, a much-touted triumph of the school choice movement, new legislation in 1988 freed parents to enroll their children in any public school in the state, with only minimal limitations. But in the 1990–91 school year, only 0.8 percent of families used the option to choose different schools. And the great majority of these choices were made for geographic convenience, not in search of academic "excellence."

A Market Without Capital Means Choice Without Choices

Even when school choice is legislated, it fails to unleash any significant new demand and therefore little real competition. One key reason is that nearly all existing schools are pretty much the same, and satisfy most parents' expectations and desires for mediocrity.

This leads to another fallacy of the school choice strategy: that the resulting "free" market by itself will goad the creation of radically new, more effective and productive educational services. Based on this erroneous belief, none of the existing school choice initiatives provides an effective built-in mechanism for financing the wide-ranging innovations the programs promise. But without an explicit means for financing innovation, the most ideal program of laissez-faire "choice" will be insufficient to achieve the large-scale, systemic advances in performance and productivity America needs in its learning enterprise.

The situation of Poland is a useful analogy. Poland has abolished the Communist apparat, made its currency convertible, and largely deregulated and opened its markets for competition and consumer choice. These policies have not made Poland competitive with Japan or even Hong Kong. What Poland urgently needs, and can't get enough of, is financing for vast investment in rebuilding its outworn and hopelessly archaic economic infrastructure.

That reconstruction hinges on two particular capital investment needs. One need is for physical capital—to replace technologically obsolete and inefficient plant and equipment.

But an even more urgent need, often overlooked or underestimated, is for massive commitment to retooling the ex-socialist economy's human capital. Hopes for creating efficient, competitive economies in Poland, other ex-Communist countries of Central Europe, and the newly liberated republics of the erstwhile Soviet Union depend on rapidly reeducating several generations of workers, managers, and consumers to perform effectively in a market environment.

The predicament of academia in America and in the world as a whole is essentially the same as Poland's. The drive for "school choice" as it has recently been undertaken is doomed to fail from lack of provision for the large quantity of investment capital needed to finance the radical improvements it hopes to achieve. Deregulation or privatization of the socialist economy of public education is essential—but, by themselves, such policies will not create or attract the necessary "venture capital" for new, productive service systems any more than building a dam will make the rain fall. "Cloud seeding" is needed.

Private Schools Are Not Private Enterprise

Much of the controversy over school choice initiatives has centered on the issue of private schools. A key part of Chubb and Moe's thesis is the argument that private schools need to be included in the range of choices available to families for real competition and market efficiencies to be achieved. Under their proposal, and a number of plans following the same approach, families would receive vouchers equal in value to the amount of per-student government funding of public schools; the vouchers could be used to pay tuition at any qualified school, public or private.

Chubb and Moe's case for including the private school option rests less on their analysis showing that independent schools are most effective than on their aim of offering an escape from the burden of public bureaucracies that "tend to rob schools of critical authority, divert schools from their core academic mission, discourage bold leadership from principals, make a mockery of teacher professionalism, drive a wedge between schools and parents (who become just another political interest), and provide accountability for following rules—not for producing results."[204]

In short, Chubb and Moe see the benefits of school choice as depending on the autonomy of schools, whether public or private. If public schools are not thoroughly deregulated, they want to be sure that at least private independent schools are available to meet family demands. Also, existing and potentially new private schools can only enhance competition by adding to the number of geographically convenient choices. Of course, if public schools were given the large degree of independence of existing private schools, it would be harder for critics to justify the exclusion of private schools from competing for public tuition dollars, except perhaps in the case of parochial schools.

Most of the criticisms hurled at the proposal for public funding of private school choice are bogus or hollow: That such "privatizing" would "destroy" public education—assuming that is necessarily a bad thing. That including parochial schools would violate the constitutional barrier between church and state—a presumed prohibition that has long been violated in higher education, and that can be remedied by a variety of tactical arrangements. That handicapped students will be excluded by private schools—a valid problem today that could be remedied by simple antidiscrimination rules and/or supplemental vouchers for "special" education. And when logic fails, the education establishment is always prepared to unfurl the most nonsensical red shirt: that taxpayers will wind up funding Ku Klux Klan schools—an unlikely result that easily can be prevented by the same kind of antidiscrimination rules that now apply to federal higher education funding.

Nevertheless, the case for the private school option in school choice fails for two reasons. One simply is that the addition of nonprofit private schools does nothing to alter the long list of inelasticity problems of school choice reviewed above.

A second, related reason is that not-for-profit private schools do not and will not offer the benefits of competition or innovation that Chubb and Moe and other school choice advocates assume. Private K–12 schools, the great majority of which are nonprofit (and in fact parochial), in reality are not very competitive. Those whose enrollment is not shrinking (and it is for many Catholic schools), and particularly the nonparochial institutions, rarely seek to expand their facilities or services to meet available demand—they prefer to maintain a waiting list for admission. Being neither profit-maximizing nor growth-maximizing, their management is mainly focused on maintenance of a satisfactory status quo. To the extent that they compete at all, it is marginally with the public school system, not with each other.

While competing with the public schools might seem just what the school choice advocates want, the "marginal" way private schools compete minimizes the potential benefits of the private choice option. Because they are more inelastic even than the public schools, private schools would not substantially expand their services to meet any greatly increased demand

Beginning last September, Milwaukee allowed a small number of low-income students to transfer to private schools, paying the private schools $2,446 for each student, money that came out of the public school budget. . . .

This fall, 341 students switched to private schools, to the delight of their parents, who believed the public schools were failing their children. . . .

Indeed, most parents and students said they were satisfied, said John F. Witte, a professor of political science at the University of Wisconsin who is studying the program. . . .

But the saga of the school that abruptly shut down in the middle of the year also shows the risks of an educational free market. The Juanita Virgil School was plagued by money troubles and personal feuds, Mr. Witte said. It accepted a large number of children from the public schools, primarily for the $2,446 that came with them. . . .

"There were problems with every aspect of the school, from picking the kids up to feeding the kids to finding books for the kids," he said. One day, the students in the choice program arrived in school and were told not to come back.

"Some kids had nowhere to go," Mr. Witte said. "They literally were not being educated. I don't believe this is similar to closing a business."

Most of the 63 students in the choice program had to return to public schools . . . and it is not clear what happened to the other students enrolled in the school.

—"The Rules of the Marketplace Are Applied to the Classroom," *The New York Times* (June 12, 1991)

that might result from a public voucher program. Rather, the private schools at best would accept only as many new students as needed—or might indulge in cream-skimming, taking the most desirable students—only to the limit of their enrollment quotas.

This expectation is supported by a study of health care institutions—which already operate in the kind of open market Chubb and Moe advocate—that compared the way for-profit and nonprofit organizations used waiting lists to ration access. The study looked at nursing homes, psychiatric facilities, and facilities for the mentally handicapped. It found that the use of waiting lists, and the length of the lists, were greater among church-owned than other nonprofits, and were greater among nonprofits in general than among for-profit organizations.[205]

As noted earlier, there is not much evidence of a very large unsatisfied demand for schools different from those which serve families now. This might not be true in a locality where the public school system is notoriously dilapidated. In those cases, many families already have opted for private, often Catholic or other parochial schools. The nagging constitutional issue aside, a private voucher policy in those places might provide welcome financial relief to families and institutions burdened by tuition costs. But that would not by itself create much new choice or competition. To its credit, what limited benefits the private choice option offers would likely accrue mostly to the advantage of the most truly disadvantaged.

Systemwide, the addition of private school choice fails to break the gridlock of inelasticity. If there is little new demand for changes in enrollment (as in Minnesota for instance), no significant competitive "force" is created—the problem of inelastic demand. But even if demand is increased, not-for-profit private schools have no incentive, and little evident inclination, to expand their services to meet surplus demand. Church-affiliated schools might well feel a religious mission to expand their services—but no legal voucher program could fund the expansion of the religious function of their services, and therefore a real voucher program would undercut the religious motivation.

School choice proponents evidently believe that the supposedly "free market" for schools would provoke the creation of substantial numbers of new, innovative schools so dramatically superior that they would stimulate a broad demand for their "excellent" services that is not now much evident. But nonprofit schools have no incentive for investing in innovation, and the fact is that existing private schools are no more technologically innovative than public schools are—which is to say, almost not at all.

Furthermore, the lack of provision for capitalization remains an unsurmounted barrier to creation of a large enough population of innovative new schools to make a competitive difference. Brand-new nonprofit private schools would have to be capitalized by vast donations from charitable

Richmond's troubles, and $24 million deficit, are widely blamed on former superintendent Walter Marks's ambitious programs, including the "system for choice" program of magnet schools in the working-class city of 87,000 residents on San Francisco Bay.

The system was designed to integrate the 47-school district, about 70 percent minority, by giving some schools specialties in, for example, classical instruction or math, thereby attracting students from the district's affluent hill towns. . . .

School officials now acknowledge they overspent and counted on grants that never came. Then cutbacks in state education allotments brought the district to the brink of financial ruin.

Much of the blame goes to Marks's programs, administrators said. "He built that reputation and generated that kind of national publicity for the district by spending money that didn't exist," said a spokeswoman for state Superintendent of Public Instruction Bill Honig. . . . Last November, Marks was bought out by the school board for $93,300, and by April, the schools had to seek protection under Chapter 9 of the federal bankruptcy law.

—"Judge Orders California to Keep Troubled School District Open," *The Washington Post* (Apr. 30, 1991)

sources—mostly by competing with the claims of other philanthropic causes, particularly colleges and universities which now receive the great majority of donations to education. Private choice advocates have yet to explain how such a drastic alteration in philanthropic priorities is to be achieved.

The "charter schools" legislation enacted in Minnesota in 1991 may help further undermine the public school monopoly, but leaves all these problems of private school choice unsolved. In essence, this new law allows groups of licensed teachers to establish independent schools that would operate under contract to a public school board. The charter schools would receive the same revenues per student from local, state, and federal sources as public schools. But they would be free of most regulatory controls, except that they may not discriminate among applicants, and must observe normal health and safety requirements.

The charter school idea, developed by education policy consultant Ted Kolderie and touted by Minnesota's Republican U.S. Senator Dave Durenberger, aims to improve the state's school choice plan by ending the "exclusive franchise" to create and operate public schools. The logic is that school choice won't work unless there are lots of new and exciting schools to choose from, and the existing bureaucracy stands in the way of such innovation.

But the Minnesota law establishing charter schools as currently written limits the total number of charters to eight, and no more than two per school district—hardly a prodigious competitive challenge to the hundreds of public schools in the state. Moreover, the law requires that the charter schools be operated by nonprofit organizations or cooperatives. By prohibiting for-profit operations and offering no government capital funds, the new law does no more than the old law to provide for capitalization of new educational ventures. The few teachers who may be bold enough to want to create such schools will have to do so with no start-up funding, no money to construct or acquire buildings to house the schools, and no ability to raise funds in capital markets. The only way to house the schools will be to lease space or have it donated.

And the schools would still be building-bound: "They must accept all applicants they have room for," Senator Durenberger boasts—overlooking the salient fact that they are therefore still free to turn away prospective customers the building won't hold. The fatal inelasticity of schools with and without choice remains unsolved. Charter schools are as useful as plastering over termite holes—the blemish may be removed but the underlying rot continues.

The charter school stratagem is doomed by ruling out the incentive and resources for growth that profits provide. But even if charter schools were allowed to be organized for profit, they probably would not make much impact.

There are a few dozen for-profit K–12 schools in America today. But their technology and form of operations are virtually indistinguishable from those of existing private or public schools. Because these institutions are compelled inequitably to compete with taxpayer-subsidized nonprofit and public schools, they are unable to accumulate sufficient profits or investment capital to develop dramatic innovations or to greatly expand their services. Instead they are limited to a few localized niches.

The kind of "privatization" needed to extricate learning from the wasteful quagmire of obsolete schooling must go well beyond merely permitting choices among public or even private schools. Privatization requires *eliminating* government ownership, operation, and subsidy of education and training institutions—freeing the $400 billion plus of annual education-related spending to become a true market for private, profit-seeking enterprise.

Stoking Political Conflict

The inelasticity of building-based schools also lies at the heart of most of the political barriers to school choice. Besides its economic inadequacies, the school choice strategy is politically self-limiting, inflaming a host of passionate objections that, in practice, obstruct the necessary legislation or cripple its effective implementation. These include serious concerns about government support for religious institutions; racial segregation; and the disparity of "choices" available in rural and urban or poor and rich communities.

School choice that includes private schools stirs up fervent arguments about public funding of religious schools. Choice advocates have several reasons for wanting to include church-related schools. Most private schools in the U.S. have church affiliations—the Catholic schools being the largest group—so it would be hard to offer private schools as an option in many places without including them. Moreover, the student populations of church-affiliated schools are economically and socially more like those of mainstream public schools than of elite private prep schools—reducing fears that public vouchers for private schools would result in exclusion of minority or disadvantaged students. An added allure is that James Coleman's and other research indicates that students in religious schools, particularly Catholic schools, do better academically than those in nonsectarian private schools, as well as public schools.

But most of the public is disturbed at the prospect of religious institutions receiving government funds. Allocation of government funds to church-affiliated colleges and universities has gone on since the 1950s, and has been found constitutionally acceptable. But where young children and schools are concerned the issue is more inflammatory and remains unsettled. On the other hand, even though many church-related schools are hurting for money, religious educators often are as anxious to keep church affairs from becoming entangled in state politics as are secular libertarians. "I want to run a religious school," Rev. John Graham, principal of New York's Cardinal Hayes High School, told a Washington Post reporter. "As long as Catholic schools are seen as adjuncts or alternatives to public schools, they are not fulfilling their mission."[206]

Racial segregation poses an even stickier quagmire for school choice policies. Choice raises intense worries in many communities, especially in the South, about segregation of blacks and other minorities in inferior schools. Ironically, where the concept of choice is compromised to give "racial balance" priority over family preferences, it invariably results in official discrimination and exclusion on the basis of race, usually to the disadvantage of the already disadvantaged. Whether in the form of "managed choice" as pioneered in Cambridge, Massachusetts, or the even more diluted version of "magnet schools" concocted in Prince Georges County, Maryland, Richmond, California, and many other communities as an alternative to busing, minority students are regularly denied access to beneficial educational programs in order to maintain racial quotas.

These problems ultimately will require fundamental rethinking of the flawed sociological rationale of the Supreme Court's famous 1954 Brown v. Board of Education decision, which laid the groundwork for court-ordered attacks on de facto (matter of fact) as opposed to just de jure (imposed by law) school segregation. In fact, the most incendiary impact of the private voucher program for black children in Milwaukee championed by Polly Williams may be its explicit demand to put educational opportunity ahead of racial mixing. While the Supreme Court recently relaxed some school integration requirements, until current legal doctrine is reconsidered further, any program rooted in the obsolete technology of bodies, buses, and buildings will risk running into the desegregation mess.

School choice also gets embroiled in the growing anger and litigation over the gross inequalities of education funding between rich and poor districts in many states. In Kentucky, where the disparity in per-student funding between urban and rural districts was as great as ten-to-one ($4,000 a year compared to $400 a year), the state supreme court ruled the entire public education system unconstitutional and required the governor and legislature to devise a completely new system to assure more nearly equal funding. In Texas, the supreme court finally impelled the legislature to enact a "Robin Hood" law to redistribute resources from rich to poor districts after several aborted attempts, but further litigation is virtually certain. Similar battles are percolating in other states. The mechanics of school choice programs get entangled in these conflicts over the equity of diverse forms and levels of school funding.

But perhaps the most intractable political problem raised by school choice is the patent inequality of its feasibility for rural versus urban communities. In densely populated areas with numerous schools, the transportation and logistical problems of school choice may seem minor or at least manageable. The same is evidently not so in rural communities where a whole school district may have only a few hundred students and the drive from one school building to another may be measured in hours.

These key political conflicts over school choice are not insoluble. But the heated debates and politicking they provoke, and the ultimate cost of solving the problems, all absorb time, energy, and resources in pursuit of a program that promises at best no more than meager benefits. The game simply is not worth the candle.

Bodies, Buses, and Buildings

To have any hope for a genuinely productive restructuring of learning systems, the learner as consumer must be the overriding focus. No matter how much it speaks of "radical change" and "revolution," any reform program that is based on "the school as the site of reform"—as America 2000 states, and as virtually all reform programs assume—is committed to a lethal error.

Again, elasticity is the central issue. The supply side of school choice—tied up in the obsolete technology of bodies, buses, and buildings—is nearly as inelastic as the status quo system of assigned enrollment. It is just as technologically incapable of responding quickly and precisely to individual learner demands as ever. The demand side of school choice is also inelastic. What families demand most urgently from schools are adequate day care, and then geographic convenience. To a lesser extent, parents seek association through the school with a community of like-minded families. Research by Chubb and Moe, Coleman, and others[207] indicates that such community involvement tends to be associated with marginally more "effective" schools.

BRITAIN

By making money follow the pupil, [the local management of schools initiative] will encourage good schools and penalise bad ones; and by delegating budgets to individual heads, it will cut down on time-wasting bureaucracy. . . .

But . . . pupil-driven financing . . . really upsets the heads. One headmistress gives a pungent summary of the prevailing philosophy: "Market forces are very dangerous when you are messing with children's brains." She hints that teachers and local officials will do their best to blunt the impact of the market. Local heads will not allow a school run by a friend to go under.

Even heads who do not share this cartel mentality may find that aggressive expansion is not worth the candle. Additional pupils bring extra costs as well as extra cash. Over-zealous expansion may be counter-productive as well as burdensome: a good school may cease to be a good school if its classes are overflowing and its playgrounds full of makeshift accommodation. Besides, some heads like to lord it over local parents—particularly pushy ones. Like National Health Service consultants, they treat waiting lists as a sign of status rather than a symptom of failure.

—"A Classroom Revolution?" *The Economist* (Feb. 23, 1991)

Because school choices are exercised only infrequently—no more than annually and usually only once in several years—and by no more than a minority of families at any given time, even totally free school choice cannot lead to much aggregate demand for new, better schools. Nor could the inelastic supply of geographically and architecturally hidebound schools respond significantly to such demands over periods shorter than decades. By then, the archaic infrastructure of campus-bound education will have been totally bypassed by new information technology. School choice simply cannot unleash the dynamism of competitive markets.

In stark contrast to the molasseslike torpor of school choice, the demands learners make for learning are naturally elastic. The individual's learning demands are genetically attuned to the moment-to-moment attention-grabbing and reward-conferring qualities of any learning product or experience. Each person's needs and demands for learning vary greatly by the hour or even by the minute. And the great diversity of individual learning styles, multiple intelligences, and current needs and interests means that the demand for learning across the student population is highly variable.

Equally elastic is the fast expanding network of learner-focused products and services that HL technology now makes both possible and inevitable. A growing array of intelligent multimedia tools has the speed-of-light flexibility to respond to these highly elastic demands of the natural human learning process. "Just-in-time" learning is the order of the new day—the relevant knowledge, expertise, experience, or tutoring can be delivered just when and where it is wanted to serve the needs of the individual learner or cooperative work group.

This powerful elasticity of HL technology cannot be matched by any reform or refinement of the "Yak in the Box" technology of traditional school classrooms—where a teacher or professor talks at a passive group of inmates in a closed room 80 percent of the time, and performs "administrivia" bureaucratic tasks the rest of the time, leaving students with at best a couple of minutes a day of interactive learning opportunities.

So another fatal error of the school choice strategy is the myth of the "good" school. Chubb and Moe's policy recipe hinges on an erroneous distinction between what they label "effective" and "ineffective" schools. But in a realistic technological perspective, there are no effective schools in America, or anywhere else in the world.

If "school" means a building-bound organization, there are only two qualities of school in the world today—the hopelessly backward and the merely obsolete. Alternatively, if the label "school" is stripped of its traditional meaning and transferred to the architecture-free channels of multimedia networks, then "school choice" cannot mean anything like what its advocates have proposed to date.

THE MICROCHOICE SOLUTION

Microchoice is what is really needed. Rather than try to salvage a bankrupt policy with semantic sidesteps, genuine education restructuring initiatives need to drop or ignore school choice and focus on the personal demands for learning made by individual learners, and on the specific products and services that respond directly to those personal demands. The economy of microchoice must be independent of geography, architectural shells, and the artifices of "attendance"; learning via multimedia technology meets these requirements.

The mechanics of a workable microchoice solution include five elements:

1. *Microvouchers*—a financing technology similar to a bank credit or debit card that puts control in the hands of the consumer.

2. *Intellectual "food courts"*—ownership of particular products or services is independent of the ownership of the structure within which they are delivered to the consumer, just as the restaurants or stores in a shopping mall are owned by companies independent of the mall owners.

3. *Attendance-free accounting*—value of any learning experience is determined by outcomes achieved, not by time or place of attendance.

4. *Intellectual "food stamp" funding*—to the extent public funds are provided to consumers via microvouchers, consumer choices are limited, as in the case of food stamps, only by the broad purposes of funding and not to particular vendors.

5. *Market-based regulation*—no uniquely "educational" regulation is needed, but only normal consumer protective health and safety, antifraud, and antitrust regulations applicable to any commercial industry.

The key differences between microvouchers and the kinds of vouchers associated with school choice are the degree and market impact of consumer choice. With school choice programs, some kind of voucher—whether called that or not—is used to transfer government funds from one school to another, as a result of the family choice of institutions. The voucher is, essentially, a check drawn on the government treasury to pay a school's "tuition" in whole or part.

In contrast, microvouchers would be specific charges made against a balance in an account under the control of the family or individual student, not of the school. Technologically, the microvouchers would work the same way as a bank debit card account. The government would periodically deposit funds representing education and training appropriations in each qualified recipient's account, presumably at least once every fiscal year. Like food stamps, the microvouchers could be spent only on eligible products and services—those that nurture the development of knowledge and skills.

Card account technology brings vastly improved elasticity to supply and demand in the learning market. Rather than paying a lump sum for tuition once or twice a year, the student can make purchases monthly, weekly, hourly, or even minute-by-minute—whatever is most appropriate and efficient. Purchases can be made by the student-consumer either with the mechanical use of a plastic, data-encoded card or by the simple use of an account number. As with commercial card systems, account security can be protected by some personal identification device such as a simple password or even more sophisticated ID systems using voiceprints, fingerprints, or eyeprints.

The procedures and economics for operating this kind of system are well established everywhere in the world outside academia. Purchasing an instructional service or material or tool would be the same as using your Visa card to buy tickets to a rock concert, a computer at a computer store, a book at a bookstore, a long-distance phone call, the use of an on-line database, or the opportunity to see a pay-per-view cable TV program. Consumers could receive account statements monthly or even daily, as is possible with most automated banking systems today.

Oxford zoologist Richard Dawkins proposed the term *meme,* as an analogy to "gene," to represent the most basic elements or quanta of cultural knowledge.[208] So, if the future of television is pay-per-view, as many analysts believe, then the future of education based on microchoice may well be "pay-per-meme."

The microvoucher is no "pie in the sky" dream. The use of personalized card account technology for payment of government benefits, including educational services, is already being developed. Special charge cards have been used with automatic teller machines (ATMs) and point-of-sale (POS) terminals to deliver food stamps, unemployment insurance, social security, and other assistance benefits in Reading, Pennsylvania, Ramsey County, Minnesota, Tacoma, Washington, Cedar Rapids, Iowa, and the city of Baltimore.[209] Maryland recently became the first state to replace checks and coupons for welfare services entirely with electronic card technology.[210] The federal Agriculture Department is now pushing to get states to replace paper food stamps with electronic cards.[211] And the Michigan "Opportunity Card" allows adult benefit recipients to do "one-stop shopping" for a range of education and training services.

This combination of information and financial technology makes the traditional school building obsolete. The delivery of specific products and services for learning can be provided in the time, place, and form of the student's choosing. Technologically, the student can change "schools" as easily as switching TV channels, or can "attend" several different "schools" at once.

To the extent younger children may still need a place to go for custodial care, that building need not be limited to ownership and administration by one school. Nor do adults who prefer to go to some kind of center to participate in instruction have to be limited to attending one institution on a given campus. Instead, buildings become discretionary, and no more than shells to cover an array of independent, competing enterprises available to serve the student-consumer.

A familiar analogy for this arrangement is the shopping mall "food court." Like a village bazaar, the food court is a hockey-rink-size dining area surrounded by stalls from which a dozen to a score or more food vendors sell their products. The food court not only empowers the consumer to choose, in one place, from among her favorite hamburger, or chicken, or Mexican, or Chinese, or whatever fast food restaurant. She also can mix and match items from several menus, creating a meal from a much wider—and more nutritionally balanced—variety of foods than any one vendor would find it efficient to offer.

The foods provided are produced by specialists whose ownership is independent from one another and independent of the ownership of the building that houses the food court. It's also irrelevant to the diners and to the restaurant businesses in the food court whether the building is owned by a commercial corporation, a nonprofit organization such as a foundation, or a government agency. There is no direct economic relationship between the building owner and the consumer—diners buy food from the restaurants, which in turn pay rent to lease space from the building owner. Nor are the food vendors limited to selling only in that building—they usually have their own freestanding stores, and often also sell their wares by home delivery services, through supermarkets, and so forth.

With the ability to deliver mental nourishment telematically, via software and communications, the intellectual food courts that will replace schools don't need to be housed in buildings at all—most can be accessed through a portable, personal telecomputer terminal. To the extent children or older students want to gather under one roof, the use of space and facilities in such a diversified learning center can be far more flexible than in the food court analogy. Some spaces could be leased for specific purposes such as recreation, or health, or child care services. Others—ranging from libraries to theaters to wireless telecomputing networks—could be provided either by building owners or by third parties as access points to other vendors' products and services. With everything paid for à la carte with the student's own money or microvouchers, the elasticity of the supply of services through the intellectual food court would be vastly greater than that of the traditional building-bound school.

The severance of the conventional connections between schools and buildings is no pipe dream either. Building-buster microchoice designs are already more established than many people realize.

For instance, one of the most notable innovations in the famous fifteen-year-old "choice" program of New York City's School District 4 in East Harlem was to throw out the idea that a "school" is equivalent to a school building. Early on, the district administration decided to allow entrepreneurial teacher teams to create as many as four or five independent schools within a single building. By thus breaking the linkage of school choice to geography, the East Harlem program achieved its greatest measure of success.

The most successful part of Minnesota's open enrollment law has not been school choice but a "postsecondary option" provision that allows eleventh and twelfth graders to enroll in courses in any college that will accept them, using state school aid money to pay their tuition. This arrangement was used by about 6.4 percent of all Minnesota juniors and seniors in 1990–91—eight times more than the number of eligible students who used the school choice option. The postsecondary option is inherently a microchoice program—it enables students to purchase specific courses, without having to change schools altogether.

A closer approach to the food court model than District 4's schools is the "higher-education shopping center" started on the campus of Portland (Oregon) Community College through the initiative of the college's president, John Anthony. Since 1985, the center has offered courses in business, computer sciences, technology, and education provided by thirteen private and public colleges.[212] This kind of multicollege learning center has since been duplicated in several other U.S. communities.

But as suggested above, attendance at a building like an educational shopping mall now is discretionary, not necessary. The very idea of "attendance" is a barrier to high-tech learning that needs to be removed. What matters for successful learning is *what* is learned, not *where* the learning occurred. And *how long* it took the student to master something should be included in the assessment of cost, not of effectiveness.

The microchoice strategy requires that the fundamental approach to educational accounting based on attendance be thrown out. Microchoice both enables and requires the student-consumer to control the source, location, and duration of learning activities. The so-called "Carnegie unit" measure of service—the familiar credit-hours based on attendance in a classroom—has no place in the modern world of hyperlearning. Most of the products and services students will buy with microvouchers will be valued by knowledge content, not "connect time." Accounting to the consumer will be based on the value of what is received; time and money will be presented as costs to the consumer that competing vendors will seek to minimize.

With microchoice, compulsory attendance and fruitless debates about the length of school days and school years become obsolete. Attendance is entirely a matter of the student's or family's convenience. Microchoice gives families a wide range of flexible options to decide to what extent children should participate in education at a centralized custodial facility, at home, at a location in or near the parent's workplace, or while cruising around in a boat or plane or Winnebago.

Microchoice enables government to fund learners and learning instead of schools and teaching. This is obviously a far more efficient way for a community to achieve real development of its human capital. But for financing to be allocated directly to student-consumers, governments will require some assurance that public funds are being used for their intended purposes.

The established food stamp program shows the way to do this. Food stamps—which are vouchers—can be used by qualified recipients only to purchase food. Within the obvious constraints that recipients cannot use food stamps to buy panty hose or motor oil, consumers using stamps are free to choose any kind of food they want from any store they want.

One of the objections to school choice that also will be made to microchoice is that the poor and disadvantaged are incapable of making proper choices for themselves or their own children. Certainly the existence of a market by itself does not assure that consumers will be well informed or educated. That is an argument for better consumer education, not for patronizing bureaucracy.

Returning to the food stamp analogy, there is an obvious risk that poor families will choose a nutritionally deficient diet—and in fact many do. But the food stamp program does not dictate what recipients can eat. Instead, the government attempts to communicate better information and education on proper diet to consumers.

In contrast, a recent study by Public Voice for Food & Health Policy, a consumer advocacy organization, found that the government program that gives food directly to children, the federal school lunch program, results in children receiving meals that are *less* nutritionally balanced than what is recommended by U.S. Dietary Guidelines or even than the average meals Americans normally consume.[213] This suggests that families are likely to nourish either body or mind more effectively when they are free to choose for themselves than when they are stuck with what government feels like giving them.

Microchoice permits and requires a robustly competitive marketplace for learning. The microchoice strategy does not demand absolute laissez-faire or zero regulation. The learning market like any other is subject to fraud, abuse, and monopolistic practices that warrant policing by the state—not to replace the market but to protect it.

There is nothing about the learning business that demands more regulation or special kinds of regulation in contrast to other businesses. That children are involved does not change this. Children may in general be more vulnerable to some kinds of harm than most adults. But many adults are as vulnerable to certain insults as children, maybe even more so. The issue in regulation is the harm, not the age of the victim. There is no less justification for laws protecting consumers in the learning market from fraud, theft, health and safety hazards, and anticompetitive business practices than in any other market—but there is no greater justification either.

Nearly all the political conflicts surrounding school choice are created or aggravated by the archaic technology of bodies, buses, and buildings. The microchoice solution based on multimedia technology makes all the major objections to "choice" either minor or moot.

With or without choice, schools are persistently bogged down in the subversive numbers game of "racial balance." But when technology is allowed to make school buildings irrelevant to the delivery of instructional services, the logic of school desegregation becomes moot. Equity becomes a matter of access to tools that are naturally portable and ubiquitous rather than a matter of building attendance. Integration—as opposed to desegregation—across racial, ethnic, and cultural boundaries becomes a matter of curriculum and competence rather than of location and transportation.

The technological extinction of "school" as a relevant organizational structure for learning also makes moot arguments about government aid to church-related schools. Existing court decisions clearly indicate that, as long as the government is funding the student's use of specific tools and services and these are not used for a religious purpose, there is no constitutional problem.[214] School choice vouchers would allocate public funds to church-run institutions, making it difficult to show real separation of public money from sectarian purposes.

But microvouchers controlled by students and families would be much more clearly targeted on specific products or services whose secular nature could be easily verified. Neither the public as a whole nor a court is likely to find constitutional objections to the idea of a student located in a church-owned building using government funds to pay for a phone call on a government-regulated or subsidized telephone network to the public library to retrieve knowledge from a commercial database. It would be hard to argue that a student in the South Bronx participating via multimedia telecomputer in a seminar on electronics being given by an engineering professor at UCLA would be violating the Constitution simply because she happened to be sitting in a chair owned by a church.

But the greatest advantage of microchoice over schooling is the vastly superior productivity of an economy based on bits instead of bricks. Communications media like the microchoice system grab the benefits of what economists call "network externalities"—the nature of networks to become geometrically more productive, and profitable, the more they are expanded.

To illustrate this important idea, suppose you own a parking lot with 100 spaces and, to make more money, you decide to buy an additional parcel of land to add 10 more spaces. If each space brings $10 a day in revenue, your revenue grows from $1,000 to $1,100 a day. So expanding your assets by 10 percent generates a 10 percent increase in revenue. Simple enough.

Now suppose you own a telephone network with 100 customers. If each day, on average, every customer calls every other customer, that's 100×100 or 10,000 calls. At 10¢ a call that would bring in $1,000 a day in revenue. But if you go out and sign up 10 new customers, look what happens to your sales: The number of calls each day grows to 110×110, which equals 12,100 and yields $1,210 of revenue. So *expanding a communication network's total assets by 10 percent produces a 21 percent increase in value,* whether value represents revenue added or costs saved.

The younger generation thinks nothing of picking up a phone to tap into a data base—for updates on preteen heart-throbs New Kids on the Block, for example. Just ask third-grader Courtney Hampton at Lew Wallace Elementary School No. 107 in Indianapolis. Courtney calls three voice-mail numbers every day after school: one to find out what's coming up in Spanish class, one to see when his other homework is due, and one to find out the next day's hot-lunch menu. (He doesn't like the mixed vegetables.)

At School No. 107, even kindergartners use the voice-mail system, donated for the semester by Ameritech Corp. Chad Hinnan, a second-grader, sums up life before voice mail in one word: "Rough." With customers like Courtney, Carisa, and Chad in hand, all the voice processing industry has to do is make the technology so easy that even adults are comfortable with it.

—"Your New Computer: The Telephone," *Business Week* (June 3, 1991)

That's what "network externalities" means. And that's why a *Fortune* magazine article on intellectual capital concludes, "In networks, you can violate the law of diminishing returns for years without getting caught."[215] Replace parking lots and telephones in the above examples with schools and multimedia microchoice networks, and the implications are evident.

Microchoice reduces the inequalities that afflict schooling, with or without school choice. Information technologies that get rapidly cheaper and more universally available even as they get more powerful inherently reduce gaps between rural and urban communities and between the wealthy and the poor. Virtually all homes in America have telephones and TV sets. VCRs are in three-quarters of homes. Six out of ten homes subscribe to cable TV. Computers, fax machines, camcorders, and other advanced tools are now as cheap as TV sets. India has been delivering televised education to poor, remote villages by communications satellites for nearly two decades. With the low-cost, high-powered technology now available there is no reason why distance or poverty need to be barriers to educational choice and opportunity.

Moreover, the network externalities built into microchoice learning will doom traditional schools to rapid extinction. Given the freedom to compete equally for academic revenues, microchoice networks, once established, will become ever more productive and profitable the more they grow, fueling them to grow faster and faster. And as microchoice networks siphon an expanding stream of consumers and revenue from old-fashioned academies, the more inefficient, unequal, inflexible institutions will shrivel to the vanishing point.

Multimedia technology makes schooling obsolete and therefore school choice irrelevant. HL technology offers students of all ages the right choice: the freedom to learn anything, anytime, anywhere, in the way that works best for each individual and family. But making this technological potential real for everyone requires a vastly more aggressive commitment to research, development, and commercial implementation of the new technology for learning.

CHAPTER 10

CLOSING THE TECHNOLOGY GAP: BEYOND PSEUDO-INNOVATION

• • •

Had the power of educational technology (not in some laboratory but in common use) grown at the same pace over the last four decades as the power of computer technology, a high school or college diploma—which still take twelve and four years respectively to produce, at an average cost for either of more than $60,000—could be "produced" in less than five minutes for less than five cents!

The point is not that the world should expect instant education for a nickel tomorrow. While human factors still limit such instant learning, the fact remains that schools and colleges are almost totally isolated from the information revolution that is so explosively transforming every other venue of human affairs. This comparison demonstrates that the technological gap between the school environment and the "real world" is growing so wide, so fast that the classroom experience is on the way to becoming not merely unproductive but increasingly irrelevant to normal human existence.

The immediate cause of this poor performance is education's gross lack of investment in technology. A four-year study of the knowledge age economy by the U.S. Congress's Office of Technology Assessment[216] (OTA) revealed that education has by far the lowest level of capital investment (another name for "buying technology") of any major industry: only about $1,000 per employee. The average for the U.S. economy as a whole is about $50,000 of capital investment per job. Some high-tech industries invest $300,000 or more in technology for each worker. Even other, relatively labor-intensive, "service" businesses provide at least $7,000 to $20,000 worth of equipment and facilities for each employee. So when it comes to investment in technology, the education industry is not even involved in the twentieth century, much less prepared for the twenty-first century.

This is a good place to call attention to a unique characteristic of the education industry, or learning enterprise, that sets it apart from all other businesses, and that makes the above and other unflattering comparisons even worse. That is: *Education is the only business in which the consumer does the essential work.* To the extent that learning is education's essential (though not only) business, it's clear that the productivity of the student or learner—not teachers or administrators—is what really counts.

If we count the student, rather than the paid staff, as the "worker" to be compared to workers in other sectors, education's productivity/technology gap looms even larger. Thus, the education sector's niggling capital investment of $1,000 per employee becomes a pathetic $100 per worker if "worker" means "student." Coincidentally, while the average U.S. public school budget now comes to about $5,000 per student annually, the typical school district expends only about $100 to $200 of that exorbitant sum on materials and tools for each student to use directly for learning.

In a world where life cycles of product and production technology now are measured in months rather than decades, scanty capital investment inevitably leads to creaking technological backwardness. So we should be dismayed but unsurprised to observe that—in the midst of a global information revolution—the instructional technology available to most students, most of the time, in most schools and colleges today ranges from a hundred to a thousand years old. While the power of information technology has been leaping upward by factors of ten every few years since the 1950s, a report by the late Ithiel Pool of MIT[217] found that classroom instruction was the only one of some two dozen communications media studied whose productivity, in terms of the cost of delivering information, sharply declined between the 1960s and the 1980s.

The fault for this festering obsolescence lies not in any shortage of

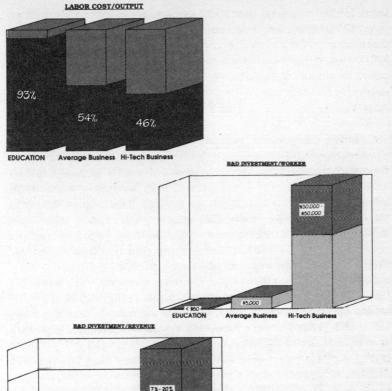

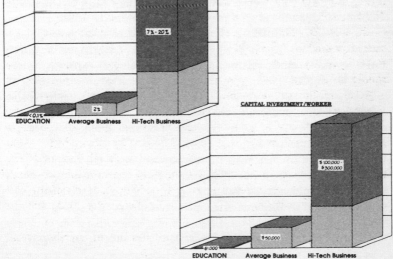

sources: Office of Technology Assessment; *Business Week.* See L. Perelman, *Closing Education-tion's Technology Gap,* Briefing Paper No. 111 (Indianapolis: Hudson Institute, Nov. 1989).

tax and tuition revenue, but is rooted entirely in the priorities of an academic establishment that has habitually replaced innovation with supplication.

THE R&D GAP

To gauge the extent to which education has shortchanged the research and development of productive learning technology, consider that the Gillette Company's high-tech "Sensor" razor blade cost some $200 million in R&D investment over thirteen years to create. Gillette, a company whose annual revenues of more than $3.5 billion are less than the education budgets of three-fourths of the U.S. states, thus spent more to invent a better shave than all the states combined spent during the same period to develop a better technology for teaching and learning than the thousand-year-old "Yak in the Box" (the lecturing classroom professor).

Compared to any other part of the modern economy, the minuscule share of the education industry's vast financial resources invested in research and development is shocking. While the federal government pays less than 9 percent of the national bill for school and college education, it pays for most of the educational research. Depending on what one counts as "R&D," the federal Education Department spent between $136 million and $388 million on some kind of research in the 1989 fiscal year. Only about a million dollars of this was devoted to development of advanced instructional technology.[218] Most of the research on high-tech teaching and learning was financed by the Defense Department, to the tune of about $200 million annually in explicit expenditures, and up to $2 billion a year in training systems development that is estimated to be buried in acquisition budgets.[219] The National Science Foundation also allocated about $15 million a year to research on innovative instruction for science and mathematics.[220]

Education researcher Myron Lieberman estimates the dollar value of the time that college of education faculty claim to devote to research at roughly $300 million a year. But precious little of this so-called "research" has any relation to the basic science and technology of learning.[221]

These hundreds of millions of dollars may sound like a lot of money for research until one considers the scale of the nation's learning enterprise. Again, the education and training sector is America's largest information industry and, depending on what is counted, may be simply the country's biggest business at $400–600 billion a year.

By OTA's accounting, the education sector's investment in R&D comes to only 0.025 percent of its annual revenues. Even if demonstration projects, program evaluations, and other activities plausibly considered "research" are included, education's R&D spending still is no more than 0.1 percent of revenues.

In contrast, R&D accounts for 2.5 percent of the entire U.S. gross national product. The average American business firm invests 2 percent of sales in R&D. But in high-tech, information-based businesses—the kind of business education ought to be but isn't—companies commonly plow 7 to 20 percent or more of their sales into R&D. For instance, in *Business Week* magazine's 1989 "R&D scoreboard" the five top-rated companies in the computer software and services sector (the fastest growing segment of today's computer industry) spent 26.9 percent, 17.2 percent, 17.9 percent, 16.1 percent, and 28.6 percent of their revenues on R&D.

But *Business Week*'s research revealed that it is the amount of R&D investment *per employee* that is the most powerful predictor of business success. By that standard, the magnitude of the education sector's failure to invest in innovation is magnified because education, being so labor intensive, dilutes its already piddling R&D expenditures over a relatively larger workforce than other businesses.

For the formal education sector (kindergarten through university), R&D spending per employee is less than $50 a year. Now consider what each of those leading companies in the computer software and services business spent annually on R&D per employee: $42,622; $36,207; $33,535; $30,389; and $30,264.[222] The composite figure for all the companies in all the industries rated by *Business Week* was $5,042 of annual R&D investment per employee.[223]

As meager as $50 a year for education's per-employee R&D investment appears, it's instructive again to recall that the student is the "worker" whose productivity matters most in the education business. So the education sector's annual R&D investment per worker realistically is something less than $5—a *thousand times less* than the norm for other major industries, and *ten thousand times less* than the amount spent by the most competitive U.S. firms in high-tech, information businesses.

That is not to say that the U.S. education sector could or should spend exactly as much on R&D per learner-as-worker as the top computer software companies—that would total over a trillion dollars a year. But an increase in learning R&D on the order of a hundred times would narrow an inexcusable chasm in R&D investment down to a plausible difference.

There are other sectors of the overall learning enterprise where major investments in R&D are being made—those in which competitive forces demand improved productivity in learning and teaching. In particular, military and corporate educators are investing in the development of more cost-effective learning systems, because if they don't their competitors will eat their lunch.

For instance, Col. Robert Seger, director of the U.S. Army's network of training schools, is investing 5 percent of his annual $600 million budget in R&D on learning and instructional technology. With some 85,000 students in class at any time, the education system Colonel Seger commands is comparable in size and cost to some of the largest and best-funded suburban or urban school districts in the U.S., such as Montgomery County, Maryland, or Fairfax County, Virginia. Yet the more than $30 million Colonel Seger's organization invests each year in R&D exceeds the total R&D expenditures on learning technology of all 15,400 school districts, 50 state education departments, and the federal Education Department, combined. And that sprawling K–12 bureaucracy has a total budget that is more than three hundred times greater, to serve a student population that is about five hundred times greater than the Army's military school system.

Ask Colonel Seger why he is making such a substantial investment in educational R&D and he'll explain that, from the Pentagon's perspective, there's really no choice: "A political commitment has been made to cut military spending. But our people have to be prepared to fulfill our mission—a mission that is getting ever more technically demanding. We simply have to seek ways to educate our people better at lower cost."[224]

If there is good news in this dismal situation, it is that—quite to the contrary of education lobby propaganda brooding about America's mythical "lag" in the global school wars—the United States does not trail behind other nations in closing education's disastrous technology gap. While specific data on national investments in educational R&D are scarce, the available information suggests that academia in other nations is as resistant to innovation and productivity as it is in the United States. So America is not yet losing the race to transform educational technology to match a knowledge age economy—if only because there is no race, so far. More important: The whole world is losing the precious opportunity for growth, prosperity, and freedom that hyperlearning offers by failing to invest in the learning technology needed to run a knowledge age economy.

THE INNOVATION GAP

Clearly, a vastly expanded investment is urgently needed to close education's disastrous R&D gap. But it's essential to recognize that merely adding dollars to the educational research budget will not, by itself, lead to more innovation or greater productivity in schools and colleges.

The failure to effectively exploit the instructional power of the computer is just one notable illustration of educational institutions' capacity to resist change. A decade and a half into the "desktop computer" revolution, sixty million personal computers are in use in the United States—about half of those are in use in American homes. Over thirty million U.S. homes also have Nintendo "game" units—computer terminals masquerading as toys.

In contrast, another 1988 OTA report[225] found that U.S. schools spent a total of about $2 billion on instructional computers over a period of ten years—that's only a tenth of what the rest of America spends on personal computers *every year*. Surveys showed that K–12 schools had accumulated a total of less than two-and-a-half million instructional computers by 1989, only about one for every twenty students on average. And the distribution of the computers is uneven—43 percent of all schools had a total of less than fifteen computers for students to use.[226] Many of the computers counted as "present" in schools are old, obsolete, or simply locked away, unused. While specialists have concluded that, ideally, all students should get to use instructional computers for about a third of their time in school, or ten hours a week,[227] the OTA report estimated that students typically get to use computers in U.S. schools only about one hour a week.

Nor are U.S. colleges and universities notably more innovative than schools. A study of PC use by the Center for Scholarly Technology at the

Education R&D Share of Total Ed. Spending (%)

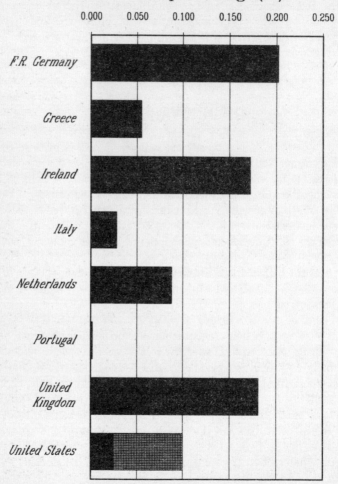

SOURCES: EUROSTAT, *Government Financing of Research and Development 1980–1987* (Luxembourg, 1989); OECD, *Education in OECD Countries 1986–87* (Paris, 1989); total ed. for Italy from UNESCO, *Statistical Yearbook: 1988.* These are the only EEC countries reporting "education" as a subset of R&D expenditures. (1986—Local Currency) U.S. data from Office of Technology Assessment, Dept. of Education, for comparison.

University of Southern California found that there is on average only about one "publicly available" personal computer for every forty-five students on U.S. college campuses. True, many students now own their own PCs—but the survey found that even at elite private universities only three in ten students own a personal computer and at community colleges or mainstream public colleges fewer than half as many students own PCs.[228]

The technological paralysis of academic institutions did not stop America's youth from joining the computer revolution: In 1989, 24 percent of high school boys and 17 percent of high school girls were using computers at home. More than a third of that use was unrelated to schoolwork—kids did not need to be compelled or "assigned" to use their own computers.[229] These data underscore the large and growing gap between the technology of schooling and the technology of living.

In contrast to the situation in schools and colleges, demand for computer-based instruction is strong in the unregulated and unsubsidized market for education that is provided by employers. An estimated 30 percent of the more than $50 billion employers invest annually in employee training is spent on computer-based instructional systems[230]—that is over seven times more in one year than public schools spent on instructional computers in the last decade. Or, to look at the same data from another angle, *employer-provided education invests a three-hundred-times-larger share of its total budget in computer-based instruction than public education does.*

The failure to consider the total market for instructional computing and other advanced technology beyond schools commonly distorts published reports of educational technology's lack of progress.[231] Contrary to what many reports imply, the problem is not that instructional computers don't work well enough, or that they are not affordable, or that educators won't use them. The truth is that computer-based and other high-tech instructional tools are being produced, sold, and used successfully and extensively *outside of schools.*

The fundamental technology of programmed instruction—focused on continuous feedback, self-pacing, timely reinforcement for success, and mastery of subject matter—has been applied successfully in military and corporate training, as well as other educational settings for over thirty years. As affordable computers have replaced paper and mechanical systems, programmed instruction has become far more sophisticated and entertaining. Over two decades of research shows that even rather ordinary computer-assisted instruction—CAI—produces about 30 percent more learning in 40 percent less time and at 30 percent less cost than conventional classroom instruction.[232] These long-term averages clearly understate the productivity benefits of state-of-the-art technology in a world where computer power doubles every eighteen months and software improvements, if not as explosive, are still prolific.

The power of multimedia for instructional technology already has been demonstrated by a generation of products linking desktop computers to videodisc players. The player and computer combine to form an "interactive video instruction" (IVI) system that enables students to access and combine large volumes of information in attention-galvanizing forms. IVI, increasingly referred to simply as "interactive multimedia" as video and computer technologies merge, permits learners to apply knowledge and to practice skills in simulated settings that are more authentic and understandable than anything the printed text can challenge. A research review by the Institute for Defense Analyses concluded that IVI was more effective than conventional teaching both for imparting knowledge and for improving task performance skills.[233]

A research survey six years ago by Douglas Ellson, a retired psychology professor at Indiana University, found some 125 instructional technologies, particularly using programmed approaches, that were shown by experiments and demonstration projects to at least *double* the productivity of teaching: They achieved twice as much learning for each unit of cost in time or money.[234] The widespread adoption of such existing, already proven instructional technology could save the U.S. economy over $100 billion a year.

The key difference is that competition makes corporate and military educators accountable for costs and results—More Better Faster Cheaper has value in those competitive environments. The principal reason for the almost total lack of investment in productivity-enhancing technological innovation, and the record of steadily declining productivity in formal education, is the inherent absence of competitive market incentives in the bureaucratic structure of government-controlled educational systems.

History argues that neither the abundance of current information technology nor further research and invention of even more exotic tools for teaching and learning will, by themselves, have much impact on the near-static pace of innovation in education. At least since Socrates groused about the threat literacy posed to the discipline of human memory, educators have addressed innovation less as a promise than as a threat. Pocket calculators have been ubiquitous for some two decades, yet their common use in precollege education is still sedulously resisted. Television has been around for half a century, yet its educational use remains minor relative to traditional classroom methods. The telephone is a century-old technology; yet hardly any schoolteachers in America have their own classroom or office telephone or even ready access to one.

Continual attempts to inject technological innovation into American schools and colleges through subsidized experimental, pilot, and demonstration projects or top-down bureaucratic mandates have failed as thoroughly as similar initiatives in the Soviet state agricultural system. (In fact, the socialist governments of both France and the former Soviet Union tried to inject computers into classrooms en masse—both efforts, which completely ignored consumer markets, wound up as costly flops.[235]) In contrast, American agriculture has become the most productive in the world because adoption of technological innovation has been motivated by the competitive forces experienced by independent, market-driven enterprises.

In essence, the public school is America's collective farm. Innovation and productivity are lacking in American education for basically the same reasons they were scarce in Soviet agriculture: absence of competitive, market forces.

At best, the public school normally provides no incentive—other than altruism or curiosity—for practitioners to adopt innovations. In fact, scarcely any schools, even those that aspire to be progressive, offer any substantive reward, or even opportunity, for professional staff to adopt productive tools.

At worst, and commonly, the typical school environment is pregnant with disincentives which, over a period of a half century or more, have proven highly effective in preventing or reversing technological change in education.

For instance, journalists and other education analysts commonly cite lack of teacher training as a barrier to adoption of instructional computers. Yet training, by itself, cannot overcome bureaucratic disincentives. Indeed, training may even prove counterproductive.

The Houston Independent School District, for example, during the mid-1980s provided an intensive, three-hundred-hour teacher training course in the effective use of instructional technology. The training also was tied to an innovative salary scale that provided extra pay to the teachers who enhanced their skills through this training. Yet graduates of the program—the most innovative and technically proficient teachers in the district—who practiced what they learned actually got negative grades on a state-imposed teacher evaluation instrument that values "teaching" according to the ability to stand in front of a blackboard and talk, rather than the ability, or even willingness, to employ modern, student-centered tools. Staff in the district told me that many of the best-trained teachers were leaving the system for jobs where their skills were in demand and rewarded.

After seven years of progressive development, the Houston program and the entire district technology department were abolished in 1989 when a new superintendent with different priorities took office. Strong pressure to kill the program came from teacher unions, most of whose members resented the extra income received by the minority that had been trained and certified as teacher technologists.

The resistance to technological innovation in education is not complete, and the exceptions are at least as telling as the rule. From three hundred thousand to perhaps a million or more supposed "hyperactive" children are required to take Ritalin or other amphetaminelike drugs as a condition of attending public schools in the U.S.[236] While *personal* computers are scarce and ill-used in school or college classrooms, VCRs are virtually ubiquitous, and have put the old 16-mm projector literally out of business. And academic organizations have been as quick to adopt computers for data processing and other administrative chores as other bureaucracies have.

What these examples demonstrate is that academia is eager to implement high technologies, even including psychoactive drugs, that increase bureaucratic *control* of behavior. The education establishment attacks only technology that *liberates* teachers from the control of the bureaucracy or learners from the control of bureaucrats and teachers.

Despite apparent institutional differences, the barriers and disincentives for innovation in higher education are broadly similar to those that hobble K–12 schools, and are equally effective. First and foremost, universities reward faculty for their demonstrated research accomplishments, not for their teaching competence. For all the sanctimonious talk about the university's educational mission, the fact remains that virtually no institutions in the U.S. hire, compensate, or promote faculty on the basis of a professor's ability to educate anyone.

Given that there is little or no reward for educating in higher education, it's unsurprising that few faculty have put any effort into developing or using advanced computer-based or other multimedia "courseware." Even those professors who have the imagination and altruistic motivation to work on creating high-tech learning products are unlikely to gain much reward for their efforts—many universities make a policy of expropriating to themselves the patents or copyrights of faculty-created products, depriving professors of much motivation to create anything that might be commercially viable.

The list of such obstacles could be extended indefinitely. But the vast majority stem from the bureaucratic structure of the formal education system, not, as some "experts" claim, from inadequate technology or lack of government subsidies.

The agenda of educational restructuring that has recently evolved from growing disillusion with conventional "reforms" will bear little fruit unless a vastly expanded share of education's resources is committed to the research that is the wellspring of progress and productivity. But the massive increase in educational R&D that is desperately needed will not pay off in actual, productive innovation in the national learning enterprise without sweeping commercial privatization.

K–12 education will remain technologically backward in the absence of genuine market competition to attract customers (students and families) who control the income earned by the providers of instructional services and products. And higher education will continue to eschew efficient instructional technology as long as instruction is subservient to the priority of faculty research, selectivity takes precedence over productivity, and institutions compete only to generate elite credentials rather than real learning.

R&D AND INNOVATION: WHAT WORKS

Within the broad context of innovation is the nitty-gritty process of inventing and introducing new technologies. This process includes basic research, transfer of the discoveries of basic research into the invention and development of new technologies, application of technologies to provide practical solutions to real problems, and development of efficient production and marketing systems to make the new technologies affordable and accessible.

To understand how to remedy education's appalling absence of innovation, it's useful to see how the processes of research, development, and innovation work effectively in other sectors of the economy.

First and foremost: Profit is primary. Without the expectation of profit, sensible private investors and entrepreneurs will not make the investments and take the risks that creating and marketing a new technology entails. Fools may try to build a better mousetrap that cannot be sold profitably, but only at peril of going broke. Governments commonly try to foist technologies on the marketplace that no one wants to make because they can't be sold for more than what they cost to produce, but the results range from feeble to disastrous.

The distinction here is commonly put in terms of "market pull" and "technology push." Management studies have shown that 60 to 80 percent of technical innovations are mainly stimulated by the pull of market needs or demands.[237] An analysis by the Industrial Research Institute concluded that "most innovations come about as a result of the recognition of a market need or opportunity. While the push of a new technology is also important, it plays a distinctly secondary role."[238]

Policies on R&D and technological innovation are complex and controversial. The proper design and distribution of public and private roles in the innovation process will be debated endlessly. What specialists in the field uniformly agree about, however, is that commercialization is the minimum measure of success. Inventions that cannot ultimately be produced, sold, bought, and adopted in practical use, without coercion, don't count as successful innovations.

As Louis Tornatzky and Mitchell Fleischer and other R&D specialists have observed,[239] the U.S. agriculture sector offers an impressively successful model of a system for technological research, development, and innovation that has paid off richly in growing productivity and global competitiveness. It is crucial to recognize that the engine that drives the highly productive system for technological innovation in agriculture is the entrepreneurial, commercial farm.

The contrast between the potent agricultural technology system and the anemic mechanisms that pass for educational research could scarcely

> There is one sector in which many of the failings of [federal technology programs] have been surmounted, and significant successes have resulted. Over the past one hundred plus years, the United States has been building one of the most successful, and internationally competitive, high-technology industries that one could imagine. It is U.S. agriculture. ... It has relied on a highly developed system of basic and applied research, funded by a mixture of federal and state monies. It has tended to be highly focused both in terms of agency home and technical scope. It has also tended to be quite intelligent about addressing the whole technology life cycle, and all the technological innovation processes embedded therein, including in particular the problems of deployment.
>
> —Louis Tornatzky and Mitchell Fleischer
>
> *The Processes of Technological Innovation* (Lexington, Mass.: Lexington Books, 1990)

be more stark. The predominant absence of private, for-profit enterprise in the school and college sector removes the prime engine of innovation. Of education's meager total investment in research, most is allocated to the study of administrative and political issues of bureaucratic management. Support for basic research in the biological, neurological, or cybernetic sciences of learning is comparatively insignificant, while investment in the further development of commercial technologies for teaching and learning is almost nonexistent.

Lessons from R&D Experience

Economists recognize that government (or foundation) support for basic research is justified because the marketplace generally does not adequately reward the researcher for the full value of his contributions. Neither patent nor copyright laws protect the discovery of basic knowledge, yet new knowledge makes a valuable contribution to economic growth. Giving grant support to researchers therefore makes good economic sense.

Government (and sometimes foundation) efforts to promote technological innovation often go beyond just "research and development" to include "demonstration" and "dissemination" (or "deployment" or "diffusion") and "commercialization." From the great variety of these efforts, we've learned some things about what works and what doesn't.

What works, so far as the government role in innovation is concerned, is when government plays an active role on the boundaries of the innovation process, but leaves most of the development and marketing of technological products to the private sector. One of those important boundary conditions is support for basic R&D. The National Bureau of Standards carried out an exhaustive study of the government role in R&D under its Experimental Technology Incentives Program (ETIP) in the early 1970s, and found, in general, that government-supported R&D was most likely to result in a commercially adopted product when planned and managed with that goal in mind from the outset.

The public interest in technology and innovation sometimes goes beyond just the creation and marketing of new products and services. In areas where critical public goods are involved—such as national security, health, food, environmental protection, and arguably education—not just commercialization but widespread adoption of new and better technology is an important goal.

To examine the government role in promoting adoption of innovations, an instructive example is the way the federal government tried in the early 1970s to promote more fuel-efficient cars as an energy conservation measure. Rather than try to tell car manufacturers how to make fuel-efficient cars, the government stayed on the boundary: Federal CAFE (Corporate Average Fuel Economy) standards defined fuel economy goals that would rise each year, and that manufacturers would be penalized for not meeting. Further, the government had the Environmental Protection Agency test the fuel economy of each model, and required car dealers to post a sticker showing the test results in every new car's window. Combined with deregulation of fuel prices, the program gave consumers the motive and the information to buy fuel-efficient automobiles, and gave the manufacturers incentive to develop cars with better fuel economy.

The most effective measures in this conservation initiative were those that removed the key barrier to better fuel economy: the absence of an informed, free market. Deregulating prices gave consumers accurate information about the cost of fuel. And providing an independent, published measure of each car's fuel efficiency gave consumers the additional information the market alone might not have provided to determine how their choice of cars would affect how much they would have to spend on gas.

Whether the government was justified in using penalties to motivate automobile manufacturers to produce more fuel-efficient cars is highly questionable. Ideally, a deregulated market should create an efficient level of demand for fuel economy. But, in the past at least, the several years of lead time required to research, develop, design, and manufacture a new car meant that supply and demand could easily get out of sync. In fact, the downsized, fuel-efficient cars U.S. manufacturers designed in the late 1970s arrived on the market in the early 1980s just when oil prices had collapsed and consumers had renewed their preference for "muscle" over economy. At best, the CAFE program had the virtue of defining a goal for technology rather than getting the government into the business of telling industry how to invent and build a better car. But a National Research Council report concluded that steep increases in fuel taxes, to raise the cost of fuel at the pump, would be a more efficient way to promote greater fuel economy than the CAFE standards.[240]

We also have learned some things that do not work. The "mousetrap" approach—where government supports research for its own reasons and then hopes that developers will beat a path to its door—doesn't work very well at all. Over 90 percent of the research the federal government has paid for over the years has failed to spawn commercially successful products.

Another approach that doesn't work is "micromanagement" of the innovation process, where the government tries to create new products and get them to be used, usurping most of the role of the private sector. An egregious example is "Transbus"—a federal program that tried to develop, from scratch, a transit bus that would be easily accessible to the handicapped, fuel efficient, and altogether ideal. The Department of Transportation's prototype was so expensive that one critic figured out that it would be cheaper to provide a chauffeured limousine for every handicapped person in the country than to have cities adopt Transbus.

One of the most popular measures intended to promote innovation also turns out to be rarely effective: "demonstration" projects or programs. Because the impulse to demonstrate change is so common among would-be education and training reformers, the shortcomings of demonstrations are particularly important to understand.

The general idea of demonstrations is to stimulate market demand for an innovation that R&D has developed to a point of technical and economic feasibility. The rationale for demonstrations subsidized by government or nonprofit organizations is that, left to itself, the private market will fail to beat a path fast enough or big enough to the door where the better mousetrap has been made. The demonstration is supposed to stir up excitement by communicating: "Look at this wonderful new mousetrap. It's better than anything you've ever seen and you really should want one."

As reasonable as the concept sounds, in practice most demonstrations fail to satisfy the rather special conditions needed to achieve the desired result. A crucial requirement is that the innovation be commercially feasible when demonstrated, and further that there is a strong production and marketing system in place that is ready to commercialize the new technology when demand appears.

Demonstrations work best under the rare circumstance when lack of knowledge among potential adopters is the main obstacle to commercial success. Demonstrating technology that is unproven and unready is unlikely to stimulate demand and even may have the opposite effect—demonstrating failure and thereby discouraging interest in effective technology when it comes along. Demonstration is unlikely to spark commercialization when there is little demand for what the innovation does, or when institutional or other barriers would make it difficult for consumers to buy the innovation even if they wanted it. The paradox of demonstrations is that when uncertainty is high they rarely work; and when there is little uncertainty about the usefulness and desirability of an innovation, demonstrations probably are not needed.[241]

In general, we know that government works best at the extreme ends of the innovation process: supporting basic R&D, and removing barriers to adoption of desirable innovations. The government role can be powerful, even essential to the success of very large-scale, high-cost, high-risk innovations—such as building transcontinental railroads, developing a national electric power grid, or creating a commercial space-satellite communications industry. Even then, markets and private enterprise are the best engines we have found for the actual creating of innovation.

Lessons from Automation Experience

Technology doesn't have much economic value if it just sits on the shelf. The real economic power of invention is realized only when innovations are widely adopted by the people who can benefit from them. From the wide experience of factory automation and office automation, we have learned some things about the adoption of the kinds of innovations that can advance learning.[242]

First, new technology has as much capability to make things worse as to make them better. Technology is a magnifier and it can magnify the bad as well as the good. Office automation, for instance, held out the vision of the "paperless office"; but many offices used word processing technology to simply expand the amount of paper produced.

Planning innovation also is as likely to make things worse as to make them better. Most technological disasters followed thorough planning. In general, things are more likely to get worse than better in the early stages of diffusion of an innovation because innovation requires learning, learning implies trial and error, and when dealing with the new and unfamiliar one is more likely to make errors.

The most important lesson from automation in these other areas is that the specific form in which automation is introduced and applied makes a big difference in the direction and magnitude of performance change. In particular, we know from widespread experience in factories and offices that changes in organization, management, and human resources account for about 80 percent of the potential productivity gains from automation. Hardware and software alone are a relatively small part of the story.

Another fundamental rule about technology, which has broad implications for innovation, is simply that *scale counts*. The scale of a technical system determines much about its impact and utility.

For instance, environmentalists among others have dreamed for years about replacing polluting gasoline-burning automobiles with electric vehicles. That replacement may occur, but it will require a radical transformation of the entire structure of our society. The reason is a matter of scale. Gasoline is an incredibly dense energy source. The power delivered to your car by a single service station gas pump is equivalent to about 10 megawatts of electricity; a service station with 15 pumps represents 150 megawatts of delivered electric power. Since about two-thirds of electric power is lost in generation and transmission, 450 megawatts of electric generating capacity would be needed to replace one gas station. That's the equivalent of one large electric power plant for every two gas stations replaced.

For similar reasons, the scale and rate of growth in the power and speed of knowledge age technology make the ongoing developments in computation and telecommunication qualitatively different from other forms of technological innovation. Nothing else has ever moved so far so fast.

Today's microchip computer that replaces a roomful of equipment of a decade ago is not just a shrunken big computer—it's a whole new set of possibilities. For instance, advanced military aircraft utilize structural designs that are aerodynamically too unstable for a human to control manually. A human pilot cannot fly these craft without the aid of tiny computers that feverishly adjust the airplane's controls hundreds of times each second. If the computers were to die suddenly (a contingency designers take great pains to prevent), a fly-by-wire aircraft such as the F-16 would likely tear itself apart in midair before it crashed. On the other hand, the airplane could fly much better without the human pilot, because it can execute and survive the stress of maneuvers that would kill its human passenger.

Research, Experimentation, and Evaluation in Education

Many innovations in education have been experimented with over a period of decades. The record shows that many innovations that offered real value nevertheless were never implemented or incorporated into the education system. Orderly plans for experimentation, demonstration, and adoption rarely lead to systemic innovation or transformation.

Why has the R&D process in education often been so unproductive? There are several reasons. One, very simply, is that the absence of competitive markets and the profit motive has been the kiss of death for attempts at innovation in education.

For example, a few years ago, two research reports appeared at the same time that showed the difference market forces make. One reported that the addition of oat bran to diet could significantly help reduce the level of blood cholesterol—an important factor in heart disease. The other report revealed that an innovative design of adult literacy programs could substantially reduce illiteracy. The clinical approach and statistical reliability of the findings in these two research efforts were very similar. Yet the oat bran study was followed within a few months by a flood of oat bran cereals, breads, muffins, and other commercial products into the market-

Du Pont's [senior vice president for research Alexander] MacLachlan observes: "Once upon a time the pearls in the oysters were so plentiful that we would just go ahead and explore the technology, bring something out and tell the customer: 'Here it is, what do you want to do with it?' That worked pretty well with nylon and teflon, kevlar, lycra and so forth. But we have shifted very fast to involving the customer earlier and having him help us figure out whether a new product would be of value to him."

The company now has a formal, ongoing relationship with potential customers in the auto, electronics and fiber industries—trying to determine what products Du Pont might develop that would be useful three to five years down the road.

It is a pattern one can find repeated at many large corporations. . . .

Bellcore, the research arm formed to serve the needs of the seven regional telephone companies . . . has always had a more practical, here-and-now orientation than the esteemed Bell Laboratories from which it sprang. But Bellcore's new president, George H. Heilmeier, is determined to pull its ties to the marketplace even tighter in the years ahead.

"We're trying to get everyone in this organization to recognize that everybody has a customer," declares Heilmeier. "Our job is to satisfy that customer."

Dan Cordtz, "Corporate R&D: A Special Report," *Financial World* (Oct. 1, 1991)

place, touting their advantages to the consumer's health. In contrast, virtually nothing followed the discovery of the more effective literacy technology—the academic monopoly denied any real market opportunity to profit from the scientific findings.

As this last case suggests, a common complaint among education researchers is that very little of what has been discovered to make teaching and learning more effective has been applied in practice. The equally common mistake in the education establishment is to attribute this failure to insufficient "dissemination"—jargon for "getting the word out."

The real reason is that what passes for education research is doomed by one fatal flaw—the absence in academia's socialist economy of a real customer. Or, more precisely, there is a division between the customer—the politicians who pay the bills—and the consumer—the student who uses educational services and products—that obliterates the normal discipline of supply and demand.

In the industrial research arena, it is now accepted wisdom that the customer must be a crucial player for research, development, and commercialization to succeed. Without the information generated by the interplay of vendor and customer in a competitive marketplace, there is no way to know what unmet needs justify the risk of R&D investments. And only the customer ultimately can determine "what works" in the fountain of potential innovations that research spawns.

But education "research" generally doesn't even lead to "development," much less innovation or anything resembling (gasp!) commercialization, because the researchers have no market or customer for their product. Nor do they care.

For instance, a critique of America 2000 by Michael Kirst, a celebrated education researcher at Stanford University, takes the president's plan to task for failing to follow the research goals defined in a National Academy of Education report Kirst codirected: "We need such overarching priorities to guide both research and practice," Kirst complains; "what we don't need is more random innovation."

In Kirst's view, the main reason that Experimental Schools and similar programs have come and gone, over a period of decades, while failing to yield any widespread innovation in schools, is that "[a]lmost all education research has not been funded at levels sufficient to allow intensive and comprehensive experimentation and collaboration with education practitioners." Instead, Kirst and company think we need "longitudinal experiments and demonstration" to create "a systematic knowledge base established over time and under varying circumstances."[243]

Cutting through all this ed-speak gobbledygook, what Kirst and his Academy cronies are saying is that, given a blank check and an eternity, they can perfect socialism in the laboratory. This is like the infamous Captain Queeg of *The Caine Mutiny* using "mathematical logic" to prove who stole the quart of strawberries that was never stolen in the first place.

Kirst and his ilk have little experience with—and less enthusiasm for—customers, markets, or capitalism in general. They disdain "random innovation," the hallmark of a free economy.

Moreover, the research cabal of our socialized education system wouldn't know a customer from a carbuncle. They see their clients as "education practitioners," ed-speak for teachers and maybe principals. But teachers and principals are neither consumers nor customers—they don't use the end product and they have little or no control of the money that pays for it. In the socialist world of academia, teachers or principals or deans are the domestic equivalent of Soviet apparatchiks; customers are commissars; and the consumers of learning are impotent serfs.

A second barrier to innovation in education is the time factor. It has been said that it takes at least twelve years to demonstrate the value of an educational innovation. Head Start took twenty years to show significant results of its effectiveness—in fact the early evaluations of Head Start were generally negative. Because many of the policy goals of childhood education are presumed to be very long-term, it is inherently difficult to show quick success from an attempted innovation.

But the rapid pace of improvement and obsolescence of many computer, communications, and other technologies simply won't wait for this kind of plodding assessment. With new generations of technology arriving every couple of years (or less), and turbulent social changes rippling off the wake of these technological revolutions, decades-long evaluations are neither meaningful nor even feasible. Educational evaluation research that takes a decade or two to complete won't describe "what works," but only "what worked" in an era that is already bygone when the results are published.

In stunning contrast to the sludgelike ooze of education's development-less "research," industrial R&D is hurtling down an ever faster track. While American firms are pressing their research labs to get closer and more responsive to the needs of the marketplace, Peter Drucker observes that the Japanese are thoroughly reconstructing their R&D programs to generate three new products with the effort previously required to produce just one. The key to the more productive pace of R&D, as Drucker sees it, is that leading Japanese companies now have a deadline in place for *abandoning* a brand-new product the first day it is marketed.[244]

But no one in the education "research" world is planning now to abandon the multimedia PC in favor of the next generation of automated learning technology. The change-o-phobic education establishment never plans

By deciding in advance that they will abandon a new product within a given period of time, the Japanese force themselves to go to work immediately on replacing it, and to do so on three tracks:

One track *(kaizen)* is organized work on improvement of the product with specific goals and deadlines—e.g., a 10% reduction in cost within 15 months and/or a 10% improvement in reliability within the same time, and/or a 15% increase in performance characteristics—and enough in any case to result in a truly different product. The second track is "leaping"—developing a new product out of the old. The best example is still the earliest one: Sony's development of the Walkman out of the newly developed portable tape recorder. And finally there is genuine innovation.

—Peter F. Drucker

"Japan: New Strategies for a New Reality," *The Wall Street Journal* (Oct. 2, 1991)

to abandon anything—it only "supplements" and "enhances." The academic apparat has yet to fully master the telephone, much less television.

Educators and politicians are still wrangling over whether to let students use pocket calculators on math tests. Meanwhile Japanese and American companies are now designing computers free of either keyboards or screens that will be worn as articles of clothing, and that will project holographic images in midair while conversing with the user in plain language.

A third barrier to wringing much innovation out of the sponge of education research is the considerable hazard in any kind of experimental process in zooming from small scale to large scale. Things that work on a small scale may not work so well on a large scale, and vice versa. Therefore, even well-crafted experiments and demonstrations may not provide persuasive evidence for implementing an innovation broadly.

But the real value or impact of an innovation may not be visible until it achieves large-scale application. A few television sets are a novelty; one hundred million television sets define a way of life.

Research and experimentation in education to some extent actually have reduced the prospects for innovation. The perceived if not actual "failure" of previous experiments, demonstrations, or attempted innovations provides fodder for resistance to innovation today: "We tried that five years ago—it didn't work." Alternatively, experimentation can serve to postpone basic change; administrators (or other institutional stakeholders) will claim that innovations should not be incorporated into standard practice until the results of long-term experimental evaluations are available. These are just a few of the ways in which pseudoinnovation becomes an instrument of what sociologist Donald Schon calls "dynamic conservatism" rather than a force for real change.[245]

A coconspirator in public education's long history of pseudoinnovation is the "add-on" syndrome: that is, reliance on "soft" money from federal, foundation, or corporate grants to finance attempted innovations that are simply added on to the established system. A wealth of experience shows that the attempt to "add-on" innovations with external support, and without internal structural change—especially commitment of resources in the educational system's core budget—has been almost totally unsuccessful.

The most surefire way to tell whether an innovation is for real or is artificial is to look at its funding. Unless an innovation is paid for directly by those who stand to benefit from it, its chances to flourish are dubious at best. Of course in the early stages of an innovation's lifetime, it may be appropriate in rare instances to subsidize its introduction, to give consumers a chance to try it out and develop a real demand for it. But an innovation that has no plan or prospect for the transition from subsidized "demonstration" to adoption as something users will pay for out of their normal budget has little prospect for survival.

CURRENT ASSETS

The effort to create an effective national hyperlearning technology development program does not have to start with a blank slate. The U.S. has some valuable R&D assets to build on, probably more than any other nation.

But the existing R&D base is woefully inadequate. Estimates are that no more than a hundred researchers are actively working on the science and technology of learning in the whole country, maybe even in the whole world. The projects that are going on are incredibly self-contained and isolated from the work in other relevant fields. Worst, there is almost no link of the existing learning technology R&D to commercialization.

For instance, the Institute for the Learning Sciences, based at Northwestern University in Evansville, Illinois, is one of the more technically solid centers. ILS founder and director Roger Schank is a real scientist with recognized stature in the field of AI research. The staff of a couple of dozen bright young techies Schank has assembled at ILS is equally impressive.

Schank has a passionate, almost obsessive commitment to applying psychological and computer science to reinventing education. So he forces the work at ILS to focus not on abstruse theory but creation of effective, working instructional products. Because many of the R&D projects have corporate sponsors such as Andersen Consulting, IBM, and Ameritech, there is even some linkage of ILS's work to the commercial world.

But ILS falls far short of an ideal HL technology laboratory. For one thing, its staff and budget are much too small to incorporate the wide range of disciplines of science and technology that need to be applied to the complex business of learning. Like many brilliant scientists, Schank's ego (or at least confidence) can seem as extraordinary as his talent. Schank is unwavering in his conviction that software engineering is far and away *the* most important thing in learning technology, and that nothing else much matters. Within the field of AI software, he further has an ardent commitment to the techniques called "case-based reasoning" and little enthusiasm or even tolerance for other approaches.

Schank may be right in some of these judgments, but I think he's wrong about others. Be that as it may, his intense focus and discipline of ILS's work gives the organization a narrow, even esoteric cast. ILS may be a shining star in learning R&D but it's hardly a constellation, much less a galaxy.

Moreover, ILS's involvement in the commercialization of the gadgets it's working on is tenuous at best. Like many academic researchers, the ILS staff evince a left-leaning view of political economy—at the least, they show little concern for the commercial development and marketing of their creations. Schank, who boasts of gourmet tastes in food and wine, took a stab at a commercial venture aimed at selling the products of his work a few years ago that didn't pan out. One of Schank's genuine charms is that he confesses his limitations as glibly as he touts his scientific encyclicals—he readily admits that politics and commerce are not the areas where his greatest interests or talents lie.

The corporate sponsors of ILS projects generally seem to be more interested in developing tools for internal training applications than in developing products that can be sold profitably. When one sponsor asked for evidence that a glitzy, multimedia training program would be cost-effective to actually use, the ILS staff seemed befuddled, even vexed, at such a "bean-counter" question.

The strengths and weaknesses of ILS can be seen elsewhere. Another center seriously studying the technology of learning is the Institute for Research on Learning. Housed in a modest one-level building on a quiet street near the Stanford University campus in Palo Alto, California, IRL was founded in 1986 with a $5 million grant from Xerox initiated by David Kearns, then the company's CEO. By focusing research on computer technologies and artificial intelligence, the Institute was to be "dedicated to train the so-called untrainable," in the word of a Xerox media campaign that aimed to induce other corporations to join in financing the program.

IRL assembled a small but talented and even visionary staff of researchers covering a healthy mix of disciplines, from computer science to anthropology. The Institute has benefited since the beginning from its association with Xerox's famous Palo Alto Research Center, and particularly the oversight provided by John Seeley Brown, a leading light in the AI field who is PARC's vice president for advanced research.

But the other corporate partners mostly failed to show up, probably in large part because of Kearns's tactical blunder of launching IRL with a blitz of self-congratulating media hoopla before securing commitments from other companies in private—bigwigs simply do not like to be viewed as me-too-ers. Any effective link of IRL's learning R&D to commercialization was largely severed when Xerox divested the one business unit, Xerox Learning (now Learning International), that might have developed and marketed the kinds of products IRL was supposed to create. IRL languished as Kearns's attention drifted to other, political objectives, and with Kearns's departure in 1991, Xerox's modest support withered away.

A new director, Peter Henschel, was hired to try to salvage the Institute. Henschel had no background in R&D but brought impressive political leadership skills honed as a deputy mayor of San Francisco and a longtime economic development activist. Henschel's immediate impact was to bring IRL's high-sounding but vague mission into articulate focus.

"Our mission is research on *learning,* not education," he told me. "IRL's role is to develop useful learning technology for clients who want to put these tools to work."

Like ILS and the rest of the sparse constellation of centers doing research on learning, IRL is far too small to cover the scope of this huge field. But, perhaps because of his real-world background, Henschel seems more concerned with commercialization than the head of any other learning lab. He appreciates that IRL's future depends on its success in helping clients develop commercially viable products. Whether IRL can retool itself as an industrial laboratory and endure the financial turmoil and staff turnover its restructuring entails remains to be seen. If so, IRL could become a valuable HL industry asset.

The short list of centers doing R&D of high-tech hyperlearning includes the Learning Research and Development Center at the University of Pittsburgh. LRDC director Lauren Resnick and a capable group of other cognitive scientists have done important research on how people think and learn. LRDC's expertise has been applied especially to issues of workplace competency. The Center is developing a set of examinations and diverse assessments to demonstrate that youth have mastered the basic abilities needed for employment, under a multimillion-dollar contract with the National Center for Education and the Economy based in Rochester, New York.

Seymour Papert, a notable pioneer of AI research and of computer-based instruction in particular, is directing an epistemology and learning group at MIT's famous Media Lab. One of the group's more celebrated projects, funded by a $3 million grant from Nintendo of America, is exploring how the entrancing power of video games can be applied to instructional programs designed by children themselves. But there is little evident concern or capability for developing commercially viable products in the Papert group's efforts.

Two small centers for instructional technology have been funded at less than a million dollars a year by the U.S. Department of Education over the past decade. After initially funding the Educational Technology Center at Harvard for five years, the department switched its support to the Center for Technology in Education, a cooperative venture based at Bank Street College in New York that also involves Brown University and Bolt Berenek Newman, a Cambridge, Massachusetts, consulting firm. While both centers have engaged talented staff, they have narrowly focused on developing a few interesting software products, and have had no impact of national significance.

Apple Computer fellow Alan Kay—a computer industry pioneer who played a key role in the development of the user-friendly Macintosh and was one of the founders of Xerox's PARC—and Ann Marion have established the Apple Vivarium Program at the Open School: Center for Individualization in Los Angeles. Their effort aims "to better understand the value computers might have as supporting media" in education, and is especially focused on the study of biology and ecology.[246] Once more, no concern or process for commercialization is evident.

These are noteworthy examples of what may be a few dozen centers, programs, and projects scattered around the U.S. that constitute the current base of civilian assets focused on learning R&D and its specific application to instruction. They are small in scale, narrowly focused, meagerly funded, and almost uniformly detached from the creation and marketing of commercially viable products.

The total of these civilian R&D efforts targeted on learning and teaching is dwarfed by the military investment in HL technology. The Office of Naval Research, the Army Research Institute, individual training arms of the armed services, and the Defense Advanced Research Projects Agency invested over $300 million in 1991 in programs staffed by scores of scientists and technicians in an array of technical fields, organized to study thinking and learning and to develop advanced instructional systems.

The dynamo driving the growing application of simulations and games and other HL products to work-connected learning is neither education nor formal military or corporate training, but the entertainment industry. Movies, music, and video games are the major magnets for the most sophisticated tools and talent.

While a few years ago policymakers tried to encourage transfer of Defense Department instructional technology to civilian use, the rapid pace of technological advance in the entertainment industry now has the flow of innovation headed back from "Hollywood" to military and other educational applications. Perceptronics, a California game designer, developed an elaborate tank battle game for the Army called *Simnet* which links a hundred or more computer-based, full-sized M1 tank simulators in mock battles. The communications "net" of *Simnet* can link NATO tank crews located anywhere throughout the United States, Canada, and Europe, in simultaneous combat exercises on a virtual-reality battlefield. Perceptronics also has worked on adapting its popular F-16 Falcon flight–simulator PC game as an inexpensive training tool for the Pentagon.[247]

Behind the Hollywood dynamo, the bulk of the key research that is laying the groundwork for the twenty-first-century hyperlearning enterprise is going on in the major industrial and independent laboratories that are concerned not with instruction per se, but with the technological "threads" of HL spinning out of work in computer science, artificial intelligence, communication, biotechnology, cognitive science, neuroscience, and molecular psychology. These include AT&T's Bell Labs, Bellcore (the joint R&D center of the regional phone companies), and IBM's Thomas J. Watson Research Center, as well as R&D organizations with multiple corporate sponsors such as MCC in Austin, Texas, and the Media Lab at MIT.

In the public, civilian sector, the most important research assets for advancing understanding of the brain and mind are the National Institutes of Health, and particularly the National Institute of Mental Health, along with corporate and university laboratories that complement their work.

The small learning research centers noted above pale beside the Beckman Institute for Advanced Science & Technology. Established in 1985 at the University of Illinois with a $40 million gift from Arnold O. Beckman, founder of Beckman Instruments, the Institute's mission is the study of the brain and the nature of intelligence. With more than 120 professors and over 450 graduate and postdoctoral students, the Beckman Institute applies a critical mass of talent to the study of the mind and thought—including learning—that is virtually unmatched.[248]

The R&D base relevant to advanced HL technology also includes a bunch of "star" researchers scattered among U.S. universities. Carnegie Mellon University in Pittsburgh contains an important cluster of leaders in the AI field, including Herbert Simon and Allen Newell, and in robotics, including the theoretician Hans Moravec and William "Red" Whittaker, director of the Field Robotics Center, who actually builds intelligent mobile robots. The list of such stars could be extended to include Marvin Minsky at MIT, Douglas Hofstadter at the University of Illinois, Howard Gardner at Harvard, Walter Freeman at UCLA, Robert Sternberg at Yale, and others. They represent the rich intellectual resources that could be—but have not yet been—galvanized into a national hyperlearning R&D program.

What are not particularly useful assets for HL technology R&D are America's hundreds of colleges of education and their more than thirty thousand faculty. What passes for "research" in these institutions for the most part has little or no connection to the real science and technology of learning, much less the more exotic frontiers of HL. Nor do most ed school faculty have the kind of scientific or technical skills needed for productive work on HL technology development—two thirds of the members of the American Educational Research Association list "education" as their primary discipline, rather than any field of science or engineering, and only a quarter of the members even claim "research" as their major professional responsibility.[249] And these organizations and their denizens in most cases have zero interest in the commercial development of educational products and services—most would actually disdain the suggestion that education should be organized as a profitable enterprise.

Ditto the U.S. Education Department. The department's research arm, the Office of Educational Research and Improvement, spends about $60 million a year on academic paper shuffling and ticket punching posing as research. Independent individual researchers, carrying out studies they have initiated themselves, are crucial to a healthy research endeavor. But while 94 percent of the work supported by the National Science Foundation and 56 percent of the research funded by the National Institutes of Health is such independent field research, only 2 percent of OERI's budget falls in this category. Less than 6 percent of OERI's funds go to support basic research, aimed at developing new scientific knowledge, compared to 94 percent of NSF's and 60 percent of NIH's budgets.[250]

OERI and the department as a whole have almost no staff capability or program focus in real science and technology or any of the key domains of HL. The department funds a dozen or so "research centers," most of whose scientific bent, such as it is, is in the sociology of academic institutions and processes, not in biological, physical, or information sciences or engineering. Another handful of "regional laboratories" the Department supports are mainly charged with "disseminating" the thin gruel of education research, rather than functioning as real scientific laboratories.

The Education Department, the ed schools, and the rest of the education establishment have not made and are unlikely to make much useful contribution to real research and development of advanced learning technology. Not only are their standards of "research" meager, but they have no capacity or conviction for "development"—the process that leads to commercialization of products and services.

To bring the benefits of the HL revolution to all people, and not just the privileged elite, as swiftly as a fast-changing global economy demands, a far bolder approach is needed. The time has come for a massive, strategic investment in the development and commercial innovation of HL technology.

CHAPTER 11

INNOVATION FOR ENTERPRISE: BEYOND THE "NEW SCHOOL" CHARADE

• • •

Prince Potemkin, Catherine the Great's chief of staff, gained notoriety in eighteenth-century Europe for his ill-fated scheme for Russia's economic development. Potemkin plotted a string of "model" communities along the road from Moscow to Odessa in the hope of igniting growth in the unde veloped corridor. But Potemkin's plan failed to provide these communities any genuine economic reason for existing. When he and the Empress took the European press on a tour of the contrived hamlets, the absence of commercial activity or even people in most of the shiny new buildings made the term "Potemkin villages" a perennial laughingstock.

Unfortunately, the scheme for a "New Generation of American Schools" that forms the second cornerstone of the Bush administration's America 2000 strategy is another in a long history of Potemkin's village blunders. The best thing about this element of the administration's plan is that it explicitly calls public attention to the need to reinvent the nation's education systems. But its good intentions are destined for failure by inept, ill-conceived tactics.

Responsibility for the "new schools" initiative of the America 2000 campaign has been vested in a New American Schools Development Corporation (NASDC—commonly called *nazz-deck*), a nonprofit organization created by a group of corporate executives at the White House's request. The original administration plan called for NASDC to raise $150–200 mil-

> One recurrent theme that appears in all the missteps and failed [technological innovation] programs over the past few decades is the ad hoc nature of how the programs are designed, implemented, and, most important, evaluated. . . . [T]here is a body of research and analytic work about how one might design technology-related programs, but for the most part, program design has been given to people who are ignorant of that tradition.
>
> —Louis Tornatzky and Mitchell Fleischer
>
> *The Processes of Technological Innovation* (Lexington, Mass.: Lexington Books, 1990)

lion in donations, to fund up to seven so-called "R&D teams" of consultants and think tank gurus. The mission of the teams was to "set aside all traditional assumptions about schooling and all the constraints that schools work under," and then "radically alter" and "redesign" the fabric of schools "to produce extraordinary gains in student learning."

The second key part of the initiative called on Congress to provide $1 million in start-up funding for each of "535 + New American Schools" intended to apply the radical innovations conceived by NASDC's would-be R&D program. The figure 535 is a magic number inside the Beltway: It is the total of the 100 senators and the 435 members of the House of Representatives. Lo and behold—the administration plan called for the creation of at least one "New American School" in each congressional district, ostensibly to assure a broad "distribution" of new schools in every part of the country.

While called a "research and development" program, NASDC resembles a genuine R&D program about as much as a lightning bug resembles a lightning bolt. NASDC will do nothing to close education's giant R&D gap and offers no promise of fomenting significant innovation in the technologically moribund education industry. Besides being ineffective, the New American Schools program risks doing more harm than good by reinforcing the obsolete notion of "school" as a building-bound entity, and by diverting energy and funds from the kinds of innovation efforts that are really needed and that can work.

If research and development in the U.S. education sector were funded at the levels of average or high-tech businesses, from $8 billion to $20 billion or more would be invested in R&D on learning and teaching *every year*—the actual expenditure is at least twenty to eighty times less.

The $200 million the Bush administration proposed to raise in private charitable donations over five years would make as much of a dent in the R&D gap as the proverbial spit in the ocean. Boeing, a leading company in an important aircraft manufacturing industry, is investing $4–5 billion in R&D to develop just one new airplane, the 777—that's twenty to twenty-five times more R&D investment than the whole proposed New American Schools program, to create just one new product in an aircraft industry that is less than one-fifth the size of the U.S. education industry. Sure, jumbo jets are expensive items—but the annual budget of the New York City public schools alone could buy over fifty of the new 777s.

What's "New"?

It may seem like a semantic quibble, but there are some real problems with the very name "New American Schools." The key point of this book is that "new" and "school" are contradictory. "New school" is as relevant to twenty-first-century learning as "new horse" is to twentieth-century transportation. "Building-less school" might be used to label knowledge age learning enterprises with the same cultural caution with which "horseless carriage" was originally applied to the automobile. But continuing to apply the name "school" to learning systems that bear no resemblance to what most people think a school is may just confuse consumers and delay progress.

In our commercial society, "new" doesn't really mean new, but maybe just improved—"New Tide" may get whites whiter and colors brighter but we know it's still just more of the same old suds. So there is a real hazard that talk of "new schools" will simply channel thinking into the same old groove of tinkering and improving instead of replacing.

There is even a problem with the use of "America" in New American Schools and America 2000. It reinforces the wrongheaded notion that American education is inferior to other countries' systems and that the purpose of radical restructuring is to catch up to these supposed competitors. The real problem is that schooling is globally obsolete and needs to be replaced everywhere. The whole world needs high-tech hyperlearning. America faces the lucrative opportunity to commercialize this truly new technology and export it, at great profit, to the rest of the planet.

The Mouse That Roared

The mechanics of the New American Schools program simply cannot produce meaningful change. First, the scale of the effort is almost pathetically puny. Even if 535 gee-whiz schools get created, they would leave the other 99.5 percent of America's K–12 students untouched and unserved, not to mention the forty million or so U.S. adults whose basic education needs a boost.

Of course the idea of the New American Schools, its advocates would argue, is not just to create five hundred to a thousand nifty new schools for a privileged few—it's supposed to inspire radical change throughout the education system. But the architects of this scheme have offered no strategy for achieving such a large-scale result and there is every reason to doubt that that's what will happen.

> "We are all seriously kidding ourselves if we believe that business-led charity is the answer to the current crisis. It costs $250 million per hour to run American K–12 education. That means all the money business currently spends annually on philanthropy could run our schools for about 90 minutes."
>
> —Chris Whittle
>
> Nancy J. Perry, "Where We Go from Here," *Fortune* (Oct. 21, 1991)

If it really takes at least a million dollars in start-up funds to create a newfangled school (the NASDC plan assumes there will be additional contributions), that means that replacing or reinventing the other 110,000

American K–12 schools would require over $100 billion just in front-end money. The NASDC crew has not had a word to say about where that kind of funding is supposed to come from. With the federal government running a $400 billion annual deficit, and many state and local governments also facing fiscal austerity, there is no evident source of new government money to meet such a demand. Philanthropy? Corporate contributions to elementary and secondary education were $264 million in 1990.[251] Total corporate donations for every kind of charitable cause are about $70 billion a year. And a hundred billion bucks is a lot of supermarket register tapes.

The large quantity of funding needed for real innovation in education exists in the present education budget, and can be acquired by reallocating some of the funds now being wasted by bureaucracy and obsolescence. But that solution requires political leadership and action, not a thousand points of light—or "pints of Lite," as one wag put it.

Models of Futility

Even if more funds were provided, the New American Schools stratagem is just another "model schools" program of the sort that has failed countless times before to foment real change in education. As Linda Darling-Hammond of Columbia University and numerous other critics have pointed out, we have had numerous experimental and model schools over the past several decades, and there are hundreds of such "break-the-mold" schools in operation in America today, all to no avail.

The pilot and demonstration strategy for promoting innovation in education has not worked, does not work, and cannot work. The America 2000 crafters, Edward Fiske (former education editor of *The New York Times*), Thomas Toch (an editor at *U.S. News & World Report*), and other fans of model schools cite "commendable efforts" such as Theodore Sizer's Coalition of Essential Schools, RJR Nabisco's Next Century Schools, and the Saturn School of Tomorrow in St. Paul as paradigms of progress. But none of these efforts has or ever will result in system-wide transformation of educational design and practice.

The thinking of model school advocates is plagued by the logical error of misplaced concreteness. This type of error is illustrated by an ancient tale from the Middle East of a man who was found one night by a passerby scrupulously hunting for his keys in the dust beneath a street lamp. When asked by the passerby where he lost them, the man explains that he dropped the keys somewhere near the door of his house. "Then why are you looking for your keys here?" the passerby asks, and the man replies, "Because the light is much better here than in front of my house."

Model schools are wimpy attempts to grope for innovation "where the light is better" instead of seizing the political keys to serious change. Model schools are Potemkin villages that create the illusion of progress without the reality. The core problem with the "Classroom of Tomorrow" and the "School of the Future" is that *they always will be*.

The obsolescence and failure of education is rooted not in the design of schools but in the design of school *systems*. Those who, undeniably with the best intentions, propose to reinvent education one classroom at a time and one school at a time simply do not understand the behavior of large-scale systems. They seem not to comprehend that in the difficult task of trying to change very big systems, the scale and form of change is critical.

For instance, Thomas Edison did not build an electric industry with 535 light bulbs. He started by changing over the entire city of New York—the biggest city in the country and the world at the time—from gas light to electric light. Edison did not create the "New American Gaslight Company"—he replaced the existing gas lighting industry with a whole new technology and organization. Doing that required an intense legal and political battle with the established, rich, and powerful gas monopoly. Edison did not intend to coexist with his competitors or inspire them to adopt his inventions—he aimed to eradicate them. And he understood that the primary change needed to make electric lighting universal was not hundreds of light fixtures or supply lines but only one thing: a change in the *law* that sought to protect the gas companies from competition.

At its best, New American Schools is a well-intended blunder. At worst, it's a cynical flim-flam. You have to be born pretty recently to believe that proposing to put a Potemkin school in each congressional district has anything to do with geographic distribution—it's the same old pork-barrel political scam that has left America's government drowning in an ocean of red ink. The plan clearly is to provide 535 photo opportunities for politicians, paid for by the taxpayer at a million bucks a pop. Ironically, even as a cynical political ploy the plan is a blooper. Over 90 percent of U.S. public education funds come from state and local governments, not from the federal level—the New American Schools pork-barrel bribe is targeted on the wrong legislators.

In any case, photo-op reformism is unlikely to help ignite the radical transformation of education the world now needs. For one thing, it's hard to take pictures of the systems and processes of HL technology, many of which are so broadly distributed and intangible that they are practically invisible. The more the camera focuses on buildings and bodies and even Tom Swift compuboxes and roboglitz, the more it risks distracting attention from what's *happening* behind the facade of Tomorrowland.

In America's high-tech and highly productive agriculture system, model or demonstration farms at most are only one minor part of a broadly developed system of research and innovation. The influence of models and demonstrations on agricultural innovation has been rather slow and incremental at best. But to the extent models or demonstrations are influential in U.S. agriculture at all it's because farmers are entrepreneurial capitalists, not state-employed bureaucrats, and "models" are economically self-sustaining.

Farmers do not look to model farms or demonstration projects only to make more corn—they also look to make more *money*. Sure, they are interested in the soil and the water and the color of the leaf and the richness of the grain. But if you want to get them actually to buy the new fertilizer or seed or whatever, you have to show them the books—the balance sheet, the profit-and-loss, the unglamorous non-photo-op financial data that tells them whether the new thing, whatever it is, is going to be profitable.

But model schools and educational demonstration projects virtually never model the *economic* conditions necessary for technological innovations to thrive. Again, the key is in the financing of these programs, not so much in the gadgetry or gimmicks they put on display.

For instance, the Saturn School of Tomorrow in St. Paul has been a much-favored example of what America 2000 and other model school programs hope to emulate. President Bush even paid a heavily publicized visit to the school in September 1991 as a model sortie into photo-op reformism.

On the surface, the Saturn School is a pretty nifty initiative. This upper elementary school has students using computers and other tools about a third of the day while spending another third of their time in cooperative learning situations; groups students by skills rather than grade levels; pays teachers about 40 percent more than average while giving them greater on-site responsibilities; and extends the school year to forty-four weeks.

> I don't think you'd see technology used in business today if there were not consequences for not using it. I mean, it's used because firms have to use it, and if they don't use it they'll be out of business because somebody else is, and it's going to do things more efficiently, and do it better—whereas, we don't have that system in education. . . .
>
> I think that if there were rewards and punishments for doing things right, that people would be out there eagerly trying to figure out what technologies they need. They would be trying it. They would be testing it. And they would be doing something that's more important—constantly trying to make it work better for them. . . . [T]he incentive systems are essentially [what] would make the whole thing work.
>
> —Albert Shanker
>
> Testimony, Hearing on Educational Technology, Subcommittee on Technology and Competitiveness, U.S. House of Representatives, June 18, 1991

Perhaps most important, the school aims to individualize instruction by using a computer-based expert system to develop a "Personal Learning Program" for each student.

But the $1.8 million cost of starting the Saturn School (named after General Motors' new Saturn automobile line, whose success as an attempt at innovation has yet to be proven) was not financed through the normal school system budget. In particular, most of the $540,000 of new technology used in the school was supplied through donations from so-called "partners," including equipment from Control Data, Apple Computer, and Pioneer, and software from the Minnesota Educational Computer Corporation.[252]

The problem with these seemingly civic-minded giveaways is that they so distort the economics of innovation that whatever successes the model school may demonstrate become almost impossible to duplicate elsewhere. If school systems are unwilling to spend their own money on innovation in the first place, they are unlikely to be more willing to do so in the second place, or the hundredth place. But if it really takes two million bucks to modernize the technology of each school, as Saturn implies, then where is the $200 billion plus needed to upgrade all of the 110,000 schools in America supposed to come from? It sure isn't going to come from corporate charity. And if the school systems refuse to spend it from their own budgets in the beginning they won't in the end either. So no matter what academic gains the Saturn School may show off, as a goad to *systemic* innovation it is bound to flop.

The excuse that these giveaways and add-ons posing as "partnerships" are really "R&D" needed to develop effective products and markets doesn't hold up in the light of real market experience. A number of higher education projects during the past decade followed the same strategy as the Saturn School—big corporations gave away equipment and other goodies supposedly in partnership with major (usually rich) universities to develop advanced instructional systems. But most of these well-publicized projects failed to bear much fruit, and were almost universally bypassed by practical innovations driven by real market forces. For instance:

- Before the $35 million IBM gave Carnegie Mellon University for its "Andrew" project to develop the perfect computer user interface accomplished much, the market already had made the Apple Macintosh's user-friendly graphic interface a widely adopted standard.

- Brown University got $50 million in grants to develop software to combine pictures, sound, and other multimedia information in a free-form database. Before anything came out of the project, Apple had developed and commercially established HyperCard as the most popular product of this type.

- While MIT's widely heralded "Project Athena" was attempting to design the ideal academic computer network with $50 million worth of equipment donated by Digital Equipment Corp., dozens of less-celebrated universities simply got on with the business of weaving thousands of campus PCs in local area networks built with equipment and software provided by smaller but more entrepreneurial commercial suppliers.

- IBM gave away $100 million of its overpriced equipment to sixteen universities to develop educational software, with little practical outcome. Meanwhile thousands of college faculty were buying cheap PC "clones" with their own money and developing useful instructional applications with popular commercial software, not so much to add to their institution's aura as to save themselves some of the time and hassles of the much-lamented "teaching burden."[253]

The Saturn School and similar giveaway strategies for innovation are not only impotent but can be downright subversive. Giveaways of educational products and services by big corporations seeking to score PR points can poison the market for entrepreneurial firms that don't have deep pockets and that are trying to make an honest living by creating and selling this stuff.

When Japanese manufacturers sell memory chips or display screens in the U.S. below cost, U.S. companies call it "dumping" and scream to the federal government for protection. But when big U.S. computer companies discount or subsidize or just plain give away products to schools, they call it "charity" or "public relations" or "corporate responsibility." But the effect is the same: to starve entrepreneurs who have no cash cows to milk, thereby subverting competitive markets and withering innovation on the vine.

It's not inherently impossible for public schools to use their own money to purchase innovations. Some plucky school leaders have done it. One is Philip Grignon, superintendent of the South Bay Union Schools, an elementary district in Imperial Beach, California. Grignon has invested over $3 million of school budget funds in classroom computer networks, Wasatch Education Systems integrated learning system courseware, electronic mail, and other tools to improve the productivity of learning.

Will, not wealth, has been the key to innovation under Grignon's leadership. South Bay is no silk stocking community. More than two thirds of the students are minority, and more than half live below the poverty line. Yet Grignon finds a million dollars a year in the core school budget to constantly upgrade learning technology.

There are hundreds, maybe thousands, of rebellious innovators like Grignon in the ranks of America's school and college educators. In fact, a study by the National Association of Secondary School Principals confirmed what most of us would have guessed: What successes schools achieve in the existing bureaucratic system are the direct result of acts of "creative insubordination" by principals.[254] That anything innovative happens is thanks to people like Grignon and others of the impertinent minority who dare to break the rules and flout tradition.

But the rebels' influence is diluted in an ocean of millions of bureaucrats who experience no incentive to follow the pioneers' lead and who,

---

Perhaps the most interesting fact about South Bay's technology program is that it was purchased with state and local monies. No Chapter 1 funds. No IBM grants. No Wasatch "model school" sites. South Bay can afford their technology plan . . . because the district keeps a thin administrative layer.

—"South Bay Union Schools: Beating the Demographics of Failure," *Electronic Learning* (Sept. 1990)

---

rather, live in a political cocoon rich with motives to resist change. Snapshots of their apparent successes in the short run miss the common trend over time for the rebels' impacts to prove temporary. The average tenure of school superintendents is measured in only a few years. It's virtually impossible in the existing legal framework of the education bureaucracy to make innovations irreversible. Once the pioneering leader retires or moves on or is simply overwhelmed by persistent political opposition or the inevitable budget crunch, the situation usually reverts to "normal."

The Lead Balloon

Reflecting all these contradictions to an ill-conceived mission, the New American Schools Development Corporation took off with all the inspiration of the proverbial lead balloon. Contrary to the springtime proclamation from the White House steps touting NASDC as a bold "R&D" initiative, by the following fall NASDC's public request for proposals was insisting that it was "a design effort, not a research program." NASDC's chairman, former New Jersey governor Thomas Kean—whose pioneering of alternative certification of teachers probably was the only true act of education restructuring of the last decade—split the difference, describing NASDC as "not your typical R&D effort."

Perhaps stung by widespread and valid criticism that NASDC was nothing but another model schools program of the sort that has failed in the past, NASDC's solicitation took pains to protest, "This is not a request to establish 'model' schools." But, at the same time, Chairman Kean was declaring in newspaper ads, "This non-profit organization is charged with designing models for the best schools in the world. . . ."

While ostensibly a private sector initiative, NASDC doomed all hope of producing meaningful change by a bizarre policy commitment to prevent any *profitable* innovation from coming out of its efforts. Specifically, NASDC insisted that any "intellectual property" developed with the aid of NASDC funds would be entirely taken by NASDC. Moreover, grants would be awarded based on the willingness of partners in the so-called design teams to give away intellectual property—technology—they already own at "no or nominal cost" to schools, or at best to freely license the use of their property to schools based on the school's "ability to pay." Since schools almost universally deny any ability to pay for anything, the latter is just another form of giveaway.

When asked by a member of the audience at a November 1991 bidders' conference why any entrepreneur worth his salt would be interested in making such a suicidal deal, NASDC staff lamely explained that the intent of their giveaway policy was "to assure widespread dissemination" of all those nifty "break-the-mold" innovations that are going to miraculously fall on academia like manna from heaven. The retread AT&T and General Motors bureaucrats running NASDC, in their shift to the nonprofit universe, seem to have rediscovered Karl Marx just when the rest of the world had given up on him.

In fact, about the same time NASDC was proclaiming its "from-each-according-to-his-ability-to-each-according-to-his-means" business strategy, U.S. Secretary of Commerce Robert Mosbacher was in Warsaw scolding the Poles for their wholesale pirating of American intellectual property. "That one person could own the rights to a film or a novel, this is not quite natural yet in the Polish way of thinking," the head of an organization charged by Poland's government with chasing down copyright pirates tried to explain to a reporter.[255] Nor is the concept of property evidently natural yet to NASDC's way of thinking.

Besides its overall befuddlement and perverse romance with Marxism, the whole NASDC venture has been plagued by conflict of interest problems. Major corporations that contributed funds to NASDC, such as IBM, also were courted as partners in teams seeking grants. Suspicions were widespread that some of the "experts" who were to evaluate the grant proposals would also be involved in projects proposed for NASDC funding of up to $3 million. The plan to deal with these issues relied heavily on what NASDC staff described as "the honor system."

The overall unbusinesslike and antibusiness aura of NASDC seems to have thoroughly put off the corporate donors whose gifts were supposed to bankroll the operation. Of the $150–200 million in donations the Bush administration had called for in April, by a year later less than $50 million had been pledged, two thirds of which had been ginned up during the first month after NASDC's much-hyped debut. If corporate America has not yet figured out how to invest in the learning revolution, at least it's smart enough not to buy condos in a Potemkin village.[256]

Further good news came in early 1992 when the key congressional education committees killed the Bush administration's proposal for the "new schools" pork-barrel grants. The bad news: Congress's Democratic leaders replaced the administration's ill-conceived and feeble plan for innovation with an even worse, more-of-the-same giveaway of $850 million directly to the public education establishment.

THE RIGHT INNOVATION SOLUTION

A realistic and effective strategy for bridging the yawning chasm that now separates the education sector from the new world of hyperlearning bears no resemblance to New American Schools or the Point O'Light tactics of America 2000. Instead, the kind of national program needed to speed up the development of twenty-first-century HL technology and to make it available for popular benefit has four key requirements.

1. Top R&D Priority. First, the science and technology of mind, brain, and learning need to be elevated to a top priority in the national R&D agenda. That's a big change from their current status, not only in terms of funding but attention. The science and engineering communities have overlooked the strategic importance of learning science and technology almost as thoroughly as the education reform crowd has.

In the past year, a White House committee and a Pentagon committee each issued a list of "critical technologies" in which America must hold a leading position at peril of becoming uncompetitive and insecure. Nearly all the items on the lists were hard stuff like semicondinkies and biogoop and photowhizzers. Nothing to hint that "technology" gets connected somewhere with human performance.

For all the political blather about our education and workforce crises, the crucial technology of thinking and learning—the technology needed to enable more humans to use, coexist with, and even to create all this whiz-bang high-tech stuff—got no mention.

Basic R&D priorities have to be redrawn. For reasons I spelled out at length earlier, the emerging science and technology of hyperlearning hold the key to the entire knowledge age economy, not just for the U.S. but for the whole world. The real threat to our security and prosperity is a set of R&D objectives that ignore this imperative.

Space romantics keep alive a federal commitment to a multibillion-dollar space station the space science community has universally and persistently condemned as useless. Still breathing (barely) is the $10 billion (or more) superconducting supercollider (SSC)—a super-duper atom smasher that aims to add no more than an incomplete increment to cryptic cosmological theories, and that promises no economic benefit other than a welfare program for subatomic physicists and a windfall for some high-tech contractors and Texas land speculators.

A multibillion-dollar project to "map" all the genes in the human genome—an undeniably invaluable venture—goes forward by impulse of the Department of Energy (?!). But an Institute of Medicine committee that called for an equally valuable undertaking to map the even more complex structure of the human brain has floundered for lack of a potent national champion. And so the committee's mandate was reduced to timidly requesting a mere $10 million over five years for an enterprise more worthy of billions than annihilating protons in Texas or flying orbital ranch houses for city slickers to play space cowboy.[257]

I've dismissed many of the favored projects of the nation's technical elite rather facetiously. In truth, the electronic, optical, material, and biological technologies that commonly appear on various "critical" lists are undeniably important to further development of the modern economy. Indeed, many are important elements in the skein of HL technology.

But physical scientists and engineers have a common and dangerous tendency, in their obsession with the tangible, to overlook the ecology of things. When stuff takes priority over process, technology becomes the master of humanity, rather than its servant.

Henry David Thoreau—no fan of the Industrial Revolution—made the mordant observation that "Men do not ride the railroads, the railroads ride men." Well, both things were true then, and remain true now. Thoreau's Walden idyll was a personal indulgence, not a social blueprint—it was as self-limiting a utopian exercise as the Shakers' devout celibacy. Technology is the defining characteristic of humanity: The creation, use, and improvement of technology are the unique features that set humans apart from all other species. Whether technology was a Promethean gift or a Faustian bargain, the deal is as irrevocable as it is ancient. The only choice remaining is whether we ride our technology or it rides us.

The process that empowers humans to use tools rather than be used by them is itself a technology. Technical specialists may refer to it as "sociotechnical systems design" or "human factors engineering." Whatever the moniker, I view it as an essential element of HL technology—as I noted at the beginning of this book, what sets hyperlearning apart from the technical "threads" that make it up is the function of empowering humans to understand, control, and thrive in an environment of ever-smarter tools. To persist in omitting this technology of human liberation from our critical objectives for science and technology is to acquiesce in our own enslavement.

2. Major Investment.   Beyond recognition of hyperlearning as a critical technology, the second key requirement is to vastly increase the sheer volume of investment in learning R&D. At least a hundred times more than currently is being spent needs to be invested annually. Given that the education sector of the economy is mainly an information-based industry and that it is comparable in size to the health care sector, a reasonable level of R&D investment would be from $8 billion to $20 billion a year.

There is no likelihood or reason that this money should simply be added on to the nation's already bloated education bill. Most can and should come from reallocation of existing funds.

3. Strategic Organization.   Third, one of the glaring weaknesses in the existing skein of learning-related research activities is a great lack of coordination or even communication among the players. HL touches a dizzying array of technical fields—neuroscience, computer science, cognitive psychology, behavioral science, psychiatry, telecommunications, cybernetics, pharmacology, sociology, epistemology, linguistics, anthropology, genetics, and others. Currently there is no central forum where work in all these fields can be brought together to advance the state of hyperlearning technology. A multibillion-dollar program spanning efforts in so many disciplines will need some kind of effective national organization as well as practical networks for combining knowledge.

The United States has been slow to accept any notion that government has a responsibility for the generation of innovations that will result in goods and services to be sold in private markets. The only exception to this has been agriculture. The conventional view is that market forces alone will be sufficient to direct innovative resources and investment into the areas of highest potential commercial return, and that government attempts to intervene in or even influence the process are more likely than not to be counterproductive. This view is reinforced by the notion that industrial innovation is driven primarily by "market pull" rather than "technology push." While government scientists and engineers may be rather good at identifying new technical opportunities, they lack the experience and knowledge to assess market potential and user needs, with the result that the typical government-driven technological development frequently tends to be a technical success but a commercial failure.

—Harvey Brooks

"National Science Policy and Technological Innovation," in R. Landau and N. Rosenberg, eds., *The Positive Sum Strategy: Harnessing Technology for Economic Growth* (Washington, D.C.: National Academy Press, 1986)

---

4. Commercialization. Finally, the high priority, investment, and organization that HL science and technology require in the national R&D agenda must entail an explicit commitment to the *commercial* development of the nation's learning enterprise. As noted often above, the billions of dollars that must be invested in learning technology development would be wasted if not aimed from the outset at the creation of commercially successful products and services.

This means that private industrial labs and R&D programs must play the central role. Government also has an important part, but it can't replace the function of private enterprise in developing products for the marketplace.

The learning industry is the second biggest business in our economy, but real private, commercial, industrial laboratories devoted to the science and technology of *learning* are essentially nonexistent. There's nothing to compare with the celebrated Bell Labs, IBM's string of five worldwide research centers, or even Chrysler's new billion-dollar R&D center. And, until the hundreds of billions of dollars locked up in education get opened to commercial enterprise, there won't be.

I got a hint of what kind of creativity might be unleashed if education were privatized as a profitable industry in June of 1991, when I had the chance to visit some of George Lucas's operations in San Rafael, California. First I met with staff of LucasArts Learning at Skywalker Ranch to discuss their business and see some of the multimedia products they were developing for classroom instruction. These included *GTV*, a mixture of geography and American history; *Paul Parkranger*, an ecology program structured as a detective story; and *Lifestory*, a dramatic exploration of the discovery of DNA.

But the real coup of my visit was a rare tour of Industrial Light & Magic's special effects factory. The faceless industrial buildings in downtown San Rafael gave no hint of the sorcery housed within—this is the Great American Dream Machine in the flesh.

Even as I was led through ILM's maze of fantastically tangible material of dream mechanics—the rubber whales of *Star Trek IV*, the real Starship *Enterprise*, the goofy green wraith from *Ghostbusters*, and multiple manifestations and pieces of C3PO—I was intrigued with the *business* of making the world's most sophisticated, popular, commercial "software."

For one thing, there is no real boundary at ILM between R&D and production—every new project aims to push the edge of the state-of-the-art. The film business is so competitive, and the audience is so fickle, that producers are under constant pressure to come up with new ways to create ever more dazzling image-sound experiences.

What most struck me, though, was the extraordinary contrast between the exotic, high-tech software ILM generates for Hollywood—like the amazing "liquid metal" robot in *Terminator 2*—and the nice but comparatively mundane computer-video products LucasArts Learning is struggling to sell for school use. It's significant in this comparison that Lucas businesses are run strictly on a pay-as-you-go basis: Lucas does not finance productions and then try to sell them—the product of any project depends on what the customer is willing to pay for up front.

With its fabulous synergy of art, science, engineering, high tech, old-fashioned showmanship, and pure entrepreneurialism, ILM's campus qualifies as one of the greatest concentrations of creativity in America, maybe even the world. Virtually everyone employed in the Lucas organization—starting with the patriarch—demonstrates superior talent, vision, and energy.

So the quality and value differences among the various products Lucas units create depend mainly on the customer and what the customer demands. If Lucas products for Hollywood are awe-inspiring while those for schools are relatively prosaic, it's because of differences in the customers and markets, not the creative talent.

ILM has about 80 percent of the market for high-end special effects used in Hollywood feature films. I estimate that ILM takes in something like a hundred million dollars annually selling world-class software to a U.S. motion picture industry that grosses about $15 billion a year.

The nagging thought that recurred as I cruised through ILM's wonder works was that this volcano of invention represented the polar opposite, on the scale of creativity, of the ed schools and would-be education research centers. Yet the bundle of exotic technology and supreme talents ILM employs are supported profitably by a movie business whose annual revenues are less than one twenty-fifth those of the U.S. education industry.

There may be no more glaring monument to the hopeless ineptitude of education's government monopoly and socialist administration than this. If education were organized like the highly competitive, consumer-focused, profit-seeking business that Hollywood is, it could support a couple of dozen ILM-type companies, producing spectacular, state-of-the-art materials for learning.

But the education industry worldwide has no source of technical innovation that could begin to compare to ILM. Academia simply will not pay for truly powerful technology to fascinate and engage an audience that institutions already hold captive by force of law or the blackmail of credentialism. LucasArts Learning's customers mostly are not even schools, but organizations like the well-heeled National Geographic Society and Visa, the credit card company, that put up modest sums to develop courseware products that these organizations intend to *give away* to schools.

The boldest step to establish a commercial, high-tech base for a knowledge age learning enterprise has been taken by Chris Whittle, founder and chairman of Whittle Communications, a $200-million-a-year media company based in Knoxville, Tennessee. Whittle may be the only education reformer in the U.S. today with a serious and competent interest in commercialization.

In May 1991, Whittle announced formation of a new division, Whittle Schools and Laboratories, with the mission of creating a profit-making education system for kids. The new Whittle company plans ultimately to invest $2.5 billion to have a network of 200 schools enrolling 150,000 students by 1996. By 2010, the firm expects to be serving at least two million students through 1,000 or more units. The plan's credibility was demonstrated a year ago when Benno Schmidt resigned his post as president of Yale University to take charge of the Whittle program.

Significantly, Whittle Communications, along with Time Warner, Philips Electronics, and Associated Newspaper Holdings, has committed $60 million to a two-year R&D effort, as the first step toward building the commercial school system. Unlike NASDC and other pie-in-the-sky model, pilot, and experimental school programs, Whittle's R&D program—dubbed The Edison Project—is the only one I'm aware of that is clearly dedicated to profitability as a necessary criterion of success. While NASDC talks about "breaking the mold," Whittle is aiming to "break the bank."

Chris Whittle just might be the Henry Ford of learning—that remains to be seen. But by investing corporate money in R&D aimed at developing technology for an independent, commercial learning enterprise, Whittle stands out as a living example of the kind of entrepreneurial leadership this book argues for.

With all the debate of government R&D policies, there is little question that government can and should support the basic scientific research—the current Washington jargon is "precompetitive"—that's the wellspring of advanced technology development. Learning research is so underfunded that billions of dollars of public investment are warranted just for the basics.

But, without duplicating the private sector, there's more that government can do to encourage commercial development of HL technology than just fund basic science. There are further public interests in hyperlearning R&D that overlap and complement private functions.

In fact, an important subject for public research investment is the nature and proper design of public policy itself. The issues raised by this book imply many questions that go unanswered here not simply because of space limits but because the investment has not been made to find the answers. A mountain of existing education, training, employment, and other public policies now thwarts the commercial development of hyperlearning. How to remove these barriers and replace them with efficient policies for nurturing the HL industry while protecting consumers is a highly complicated problem that warrants intense study in its own right. One of the main government responsibilities in commercializing advanced technology is to figure out what the proper government roles in commercialization are.

One of those proper and probably essential roles is setting technical standards. Not the "world class standards" for spurious academic tests that America 2000 calls for, but the kind of standards for technology, products, and systems that the National Bureau of Standards—now called the National Institute for Standards and Technology—has been helping establish for a couple of centuries.

There's an overlap of public and private roles in standard-setting. Sometimes standards—like the Microsoft DOS and IBM PC standard for desktop computing, or the VHS standard for video recording—evolve entirely through private enterprise. Sometimes—as for standard weights and measures—government takes the lead in establishing standards. And frequently standards come about through discussion and cooperation between government and industry.

Standards by their very nature are less than ideal—as soon as a standard is established, it limits the adoption of improvements. The American standard for television transmission, called NTSC after the committee that created it, is clearly inferior to the standards adopted later by the rest of the world. But the standardization of television led to mass production of TV sets, the quick spread of compatible broadcasting stations, competition that drove prices down, and the rapid universal adoption of a communication medium that not only created great wealth but transformed society, marking a new "age" of history.

The very success of a powerful standard like the NTSC television system becomes a tough barrier to progress. It's hard to trash a zillion dollars' worth of TV sets and recorders, tapes, cameras, and other studio and broadcasting equipment just because a better gizmo comes along. Which is why the struggle over a standard for high-definition television, HDTV, has been so long, so complicated, and even brutal—the stakes are very high.

Most of the standards relevant to the dawning age of hyperlearning are embedded in the broad spectrum of knowledge age, multimedia technology—computing, information storage, telecommunications, and so forth. But some specific to the business of learning will also be needed, and government has a legitimate social interest in facilitating their establishment.

A MEASUREMENT CRISIS

One of the most important and technically complex needs for HL industry standards is in measuring the *value* of what hyperlearning technology delivers. A key breakthrough in the establishment of a prosperous and efficient telephone industry was the development by Claude Shannon and other Bell scientists of mathematical tools to measure the economic value of a telephone call. The intangible mathematical technology needed to manage the telephone business was probably more important to creating the powerful, globe-spanning system we now take for granted than the invention of the telephone's physical hardware.

Similarly, the growth of learning productivity will be limited by the technology for measuring the productivity of HL tools and services. The efficiency of competition in the learning market will depend on the ability of the learner-as-consumer to compare the cost and effectiveness of what different vendors have to offer. There are many ways to solve this problem. But—just because modern technology is so powerful in creating and manipulating data—they are technically far more complex and sophisticated than useless "report cards" or the trivia of standardized academic tests.

For instance, every year seems to bring a new crop in a slew of national reports proclaiming that some element of American students' knowledge—such as math and science—falls at the bottom of the test curve. But, writing in *The Wall Street Journal* a couple of years ago, Mark Hartwig of Colorado College justly complained that "the problem is not with our children, not with the educational system, and not with the teachers.

Despite the ubiquity of traditional report cards and grading schemes, their usefulness has been questioned by many educators. . . .

"Report cards are such an ineffective way of improving a child's learning," said Dr. Jane C. Conoley, a professor of psychology at the University of Nebraska at Lincoln and president of the American Psychological Association's division of school psychology.

"One summary score every few months doesn't tell a child where she's strong or weak, and what she needs to do differently," Dr. Conoley continued. "The report card serves as a punishment or reward that's too distant from the behavior."

Dr. Sidney B. Simon . . . who has written extensively about grading and is a professor in the school of education at the University of Massachusetts at Amherst . . . claims that traditional report cards cause both parents and children to focus on the wrong things when grades are low and to become inappropriately complacent when they are high.

"There is no research evidence to support grades as measures of achievement," he said. "There's no research that shows grades have any connection with success in future life."

—"What Do Report Cards Really Show?" *The New York Times* (May 25, 1989)

The problem is the tests that we use to measure our children's achievement."

Curricula that nurture the "higher-order" reasoning skills called for in recent reports in fact have been developed and used effectively in U.S. schools, Hartwig observed, only to be subsequently abandoned. Why? Because "the programs were given thumbs-down by [standardized] tests, which were measuring how many arcane facts the children had memorized," instead of the more sophisticated skills they had actually been taught. Because developing relevant tests is more costly and less profitable for commercial test firms, "our schools are being held accountable," Hartwig concluded, "to standards determined by what is convenient to the testing industry, not by what is best for our children and our country."[258]

There's a powerful economic reason the testing industry finds it profitable to develop tests that show that obsolete teaching is working, and, on the other hand, finds it unprofitable to create instruments showing the superiority of truly innovative learning methods: The test manufacturers are paid by the academic bureaucracy, not by learners or employers who are looking for indicators of genuine competence rather than trivial pursuits.

A few years ago, Targeted Learning Corporation, a producer of computer-based courseware owned by Beverly Hunter, developed an innovative instructional program for Macintosh computers called "Scientists at Work," a detailed simulation of biological research aimed at cultivating students' higher-order skills in acquiring and applying scientific data. Conditions of the government grant that funded the project required TLC to evaluate the program's effectiveness. But the only available testing instrument coming remotely close to the program's objectives showed no effect, contrary to the insights and enthusiasm that could readily be *seen* in the students' behavior. "It's crazy to use paper and pencil tests to measure the multiple skills required to interact with a computer-automated, complex knowledge base," protests Hunter, who is now a National Science Foundation program director. But, she points out, developing an adequate computer-based test to measure the effects of this kind of instructional program is expensive, and could cost more than developing the program itself.

The federal Job Training Partnership Act program was designed to make continued funding of training programs contingent on measured success in placing trainees in private-sector jobs within a limited period of time. Some critics of JTPA have argued that this kind of program accounting promotes "cream-skimming": That is, program councils are encouraged to select for "training" the portion of the disadvantaged worker population that is most trainable and readily employable, and to screen out those who need basic education or other kinds of help even to become trainable.

These are but a few of the countless examples of how measurement processes affect every aspect of the normal operation of national education and training systems. They also show how measurement problems commonly thwart attempts at innovation, reform, or restructuring. Here are some further illustrations:

- Researchers such as Anthony Carnevale of the American Society for Training and Development have struggled for years simply to measure the amount of money U.S. employers spend annually on employee education and training. The key obstacles, Carnevale observes, are not only that business firms lack consistent procedures to account for such costs, but that many managers see an advantage in hiding the costs to protect their budgets from cuts during hard times. Former IBM training director Jack Bowsher reports that, when a thorough accounting was undertaken, his company found that it was actually spending about 50 percent more on employee education than management had believed.

- As a burgeoning number of baby boom generation college faculty compete ever more intensely for a dwindling number of tenured positions in the United States, the dominant criterion for tenure award—number of publications—has led to increased publishing fraud, from the multiplication of spurious journals, to a proliferation of "coauthors," to simple plagiarism and outright faking of research.

- Growing use of standardized testing and grading in kindergartens and even preschools has fed a "hurried child syndrome" of debilitating stress.

- While publicly promoting continuing education as an inducement for military service, the U.S. Defense Department, as a matter of policy, does not generally recognize the General Equivalency Diploma—based on achievement tests rather than school attendance—to satisfy high school graduation requirements for promotion.

- A high court in New York State ruled that the Scholastic Aptitude Test could no longer be used as the sole criterion for awarding state scholarships, on the grounds that females, on average, receive lower SAT scores than males, and therefore are effectively denied an equal share of such grants. In a related story, a number of minority leaders expressed outrage at the NCAA's Proposal 42—which prohibited member colleges from granting athletic scholarships to freshmen with inadequate SAT scores—because such tests generally are unfavorable to blacks and other minorities.

- With rare exceptions, no evidence that the students of a U.S. school or college actually learn anything is required for the institution to be "accredited."

These anecdotes are only symptoms of a pervasive crisis of measurement in an American learning enterprise that is hobbled by ignorance of its own purposes and performance. Like other services, teaching and learning, or education and training, are difficult to measure. Such measures that are used in practice are more convenient than valid. The result is a fog of uncertainty and confusion that obscures any discernible path to progress, and increasingly suffocates the productivity of this strategically critical industry.

The measurement crisis is a problem of both omission and commission. The physicist Lord Rutherford once said, "Only when you can measure a thing can you say you know something about it." Many efforts to manage or reform the nation's education and training systems founder for lack of any measure of relevant causes or effects.

This is not to say that the need for measurement has been overlooked. To the contrary, education and training programs are riddled with accounts and measures of many kinds. Educational testing is a huge business in the United States. A former director of testing in the Montgomery County (Maryland) Public Schools estimated that 15 percent of students' time in that district was consumed by tests of one sort or another—representing $90 million worth of school time annually. An estimate for the U.S. as a whole concluded that twenty million school days are consumed annually by mandatory testing, at a total cost of over $700 million a year.[259] The proliferation of computers and government regulations has unleashed a blizzard of statistics from monitoring, evaluation, accounting, and testing procedures.

The blizzard has been kicked up by both administrators and managers focusing narrowly on specific measurement solutions to parochial problems. Many common measures are inaccurate, invalid, unreliable, or misapplied. The overhead costs of the clutter of measures and reports are rarely considered by those demanding regulation or accounting. As several of the anecdotes cited above demonstrate, the systemic impacts of specific measurement solutions often create new, even greater problems. Or, as specialists in the field commonly observe: "Be careful what you measure—you are likely to get it."

Cybernetic science teaches that understanding the creation and flow of information within a system is the key to controlling the system's behavior. More simply put: Knowledge is power. Any attempt to restructure education and training systems must begin with—or will end with—the search for education's bottom line.

But that search is a problem of research and development of accounting technology. Measurement of information, services, and the psychological and behavioral conditions associated with learning entails difficult, complex, and often costly research problems. The sophistication of facile "report cards" and simplistic multiple choice tests falls far short of the measurement technology that is needed and possible.

The failure of accountability in education stems not merely from a shortage of integrity or political will. The learning enterprise's huge shortfall of R&D investment prevents creation of effective measurement technology as much as it stymies development of productive learning tools. Especially because the technology of measuring performance is increasingly embedded in the technology of teaching and learning, shortchanging one winds up shortchanging the other.

CHAPTER 12

ECONOMIC ACCOUNTABILITY: BEYOND "NANNYISM"

• • •

"Accountability" has been a favorite theme of education "restructuring" for at least the last decade. But the laudable movement for accountability has been hampered by two key errors. First, what most reformers persist in overlooking is that accountability is only a wish without effective means for accounting—and accounting is a problem of technology, not theology. Second, whether accountability is a good thing in practice depends very much on specifically who is accountable to whom for what—and both the education establishment and the reformers have a strong tendency to get these specifics wrong.

ACCOUNTABILITY AND RESPONSIBILITY

A decade of failed education reformism in the U.S. has been punctuated by continual demands for accountability. Noting that "we've increased the state's funding for our public schools about 76% over a six-year period," North Carolina Governor James Martin recently admonished that "we're going to have to find ways of holding our local school systems and local school buildings accountable for getting results with that money."[260]

America's school employees want to be held accountable for their students' achievement in schools that are adequately funded and staffed and equipped with up-to-date instructional materials. But as *America 2000* points out, our young people are in school only 9 percent of their first eighteen years. And we refuse to be held accountable for the deprivations and missed opportunities for learning in the other 91 percent of students' lives.

—Keith Geiger

"Holding America Accountable," National Education Association advertisement (May 1991)

The governor echoes the sentiment of most public officials and business leaders involved in education reform. The concluding statement from the education "summit" meeting of President Bush and the governors in late September 1989 called for "a system of accountability which focuses on results rather than compliance with rules and regulations," and charged, "We must establish clear measures of performance."[261] And the whole first plank of the Bush administration's America 2000 platform aims to concoct a flurry of national testing to encourage "parents, teachers, schools and communities . . . to measure results, compare results and insist on change when the results aren't good enough."

While accountability is hard to attain without accurate accounting tools, the creation of precise accounts alone would not solve education's profound problems of accountability. The most acute problems are politically loaded issues of responsibility: Who is going to be responsible to whom for what?

It's popular to assume that accountability is inherently a good thing. Certainly the absence of accountability runs a high risk of letting irresponsible behavior run free. But the wrong system of accountability can still leave the same subversive conduct unchecked.

In fact, misconstrued accountability arrangements can wind up being irresponsible in their own right. An egregious historical example is the

Treaty of Versailles. As John Maynard Keynes warned (fruitlessly) in *The Economic Consequences of the Peace,* the vengeful attempt to hold Germany fully and uniquely accountable for the cost of the Great War made economic disaster and a Second World War inevitable.

America's festering conflict over "quotas" and "affirmative action" is rooted in a similar perversion of accountability. Holding persons accountable for redressing discriminatory wrongs they did not commit, to the benefit of some persons who were not themselves demonstrable victims of any wrongdoing, creates the kind of invidious atmosphere that only serves the vindictive purposes of once an Adolf Hitler and now a David Duke.

As desirable as greater accountability may be, the why and how of accountability can be overlooked only at great peril. The wrong vision and means of accountability entail a substantial risk of doing more harm than good.

THE NANNY TRAP

Behind much of the reasonable-sounding quest for academic accountability lurks a reactionary cult of political Nannyism. The Nannies are the self-appointed guardians of the national covenant, the presumptive protectors of the cultural genetic code, the roving Knights Templars of the true faith. Their motto is *in loco parentis* ("in place of parents") and their anthem could be the pop tune "Kids" from the musical *Bye Bye Birdie,* whose cadenza goes: "Why can't they be like we were, perfect in every way? Oh what's the matter with kids today?"

The Nannies can be found all over the political spectrum, among liberals and conservatives, Republicans and Democrats. At its most sinister, Nannyism is an inexorable feature of totalitarian regimes, whether expressly communist or fascist or monarchial. More commonly, Nannyism crops up in all sorts of American political movements: Know-Nothings, Wobblies, New Left, New Right, Neo-Con, Neo-Lib, America First, Afrocentrism, Multiculturalism, Political Correctness, Black Power, White Power, Green Power, you name it.

But the mission is always purification. Nannies of all stripes share the vision of education as the engine of culture, the factory of "correct" citizenship. To the Nannies, *public* education policy is a mallet to pound the form-

HOLYOKE, Mass.—The education system here collapsed this year. One-third of the teachers were laid off. More than 40 students have been jammed into some classrooms. . . . Students often share text-books. . . .

But the majority of Holyoke's voters don't seem to care. Twice in six months they have rejected tax increases for the schools even as they approved increases for the police and fire departments and for the senior citizen center. . . .

Some voters are angry at school administrators. . . . Others are bur-dened by taxes and disgusted with modern education. But interviews with a number of Holyoke residents also indicate a more fundamental problem: The town's mostly white, working-class voters, many aged and childless, are alienated from its mainly Puerto Rican public-school children. . . .

Michael Donohue, a retired municipal court judge who publishes a bimonthly newspaper . . . says, "It wasn't a vote against the children. We just want the administration to be accountable." He contends the administration doesn't fully disclose finances and doesn't teach what's needed. "We have to get back and teach basic things such as respect for people and property."

—"As Schools Crumble, Holyoke, Mass., Voters Reject Tax Increases," *The Wall Street Journal* (Nov. 25, 1991)

less putty of free thought and behavior into the rigid mold of social conformity. Blame and shame are the Nannies' favored instruments of "ac-countability."

Nannyism follows an understandable, even benign impulse: to mobilize education as an instrument to preserve and strengthen the identity of our community. Nannyism begins when this healthy quest for community flirts with ethnic nationalism, racism, and theocracy—using secular politi-cal power to enforce its cultural ambitions on those who, in Thoreau's words, "step to the music of a different drummer."

In the American context, the problem of Nannyism stems in part from confusion about the nature of the American community. While we commonly speak of America as a "nation" with a distinctly American "culture," America actually is a nation of nations, a culture of many cultures. The American system was designed, willfully and constitutionally, to prevent the *political* establishment of ethnic, racial, religious, and therefore cultural orthodoxy.

For this very reason, America seized on education from the beginning as a means to glue together people of diverse roots and creeds joined by no other common bond than adherence to the constitutional contract. Education took on a philosophical role in the peculiar American setting that a state religion or official church plays in other societies. As the alloying process unfolded in the mid-nineteenth century—capped by the Civil War—that melded the United States from a "they" into an "it," education became suddenly and expansively more "public." The intrusion of government compulsion, finance, ownership, and regulation of education progressively raised the stakes of education politics.

The result, a century later, is the arithritic gridlock of public education politics John Chubb and Terry Moe exposed in their Brookings report. Unfortunately they attributed the stalemate between inertia and reform to what I would say they mislabeled as an excess of "democracy" in scholastic governance. Rather, the endless conflict of school politics Chubb and Moe described is ritual Nannyism—using political clout in the attempt to impose parochial values as a universal culture. As Chubb and Moe accurately conclude, as long as America remains a richly diverse, plural society, this wrangling of special interest Nannies is a game without end, yielding only bureaucratic stagnation and dynamic mediocrity. It's the kind of "accountability" we need less of, not more.

The alternative to Nannyism is not the amorphous narcissism often identified with "progressive" education (also commonly but unfairly linked with the philosophy of John Dewey). The alternative is rooted in science, pluralism, economic democracy, and common sense.

BACK TO THE FUTURE?

A central motive behind the movement for educational accountability is the belief that education has an important role to play in strengthening the nation's capacity to meet the challenges of the future. Related to this is the popular sense that education is a powerful and essential instrument of innovation and social change. Much of the impulse for innovation in schooling is couched in the language of futurism—such as "School of the Future," "Classroom of Tomorrow," and "America 2000."

But functionally and structurally, education is far more concerned with the past and tradition than with the future and innovation. The historical function of childhood education in most societies is one of cultural cohesion and stability. College prolongs adolescence in its claims to further or complete cultural infusion even as it steers toward "commencement" of adult vocation. Education's mission is "normative"—to make people normal. It aims at integrating the individual into the community and at perpetuating cultural values, knowledge, standards, and practices.

So in demanding accountability, education leaders and reformers are immediately confronted with a paradox, really a dilemma, about education's core mission. Is the fundamental role of education to prepare the young (or "alien" adults) for the future, or to connect them with the past? Are educators ultimately to be accountable for creation or preservation? For innovation or tradition?

To some, these questions will sound trivial. They will say: Education can do both; in fact, it does do both. Education prepares people for the future by arming them with the knowledge, virtues, and traditions of the past—the "tried and true."

Throughout most of human history, that answer was valid because hardly anything changed for centuries at a time. The future was the past. A child would be well prepared to take on the challenges and responsibilities of the rest of his life by learning the wisdom and skills of his ancestors, because the world in which he would spend the rest of his life would be virtually identical to that of his father's life, and his grandfather's. (Or, her experience, her life, her mother and grandmother, and so forth; though, throughout much of history, in many societies, education was an investment not made in females.)

The birth of the scholastic tradition in the reign of Charlemagne over a thousand years ago—a tradition in which our "modern" education system is still firmly rooted—came at about the midpoint of a millennium of Western history during which virtually nothing changed in the lives of most ordinary people. It was a time and a society, as historian James Burke observed, when everything that people knew was *old*. Confronted with the frustration of trying to meld together an empire of illiterates, Charlemagne resurrected an old Carthaginian concept of "liberal arts" education and made its main mission to recuperate, inculcate, and disseminate the knowledge of the classical age.

But that was then, and this is now. We live in an age of the unprecedented. Our knowledge is exploding—almost everything we know is new. Our future is drastically different from our past, or anyone else's past. For our generation, much of what's been tried is clearly no longer true; whatever may be true in the world our children will inhabit in the twenty-first century in many cases hasn't yet been tried.

Things would be simple if all traditional knowledge and culture could be trashed as obsolete, and we could use education as a loom to create a brand new culture from whole cloth. Too simple. In fact, disastrously simple. That kind of scouring of history is the simplistic dogma of a Khmer Rouge that reaches its logical, inevitable conclusion in the "killing fields."

Therein lies the dilemma. An education embalmed in tradition will surely not prove adequate to prepare children or adults to live in an unprecedented world. But we cannot survive by plunging into the future stark naked, ignorant, and mute. The only tools we have to build and maintain the future are in the kit of the past.

Our problem is analogous to that of explorers embarking on an irreversible journey to a strange, new, mostly unknown and uncharted land, trying to figure out what to take along and what to leave behind. The hold of their vessel is finite; only limited supplies can be brought. What should they take? How much and what kind of: Food? Clothing? Weapons? Tools? Money? Navigational instruments? Musical instruments? Books? Gifts? Seeds? Livestock? Medicines?

The problem is not unprecedented. The explorers, pilgrims, and pioneers of America, a truly new world, had to face that problem and resolve it. We know that they brought a good deal of tradition with them. But they were also remarkably inventive, enterprising, and adaptive people. There is no more stunning example than the Mayflower Compact. That extraordinary little band of pioneers—finding themselves stranded on a foreign and hostile shore, their plans gone totally awry, confronted with the necessity of surviving a long deadly winter with scanty provisions—sat down and summarily invented a government.

They and those who followed were practiced revolutionaries for two centuries before the American Revolution—they reinvented government, reinvented religion, reinvented education, in many ways reinvented invention. And that leads to the core irony in our current dilemma of change and preservation: The American culture is one whose most essential tradition is transformation.

In practical terms, the innovation-versus-tradition dilemma for education leaders and policymakers comes down to the tug and push of two archetypal political demands. One set of demands is saying to schools and colleges: Our country's future is threatened by intensifying international competition, technological upheaval, environmental hazards, and social trends that all demand radical changes in our way of working and living. Our youth—in fact most of us adults too—need to become more competitive, more creative, more flexible, more literate, more technologically competent, more enterprising, and generally more "excellent" individualists than ever before if our nation is going to stay a step ahead of its many challenges.

But another set of demands is saying: Our country's traditional way of life is threatened by intensifying international competition, technological upheaval, environmental hazards, and social trends that all demand a return to the historical values and institutions that made our country great. Our children—and many of these immigrant, and underclass, and other adults who are off the true path—need to get back to basics, work harder, be more disciplined and respectful of authority, and more strictly inculcated with traditional religious and cultural beliefs if our nation is going to prevail over the subversive forces that are threatening its stature and way of life.

The two demands made on education both are legitimate and at least partly valid. But they are not equally balanced. While the process of debating or deciding whether to embrace the new or stick with the old goes on, you are, by default, sticking with (stuck with?) the old. In the absence of aggressive and dogged commitment to innovation, the status quo persists through inertia. As management consultant Maurice Mascarenhas says, "Even a corpse can swim downstream."

Preservation of the traditional is an essential social function that we cannot afford to extirpate. Yet we clearly must also get on with the work of innovation and transformation.

The solution to this dilemma is to accept that education—as an institution, as a technology, as a system—is obsolete. Society needs its cultural flywheel to preserve its inheritance from the past, and to maintain its stability. But only up to the point of buffering change, not halting progress. When conservation becomes stagnation, death follows.

The politically sanctioned bureaucracy of academia has become too big, too rich, too powerfully self-serving—and thus too good at clinging to the past. Government-owned, -operated, and -controlled education has bloated from a necessary flywheel to a stifling millstone.

At the same time, political control has made education far too turgid and inert to keep up with the electric pulse of change that marks not only the threshold of a new economy but the normal life tempo in the knowledge age. Education, as traditionally and popularly conceived, simply cannot coexist with the learning technology of the unfolding new world. Science and technology have now condemned academia to be either the victim of progress, or its assassin.

The time has come to restore the independence of the institutions of economic progress from those of cultural stability—in the words of the Christian Gospel, "to render unto Caesar the things that are Caesar's and unto God the things that are God's." Americans need to give up their sacramental attitude toward public education: The school is not a church; the professor is not a priest; the textbook is not Scripture; the teachers colleges are not seminaries; the education secretaries are not cardinals, much less popes; and the mission of public education is not *propaganda*—literally, the propagation of the true faith.

"Education" is a word that can mean anything, but not everything. The role of religious, parochial "education" *is* propaganda, appropriately. The philosopher Alfred North Whitehead even insisted that "the essence" of education in general "is that it be religious," at least in the sense that it "inculcates duty and reverence."[262] But under the American Constitution and system, if education is public it must not be parochial propaganda. And if education is parochial, it cannot be public.

Compulsory public education was consciously contrived by Horace Mann in Massachusetts in 1851 to protect the native WASP culture by diverting the children of Catholic immigrants from parochial to public schools. The notion of public education as a burner under the American "melting pot" may even have been a good idea in the context of those times. But the times have changed. Big.

Modern information media have put a torch under the melting pot that has it boiling over, all over the world. It's said that, through the power of communication and commerce, American culture has conquered the world—the Japanese may make the recorders and the players, but they can only buy, not duplicate, American "software."[263] What's called American culture, though, is actually the eclectic product of every race, creed, tribe, nation, and lifestyle on earth collected in a plural country of immigrants.

The classroom as an integrating force pales to insignificance next to Disney, Nintendo, and the NFL, not to mention CNN. This bugs the Nannies to distraction. They whine about culture being vulgarized and homogenized at the same time they insist on imposing national academic "standards" on everyone, but what really bothers them is that the America-inspired, knowledge age culture of economic democracy is sweeping the world without their arthritic fingers on the multimedia broom. So the Nannies chant the alarum of the flim-flam Music Man, with the corrupting siren updated from billiards to video: "Oh we got trouble! Right here in River City! And it starts with T and it ends with V, and it's bland, you fool!"

The truth is that television has done more to spread and perpetuate classical culture than schools could ever dream of. The relatively low ratings of public or educational or specialized cable TV networks may mask the real scope of TV's impact. The Metropolitan Opera's live TV debut of *The Barber of Seville* on the U.S. public television network a few years ago was seen by more people that night than had attended all the performances in all the opera houses in the world that had staged that opera in the century-plus since it was first composed.

Outside the classrooms, the genuine, living institutions of culture—churches, associations, museums, artists, tribes, cults—are hip to using modern media to advance their mission. Only the die-hard academics—lashed like Captain Ahab to the white whale of political and cultural correctness—are sinking to irrelevancy under the wave of an implacable technology revolution.

It's time to leave the business of tradition and culture to the people's own relations and institutions. In the plural society of the American system, government has no more business in the establishment of culture than of religion—which is none.

The American government was proclaimed and constituted by its founders to "secure the blessings of liberty for ourselves and our posterity"—they didn't mention ancestors. The business of a government of the people is the future; its job is to prepare for and adapt to change.

Public policy now must be fundamentally refocused from education to hyperlearning—the essential instrument of liberty in the world of today and tomorrow.

Academic stalwarts want education to be accountable only for continuing to do more of the same. Would-be education reformers want to hold academia accountable for doing more of the same *better.*

But education cannot be reformed—it needs to be replaced. By trying simultaneously to serve two important but opposed social needs—tradition and innovation—academia increasingly is failing both. The only thing education should be accountable for now is *phasing out* as smoothly and swiftly as possible.

Accountability is much to be desired. But the new hyperlearning enterprise that is emerging to supplant the archaic architecture of academia—and that public policy must now embrace and nurture—demands a vision of accountability as different from the past as its media and mission.

THE NEW ACCOUNTABILITY

What is the learning enterprise to be accountable *for?* First and foremost, for economic democracy, not cultural correctness. The engines of cultural knowledge certainly are part of the overall learning enterprise. But, for reasons I've expressed, public policy need not and should not account for that role.

The United States was dedicated in its inception to secure the natural and unalienable rights of life, liberty, and the pursuit of happiness—the latter being Jefferson's embellishment of Locke's more mundane right of property. A necessary condition for all these rights is the opportunity for each individual and family to enjoy economic self-reliance and hope of progress.

It has become unfashionable in academic circles to give the economic mission of learning much priority. Yet numerous surveys show that the overwhelmingly top value Americans place on education is economic opportunity. A 1984 Gallup poll aimed at rating the goals of education found that 56 percent of the U.S. public ranked as their highest priority "To develop an understanding about different kinds of jobs and careers, including their requirements and rewards." But only 20 percent of teachers given the same survey gave the same goal a high rating. Similarly, 46 percent of the public but only 6 percent of teachers gave their top rank to the goal, "To help students get good/high-paying jobs."[264] A central part of the mythic American Dream is the illusion that education is an effective conveyor of career opportunity and economic advancement.

But, in reality, the "solid gold life jacket" of education is dragging us down. As the shortcomings of America's workforce are continually exposed, as the ranks of its overeducated unemployed swell, as the price tag for schooling continues to grow, and as parents financially exhausted from finally paying for college find themselves besieged by twenty-five- or thirty-year-old offspring boomeranging back to the nest because their elite academic credentials have failed to win them gainful employment, the public is getting appropriately skeptical and restive.

Pressed for an accounting of education's benefit and cost, academicians rebel. You can't expect education to be productive, they admonish, after all it's not a business. (That's funny; how come you guys always complain you're not paid as much as other *professionals* in other businesses?) Education has a greater value than mere *vocationalism,* they sniff. (Oh, like what?) Like enlightenment, understanding the universe, appreciating the finer things in life, being a liberally educated person. (And how is that going to pay my rent, not to mention my health insurance?) The benefits are *intangible.* (Then why aren't the costs intangible too?) Look, you twit, you have to have a solid, liberal education to be a good citizen. (Washington and Lincoln had almost no education; weren't they good citizens?)

And so it goes. One of the more influential consultants on education reform I know likes to quote the nineteenth-century Catholic educator John Henry Newman's conviction that "the only truly vocational education is a liberal education." The way I see it, the truth is more like the reverse: The only truly liberal education is a vocational education.

Well, sort of, anyway. The term "vocational education" has a bad image of wood shops and welding classes as a result of a sinister tradition of "tracking" the academically disfavored into voc-ed ghettos that were rarely either vocational or educational. Actually, in the mindcraft economy, where the great majority of work is knowledge work, the content of the knowledge filed under the umbrella of "liberal" arts and sciences has considerable economic utility. But most self-styled liberal educators are so thoroughly contemptuous and ignorant of the economic world that they are utterly incapable of communicating the practical application of their "expertise."

It never ceases to amaze me that anyone could call "liberal" an education system that *fails* to meet the fundamental human need for economic security, freedom, and development. Even as impeccably liberal a humanist as Abraham Maslow sensibly made basic safety and economic requirements higher priorities in his famous hierarchy of human needs than the ultimate attainment of what he called "self actualization."

To show that my dismissal of the economically intangible mission of academia is not the mere ranting of a philistine, I'll tout Regis University in Denver as a model of a traditional academic institution that has almost completely transformed itself into the kind of modern, competitive, profitable, and economically productive enterprise I'm advocating.

When Father David Clarke took over as Regis's president a decade ago, he began to turn around a small liberal arts university, which was verging on bankruptcy, with what in academia is an almost unprecedented act: *market research.* He actually went out and asked the business community in the Denver region what Regis could do for them, and found that, at a time when the baby bust meant a dwindling supply of traditional college kids, *adults* and their employers had all sorts of needs for workforce and career development that other institutions were not meeting.

Father Clarke's transformation of Regis met the two quintessential criteria of "excellence" that management consultant Tom Peters has made a career (and fortune) trumpeting for the last decade: an obsessive focus on the customer and an unrestrained passion for innovation.

Beyond concentrating on meeting employers' and workers' vocational needs, Clarke transformed the whole process of the university to serve the adult consumer: Registration materials and books are delivered to students. Promising no student would have to travel more than twenty minutes to get to class, Regis established ten satellite centers near its customers' offices and also provides on-site classes for major area companies such as IBM. Clarke laid off a quarter of the old faculty and has 85 percent of the adult, business-oriented courses presented by adjunct professors who can leaven their academic expertise with practical, real-world experience.

Regis represents a big step toward a twenty-first-century enterprise for learning, but still falls a little short of ideal. Its outreach to students is hampered by the same old Yak in the Box technology. And Regis is still wrapping its services in what I consider spurious sheepskins—though purists may take solace in knowing that the university continues to churn out bachelor's and master's degrees.

Because of the idiosyncrasies of America's surreal tax laws and accounting gimmicks, Regis is still classified as a "not-for-profit" organization. But Father Clarke emphasizes that "we're not for loss either," and in fact, Regis consistently generates a budget surplus that in a saner world would be called profit. Regis actually has been so prosperous under its president's entrepreneurial piloting that the university is now franchising the design and tactics of its productive adult program to other colleges.[265]

Specifically then, what does it mean for the learning enterprise to be accountable for economic value? First, serving the hunger for economic independence means conveying knowledge and skills that empower individuals to be economically productive. And, as I explained in an earlier chapter, being economically productive in the knowledge age increasingly will mean being prepared to be entrepreneurial, not just an employee.

Meeting these needs leads to a set of learning objectives virtually everyone who's not a Rockefeller heir will have to attain that is quite different from the vapid "world class standards" sought by America 2000 and other academic strategies. All youth, and adults too, should be prepared to enter economic life equipped with an essential set of competencies.

While I'm obviously not much impressed with many of the would-be education president's accomplishments to date, the Bush administration deserves credit for generating important guidelines for the basic competencies all workers should have in the modern economy. This list came not from the Department of Education but the Department of Labor, and was initiated by then-Secretary Elizabeth Dole months before Lamar Alexander arrived on the scene or the misbegotten America 2000 was even pondered.

Dole convened a Secretary's Commission on Achieving Necessary Skills (SCANS), chaired by former Labor Secretary William Brock, to define the essential skills needed to work effectively in a fast-changing economy and to recommend ways to assess proficiency in those skills.

After a year of studying real jobs in today's workplace, SCANS came up with a detailed, eight-part toolkit of abilities nearly all workers are likely to need. The list includes five key competencies that must be applied in just about any productive job, and three more fundamental abilities required to develop those competencies or others.[266] The SCANS report goes into considerable detail to describe exactly how these abilities would be demonstrated in practice, at work. Only one of the eight clusters of abilities includes the traditional "three Rs." Significantly, these abilities

SCANS: WORKPLACE KNOW-HOW

COMPETENCIES—effective workers can productively use:

- Resources—allocating time, money, materials, space, and staff;
- Interpersonal Skills—working on teams, teaching others, serving customers, leading, negotiating, and working well with people from culturally diverse backgrounds;
- Information—acquiring and evaluating data, organizing and maintaining files, interpreting and communicating, and using computers to process information;
- Systems—understanding social, organizational, and technological systems, monitoring and correcting performance, and designing or improving systems;
- Technology—selecting equipment and tools, applying technology to specific tasks, and maintaining and troubleshooting technologies.

THE FOUNDATION—competence requires:

- Basic Skills—reading, writing, arithmetic and mathematics, speaking, and listening;
- Thinking Skills—thinking creatively, making decisions, solving problems, seeing things in the mind's eye, knowing how to learn, and reasoning;
- Personal Qualities—individual responsibility, self-esteem, sociability, self-management, and integrity.

---

are recommended not as "world class standards" or requirements for a diploma, but as essential capabilities that should be demonstrated to get a job.

To achieve such economically valuable results of the sort SCANS has identified, the enterprise that aims to aid human development needs to be accountable for, and therefore account for, competence—not what academia generally views as "excellence." The difference may seem only semantic, but is actually costing America hundreds of billions of dollars a year in wasted education spending.

The key to this distinction lies in understanding the difference between what are called in technical jargon "criterion-referenced" and "norm-referenced" tests of achievement. A criterion-referenced test aims at an absolute standard of proficiency: Either you know it or you don't; either you can do it or you can't. A common example is a driver's license exam. If you show that you know what you need to know, and can do what you need to do, to drive a car with adequate competency, you get your license. If you fall short of the standard you don't get your license—but you can study and practice some more and come back when you're ready and try again.

Norm-referenced testing is what nearly all of us experienced in school as the sinister process of "grading on the curve." In the previous example of the driver's test, it doesn't matter how other people do on the test; what matters is whether or not you can drive a car safely. Norm testing aims to show how your performance compares to what's normal or average. It doesn't matter what you know or can do, but how your test score or grade stacks up against everyone else's who took the test. The infamous "standardized tests" don't necessarily have to be norm-referenced, but almost always are.

The difference is a matter not merely of mathematical technique but of the core philosophy of what education is all about. Norm-based accounting is the tangible expression of a social Darwinist creed that views educational accountability as a zero-sum competition for survival of the fittest. The mission of education becomes grading, testing, and sorting to filter out the excellent from the mediocre. This process *requires* that 90 percent or so of students must be made to fail, more or less, so that the elite few can be extracted and labeled the "best and brightest."

Academia's obsession with norm-based sorting is one more ploy of the Great Bamboozlement that has led most people to believe that this orgy of failing and filtering is what "education" has to be about. And if that is all it can be, that's one more reason to consign "education" to the scrap heap of extinction—because norm-targeted practice may be the single most fundamental cause of the epidemic of waste, cheating, and corruption that plagues what passes for education today.

The norm fetish lurks behind most of the public outrages over academic accountability. In 1989, a report released by Friends of Education, organized by John Cannell, an Albuquerque psychiatrist, revealed that over 80 percent of all the school districts in America reported "above average" scores on standardized tests. This phenomenon came to be labeled the "Lake Wobegon" effect, after humorist Garrison Keillor's mythical town where "all the women are strong, all the men are good-looking, and all the children are above average."

> [John Jacob] Cannell cites evidence that teachers are tailoring their curricula to fit the test questions, that teachers and administrators are teaching the test to their students, even that teachers are walking around during a test and indicating to their students where an answer should be "doublechecked." What is more shocking is that in those states where cheating has been discovered, disciplinary action was either not taken at all or relatively mild.
>
> —"Cultural Revolutions," *Chronicles* (Feb. 1990)

The technical reason for Cannell's finding was that districts were commonly comparing scores of current students to the norm (median or average) of students tested several years earlier. But the real reason was the intense political pressure on teachers, schools, and bureaucracies to show that they are doing "better" than everyone else. The result, as further studies by Cannell's group and others revealed, is that the whole business of education testing and assessment is rife with deception, cheating, and downright corruption.

In the fall of 1989, a popular social studies teacher at Greenville High School in South Carolina, Nancy Yeargin, was arrested and prosecuted for helping her students with coaching and crib sheets to win high scores on a standardized test. Her motives were not entirely compassionate: South Carolina's scheme for teacher "merit pay" paid Yeargin $5,000 in bonuses above her annual $23,000 salary mainly on the basis of points she earned for "producing" huge leaps in student test scores.[267]

The Yeargin story got national media attention, not because it was exceptional but because it revealed what was commonplace. Teachers and other bureaucrats harried to show "excellent" test results are aided and abetted by an obsequious testing industry that commonly provides practice kits and booklets that all but give away the right answers.[268]

But there is no testing scam that rivals the cost and folly of the vaunted Scholastic Aptitude Test, produced by the Educational Testing

Service and administered by the College Board. Despite the fact that the SAT has been exposed as useless and meaningless by a slew of analysts,[269] millions of U.S. students continue to spend big bucks on the SATs and test preparation courses, journalists continue to report the test results as newsworthy, and education advocates and critics continue to cite SAT scores as significant indicators of educational performance. In case you haven't heard, the truth is that the SAT is rarely used to make college admission decisions, doesn't help either colleges or students to make such decisions when it is used, is harmful to minorities and the poor, and does not indicate whether schools or colleges are getting better or worse. The only tangible benefit of the SAT is the enrichment of the test givers and coaches, to the tune of some $150 million a year.[270]

Announcing test scores has been one of the happier duties of the Board of Education during this decade. The board has been using test results to lead us to believe that our schools are making the grade. You can't argue with cold, hard figures can you? Unless you investigate how these figures are arrived at. At the bottom of every pupil answer sheet for standardized tests is a small box on the extreme left labeled "Test Status." Below this heading, under the categories "Tested with Modification" and "Absent," can be found "Exempt Special Education," "Exempt L.E.P. (limited English proficiency)" and "Excused Other." These refer to students numbering in the tens of thousands. They form a significant population of potentially poor scorers whose tests, if honestly averaged in, would lower the citywide averages dramatically.

—Marc Sacerdote

"They Flunk but Make the Grade," *New York Newsday* (Nov. 9, 1989)

Even when norm-referenced tests are accurate and honest, the process still breeds confusion and deceptive shenanigans. Several states and communities have committed themselves to "goals" that include having all students "reading above grade level" by some date. But "grade level" is defined in norm-referenced terms simply as the median, or middle, of all scores—half of all students taking the test *always* will come out below grade level, and the other half above grade level, by definition. Nevertheless, taxes have been raised and bloated budgets further padded to chase a statistical will-o'-the-wisp.

The academic pursuit of norm-based "excellence" is a treadmill that can lead only to bankruptcy or corruption. If we spend 100 percent of our gross national product on education reform through the end of the century, by the infamous year 2000 half of all the states, school districts, schools, and students will still fall below the median on honest norm-based tests—that's how "median" is *defined.* The only alternative is cheating.

In reality, norm-focused education inevitably breeds book-cooking of all kinds. Costs, payrolls, and inventories are obscured, grades are inflated, tests are tweaked, problem students are tracked into "special education" and other deadwood categories off the books of the "excellence" accounts. Driving all this costly finagling is the constant pressure from failure-loving Nannies for institutions and their staff to be held accountable for "excellent results" that they are not truly responsible for, that they cannot realistically "produce," and that are mostly irrelevant to anything students, families, employers, and society in general really need.

It doesn't have to be this way. Competency-based instruction has been around a long time and is widely practiced in military and corporate education programs as well as consumer-oriented vocational schools and community colleges.

Competency-based instruction focuses on serving, not sorting students. In contrast to the social Darwinist obsession with the virtue of failure, competency-focused teaching recognizes that failure to learn is both scientifically and technologically obsolete—any modestly healthy student can master any subject, given the right circumstances and tools.

Because the successful attainment of "grade A" competence is expected for nearly the entire student population, the idea of accountability for the failure of schools, teachers, classes, or even whole communities or states—the objective of America 2000's national testing stratagem—makes no sense at all in a competency-directed learning enterprise. Instead, such a learning enterprise takes mastery of learning as a universal result and seeks accountability for cost, convenience, accessibility, enjoyment, and other indicators of service quality and efficiency.

In particular, a leaning enterprise accountable for competency and eco-

In 1960, in Roanoke, Virginia, an 8th-grade class, using primitive teaching machines and a hastily prepared program, went through all of 9th-grade algebra in half a year. Tested in the following year, their retention was above normal. I visited that program. When I entered the room with its director, Allen Calvin, not a single student looked up at us. When I commented on that extraordinary fact, Calvin gave me a better demonstration. He went up to the teacher's platform, jumped in the air, and came down with a loud bang. Not a student looked away from the materials on the teaching machines. That is "motivation," not from fascinating subject matters, but from the assurance of success.

—B. F. Skinner

Letter in *Science* (Mar. 24, 1989)

nomic value furthermore will focus on productivity, not merely on effort. This completely upends the conventional practice in academia of treating inputs of money, staff, time, real estate, widgets, and so forth as indicators of good intentions to be maximized instead of as costs to be reduced.

A productive learning enterprise is also responsible for results. But in accounting for results, the emphasis needs to be on serving, not producing. The fruitless quest to hold schools "accountable" founders on the common but crazy analogy that school is to student what Starkist is to tuna. Schools and teachers do not produce graduates, or learners, or learning. Only learners produce learning. Instructional institutions or tools offer services that may help the learner to learn, but they don't "make" learning. Perhaps as ever more intelligent HL machines perform learning we might say that they produced something; but even then the smart machine, not the machine's manufacturer, would deserve the credit for whatever was produced.

Four decades ago, when W. Edwards Deming and J. J. Juran began to preach the gospel of quality, their advice was largely ignored by American manufacturers but absorbed with rapt appreciation by Japanese firms. U.S.

industry now is racing to adopt the lessons of Total Quality Management that Japan brought home to America with such dazzling impact.

Academia clings to the earlier, industrial age factory model of producing in mass and then inspecting and sorting out defects at the end of the assembly line—a model that the pressures of competition and technology have forced other businesses worldwide to replace with an organizational strategy in which, in the famous slogan of the Ford Motor Company, "Quality Is Job One."

The most essential requirement of Deming's Way and Juran's vision of Total Quality Management is to stop inspecting for failure and to empower the people who do the productive work to *prevent* failures from happening in the first place. Yet even while U.S. companies are striving to master the discipline of TQM, which works to steadily reduce the rate of defects through the practice of "continuous improvement" *(kaizen),* Peter Drucker reports that Japanese firms now are aiming at an even higher standard of perfection, "Zero Defect Management"—eliminating failure completely.[271]

Schools are factories of failure. That's what their genetic program of norm-based accounting makes them. In an emerging economy where failure has become intolerable to the point of obsolescence, to perpetuate such an institutional design would be folly.

In the domain of learning, "competency-based" is just a specialized name for "total quality" or "zero defect." A competency-based learning enterprise—the only kind that can serve or even survive in the knowledge age—must be accountable for one ultimate mission: the extinction of failure.

CHAPTER 13

A FREE LEARNING ENTERPRISE: BEYOND CREDENTIALISM

• • •

A system of accountability in a learning enterprise in which total-quality, zero-defect, failure-free learning is "Job One" will work very differently from what academia is used to and from what many reform Nannies seek. In this new learning enterprise, accountability will be:

- TO the consumer—not politicians, not academics;
- OF competitive vendors—not teachers, schools, or public bureaucracies;
- IN real time—not a few years or months;
- BY certification of competency—not credentials of attendance.

The education establishment's creed of accountability can be summed up in two words: Trust me. Reformers have been seeking to make education institutions accountable to politicians or political committees such as the National Education Goals Panel, or, among the more disastrous examples, soviet-style neighborhood school councils in Chicago and Denver.

What we need is a learning system that is accountable primarily to the consumer through the mechanism of the market. The learning enterprise's consumers, again, are individual learners, families, and employers of human capital. Market accountability means, more than anything else, that the consumer controls the flow of revenue. And accountability to the consumer does not mean responsibility to committees or commissions or representatives or proxies—it means being responsive to the specific needs and wants of each individual consumer. School choice aims in the right direction, but for reasons I've explained at length, falls far short.

What the consumer wants to be accountable is each specific source of knowledge or instruction used to support learning, not a collective bureaucracy or institution. We may be attracted to a particular shopping mall by its ambience or parking facilities, but if we're going to shop there it's in particular stores for specific things. And if the AT&T telephone you bought at Sears doesn't work, you're going to ask the store or the manufacturer to repair it, not the owner of the mall, much less the local chamber of commerce or the state department of economic development.

As a learning consumer you want a teacher, as a vendor or service provider, to be responsive to your needs. But unless the teacher is an independent contractor you've hired directly—such as a tutor—you don't want to have a compulsory relationship that forces you to be concerned with how that person is going to be accountable to his or her employer. If you're not satisfied with the service, you want the freedom to complain or take your business elsewhere.

For instance, if you're in the market for a new pair of loafers, you don't want to have to take a political position on how Nordstrom's should hire, train, manage, and compensate its salespersons, or whether Nordstrom's workforce should belong to a union, or the merit of Nordstrom's stock as a long-term investment before you can buy a pair of shoes there. Nordstrom's accountability to its workers, or its managers, or its stockholders, or its bankers, or to the EPA, or to God are all valid issues of accountability—but not for you. As a consumer, the accountability you care about is a good-looking comfortable pair of shoes with a fair price and service with a smile.

Also as a consumer, you don't want to wait for the government to issue a "report card" every four, eight, and twelve years to find out if your barber or hairdresser gave you a good haircut. You want accountability in real time—right now. You want to look in the mirror now. If you're a little uncertain of the result, you might go have lunch with your spouse, and if your significant other thinks you look goofy, go back to the shop and get your hair fixed this afternoon.

Science knows that learning requires feedback properly scheduled in real time and tied to performance to meet the personal style and needs of the individual learner. HL technology exists, and is coming, that can do that with ever greater precision and efficiency. We know that, in contrast, academic report cards are junk. Political report cards are junk writ large.

Finally, an accountable learning enterprise must cure the cancer of academic credentialism that is eating the marrow out of the modern economy. While it may again seem like a semantic quibble, making a clear distinction between certification of competency and credentials of attendance could save hundreds of billions of dollars that now are wasted annually by the academic paper chase in America alone.

Now the distinction I am making between certification and credential is not yet commonplace in the world of education and training. But we need to get some kind of verbal handle on the difference between an education system that primarily values seat time and a learning enterprise targeted on the demonstrable attainment of knowledge and skill.

I want to make it clear that certifying human ability by functionally relevant examinations absolutely serves the interests of both individual learners and the employers of human capital. But, as noted above, such competency-based assessments must focus on what you know and what you can do. *How* you came to learn what you know or can do and *where* you learned these things basically should be nobody's business in a truly meritocratic economy.

Objective assessment of working abilities is not just a metaphysical ideal. HL technology makes it an eminently practical reality.

Simulation technology, for instance, is valuable not only for learning but at least equally for testing and assessment. Performance Factors Inc. markets a kind of simple "game" software called Factor 1000 that tests a worker's hand-eye coordination. The test is a far more reliable and feasible measure of fitness for duty than chemical drug tests.[272] The Ergos Work Simulator developed by Work Recovery Inc. in Tucson is a more elaborate computer-based machine that precisely measures degrees of physical disability—important for making decisions about rehabilitation plans, compensation claims, and compliance with laws such as the Americans with Disabilities Act.[273]

These examples are notable for their precise and effective focus on performance rather than history. Similar assessment technology either exists or could be developed (with sensible national R&D priorities) to gauge functional abilities across the spectrum of cognitive, interpersonal, and other human intelligences listed by Howard Gardner.

For instance, applicants for jobs at Toyota's factory in Kentucky are put through three weeks of evaluation before a final hiring decision is made. The instruments Toyota uses to assess worker abilities include individual interviews, group interviews, a variety of tests, simulation exercises, auditions, and probationary employment.

That's not the way the paper chase for academic credentials works. Diplomas are awarded for classroom seat time in the form of credit hours or Carnegie units. To get the diploma, you and/or the taxpayers have to pay a school or college for time attended, not for the value of service received.

In the criminal underworld, the credentialism scam would be called what it is: a protection racket. If you don't pay the mafiosi their tribute, they send the enforcer to break your fingers, maybe taking away your ability to work. If you don't pay the academiosi their tribute, they put black marks on "your permanent record." Academia's enforcers are coconspiring employers who may take away your ability to get work, who will "make you an offer you can't refuse"—play and pay, or starve.

The only learning the credentialing game requires is learning how to play the game itself. The rules are simple: Don't get thrown out. Don't get flunked. Butter up the "dons" so they will give you good grades and recommendations

We were all told that this was the way the real world works. That learning to play the diploma game would be valuable "preparation for life." Hogwash. All the paper chase teaches is academic arrogance and cronyism—the phony importance of being accepted by the "right" people, school, college, company, community, club. It's utterly contrary to working and living successfully in the economy and society of the knowledge age, where progress and prosperity absolutely depend on economic democracy.

Let's get clear about this: There is no job in this economy that *requires* an academic diploma for its successful performance. None. Nada. Zippo.

Yes, there are lots of jobs that may force you by regulation or even law to get your academic ticket punched before they'll let you practice or perhaps get licensed. But that's just extortion; it's not because you really *need* to go to school to learn what's needed to do the job well. And you will find exceptional people who made it into almost every career who didn't have the right credentials but who got in through some combination of fortunate circumstances and irresistible ability.

One outstanding example is Peter Jennings, America's number one broadcast news anchor, who holds no diploma from any university, college, or even high school. That meaningless disability would prevent Jennings from being hired as a permanent, certified teacher of, say, English, or journalism, or history, or social studies, in any U.S. public school. Ponder the idiocy of that for a while.

Also, American historians who are polled periodically to rate the "greatness" of modern U.S. presidents frequently pick Harry Truman as the overall greatest president of the twentieth century—the one occupant of the Oval Office in this century not to have a college degree. In fact the only qualification the Constitution requires for the most responsible job in the country—president—is that you be born in the United States at least thirty-five years before taking office.

Okay, you say, but *you* wouldn't want to be operated on by a brain surgeon who had no diploma. Well, actually much if not most brain surgery today is performed by robots—who didn't go to school—under the guidance of surgeons. While the FDA probably gives considerable attention to see that these robots work as advertised, I don't know that regulators inquire all that scrupulously into the academic credentials of the engineers and technicians who design, build, and program the machines. All that aside, if the choice came down to it, I'd rather be operated on by a skilled surgeon who maybe forged his medical school diploma in an act of ambitious desperation (these guys do pop out every once in a while) but who has performed a thousand operations successfully without ever losing a patient than some bozo with a string of Ivy League BAs, MAs, PhDs, and MDs who is under indictment in six states for criminal malpractice.

And you can't practice medicine or law in America just by getting a diploma—you have to be "board certified" or "admitted to the bar" based on a competency examination. In the not-so-old days you didn't necessarily have to attend school at all. For instance, in most states you could become a lawyer by "reading for the law"—studying law books on your own—and passing the bar exam. That's how Lincoln did it. Now, as a result of political pressure from law schools, nearly all states make you get a law school diploma before you can take the exam. A dramatic enhancement of either the stature of lawyers or the quality of jurisprudence as a result of this innovation has not been widely observed.

The final word on the folly of credentialism was provided by the wise Wizard of Oz, who explained to the cunning but self-doubting Scarecrow that he had no less brains than other self-styled thinkers of great thoughts—all they had that the Scarecrow didn't was a diploma. So the Wizard gave him one, just as valuable as all the others.[274]

Shedding corrupt credentialism in favor of the honest accountability of certification also requires a fundamental shift from the aim of traditional education and testing practices to "screen out" the unqualified and incompetent. In contrast, the whole philosophy of competency-based certification must be to "screen in." The screening-in metaphor came out of an industry workshop organized in the fall of 1989 by Arnold Packer, a Hudson Institute fellow who subsequently became executive director of the SCANS commission.

The practical implications of screening in are potent. Screening in means a re-vision of testing, not as a hurdle or barrier to advancement but as a diagnostic tool aimed at devising a specific prescription for achieving competency. Screening in makes the idea of "flunking out" utterly obsolete. Instead of "failing" a qualifying test and having the door slammed in your face, you find out precisely what your shortcomings are, and get directed immediately to the learning resources needed to remedy the deficits as quickly and efficiently as possible.

As part of the whole movement toward Total Quality Management, screening in will lead to a progressive merger of assessment with instructional technology, ultimately making failure to learn statistically nonexistent. Most important, it represents a fundamental power shift from education/training institutions to learning consumers—students, workers, and employers. At its heart, screening in means giving power to those whom traditional academic practice and conventional education policy have usually left powerless.

To clean up the corrupting effects of norm-based testing and credentialing, the testing fox must be removed from the teaching henhouse. Specifically, a new learning accountability system must make the diagnosis and assessment processes independent of the providers of learning services and products. We would think it crazy to give the S&Ls or banks authority to audit their own performance and just trust them to let us know how they are doing. But that's the common practice of what passes for educational accountability—schools and teachers test their own students, evaluate their own performance, and "certify" their results with self-issued diplomas. As John Cannell's and other studies show, even "independent" standardized tests commonly are paid for and administered by employees of the same institution whose students are being assessed.

While it's not only appropriate but necessary for instructional providers to include what's called formative tests or measures to provide feedback on how the student is doing, accounting for the value of what's provided—in terms of what the student needed and what the student learned—simply must be performed by sources independent of the vendor to be credible and honest.

In a competitive, competency-focused learning enterprise, you as a consumer must be able to get an independent, unbiased diagnosis of what you need to learn, what skills you need to develop, to be able to achieve whatever your goal may be. Having then learned what you needed to from whatever products or services you used to do it, you then want to have your competency examined and truly certified by an agency wholly independent of whoever sold you that stuff.

There are places in the economy today where you can find independent diagnosis of learning needs and independent assessment of knowledge and ability—for example, in the military. But they still are far from being the standard procedure throughout the economy's entire system of learning and employment.

"Accreditation" of educational institutions is a related part of decadent credentialism that needs to be swept away with the same broom. Accrediting agencies are basically fox clubs that sanction the ability of foxes to guard the henhouses in the first place. Specifically, what accrediting agencies do is give applicant institutions a checklist of *inputs* to the instructional process—building facilities, library books, faculty with the right diplomas, and maybe some curriculum requirements—that, in their profound wisdom, they have decided are necessary to be accredited. Why are these inputs needed to be accredited? Because all accredited institutions have them. Why do all accredited institutions have these standard inputs? Because they had to in order to be accredited.

Usually lost in the circular accrediting shuffle is any consideration of the outcome, value, or even existence of any learning that might be achieved. A notable exception may be the organizations that accredit the often-maligned for-profit trade and technical schools—accredited schools can be required to report the numbers of graduates actually placed in the kinds of jobs they were trained for.

While accreditation seems on the surface to be a reasonable consumer protection measure, in practice it provides precious little information or assurance of the quality or value of the services the learning consumer actually receives. Because accreditation is often linked to an institution's ability to receive government financial aid, the process is stirred by the polluting finger of politics.

Accreditation of providers would be an acceptable practice in a free market learning enterprise, as long as it served only to provide information and not to restrict the consumer's freedom to choose. But to be a useful practice, it would have to perform the way organizations such as Consumers' Union or Underwriters' Laboratories do in other sectors of commerce—giving the consumer information about the value of the product, not just about the size of the factory or the number of MBAs on the manufacturer's payroll.

Ultimately, creating a competency-based system of learning and employment will require slashing a path through the existing thicket of civil rights law. In fact, while the legal history is somewhat complicated, understanding the link of civil rights to credentialism is crucial to the political action needed to break the academic establishment's stranglehold on the modern economy.

The central issue in the long-fought civil rights legislation sponsored by Senator John Danforth and finally passed by Congress and signed into law by the president in late 1991 hinged precisely on the problems of competency and credentialism. The problem stemmed from a 1989 Supreme Court decision in the case of *Wards Cove* v. *Atonio* which overturned the court's ruling in the 1971 case of *Griggs* v. *Duke Power Co.* Basically what happened in the *Griggs* case was that an employer wanted to require that applicants for a job like janitor either have a high school diploma or pass an IQ test. The court found in 1971 that that business policy was unlawfully discriminatory, because the qualifications demanded did not show "a manifest relationship to the employment in question." The result of the *Griggs* decision put the burden on employers to show that job qualifications are fair and "fulfill a genuine business need." And any "adverse impact" on minorities of an employment procedure would be treated as evidence of discrimination.

The more recent *Wards Cove* decision flipped the court's *Griggs* finding around, giving employers rein to set job requirements more freely and putting the burden of proof back on applicants or employees to show that the effect of qualifications is clearly discriminatory.

To Senator Danforth and other ardent civil rights advocates, the *Wards*

Cove decision was the most egregious setback for civil rights protection of several recent reversals. Restoring the *Griggs* standard became, to Danforth, the heart and soul of the bill he championed to redress these findings, which finally became law after a prolonged and heated squabble with the White House over the meaning of "quotas" in all this.

The crux of the matter is that it remains legally and economically difficult today for U.S. employers to establish the kinds of objective and technically sophisticated assessments of workplace competency that SCANS, the Commission on the Skills of the American Workforce (CSAW), and other analysts (including this author) are calling for.

As a result of *Griggs* and other lawsuits, employers were pressed to define and assess employment qualifications in a very job-specific way. This created several problems that all the back-and-forth of litigation and legislation has left complicated and less than ideally resolved.

While job-specific tests would seem a perfect expression of competency-based employment, and could pass legal muster, the large costs of developing and applying a slew of tests for the different kinds of jobs employers have to fill motivated most employers to drop testing altogether and use more subjective means for screening such as interviews. But it's been generally more difficult for employers to determine applicant qualifications accurately; so avoiding the cost of testing has often resulted in increased costs for turnover or education of employees who wound up not being adequately prepared to do the work for which they were hired. The costs of inefficient job screening have been estimated at up to $80 billion a year.[275]

Another costly problem with the narrow interpretation of "business necessity" many civil rights advocates drew from the *Griggs* decision—and which seems to be restored by the 1991 law—is that, during the nearly quarter century since the *Griggs* case, U.S. business has been steadily driven by the pressure of foreign competition and the move toward quality management to require a much more flexible workforce. In the most competitive firms, narrow job classifications have been abolished, and workers must function in teams, rotate through a variety of job assignments, and continually revise their skills to match the pace of fast-changing technology.

For all these reasons, rather than rely on either narrowly focused job exams or vague subjective judgments, employers would prefer using one or a few general but objective tests of employment capability, such as the popular General Aptitude Test Battery, which is designed to assess general cognitive ability, perceptual ability, and psychomotor ability. Scientific analyses show that these tests actually are valid predictors of performance across a wide range of job categories. But, because blacks and Hispanics tend to get lower scores on these kinds of tests than other people, using the tests raises the risk of suits for "adverse impact."

To avoid such litigation, some employers have tried adjusting minority scores upward. But such "race-norming" has precipitated complaints about "reverse discrimination," leading in turn to further litigation. Caught in the middle, many employers are believed to be skirting lawsuits by using informal hiring "quotas" that avoid adverse impact on minorities while being too subtle to be exposed in court as reverse discrimination.[276] While the new civil rights law eliminates race-norming, the general sense among employers is that it still leaves a considerable risk of costly litigation.

For the goals of a truly egalitarian society, neither the *Griggs* nor the *Wards Cove* decision is fully satisfactory. Unfair discrimination that is unrelated to valid economic roles and values obviously must be combatted. But it's also wrong to presume willful bias simply because of differential results, whether it be in hiring, lending, housing, or other areas of economic life.

A truly meritocratic, competency-based economy of learning and work requires technically sophisticated tests to certify individual ability. Minorities are wrong to conclude that the solution to low scores on objective, valid, relevant examinations (creating which is a difficult but solvable technical problem) is a legal remedy that itself is discriminatory. As Dinesh D'Souza correctly argues, the right solution to the problem of a poor score on a valid test, for a minority or any other person, is simply to do better.[277] Where D'Souza and other would-be cultural conservatives go awry is their false assumption that norm-based academic "excellence" is a valid indicator of economic competency.

The philosophy and technology of screening in are crucial to resolving these dilemmas. High-tech learning and assessment make low scores no longer stigmas of "failure" that shut the doors of opportunity, but only one diagnostic step along a path toward future learning and ultimate mastery.

None of this civil rights wrangling has directly attacked the patent inequity of academic credentialism—preventing the employment of a fully competent person of any race, creed, gender, or origin who simply lacks a diploma. But credentialism was thrown into the tangle of the civil rights debate when Education Secretary Lamar Alexander lobbied against the Danforth bill's resurrection of the *Griggs* decision with the harebrained argument that the bill would "seriously if not fatally" undermine education reform by "send[ing] precisely the wrong message to students and teachers . . . [that] staying in school doesn't matter."[278]

In truth, staying in school does not matter. Staying in learning matters vitally. Or perhaps school matters negatively: Modern science and technology show that schooling and academic credentialism are adverse to the kind of learning needed to thrive in the knowledge age.

Senator Danforth sharply disputed Secretary Alexander's contention that the *Griggs*-renewing law would fatally undermine the academic paper chase. Unfortunately, Danforth was right. The substance of *Griggs* and subsequent law including the 1991 act still permits diplomas to be at least partly considered in the employment process.

The right message was well stated by Chief Justice Warren Burger in the *Griggs* decision when he wrote: "History is filled with examples of men and women who rendered highly effective performance without the conventional badges of accomplishment in terms of certificates, diplomas or degrees."[*]

The law has not yet fully embraced the necessary conclusion of Justice Burger's sage vision. Further steps remain to establish a true economic democracy where, to paraphrase Martin Luther King, people will be judged by their competency's character and not by the colors on their sheepskins.

CHAPTER 14

TO LIBERATE LEARNING: AN ACTION PLAN

• • •

The action plan for moving the learning reformation swiftly forward has several key steps. Taken as a whole they may seem like a daunting legislative agenda: privatizing public education, establishing set-aside innovation funds and new institutions to manage them, untangling the telecommunications policy nettle, expanding distance learning programs and setting media standards—it's a full plate. It might seem impossible to accomplish all this in the face of public apathy and strident resistance from the education establishment.

But an assault on every one of these fronts at once is not needed to overthrow the establishment's ability to resist change, and to get momentum steaming ahead to accomplish these revolutionary changes. The keys to toppling entrenched power with a smaller force lie at the heart of martial arts such as kung fu and mythic tales like those of Achilles' heel and David's conquest of Goliath, and for that matter, Luke Skywalker's destruction of the impregnable Death Star: focusing on the most vulnerable spot, and using the opposing force against itself.

In reality, a long legislative shopping list is not needed to erase the opposition to the learning reformation. A single, relatively modest legislative act can do the job. It is so basic, effective, and nearly the true "panacea" to the malignancy of education that I call it "step zero" to emphasize its precedence over all other actions needed.

> Credit must be given Gorbachev for launching political reform precisely by advancing the idea of a law-governed state. Neither Party ideologues on the lookout for heresy nor liberal-minded jurists seemed to realize that a *law-governed state* not only required observance of justice and human rights, it represented a knife in the very heart of the system.
>
> —Anatoly Sobchak
>
> *For a New Russia: The Mayor of St. Petersburg's Own Story of the Struggle for Justice and Democracy* (New York: Free Press, 1991)

STEP ZERO: OUTLAW CREDENTIALISM

That act is: Prohibit discrimination in employment on the basis of academic credentials. In short, just outlaw credentialism.

This is not as far a leap as it may seem. The civil rights bill Senator Danforth fought successfully to enact renewed a legal rule that already limited the extent to which employers could use diplomas to only those situations where "business necessity" clearly can be demonstrated. The argument presented earlier in this book is that diplomas, based on attendance, *never* are truly necessary to the performance of any job. Assessments can and should be based only on a person's ability to perform the work required, not on where she went to school or how long she stayed there.

Prohibiting the use of academic credentials in employment—which is close to what many leading employers already have done in practice anyway—would bring down the academic establishment's political hegemony as effectively as a small charge of dynamite, placed at a critical stress point, can bring down a whole building. The demolition expert doesn't use tons of high explosive to tear down a skyscraper—he just loosens things up enough to let gravity do most of the work.

The result of such a law would be to induce employers to develop, or more likely buy, assessment devices that can measure actual competency.

This would establish a competency-based testing system not only to implement SCANS basic standards but to drive all employment decisions. The tests themselves then would provide objective standards to help people plan their learning investments. An industry would spring up to diagnose what individuals need to learn to qualify for their career goals, and then to steer them to the specific learning services and products that could help most cost-effectively to achieve those objectives. A phase-in period of a year or two would give employers time to prepare for the new law.

With diplomas no longer having economic value, the public would quickly turn its attention to what it should have been paying attention to all along: What do you need to learn to get the economic opportunities you want? And, what's the fastest, cheapest, best way to learn that?

Public enthusiasm for paying exorbitant taxes and tuition for diploma mills would wane swiftly in a diploma-less economy. The government education establishment would last about as long as the postcoup Soviet Union without the force of economic extortion behind it.

Wouldn't education institutions resist? Probably. But after years of decrying "vocationalism" and insisting that education is more valuable than just a means to employment, what would they say? No one would be prohibited from pursuing diplomas for the sake of intellectual or spiritual enlightenment, if they wanted to. If schools and colleges could persuade paying customers that academia will improve the quality of their lives, more power to them. But no one should be blackmailed by threat of prosecution or unemployment to have the quality of their lives improved whether they like it or not.

Outlawing discrimination by credentialism strengthens the civil rights of all citizens, regardless of race, creed, gender, or national origin. And it would open the greatest flood of economic opportunity since the great land rushes of the American frontier.

To replace hollow diplomas, there will need to be a means to certify that all members of the workforce have the essential skills and knowledge to be initially employable and trainable. A specific device I proposed in a report for the National School Boards Association, echoed in the later report of the Commission on the Skills of the American Workforce, is a Certificate of Basic Competency, a replacement for the high school diploma and GED.

The CBC would be awarded on the basis of assessment tests of the set of abilities needed to qualify for entry-level employment in a broad spectrum of occupations—as well as the essential capabilities needed for *entrepreneurship*. The latter requirement generally has been overlooked in other calls for "standards" that focus either on employment or college admission—both of which will be vanishing species in the twenty-first-century economy. The specific abilities to be demonstrated probably would be very similar if not identical to those recommended by the Labor Department's SCANS report, with entrepreneur skills added.

Given the trend toward human capitalism noted earlier—the ongoing shift from labor to ownership of capital, especially intellectual property—the entrepreneurial competencies warrant significantly greater emphasis in the CBC than what SCANS and other reports have suggested. The CBC should be viewed as a ticket not only to employment but to economic opportunity and participation more generally. For instance, it might be required for budding entrepreneurs to qualify for bank loans or for government programs like the Small Business Innovation Research program.

The CBC would serve not just the need for basic vocational or economic competency, but the goals of social integrity and competent citizenship as well. But these broad social objectives would be represented in the form of specific, observable skills. For example, the SCANS criteria for social and communication skills incorporate much of the substance of what is commonly sought in the name of "socialization"—without the propaganda. The abilities to communicate with people of different backgrounds, and to cooperate to solve problems and get things done, are as relevant to good citizenship as to good business.

Should the CBC standards be national? Maybe national, but probably not federal. They certainly should apply statewide in a system funded and directed by the state government. It's hard to deny the state government the prerogative to establish objectives it wants to satisfy with its own taxpayers' dollars. But it would be imprudent of the states to institute minimal standards for human capital that are overly fine-tuned to the local economy. Given the degree of mobility in America, truly essential competencies should be national if not even global in their utility.

The crucial pitfall for the CBC to avoid is becoming an excuse for renewed "tracking" and "screening out." The CBC needs to be presented as an essential standard of economic competency for everyone, not just the so-called non-college-bound. And it must be used to open doors of opportunity, not close them.

STEP 1: BYPASS

Attempts to transform the education establishment through reasoned persuasion, incremental conversion, collaboration, and "partnership" have proven historically and continually ineffective. History offers no example of established bureaucracies restructuring themselves from within or voluntarily yielding to their replacements. A major force for actual restructuring in other industries has been the opportunity created by new technology itself for consumers to bypass the control of the establishment.

For instance, legal windows in the regulatory structure combined with new transmission and terminal equipment to enable telephone consumers to bypass the economic turf of the century-old "Ma Bell" monopoly. Now cellular phones, personal communicators, and private fiber optic networks are bypassing even the local phone company monopoly. Similarly, the 1978 federal Public Utilities Regulatory Policy Act (PURPA) legislation combined with new cogeneration technology to enable large electricity users to pull the plug on the local electric utility. In a more subtle and complex way, the evolution of electronic financial transaction systems has progressively bypassed the control of traditional money, banking, and trading institutions. And the spread of cable TV, VCRs, and remote controllers has increasingly empowered the TV audience to bypass the advertising base of the shrinking broadcast TV networks.

Such technology bypass strategies are clearly sufficient (and may be necessary) to topple the hegemony of established monopolies such as the American school and college system. What is clear is that in each of the above cases technological bypass ignited vast, swift, and irrevocable changes in the structure of huge, deeply rooted industrial establishments. Furthermore, the dynamic changes unleashed through bypass circumvented either the control or consent of the dominant institutions. In the words of the Godfather, bypass "made them an offer they could not refuse."

The new generation of hyperlearning technology is not merely an "add-on" to traditional teaching systems. New HL technology replaces many traditional practices with far more cost-effective means of serving established instructional objectives. Perhaps more important, hyperlearning creates new possibilities and forms of learning that could never before be achieved on a comparable scale, or even attempted—and that traditional institutions simply can't compete with.

Distance Learning and the National Information Infrastructure

Of the wide variety of technologies available to transform learning, distance learning—the use of telecommunications to deliver learning resources and services—has special strategic value: Distance learning inherently tends to bypass and undermine the control of the orthodox education bureaucracies. Ultimately the nation needs to extend broadband, digital, fiber optic networks to every work, residential, and other facility. But business-led coalitions of learning consumers should give immediate priority to supporting all efforts to provide distance learning services, through whatever media are available, to every learner of every age.

The telecommunications revolution that must arrive sooner or not

[W]hen broadcast signals or data transmissions link teachers to students thousands of miles away, some of the most sacrosanct structures in American education are fundamentally transformed. Individual principals no longer assign teachers and set class size. . . .

Local control takes on new meanings when school districts can choose among many televised offerings. But local leaders cannot then dictate the course contents.

State boards of education are faced with giving reciprocal accreditation to teachers from places with greatly different standards and traditions. And college campuses are no longer hermetically sealed intellectual breeding grounds. Breaking these boundaries changes not only the types of programs offered but also the kinds of people coming to school, with adults learning at a distance everything from a rudimentary appreciation of art to course material for a college or graduate degree.

—William Celis 3d

"Inventive Curriculums," *The New York Times,* Special Report on Education (Apr. 7, 1991)

much later may be the single most powerful force to achieve the genuine "systemic restructuring" of education and training that has been much talked about but so far unrealized. The power of telelearning may prove irresistible even to academic institutions that have a long history of successful resistance to change. But there is no way distance learning can be adopted without violating and ultimately reconstructing the fundamental bureaucratic structures that tie established institutions together.

For instance, school districts in the Oklahoma panhandle developed an advanced two-way video distance learning network by linking in to a long-distance phone company's fiber optic trunk. After two years of pilot-testing the system, participating schools agreed to give up one teaching position each to use the freed salaries to help pay for the network. In the short run at least, the technology did not necessarily "eliminate teachers" or jobs; probably the opposite. In this rural region, the network permits teachers with a few or even no students in one school to teach large classes spread over hundreds of miles. Normally, the alternative would be to cancel courses with insufficient enrollment—depriving both teachers of jobs and students of learning opportunities—or to consolidate schools into larger units, requiring longer travel or possible relocation, and eliminating some number of school jobs. Nevertheless, the allure of distance learning technology induced these schools to do what might have been thought impossible to propose: to pay for capital investment in new technology by reducing labor costs.

Alternatively, education bureaucracies are powerless to exercise an effective veto over the spread of telelearning. As broadband, multimedia channels proliferate and take root, they geometrically expand the lucrative opportunities to bypass academic institutions and deliver learning services directly to consumers—families, employers, associations, and various other private organizations. The quasi-monopoly of public education is far less formal or exclusive than the explicit legal monopoly conferred for a century on AT&T and now on its offspring, the regional phone companies. It seems improbable that the education establishment will be any more able to permanently resist the onrushing tide of technological competition than the telephone monopolies have been. Which is to say that, for either institution, technology makes a policy of "business as usual" not merely undesirable but ultimately impossible.

But distance learning initiatives, while helpful, are only an intermediate measure. The key to transforming not only the learning enterprise but the entire economy lies at the focal point of current telecommunications policy. Everything now depends on constructing a "National Information Infrastructure" for the knowledge age.

The basic problem is that the technology for creating, processing, and visualizing information is zooming ahead far faster than the in-place technology of the communication infrastructure. While nearly every home, office, and other business and facility in the U.S. is connected to a national telephone grid, most of those connections still are tied together by copper wires. Those wires can carry information at rates on the order of ten to twenty thousand pieces per second. Graphic workstations generate pictures at sixty million bits per second. Networks to link more powerful computer and imaging tools need to transmit hundreds of millions to billions of bits each second.

This is why telecommunications policy now is focused on the replacement of copper wires with the glass threads of fiber optic cables. Transmitting the entire contents of the Library of Congress over copper would take about two thousand years. The kind of fiber optic cables now carrying long-distance calls at more than eight million bits per second could accomplish the same result in eight hours; a 140-million-bits-per-second network like those being developed in Germany and Japan could zip the whole library through in about half an hour. Tomorrow's "teraflop" and "terabyte" technology will need to move *trillions* of chunks of data with each tick of the clock—the information content of the Library of Congress could be delivered in less than half a minute.

While we await the information equivalent of our national interstate highway system, engineers have devised several clever gimmicks to "compress" data, effectively stretching the carrying capacity of today's cow-path communications grid. Data compression techniques all hinge on the fact that most messages of interest to humans contain a lot of data bits that are boring, irrelevant, or useless. Just as the DNA required to reproduce an elephant can fit comfortably in a raindrop, the essential parts of a message can take up much less space than the whole. For instance, transmitting a picture of an eagle soaring high against a clear blue sky does not require sending the message "this is blue" for each of the million or so blue dots the picture may contain. Rather, a computer program could boil the whole message down to something like: "Every dot in this picture is blue, except for the following. . . ."

Compression gizmos bring some welcome efficiency to data communication. But compressing data more than a few times eventually comes at the cost of some loss of information. Compression is destined to be overwhelmed by the explosion of information from processors spewing billions and then trillions of pieces of data each second. Trying to pump such vast oceans of data through the soda straws of copper wire or scarce electromagnetic channels recalls the biblical challenge of passing a camel through the eye of a needle.

Solving this problem will require untangling a Gordian knot of confused and outmoded local, state, federal, and international communications policies. The rearrangement of communication media sketched by Nicholas Negroponte of M.I.T. and touted by George Gilder—portable, personal communication by air, the big pictures by glass wire, and everything digital—will come eventually. The knot either will be untied by farsighted political leadership or will be ultimately cut by the brute momentum of economic necessity: By the beginning of the next century, George Keyworth and Bruce Abell forecast in a Hudson Institute report, about a third of Japan's GNP will be generated through the broadband (high-speed) digital communications network that country is developing.[279]

While regulatory policy seems stuck in a gridlock of political interests, advancing telecosm technology itself is fomenting competition that promises imminent upheaval in the telecommunications infrastructure. Private networks and other technology that bypassed the telephone monopoly led to the breakup of the AT&T system under a court settlement in 1982.

Newer technologies now are undermining the monopoly of the regional phone companies—the so-called RBOCs or Baby Bells—that were born in the 1982 judgment.[280] Cable TV companies like Time Warner's subsidiary in New York are building two-way fiber optic networks that will be able to carry phone calls as well as movies and other information services. Cellular telephones already offer a way to bypass the local phone company, a capability that new, digital cellular technology will expand. And AT&T and other companies are rushing to develop shorter-range but higher-volume personal communications networks (PCNs) that also will skip the local phone network.[281]

The vast capacity of fiber optic cable, plus the options offered by satellites, microwave carriers, and cellular and other channels, is quickly unraveling the century-old notion of "natural monopoly" on which much current communications policy still rests. Tiny glass fibers can carry so much phone and other traffic in a small space that it's not impractical to have two or more competing lines sharing space under streets, on poles, and in building walls.

Building the broadband digital "superhighways" that fiber optic and other advanced technologies now make possible is at least necessary and may be sufficient for the revolutionary transformation of learning the knowledge age economy requires. A comprehensive policy framework urgently is needed to end and replace the current deadlock among cable TV, print publishing, broadcast, and telephone company interests that is thwarting the evolution of a coherent national media network.

Key technologies for the learning enterprise such as multimedia and distance learning can be made far more affordable, useful, and productive for consumers by being standardized. Standards are an important instrument to assure "choice" and competition in high-tech learning systems. Business leaders and their allies should support national and state programs that help establish broad-based standards for HL media. An essential guideline for this effort is to insist on "open systems" architectures—that is, technologies that are not proprietary but are available through multiple producers and vendors.

Appropriate objectives for standard-setting would be telecommunications protocols, computer hardware and operating systems, and software user-interface designs. Other appropriate objects for standardization are accounting and assessment methods, including measures of competency and learning outcomes. To be avoided is the kind of centralized state purchasing and content control that has desiccated textbooks, or any effort to standardize media/software content or teaching/learning methods.

STEP 2: PRIVATIZE

The time has come to make privatization the primary goal of restructuring education and training. The outcome of this effort would be the kind of microchoice market for learning I described in an earlier chapter, in which each learner is free to choose the products and services that person needs from the variety offered by profit-seeking vendors, freely competing in an open marketplace. Creating that kind of free enterprise for learning has a number of practical policy requirements.

I've taught public school for 26 years but I just can't do it anymore. . . .

Government schooling is the most radical adventure in history. It kills the family by monopolizing the best times of childhood and by teaching disrespect for home and parents. . . .

The whole blueprint of school procedure is Egyptian, not Greek or Roman. It grows from the faith that human value is a scarce thing, represented symbolically by the narrow peak of a pyramid. . . .

Socrates foresaw that if teaching became a formal profession something like this would happen. Professional interest is best served by making what is easy to do seem hard; by subordinating laity to priesthood. School has become too vital a jobs project, contract-giver and protector of the social order to be "re-formed." It has political allies to guard its marches. That's why reforms come and go—without changing much. Even reformers can't imagine school much different.

. . . Good schools don't need more money or a longer year; they need real free-market choices, variety that speaks to every need and runs risks.

—John Taylor Gatto

"I May Be a Teacher, but I'm Not an Educator," *The Wall Street Journal* (July 25, 1991)

The foremost problem in creating a microchoice learning economy to replace the public education bureaucracy is to rearrange the existing finance structure to fund the microvouchers that form the heart of the new design. The current fragmentation of funding sources makes that task more difficult and inefficient than it needs to be.

The local property tax that now funds a share of the costs of K–12 schools (and some public colleges)—a share that varies from minor to major across U.S. communities—should be ended as a source of educational revenues and replaced with state government sources. Using property taxes to finance education never had any philosophical rationale, but was just an arbitrary expedient in earlier times when America had a lot more land than cash. The result has been a continuous and growing flurry of court challenges to the inherent inequality and inequity of funding schools by this mechanism.

The thrust of recent state court decisions in Kentucky, New Jersey, Texas, and elsewhere is clearly headed toward the logical, inevitable conclusion that there simply is no reasonable or fair way to finance the learning opportunities of individual persons by a randomly variable revenue source like the property tax. Attempts at "leveling down" by so-called Robin Hood strategies that reallocate taxes from rich to poor communities will never be politically acceptable. "Leveling up" by increasing the total tax burden is equally infeasible. The U.S. tax burden is as high as the public will tolerate; if anything it's become too high. And leveling up arrangements never last long anyway, because the wealthy believe that they have to spend more on education to get the better results they think their station deserves—the inequality eventually returns, with the only result that total costs have been further inflated.

Nostalgic mythology about "local control" should not mask the reality that the state governments in America have the constitutional authority, call the shots, and pay most of the bill for education. A big step in the right direction is represented by the state of Hawaii, which has no local school districts and which funds education by collecting all property taxes, combining them with other revenues, and allocating almost equal per-pupil funding to each school. It's true that Hawaii has a relatively small population. But there's nothing about the structure of its educational system that could not be duplicated in other states.

Keep in mind that a microchoice learning enterprise makes the technology and structure of "school" obsolete anyway. A system with no schools in the traditional sense needs no local school districts, boards, superintendents, and bloated bureaucracies. The traditional argument for local control is that it is more responsive to a community's people than a distant authority in the state capital. But microchoice provides *individualized* services to meet the needs of each family and student—a system that is far more responsible to learning consumers than a collective local government structure.

So consolidating both funding and governance of the learning enterprise at the state level not only is administratively simpler, but, by eliminating a superfluous layer of bureaucracy, will immediately start saving a substantial chunk of taxpayer dollars. Local governments—counties and cities—should still have a formal learning policy expressing local priorities and interests, and agencies to oversee local learning services, just as they do for health, transportation, water, or other services. But government, local or otherwise, no longer needs to own and operate school systems or academic institutions.

Again, the government responsibility in a microchoice system is to provide financial support directly to learners and the normal consumer protection and other regulation appropriate to any business. Everything else will be left to private enterprise. That's what "privatize" means.

While states may prefer to continue to use property or other kinds of taxes to fund learning and other human development services, there is merit in earmarking a source of revenue specifically for this purpose. One possibility would be a human capital tax. The human capital tax might be simply the same as a personal income tax, or might be calculated or earmarked in a more limited way. Technicalities aside, it's logical that if the government is going to help fund investments in the development of the community's human capital, taking back a share of the resulting gains is a good way to pay for it. In effect, each generation of beneficiaries of such investment pays back some of the benefits it received to the next generation.

Recall that the microchoice system pays for products and services, not for attendance in the traditional sense (although many services have to be "attended" to be consumed). So part of the legislation for privatizing public education includes revoking compulsory school attendance laws.

This is necessary to assure a truly consumer-focused system, and it is not as radical a change as it may at first seem. There is no reason to believe that if compulsory attendance were scotched tomorrow notably fewer students would attend school. If anything, the great unmet need of most of today's working-parent families is for more day care for their children, not less.

What about the kids who would play hooky and whose parent(s) either doesn't care or can't do anything about it? Most of the ones that want to cut or drop out of school are doing it anyway—truancy laws are not all that well enforced or effective. A privatized, microchoice system by its very design would be far more attractive and engaging for the legions of kids who are tuning out now.

I'm not suggesting we simply write off the small minority of cases in which parents are not effectively caring for their children and are not getting their kids the developmental services they need. But we have other legal tools to take care of those problems—the laws governing child neglect and abuse. We should deal with parents who are starving their children's minds with the same legal remedies we use to deal with parents who are starving their children's bodies. The HL media through which a microchoice system is provided will give public authorities more accurate information on what individual families and kids are doing than is currently available, making it easier to identify instances of negligence or misuse.

How will we know what's happening with the public money invested in a privatized learning system? Development and implementation of an effective technology of accounting for specific results and costs is one of the essential planks in the basic platform for restructuring the nation's educational systems—improved productivity cannot be attained if it cannot be measured. Development of this technology is a key mission of an expanded R&D program.

But accounting processes also need to be institutionalized. One step in this direction could be the creation of the instructional equivalent of the Financial Accounting Standards Board, at least at the state and perhaps at the national level. Just as FASB exists to protect the interests of investors, an instructional accounting standards organization must be designed to serve the interests of the learning consumer. At a minimum, this means that the membership, organization, and control of an instructional accounting board need to be independent of institutions and bureaucracies responsible for providing instructional services and products.

The commercial privatization of public education would include higher education, by the way, as well as the elementary and secondary levels—in fact these labels to distinguish education "levels" would be obsolete in a learner-focused enterprise. People of any age will simply learn whatever they need and want to. The state may want to focus its financial contribution on a certain range of human needs—almost certainly including at the very least attainment of those "basic" abilities represented by the CBC. But there is no reason to discriminate by age—a thirty-year-old immigrant who needs to develop English literacy and some other of the "basics" should be as eligible for public support as a ten-year-old native-born child.

Current higher education aid to students would be lumped into the same microchoice account as other education and training funds—all learning that is eligible for government assistance should be payable with the same card from the same account. While an argument can be made that the state would want to limit funding to persons who reside within the state's borders, there's no good reason why the learner should not be able to purchase services or products from any provider—whether public or private, in-state or out-of-state. The point is to get as much competition as possible to maximize choices and drive down costs.

I've advocated—actually predicted—the extinction of public schools . . . what about public colleges and universities? As educational institutions and technologies they are as obsolete as other kinds of schools. As research institutions, though, they are as valuable as ever—possibly more so, since the faculty can be eternally freed of the onerous "teaching burden" if they like.

I'm not seeking to deny anyone any kind of opportunity, and those who crave the pageantry, ambience, and experience of a campus community ought to be able to have it. But in a multimedia, telematic, and so forth knowledge age environment, attendance and residence are not generally essential to learning or to apprentice participation in a community of practice. Rubbing elbows and hanging out with sympathetic fellows certainly is a very enjoyable experience to most of us. And those who want it should be able to buy it. Whether the state taxpayer wants or should want to pay for someone to enjoy that "experience" is another question.

Privatization of education may seem like a giant step, utterly unimaginable to educators, but it's actually the culmination of a process that is already under way. The commercial Berlitz International is contracting with public as well as private schools to teach Spanish, Japanese, and other language courses. Schools also have purchased the Evelyn Wood brand of speed-reading and study skills courses. Hundreds of for-profit Sylvan Learning Centers, Britannica Learning Centers, and Huntington Learning Centers now dot the country, providing supplementary instruction in basic skills to thousands of parents more than willing to pay for after-school teaching for their kids.[282]

In 1991, Gateway Educational Products Ltd., based in Orange, California, sold over a quarter million *Hooked on Phonics* audiocassette programs that teach reading skills. A number of academic critics carp about the $180 program's limitations. But John Shanahan, the company's president, points out, "If there weren't a need for our product, we wouldn't be here."[283] Moreover, the product's thirty-day unconditional money-back guarantee is rarely used, according to Shanahan. While the Council of

Better Business Bureaus got Gateway to tone down its ads slightly, there's no evidence that the product or its marketing are illegitimate.

Hooked on Phonics is hardly high technology, and critics such as Ken Komoski of Educational Products Information Exchange and Jeanne Chall, a reading specialist at Harvard, are correct in asserting that there are more effective tools to learn reading. But Gateway's marketing strategy deserves credit for motivating thousands of people to overcome their school-induced fear of failure, and to tackle learning to read as a fun and rewarding task. Instead of whining, Shanahan's academic critics would do better for all concerned by simply bringing superior products to the commercial market and trying to beat Gateway in head-to-head competition.[284]

As employers are compelled to meet the acute child-care needs of the working-parent workforce of the 1990s and beyond, they are moving progressively to develop high-quality corporate-owned centers rather than just referrals. And rather than bear the cost and liability risks of company-owned facilities alone, major employers are forming multicorporation partnerships to develop community centers for their own employees that also are open to the public.[285] As the line between child-care and learning centers increasingly dissolves, corporations are going to find themselves more and more owning, operating, managing, subsidizing, and generally providing community-wide "educational" services for workers' and other families.

But what about privatizing a whole school? The new South Pointe Elementary School in Miami Beach, Florida, is at least a partial step in that direction. The school is designed around an integrated curriculum and operating plan developed by Education Alternatives Inc., a for-profit Minneapolis company that owns and operates private schools in Minnesota and Arizona. EAI's founder and president, John Golle, originally proposed a contract to the Miami-Dade school district that would have had his company operate South Pointe on its own. But the current contract has the district running the school, with EAI paid $700,000, in addition to the district's budget for the school of $1.7 million, to cover costs of implementing the company's curriculum design, marketed under the brand name Tesseract.

While Golle is taking an entrepreneurial stab at commercializing schools, EAI's particular approach may not be a feasible business strategy. While EAI's system is supposed to be profitable at the same cost per pupil of public schools, the two private schools EAI operates so far have not made a profit, despite tuition charges of $5,000 to $6,000 a year. And EAI's costs plus its $1.2 million fee for the South Pointe school were to be funded not by the school district but by $2.2 million of private donations raised over a five-year period, which so far have proven difficult to raise. Depending on charity to cover costs, much less profits, is a pretty bizarre concept of "commercialization" that offers little prospect of being sustained, let alone duplicated. Still, EAI is a young company and Golle is trying to bootstrap it to a large enough scale to become efficient.[286] EAI recently joined with KPMG, Peat Marwick, and Johnson Controls World Services (which helps manage the Kennedy Space Center) in a contract to take over management of an entire Florida school district.

Another private, for-profit company, Ombudsman Educational Services, based in Libertyville, Illinois, is running special programs for students at risk of dropping out of school under contract to twenty-three school districts in Illinois, Minnesota, and Arizona. OES got its charge down to $3,500 per student—$2,000 less than the average expenditure per pupil in Chicago's public schools—by cutting out study halls, lunchtime, and as much noninstructional time as possible. The short school day enables OES to run three shifts of students a day, achieving more efficient use of resources, with the added benefit of enabling older kids to continue their studies while holding down jobs.[287]

These examples at least show that some public school systems are willing to consider privatizing by contracting out school operations. The Minnesota Educational Computing Corporation, MECC, was founded as a state-owned agency to develop and distribute K–12 school software. After operating nearly fifteen years as a government organization, MECC went private about a year ago. MECC "evolved into a viable commercial enterprise," the state's former finance commissioner, Peter Hutchinson, pointed out.[288] So much so that commercial software firms complained to the state about the unfairness of the government subsidizing MECC to compete with them.

The most important move toward privatizing K–12 education is Chris Whittle's plan, mentioned earlier, to invest $2.5 billion in developing a profitable commercial system of at least two hundred centers by 1996. While the plan seems ambitious, Whittle is a savvy entrepreneur who has a track record of success. Despite the armed resistance of the state education pooh-bahs of California and New York, Whittle's Channel One program—which provides commercial-sponsored news and other television programming, along with satellite equipment and TV sets, at no charge to subscribing schools—within two years of its introduction had been adopted by over ten thousand public schools nationwide, reaching about a third of U.S. secondary school students. While an independent evaluation of Channel One after its first year, commissioned by Whittle, found only minor and inconsistent learning gains, 60 percent of the teachers in the participating schools surveyed said they would recommend the program strongly or very strongly.[289]

Privatization is less alien at the postsecondary level of education, which long has included hundreds of "proprietary," meaning for-profit, institutions—mostly trade and technical training schools. In fact, critics of privatization likely will pick on the troubles of this industry to discredit the idea of commercial learning ventures.

Continual controversy over the relatively higher default rate of government-insured student loans among the proprietary institutions has generated an undeserved aura of scandal. Most proprietary schools are well-run, professional organizations that are successful in providing the kinds of job-specific training services for which they were designed. The higher loan default rate mainly reflects the needier student population they serve, many of whom have been failed by the public education system and come to the trade schools in search of a "second chance." The proprietary schools are often held to higher standards of performance than public or nonprofit colleges—they are expected to actually place their graduates in jobs. Students occasionally are stranded when schools go bankrupt, but other proprietary institutions usually pitch in to help the students complete their training.

The for-profit schools have had their share of smarmy, fly-by-night operators. But the industry associations have a vested interest in working with the government to police these crooks. And such corruption is not unknown in nonprofit education circles—for instance, witness the recent history of the University of South Carolina, whose president was caught with his fingers in the fiscal cookie jar, or the esteemed Stanford University, which was tagged for misusing federal research funds to buy such niceties as bed sheets and furniture for the president's house, a yacht, and a shopping mall.

Privatization is not just the wave of the future—it's sweeping the whole world. Just about every state industry other than education is going private somewhere in the world today.[290] The former Soviet Union is struggling to imminently privatize about five hundred times as many state-run businesses as the whole rest of the world has taken private in the last decade.

Everything new has to happen somewhere for the first time. Sooner or later, Argentina, Mexico, Mongolia, Poland, or any other of the slew of nations rushing to privatize government bureaucracies will grasp the message of this book—that the same bloated inefficiency that plagues state-run oil companies, telephone companies, banks, or airlines infects state-owned education businesses with the same cancerous result.

In the beleaguered nations of the ex-Soviet empire, no form of privatization is unthinkable. A software entrepreneur from St. Petersburg with whom I recently dined in Washington told me that Russians, distrustful of any state institution, are setting up their own private schools. So maybe the Russians will do with American innovations in hyperlearning what the Japanese did four decades ago with American innovations in manufacturing quality control.

There's no reliable textbook on how to privatize large numbers of big public organizations—the privatization wave is too new and too swift. But to privatize education, there's plenty of ongoing experience in other industries and countries all over the planet to observe and learn from. This experience offers at least two key lessons.

One is that there's not much to be gained by simply "commercializing" a public monopoly into a private monopoly.[291] "That's market socialism, and it is sure to fail," warns Jeffrey Sachs, a Harvard economist who has been closely involved in advising Poland's government on restructuring its economy. The benefits of free markets come from competition, not just private ownership. Some education consultants think public education can incrementally commercialize by having the same public bureaucracy "contract out" for services and products—a "mixed economy" approach. That's just another name for market socialism. "There is no valid 'third road,'" Sachs concludes.[292]

The other basic lesson is that faster is better. "Rapid privatization is needed to combat the inevitable social, political, and economic problems associated with the lack of corporate governance," say Sachs and David Lipton in a Brookings Institution paper on the Poland situation.[293] Tinkering with reform for ten years only left Poland poorer and deeper in debt when the country finally was forced to face the inevitable collapse of socialism. Seven years of plan after fruitless plan for incremental *perestroika* left the Soviet Union shattered, hungry, and facing frightful chaos.

Experience in many countries and large industries shows that, while privatization is never painless, the most rapid and thorough process is far less painful and costly than procrastination and half-measures. The best strategy, as the pithy wisdom of the marketing slogan for Nike sneakers goes, is "Just do it."

STEP 3: CAPITALIZE

Privatization of education's socialist economy is necessary but not sufficient to turbocharge the new reformation of learning. Even after the legal barriers to a private, commercial learning enterprise are removed, there will remain the same yet-unmet needs for capital investment—technical, working, and human—that hamper the reconstruction of Central European, ex-Soviet, and other ex-socialist countries. In the case of America's learning enterprise, I've estimated earlier that at least $8–20 billion annually needs to be invested in research, development, innovation, and commercialization of the hyperlearning systems suitable to a knowledge age economy.

To achieve this goal, we need, first, to reallocate funds from existing education and training budgets to these purposes. Second, we need to create and reorganize institutional structures to carry out these tasks.

Set-aside Funding for Technology Development and Implementation

The near-total lack of funding of technological development and innovation in the education sector can best (and probably only) be remedied by reallocating a substantial portion of existing education budgets. Since state governments provide about half of K–12 school funding in the U.S., and a larger share of total higher education funding, the states are in the best position to swiftly and effectively close education's technology gap. At least 5 percent of the total education and training expenditures in the state need to be redirected to finance innovation.

Specifically, states should set aside (by mandate or direct appropria-

> . . . [A] market economy cannot succeed in a country where hardly any-
> one understands how the free enterprise system works. In addition,
> very few Soviet enterprises are capable of competing with businesses
> in the industrial nations, and steps such as privatization and price reform,
> by themselves, will seldom make Soviet enterprises competitive. In a
> market economy there is no market for inferior products based on out-
> dated technology. As we have seen in eastern Germany, where quick
> reform has idled one-third of the work force, competitiveness requires
> not only reform but large investments.
>
> —James Hecht
>
> "Won't the Soviets Use the Aid to Preserve a Failing System? There's a Better Idea,"
> *The Washington Post* (July 7, 1991)

tion) at least 2 percent of the total funding they provide to schools, colleges, and other education and training organizations within their
jurisdictions for a research and development fund. Comparable contribu
tions should be either solicited or mandated from local governments in
the state. Because there are inherent economies of scale in research, the
state R&D fund should be centrally accumulated, to be utilized by one or
more state research organizations. (Some alternative organizational forms
are suggested below.)

A second set-aside of 2 to 3 percent of educational organization budgets
should be mandated for either centralized or distributed "innovation
funds" to support the commercialization and implementation of new technologies for learning and teaching. It is essential that the total program
supported by these funds be managed in accordance with the kinds of
guidelines suggested earlier. In particular, the funds must be invested to
achieve the goals of (1) increased productivity of learning and teaching and
(2) self-sustaining commercialization of innovative products and services.

The 2 percent level of funding proposed here for R&D would still leave
research and development in the education sector funded at the level of
the average U.S. business, and well below the levels found in major infor-

mation and high-tech industries. It would generate R&D funding some-what in excess of $8 billion annually at the current level of school and college spending—about the same as the budget for the National Institutes of Health.

The additional 3 percent to capitalize commercialization and innova-tion would produce at least $12 billion of venture capital that could be leveraged to generate several times more investment capital needed to launch a dozen or more entrepreneurial ventures like Chris Whittle's, to help educate consumers and policymakers about the new learning options available to them, and to help train, retrain, and recycle the learning en-terprise's workforce.

While the 2 percent plus 3 percent mix of funding suggested here is admittedly arbitrary, it's important to keep in mind the importance of developing a program that focuses on commercialization and innovation, not just R&D. Education's shortfall in R&D investment is huge, and needs to be closed. But throwing billions into research laboratories without as-suring that results will be translated into commercially successful products and services would simply be a new form of waste. Dogma about focusing public investment on "precompetitive" research and not "picking winners" should not obscure the necessity of linking R&D investments intimately to the achievement of practical marketplace results.

The education establishment and its apologists will claim that they can't *afford* to take 5 percent off the top of budgets they always feel are inadequate. But the real cost of implementing this proposal is: nothing. The whole point of making these investments in innovation is that they will be paid back many times over by greatly increasing the productivity of our expenditures on learning. The real cost of education's vast technol-ogy gap is the huge cost of doing nothing to close it.

If education politics are good for anything, it's to provide an infinite variety of excuses for inaction. When I made these proposals last year to a conference of state legislators, they argued that, in the midst of a reces-sion when education budgets were frozen or even being cut, it would be politically impossible to take away another 5 percent from current opera-tions. But a few years earlier, when I suggested a similar investment strat-egy to a meeting of senior officials in the state of Connecticut, I was told that the state government was running a revenue *surplus* of more than $200 million and the governor therefore would have no interest in propos-als aimed at saving the taxpayers' money.

Which brings us full circle back to public schools as America's collective farms. A socialist economy never can find reasons to invest in innovation and productivity because it gets its money from political extortion, not what an old TV commercial used to call "the old-fashioned way"—by earning it.

So it's unlikely that the proposal to take some of the money now being shoveled into the incinerator of education bureaucracy and to invest it instead in productive innovation is going to be enacted unless it's linked to the larger agenda of privatization. But that should not obscure the reality that the money exists in the current budgets and that there is every reason it should be invested now.

For one thing, it's odd that politicians think it's "practical" to try to convince voters to accept education budget cuts in the name of fiscal austerity, when the result usually is to reduce services and increase out-of-pocket costs for fees and tuition, leading to stormy public protests. Yet the politicians doubt the feasibility of offering voters the option of redirecting some of the costs of bureaucratic overhead into investments that will give back more bang for the tax and tuition buck.

The simple fact is that the most competitive companies and communities invest *more* in innovation in hard times. The current recession affects Japanese firms as much as anyone else—yet they generally are increasing their investments in innovation, not using "austerity" as an excuse to cut back. So, in the midst of a slump in the U.S. car market, Toyota opened a $46 million prototype-vehicle evaluation center in California, began construction of a $110 million proving facility in Arizona, doubled the size of its U.S. design center with a $19 million addition, and opened a $41 million parts and materials evaluation laboratory in Michigan.[294]

Some American companies have learned the lesson. Faced with sagging prospects in the computer and consumer electronics industries, Motorola chairman George M. C. Fisher nevertheless planned to raise R&D expenditures as a percentage of sales and profits. And Chrysler proudly debuted its new billion-dollar R&D center—an investment made not in spite of the most ruthlessly competitive automobile market in history, but because of it. Even cash-strapped U.S. corporations that have trimmed total R&D budgets have restructured those investments to get more bang for their bucks by shifting the focus from basic research to product- and profit-generating development.[295]

A total set-aside of 5 percent of existing public education and training budgets would impose no undue strain on existing programs. By vastly expanding the current degree of investment in research and technology, these set-asides would generate unprecedented momentum for innovation in learning, and establish a base for further expansion of innovation funding in the future.

The obsolescence of the job of "classroom teacher" or "college professor" need not be a threat to the people who now hold that position. They won't be thrown on the scrap heap or sent to the glue factory. Indeed, the learning revolution is opening a golden age for professional educators who are truly dedicated to serving the consumer. But the resources needed to recapitalize these professionals—to acquire new skills and to create their own entrepreneurial enterprises for learning—won't be available without the kind of major funding program proposed here. Professional educators are at a technological and economic crossroads: "More of the same" is not an option. Teachers now must decide what role they will play in the HL revolution: vanguard or victim, leader or Luddite.

National Institutes for Learning

A powerful organizational structure is needed to implement the large-scale research, development, and innovation program the education sector so far lacks.

An institution roughly analogous but not identical to the National Institutes of Health could serve this purpose. The National Institutes for Learning would focus on the research and development of advanced hyperlearning technologies.

NIH itself has only limited relevance as a model for a national learning R&D program. What's relevant is that the federal government's investment of nearly $9 billion a year in NIH represents roughly half the total R&D spending in the health care industry, and this mix of public and private investments seems to have been quite effective in spawning a dazzling array of new medical technologies that are both powerful and profitable.

But the same peculiar economics of health care that make NIH a more productive engine of commercial products than other government R&D programs also make technology a major contributor to the health care sector's disastrous cost explosion. An Institute of Medicine study indicates that the continual introduction and overuse of advanced technologies accounts for up to half the ongoing growth in health care costs.[296]

In other industries, technology usually reduces costs while adding new or better abilities. Technology increases health care costs because the majority of the public so far continues to feel that any gadget that can alleviate disease or extend life should be provided to anyone and everyone who needs it, no matter what the cost. We cling to the notion that insurance or the government can pay the price, even though that increasingly means all of us. So the national bill for health care—which really should be called "disease care"—now demands about one of every eight dollars of U.S. national income and continues to grow at a rate that will double the tab in five years.

I mention this only because it explains why NIH is not necessarily a good model for a national learning R&D program. As long as the nation gives health care a blank check, NIH research can continue to be indifferent to cost and still score success in commercial spin-offs. But a learning R&D program must make cost reduction a primary goal.

The NIL should emulate the high quality standards of NIH in programs, staff, and facilities. The organizational structure of the National Institutes of Learning should be quite different, however.

A better model for the overall organization of learning R&D may be the very successful U.S. agricultural research system. That system combines federal, state, and local organizations, and mixes public and private roles, in a way that has been highly effective in pushing research toward innovation and commercialization. Agricultural R&D resources are split between a federal Agricultural Research Service and a Cooperative State Research Service based in each state. ARS's 1991 budget of $661 million was distributed among several federal laboratories across the U.S. The unique part of the agricultural R&D system is CSRS. Funded at $347 million in 1991, with matching funds contributed by each state, CSRS gets hands-on, local involvement in the R&D process.

The third arm of the process that powers the translation of research into practice is the Agricultural Extension Service, also budgeted at $347 million in 1991. The extension services are based in the state land grant universities, with the mission of getting R&D results out to farmers in the field. In addition to county agents, the AES employs university agricultural research professors as extension agronomists, to bring their technical expertise directly to the entrepreneurial farmers who can put productive new developments into commercial practice.

Rather than being closely tied to the federal government, NIL should be primarily a consortium of state-based and -funded institutions, following the decentralized structure of the nation's agricultural research system. This reflects the reality that the states provide over 90 percent of the funding and virtually all the policy control of public education and training programs (which represent about half or more of the total learning U.S. enterprise). Also: The federal government will be fiscally incapable for the foreseeable future of providing R&D funding on the scale needed to close education's technology gap. There are significant handicaps in federal political control of R&D institutions, as now can be seen in the malaise of NIH. And a decentralized R&D structure offers substantial benefits in diversity, diffusion, and commercialization, as the agricultural system demonstrates. The decentralized, state-based structure of NIL also would fit the set-aside funding mechanism recommended above.

This is not to rule out federal participation entirely. The federal government's $23-billion-a-year constellation of national laboratories is now actively seeking a new mission and role to replace its major function to date of developing nuclear and other strategic weapons—no longer an important priority with the passing of the Cold War. Some of the labs' powerful technical capabilities—in fields such as supercomputing, software engineering, imagery, and bioscience—not to mention a welcome share of their generous budgets, probably could be applied usefully to the development of advanced hyperlearning technology.

On the other hand, the labs are not particularly experienced or effective at bringing technology to successful commercial application. As columnist Jessica Mathews quoted one skeptical CEO: "It's just hard to find a profit-driven attitude there."[297] It may be more efficient to simply reallocate some of the national lab budget to learning and other civilian purposes. Former Defense Under Secretary Robert Costello figures that 20 to 30 percent of the national lab budget could be saved by closing down some of the seven hundred or so laboratories and paring down others.

The most productive model of a government R&D effort that might be applied to the quest for learning innovations is the federal Small Business Innovation Research program. A 1991 study by the General Accounting Office, an arm of the U.S. Congress, concluded that the eight-year-old SBIR program had achieved impressive success in translating research dollars into commercially useful products. A Small Business Administration study found that one-fourth of the eight hundred grant recipients it reviewed were selling products developed from their grant-sponsored research within four years—a much higher success rate than other government R&D programs.[298]

The SBIR program was set up to assure small firms the chance to get a fair share of the large sums the federal government spends on R&D. Because small businesses in the past found it hard to compete against giant corporations for R&D contracts, the SBIR act earmarked a minimum percentage of all R&D budgets to go to small companies only.

Under the SBIR program, companies submit proposals for projects that serve government agency missions and that also have commercial potential. The first phase of funding gives winning proposers $50,000 to explore the feasibility of the innovation, and the second phase grants successful bidders up to $500,000 to start developing their inventions. The aim of the program is to boost innovators so that, in phase three, they can raise private-sector investment to bring their ideas to market.

So, while there is a variety of ways a learning R&D program and the structure of National Institutes for Learning could be worked out, an arrangement combining the agricultural system's effective outreach and technology transfer with the SBIR program's productive support for new business start-ups would seem to have promise.

Strategically, the Institutes can be realized most expediently by business led coalitions motivating the legislatures in a number of bellwether states to create simultaneously a state R&D set-aside funding program and a state Institute for Learning to administer it. As more and eventually all states replicate this model, it will become feasible to organize the national Institutes as a collaborative consortium of these organizations.

As Robert Hutchins once noted, "Anything worth doing is worth doing badly." The mere creation of these learning institutes offers no assurance that they will be organized and managed well. That's one advantage of having them based in the states—more chances of finding a successful design. In reality, a number of state government programs aimed at supporting R&D and promoting new technologies have proven not terribly productive—Virginia's Center for Innovative Technologies is a disappointing but instructive example. Nor have state agencies—such as the Kansas Public Employees Retirement System—always been notably brilliant in using public monies to spark local business creation.[299]

So care must be taken to design and manage these institutions well. At the least, it would be desirable and perhaps essential for the Institutes to be incorporated as entities independent of direct government administration, and especially of civil service regulation. The Institutes should have the autonomous governance of such organizations as Fannie Mae.

The federal government could play a facilitative role in initiating and supporting the National Institutes for Learning. In cooperation with the states, the federal government could charter the Institutes and/or the national corporation that would coordinate the activities of the consortium. Existing or future federal research centers could join the consortium as equal, participating members. The modest federal funds likely to be available could be used as "seed money" or to supplement and hence encourage state, local, and other R&D funding. For instance the federal government could offer to add 10 percent to either all or perhaps the first ten state R&D funds. The federal government also could target certain large-scale and broadly useful research projects such as the "brain map." A more urgent and perhaps intrusive federal strategy would be to require states to establish adequate learning R&D funds and institutions as a condition of eligibility for any federal education/training funds—such mandates exist in a variety of federal programs, from highways to health care.

All this government funding and organization should not cloud the fact that, in a privatized learning enterprise offering lucrative profit opportunities, most investment in the development of advanced HL technology will and should be in the private sector. How that private R&D role can be best stimulated and organized is a matter of open discussion.

While there is a seductive allure to the idea of creating an industrial consortium like a Sematech or MCC for learning, the track record of these corporate research collaboratives to date has not been all that impressive. For example, Britain's "Alvey" program spent $360 million of government funds over five years in a largely unfruitful research attempt to compete with Japan in developing so-called "fifth generation" computer technology. Bringing companies together in consortiums to pursue research jointly achieved research objectives well enough, but failed to yield marketable products. Brian Oakley, former director of the Alvey program, concluded, "The lesson we failed to learn from the Japanese was that their research centers tend to be staffed by people from companies on short-term assignments who then go back to their firms to develop technology for the market, fighting furiously as they do so." The Alvey experience also reflected the finding of a U.S. National Academy of Sciences study that companies would rather make their own research arrangements with universities than risk losing their technical edge by teaming up with competitors in consortia.[300]

Bank for Innovation and Redevelopment

These R&D arrangements will not, by themselves, suffice to meet the need to develop and commercialize learning products and services that will be widely adopted in the marketplace. Innovation must go beyond just invention to achieve widespread commercial sales and popular use.

Because complex innovation processes take place through both centralized and decentralized mechanisms, innovation funds probably should be organized at several levels. For instance, it would seem desirable to require or at least allow individual organizations to retain some portion of innovation funds internally for their discretionary use. Some funds also should be pooled at the regional or state level to support larger-scale services such as training support, consumer information, product evaluation, and so forth. It also would be useful to centralize funds in a state-level innovation "bank" that, like the World Bank or similar development financing institutions, would provide loans in response to competitive proposals.

Replace the Ed Schools

Colleges and graduate schools of education are costly, wasteful institutions that currently absorb resources that can better be applied to technological innovation and structural transformation of the education sector. In most states, the total funding now absorbed by these institutions could provide a major share of the minimum R&D set-aside called for elsewhere in this strategy. The research and training functions the ed schools now nominally perform with negligible useful effect should be reallocated to a completely different form of organization.

Specifically, business leaders—in alliance with their employees and other families in their community—should press the state governments to abolish the existing ed schools (most of which are state funded) and the statutory credentialing requirements for academic employment that seem to justify the existence of the ed school diploma mills. These institutions should be replaced by two new structures.

First, the university ed schools should be converted into R&D centers of the proposed state Institutes for Learning. This would adapt one of the productive features of the agriculture research system's network of research centers based in the traditional land-grant institutions. Some ed school faculty with genuine research competencies could be retained in the new organizations, while faculty and scientists from other disciplines would be invited in. However, R&D center/laboratory staff would be employed to perform research, not to teach; they would work under contract, with no tenure. Relevant models of the R&D centers are the German Max Planck Institutes and the federal national laboratories, particularly the ones that are operated by universities or consortia under contract to the federal government.

Instead of the inefficient and ineffective ed schools, professional development for careers in the learning enterprise would be provided mainly on the job, utilizing distance learning and other advanced media. The new system would combine something like the "alternative certification" structure pioneered in New Jersey with the kind of distance learning network demonstrated by the National Technological University.

YOUR OWN BACKYARD

If we are going to seize the opportunity the learning revolution offers, and make its benefits fairly available to all, joining forces in political action is essential. But you may be more of a joiner or supporter than a political organizer. You want to know what you can do on your own, right now, to take advantage of these new learning opportunities, and maybe help the revolution along in your own backyard.

First, if you are a business leader, the most important action you can take altogether is to manage your own business as if learning matters —because it does. Not only will a strong pro-learning business policy reward your bottom line, but as the old saying goes, practice is better than preaching if you want to influence other people's behavior. As *Harvard Business Review* editor Nan Stone rightly concludes, "business leaders can affect what happens in schools by changing what happens in their own companies."[301]

Perhaps the most powerful and needed initiative in this category is for business to implement completely "competency-based" employment systems. This means, first, developing and using the kind of objective, context-relevant screening-in assessments for entry-level workers called for by the SCANS commission. Beyond the entry level, compensation, promotion, and other employment policies should be revised to focus on demonstrated knowledge and skills rather than academic credentials or general tenure.

In other words, employers don't have to wait or rely on new law to start eradicating credentialism. A uniform legal framework would level the playing field and reduce worries about litigation, but there's much that employers can do now to pave the way to a credential-free economy. And the more employers do in their own backyard, the easier and more persuasive legislative reform efforts will be.

Employers can accelerate the technological restructuring of education and training by committing their companies to continuous improvement of the quality and productivity of their own employee development systems. This is not just a matter of targeting a certain level of expenditure on training. Rather, it means creating a strategy that applies "just-in-time" learning to every phase of operations; that links learning objectives to business productivity and quality; and that serves every employee as needed "on demand," not just the managerial elite.[302] Employee education services further should be extended from just workers to workers' families, especially children.

The Schoolproof Family

Well, all this political action and business leadership sounds swell, you say, but what about my family—what about my kids? You want to know what you can do to get your children prepared for the radically new future this book describes.

First, don't overlook your responsibility as a learning consumer to participate in the kind of political action I called for earlier. After all, this education mess is costing you a fortune. A big chunk of those taxes you're sagging under is going to an education system that's barely serving your family's needs, at best, and may be downright harmful. If you've got a couple of little tykes, the ongoing cost spiral means you might have to shell out close to a million bucks to send them to college, not counting the thousands for private school. If you don't want to keep getting shafted, you have to fight back.

Meanwhile, caring for your family's needs right now is a lot simpler than you might think. The key thing is to create a home where learning is a necessary part of your way of life. Make learning a normal, daily activity for the whole family.

Children become what they behold. Parents who are learners have children who are learners. Learning is as natural a human passion as sex. School may have stomped a lot of that passion out of you, but your kids still have gobs of it and you can renew yours by exercising it. How "smart" or "educated" you are doesn't matter—it's eagerness and openness to learn new things that counts. Rather than harangue the kids about doing their homework, let them see you doing yours. One of the best investments you can make in your children is to invest in your own economic advancement, and that almost invariably means learning new stuff. Most of this has nothing to do with taking courses or passing tests.

One of the best ways research has found to nurture kids' learning is simply for the family to have dinner together and talk about what's going on in their world. A learning family needn't be ponderously serious or "intellectual." It's a matter of being ardently engrossed in whatever interests you, staying insatiably curious, and never letting the need to know something go unsatisfied.

I've noticed that high-learning families I know often are avid sports fans—especially for baseball, which demands constant study of history and statistics to be fully enjoyed. High-learning homes also are information-rich, even those that are not money-rich. They are full of books, newspapers, magazines, stereo, video, computers, Nintendo, toys for grownups as well as kids—all sorts of things that stimulate and nurture curiosity. Providing a brain-stimulating home environment is valuable to kids at all ages, but is especially critical in the first year of life.

The lesson of learning "in context" and participating in "communities of practice" is that the most valuable learning takes place not in classrooms but in doing real things in real places connected with real people in real social institutions. All sorts of community organizations give kids opportunities to learn by practice, to be socialized by real society—scouting, Junior Achievement, 4-H, Little League, churches, museums, libraries, service clubs, the Y, jobs, you name it.

If it fits your family's circumstances, home schooling of children is an option that deserves your serious consideration. While there is some uncertainty in the numbers, estimates are that more than half a million American children are now being schooled at home, an increase of ten times over the last decade. Home schooling is fairly easy to adopt in thirty-two states that only require that parents who teach their own children have a high school diploma. Other states make it more difficult, requiring parents to have a college degree or to pass a teachers' exam, but home schooling is possible almost everywhere in the U.S. The home school option has the attraction of strengthening both families and children while striking a powerful political blow against the education establishment.[303]

Remember: Learning and schooling are on a collision course. Report cards, grades, SATs, diplomas, degrees are all phony claptrap. Celebrate and invest in learning with passion and confidence, and your family's economic prospects and self-esteem will be well taken care of.

CHAPTER 15

EPILOGUE: TOWARD THE TWENTY-SECOND CENTURY

• • •

The belief that education is a key factor of global competitiveness has been expressed in self-defeating strategies of reform aimed at closing imagined "gaps" between the reputed quality of America's schools and those of other nations. Analysts of competitive strategy from David Ricardo to Michael Porter and from Sun Tzu to Douglas MacArthur have known for centuries that the least promising path to competitive advantage is that of catch-up or copycat.

As James Fallows has argued persuasively, America can renew its tarnished leadership not by envy and emulation but only by building on its unique strengths.[304] In regard to education, this means not wasting further time and treasure trying to close mythical "lags" behind the academic budgets and test scores of other nations. Rather, *leadership* means leapfrogging ahead of others, and being first to replace medieval academic structures with the high-tech, hyperlearning industry a knowledge age economy demands.

Ironically, while some Americans view Europe's schools as objects of envy, European industrialists and government leaders increasingly view their traditional education systems as a barrier to the successful integration of what they call the European Economic "Space"—comprised of the Continent's suddenly expanding universe of democratic, market economies. Europe's leaders are laying the groundwork to replace provincial, academic institutions with a new Continental system, blending basic, higher, professional, and vocational education, internationally integrated by a "telematic" network[305] linking the entire "space."[306]

But the precedent for radically reinventing education can be found in America's own history. Despite the fact that the Industrial Revolution began in Great Britain, in the course of the nineteenth century the United States leapfrogged ahead of the British to seize the leadership of the industrial economy. Historians note that the key to America's competitive success in the industrial age was this country's unique education system, which consciously did not attempt to emulate or catch up with the academic establishment of Britain, America's "mother country" and then the world's leading industrial power. Instead, the pioneering Americans of the last century, through eclectic borrowing and novel designs, developed a completely new kind of education system focused on the practical, vocational needs of an industrial economy and a democratic society.

Despite [the] brilliant success [shown at London's Great Exposition in 1851], the reality was that Britain was already in decline. . . . [T]he consensus of opinion was that the English educational system was totally unsuited for the needs of the day. . . . The old prestigious universities of Oxford and Cambridge virtually ignored science, as did the public schools from which most of their students came. . . . The plain fact was that the ruling classes saw no need for technically trained men. . . . [T]he leading countries of Europe set up technical education systems. . . . In the United States, where labour shortage encouraged mechanization and a flood of European immigrants brought new ideas about education with them, land grant colleges were endowed from 1862. . . . Britain reacted too slowly and inadequately: the lead which had seemed unassailable at mid-century had been irretrievably lost by its end. . . .

—Trevor I. Williams

The History of Invention (London: Macdonald & Co., 1987)

After World War I, the conventional wisdom of the world's navies was so convinced of the strategic preeminence of battleships that in the 1920s arms control negotiators desperately sought to avert a battleship-building "race." Once the resulting treaties failed, the world's naval powers each launched an equally urgent effort to avoid a national battleship "lag." Lost in all this rigmarole were the voices of the few visionaries like Mitchell in the United States and Yamamoto in Japan who could plainly see that airpower, not gunpower, had become the key to victory. As the Second World War unfolded, it became increasingly clear that the aircraft carrier had rendered the battleship obsolete.

Similarly, the "battleship" mentality that drives the more-of-the-same-only-better vision of education reform is leading America toward an intellectual and economic Pearl Harbor. For the true threat to American economic security today is not a schooling lag but a *restructuring gap* that is widening with breaktaking speed.

While "restructuring" in America remains little more than a hollow platitude, in Europe the collapse of socialism that followed years of often dilatory talk of *perestroika* has unleashed winds of change that now blow, both east and west, with gale force. In the Orient, and Latin America, and even now in Africa, the passion for democracy is bursting the bondage of Marxist and authoritarian regimes. China's doddering Communist warlords struggle vainly against time and tide to suppress the flood of liberty that sprang forth in Tiananmen Square. Japan's worn-out political establishment remains untoppled, but continues to teeter as that fast-aging society reassesses all its basic assumptions and plots its next great leap. India's establishment has fallen, unleashing new upheaval in the world's biggest democracy.

From Czechoslovakia to Chile, from South Africa to Nicaragua, from Mongolia to Ethiopia, the status quo is on the rout, the unthinkable has become the commonplace, and the fabric of whole societies is being rewoven. As every major social structure in these lands is reappraised and redesigned or replaced, the most conservative social glue—education —inevitably will be reinvented as well.

The same HL technology that is driving the overthrow of arthritic bureaucracies holds the key to achieving this social reformation swiftly and productively. In the words of the immortal philosopher Pogo, we seem to be confronted with an insurmountable opportunity.

NOTES

• • •

1. See John Immerwahr, Jean Johnson, and Adam Kernan-Schloss, *Cross-Talk: The Public, The Experts, and Competitiveness,* A Research Report from The Business-Higher Education Forum (Washington, D.C.) and The Public Agenda Foundation (New York, February 1991).
2. Tony Swan, "Microchip Mechanic," *Popular Science* (July 1987); Martin's Chevrolet account from "Mr. Chips, Meet Mr. Goodwrench," *Human Capital* (Nov.-Dec. 1989).
3. George Gilder, *Microcosm: The Quantum Revolution in Economics and Technology* (New York: Simon & Schuster, 1989).
4. Hans Moravec, *Mind Children: The Future of Robot and Human Intelligence* (Cambridge: Harvard University Press, 1988).
5. "Smart Programs Go to Work," *Business Week* (Mar. 2, 1992).
6. "Some Computers Manage to Fool People at Game of Imitating Human Beings," *The Wall Street Journal* (Nov. 11, 1991).
7. Personal communication.
8. See Kalman A. Toth, "The Workless Society," *The Futurist* (May-June 1990).
9. "Smart Programs Go to Work," *Business Week* (Mar. 2, 1992).
10. Personal communication, Oct. 22, 1991.
11. Andrew Tanzer, "War of the Sales Robots," *Forbes* (Jan. 7, 1991).
12. "Fuzzy Logic Puts Minolta in Sharp Focus," *Business Week* (June 17, 1991).
13. Victoria Kader, "Japanese Companies Are Incorporating 'Fuzzy Logic' in a Growing Number of Products and Services," *Business America* (Sept. 24, 1990).
14. "Neural Network Software Is Getting Brainier," *The Wall Street Journal* (Feb. 28, 1991).

15. "Smart Programs Go to Work," *Business Week* (Mar. 2, 1992).

16. M. Mitchell Waldrop, "Toward a Unified Theory of Cognition," *Science* (July 1, 1988) and "Soar: A Unified Theory of Cognition?" *Science* (July 15, 1988).

17. "Computers Gaining a Way with Words," *San Francisco Chronicle* (June 13, 1991).

18. "Japan shows progress in machine translation," *The Institute* (IEEE; May-June 1991).

19. George Gilder, "Into the Telecosm," *Harvard Business Review,* March-April 1991.

20. "Wireless personal links, office LAN under test," *The Institute* (IEEE; May-June 1991).

21. "Computer Makers Are Hurrying to Create Portables Incorporating Cellular Modems," *The Wall Street Journal* (Mar. 6, 1991).

22. "The Baby Bells Learn a Nasty New Word: Competition," *Business Week* (Mar. 25, 1991).

23. "Your New Computer: The Telephone," *Business Week* (June 3, 1991).

24. "Electronics Newsfront: Compressing Cable Video," *Popular Science* (May 1991).

25. "Talking Back to the Tube," *Newsweek* (Dec. 3, 1990).

26. On "just-in-time" learning, see Steve Floyd, "J.I.T. Learning Fulfills Technology's Promise," *Human Capital* (Nov.-Dec. 1989).

27. "Word Wizards," *Popular Science* (Dec. 1989).

28. "Products to Watch," *Fortune* (June 17, 1991).

29. "Products to Watch," *Fortune* (Mar. 25, 1991).

30. Dawn Stover, "Hypermedia," *Popular Science* (May 1989).

31. "Insight aided by computer graphics, more education urged at IBM conference," *The Institute* (IEEE; May-June 1991).

32. "Computers Are Making Strides in Portraying Scientists' Ideas," *The Wall Street Journal* (Nov. 6, 1987).

33. "MCA May Offer a New Reality at the Movies," *The Wall Street Journal* (Apr. 15, 1992).

34. "The Roar of the Engine, The Glow of the Screen," *Business Week* (Oct. 9, 1989).

35. "Fighting Back Against Data Overload," *The Wall Street Journal* (Oct. 20, 1989).

36. Tekla S. Perry, "Hypermedia: finally here," *IEEE Spectrum* (Nov. 1987).

37. "A Machine with a Mind of Its Own," *Insight* (Dec. 3, 1990); "USA Today Profile: Doug Lenat," *USA Today* (Mar. 9, 1988).

38. Lecture by Walter Freeman (University of California at Los Angeles) at Smithsonian Institution, Washington, D.C. (Aug. 8, 1991).

39. Paul Willbust, lecture at Smithsonian Institution, Washington, D.C. (July 25, 1991).

40. See "Medicine's Next Marvel: The Memory Pill," *Fortune* (Jan. 20, 1986).

41. "Brain Research Spawns a Race for New Drugs," *The Wall Street Journal* (Feb. 15, 1989).

42. Michael Schrage, "Soon Drugs May Make Us Smarter," *The Washington Post* (Feb. 3, 1985).

43. "Can Lab-grown Cells Thwart Parkinson's and Alzheimer's?" *Business Week* (Mar. 25, 1991).

44. Personal communication (Feb. 27, 1992).

45. L. Roberts et al., *Linking for Learning: A New Course for Education* (Washington, D.C.: Office of Technology Assessment, 1989).

46. Peter H. Lewis, "The Electronic Edge," *The New York Times,* Special Report on Education (Apr. 7, 1991).

47. Therese Margeau, "Teaching and Learning On-line," *Electronic Learning* (Nov.-Dec. 1990).

48. Bernie Ward, "Corporations and Kindergartens," *Sky* (April 1991).

49. "Trade Show Targets the Home Office," *The Washington Post* (June 4, 1991).

50. See "Tolerance Rises for Businesses Run in Homes," *The Wall Street Journal* (July 9, 1991); Terri Shaw, "The Perils and Pleasures of Home Offices," *The Washington Post* (Apr. 25, 1991); Christopher O'Malley, "High-Tech Tools for the Home Office," *Popular Science* (May 1991); Michael Alexander, "Travel-Free Commuting," *Nation's Business* (Dec. 1990).

51. See Chapter 4.

52. George Gilder, *Life After Television* (Knoxville, Tenn.: Whittle Direct Books, 1990), p. 43.

53. "Smart Programs Go to Work," *Business Week* (Mar. 2, 1992).

54. David Kirkpatrick, "Here Comes the Payoff from PCs," *Fortune* (Mar. 23, 1992).

55. *An America That Works: The Life-Cycle Approach to a Competitive Work Force* (New York: Committee on Economic Development, 1990).

56. Evolution of the term "automobile" is from Frank Donovan, *Wheels for a Nation* (New York: Thomas Y. Crowell, 1965).

57. Data are from U.S. Census Bureau. A spurt in construction employment from the building boom of the 1980s has now reversed and is likely to recur soon. It does not alter the trend toward service employment. In fact, the service trend is understated as an increased number of jobs in manufacturing or even agricultural firms involve services. IBM, for instance, is a major "industrial" firm that nevertheless employs a large number of its people in services and is committed to expanding the share of its total revenue from software and services.

58. *Capital Formation and Economic Growth,* Center for Economic Policy Research Publication No. 214 (Stanford: Stanford University, August 1990).

59. See "The Analytical Economist: Sixteen Tons of Coal," *Scientific American* (June 1990); "Productivity's Progress," *The Wall Street Journal* (Sept. 25, 1989).

60. Interstate Conference of Employment Security Agencies. *The Wall Street Journal* (July 23, 1991).

61. Alfred Bork, "Technology in education: work toward goals," *Electronic Education* (Jan. 1987).

62. National Center on Education and the Economy, *America's Choice: high skills or low wages!* (Rochester, N.Y.: NCEE, 1990).

63. Louis Uchitelle, "High Technology in Plants Abroad," *The New York Times* (Mar. 12, 1990).

64. Michael Schrage, "Making Sense Out of a Firm's Greatest Asset—Smarts," *The Washington Post* (Apr. 17, 1992).

65. "Key Economies Seem Likely to Avoid Risk of a Global Recession," *The Wall Street Journal* (Apr. 17, 1992).

66. Charles Handy, *The Age of Unreason* (Cambridge: Harvard Business School Press, 1989).

67. "Technology Firms Are Finding Their Expertise Elsewhere," *The Washington Post* (July 29, 1991).

68. Kathleen K. Wiegner and Julie Schlax, "But Can She Act?" *Forbes* (Dec. 10, 1990).

69. "Walt Disney Agrees to Distribute Film by Jobs's Pixar," *The Wall Street Journal* (July 12, 1991).

70. "Five U.S. Companies Form Computer Group," *The Washington Post* (Apr. 25, 1990).

71. Anthony Patrick Carnevale, *America and the New Economy* (Washington, D.C.: American Society for Training & Development, 1991).

72. At the Dobelle Institute Inc. in Glen Cove, N.Y. See "Pacemakers That Let Patients Escape from the Iron Lung," *Business Week* (June 3, 1991).

73. "Homemade Music Is Going High Tech at a Low Price," *The Wall Street Journal* (Feb. 15, 1989).

74. John McDonough, "Pop Music Without Pop Performers," *The Wall Street Journal* (May 4, 1991).

75. "How Iris Gillon Keeps an Orchestra in Her Apartment," *Business Week* (Oct. 27, 1987).

76. "Making Music the PC Way," *The Wall Street Journal* (Oct. 21, 1991).

77. "Giving Greater Weight to the Jobless in Making Policy," *The Washington Post* (Jan. 26, 1992).

78. "If It's a Mild Recession, Why Is It So Painful?" *Business Week* (Feb. 10, 1992).

79. "Torrent of Job Cuts Shows Human Toll if Recession Goes On," *The Wall Street Journal* (Dec. 12, 1991); "Labor force is changing permanently," *USA Today* (Dec. 20, 1991); "Downward Mobility," *Business Week* (Mar. 23, 1992).

80. "Where the Schools Aren't Doing Their Homework," *Business Week* (Nov. 28, 1988).

81. "Law Firms v. Layoffs: The Case of the Bottom Line," *The Washington Post* (Dec. 4, 1991); "Big Law Firms Are Trimming Associates' Pay Scales," *The Wall Street Journal* (Mar. 10, 1992).

82. Lewis J. Perelman, "Learning Our Lesson: Why School Is Out," *The Futurist* (Mar.-Apr. 1986).

83. "Is Your Job Safe?" *U.S. News & World Report* (Jan. 13, 1992).

84. "A Sea Change in Confidence," *Fortune* (Dec. 2, 1991).

85. "The Future Deferred," *The Washington Post* (Sept. 15, 1991). Also, "The Boomerangers," and "When 7 Is More Than Enough," *The Washington Post* (Aug. 3, 1990).

86. "The Case of the Missing Productivity," *The Washington Post* (Jan. 21, 1990).

87. For instance, see Richard B. Freeman, *The Market for College-Trained Manpower: A Study in the Economics of Career Choice* (Cambridge: Harvard University Press, 1971); Richard B. Freeman, *The Overeducated American* (New York: Academic Press, 1976).

88. "The Rich Are Richer—And America May Be the Poorer," *Business Week* (Nov. 18, 1991).

89. Marvin H. Kosters, "Be Cool, Stay in School," *The American Enterprise* (Mar.-Apr. 1990); also "The Measure of Measures," *The American Enterprise* (Jan.-Feb. 1991).

90. Peter Passell, "Blue-Collar Blues: Who Is to Blame?" *The New York Times* (Jan. 17, 1990); William B. Johnston and Arnold H. Packer, *Workforce 2000* (Indianapolis: Hudson Institute, 1987).

91. A. Gary Shilling, "Good News: More Productivity; Bad News: High Unemployment," *The Wall Street Journal* (Dec. 10, 1991); Marvin J. Cetron and Margaret Evans Gayle, "Educational Renaissance: 43 Trends for U.S. Schools," *The Futurist* (Sept.-Oct. 1990); Stephen L. Mangum, "Impending Skill Shortages: Where Is the Crisis?" *Challenge* (Sept.-Oct. 1990).

92. "Look for Jobless Rate to Stay High in '90s," *The Wall Street Journal* (Mar. 2, 1992).

93. U.S. Dept. of Labor, *Monthly Labor Review* (Nov. 1989).

94. Michael Porter, "Why Nations Triumph," *Fortune* (Mar. 12, 1990).

95. "With Cold War Won, Jobs Are Being Lost," *The Washington Post* (Feb. 14, 1992); Louis S. Richman, "America's Tough New Job Market," *Fortune* (Feb. 24, 1992).

96. "Soviet Scientists Sign Pact to Help Sun Microsystems," *The Wall Street Journal* (Mar. 4, 1992).

97. "Tapping Foreign Talent Pool Can Yield Lush Growth," *The Wall Street Journal* (Mar. 23, 1992).

98. "Lower-Paid Russian Immigrants Offer Competitive Edge to Some Israeli Firms," *The Wall Street Journal* (Mar. 4, 1992).

99. Richard R. Verdugo and Naomi Turner Verdugo, "The Impact of Surplus Schooling on Earnings," *The Journal of Human Resources* (Fall 1989).

100. "State College Tuition Soars While Private School Costs Top $23,000 a Year," *The Wall Street Journal* (Mar. 26, 1992).

101. Lewis J. Perelman, *The Learning Enterprise: Adult Learning, Human Capi-*

tal, and Economic Development (Washington, D.C.: Council of State Planning Agencies, 1985).

102. Henry Kelly, *Technology and the American Economic Transition* (Washington, D.C.: Office of Technology Assessment, 1988).

103. Ithiel de Sola Pool, "Tracking the Flow of Information," *Science* (Aug. 12, 1983).

104. Michael E. Porter, "The Competitive Advantage of Nations," *Harvard Business Review* (Mar.-Apr. 1990).

105. "Productivity Looks Promising," *Fortune* (Mar. 9, 1992).

106. See Anthony Patrick Carnevale, *America and the New Economy* (Alexandria, Va.: American Society for Training and Development, 1991).

107. Eric A. Hanushek, "The Impact of Differential Expenditures on School Performance," *Educational Researcher* (May 1989).

108. Deborah Inman, *The Fiscal Impact of Educational Reform* (New York: Center for Educational Finance, New York University, 1987).

109. Dana Wechsler, "Parkinson's Law 101," *Forbes* (June 25, 1990).

110. Richard Meinhard, "Education by Committee in Oregon," *The Wall Street Journal* (Aug. 23, 1991).

111. "The Exodus," *U.S. News & World Report* (Mar. 9, 1991).

112. "Bush's Education Vision," *The New York Times* (Apr. 20, 1991); "'Education President's' Ambitious Agenda Faces Formidable Obstacles Nationwide," *The Wall Street Journal* (Apr. 19, 1991); "In New York City, Altering School Aid Insures a Fight," *The New York Times* (Apr. 19, 1991).

113. "A Bush Push for His Education Reform Plan Is Likely Soon," *The Wall Street Journal* (May 17, 1991).

114. See, for instance, F. Howard Nelson, *International Comparison of Public Spending on Education* (Washington, D.C.: American Federation of Teachers, 1991); Edith Rasell and Lawrence Mishel, *Shortchanging Education* (Washington, D.C.: Economic Policy Institute, 1990). For a detailed analysis of the statistical errors and misrepresentations in these reports, see Lewis J. Perelman, *The "Acanemia" Deception,* Briefing Paper No. 120 (Indianapolis: Hudson Institute, 1990).

115. See Diane Ravitch, *The Troubled Crusade: American Education 1945–1980* (New York: Basic Books, 1983). Also see Carl F. Kaestle, "The Public Schools and the Public Mood," *American Heritage* (Feb. 1990).

116. "Forecast Is Bleak for State Finances," *The Washington Post* (Aug. 13, 1991); "States' Tax Increases for Year to Show Biggest Jump Since 1971, Survey Finds," *The Wall Street Journal* (Aug. 13, 1991); "Recession, Soaring Medicaid Costs Put the Squeeze on State Budgets," *The Washington Post* (Apr. 18, 1991); "The Sad State of the States," *Business Week* (Apr. 22, 1991).

117. June 19, 1991.

118. "School Cuts Endanger Boston U. Experiment," *The Washington Times* (May 30, 1991).

119. "Cheney Says Taut Reins Will Save $70 Billion," *The Washington Post* (Apr. 26, 1991).

120. "Be Willing to Fund Education Reform with Tax Hikes, Business Leaders Told," *Education Week* (June 19, 1991).

121. Robert B. Reich, "Big Biz Cuts Class," *The Washington Post* (Apr. 21, 1991).

122. "Schools Lose Money in Business Tax Breaks," *The New York Times* (May 22, 1991).

123. See Anthony P. Carnevale, Leila J. Gainer, and Janice Villet, *Training in America* (San Francisco: Jossey-Bass, 1990).

124. "Firms Put Their Weight Behind Early Education," *The Wall Street Journal* (Jan. 7, 1992).

125. "Schools Lose Money in Business Tax Breaks," *The New York Times* (May 22, 1991).

126. Various public statements, including *Educational Technology,* NEA Special Committee Report (Washington, D.C.: National Education Association); "Schools Giving TV Warmer Reception," *The Wall Street Journal* (Dec. 26, 1989).

127. Mikhail Gorbachev, *The August Coup: The Truth and the Lessons* (New York: HarperCollins, 1991).

128. Ellen M. Pechman, "The Child as Meaning Maker: The Organizing Theme for Professional Practice Schools," unpublished paper commissioned by American Federation of Teachers, 1990.

129. John Seeley Brown, Allan Collins, and Paul Duguid, "Situated Cognition in the Culture of Learning," *Educational Researcher* (Jan.-Feb. 1989).

130. Sylvia Farnham-Diggory, *Schooling* (Cambridge: Harvard University Press, 1990).

131. A. Collins, J. S. Brown, and S. Newman, "Cognitive Apprenticeship: Teaching the Craft of Reading, Writing, and Mathematics," in L. B. Resnick, ed., *Knowing, Learning, and Instruction: Essays in Honor of Robert Glaser* (Hillsdale, N.J.: Erlbaum, 1989).

132. C. P. Childs and P. M. Greenfield, "Informal Modes of Learning and Teaching: The Case of the Zinacanteco Learning," in N. Warren, ed., *Studies in Cross-Cultural Psychology,* vol. 2 (New York: Academic Press, 1980).

133. Albert Shanker, American Federation of Teachers editorial advertisement, *The New York Times* (July 8, 1990). See also T. N. Carraher, D. W. Carraher, and A. D. Schliemann, "Mathematics in the Streets and in Schools," *British Journal of Developmental Psychology,* no. 3 (1985); and Thomas Sticht, "Adult Literacy Education," in E. Z. Rothkopf, ed., *Review of Research in Education, 1988–89,* vol. 15 (Washington, D.C.: American Educational Research Association, 1989).

134. A general discussion of this issue is in Howard Gardner, *The Unschooled Mind* (New York: Basic Books, 1991). Also see: J. Clement, "Student Preconceptions of Introductory Mechanics," *American Journal of Physics,* no. 50 (1982); M. McCloskey, A. Caramazza, and B. Green, "Curvilinear Motion in the Absence of External Forces: Naive Beliefs About the Motion of Objects,"

Science, no. 210 (1980); and A. A. diSessa, "Phenomenology and the Evolution of Intuition," in D. Gentner and A. Stevens, eds., *Mental Models* (Hillsdale, N.J.: Erlbaum, 1983).

135. Lauren Resnick, "Learning in School and Out," *Educational Researcher* 16, no. 9 (1983).

136. James Herndon, "How to Survive in Your Native Land" (New York: Simon & Schuster, 1971); as quoted in Jean Lave, *Cognition in Practice* (Cambridge: Cambridge University Press, 1988).

137. Roy D. Pea, *Socializing the Knowledge Transfer Problem,* Report No. IRL89–0009 (Palo Alto, Calif.: Institute for Research on Learning, 1989).

138. M. Pressley, B. L. Snyder, and T. Cariaglia-Bull, "How Can Good Strategy Use Be Taught to Children?" in S. M. Cormier and J. D. Hagman, eds., *Transfer of Learning* (New York: Academic Press, 1987); D. N. Perkins and Gavriel Salomon, "Are Cognitive Skills Context-Bound?" *Educational Researcher* (Jan.-Feb. 1989). See also J. R. Hayes and H. A. Simon, "Psychological Differences Among Problem Isomorphs," in N. J. Castellian, Jr., D. B. Pisone, and G. R. Potts, eds., *Cognitive Theory* (Hillsdale, N.J.: Erlbaum, 1977).

139. Jim Schefter, "Air Traffic Training Gets Real," *Popular Science* (July 1991).

140. "Coming: Embedded Training Systems," *Electronics* (Dec. 17, 1991); Greg Kearsley, "Embedded Training: The New Look of Computer-Based Instruction," *Machine-Mediated Learning* 1, no. 3 (1985).

141. Jean Lave, *Cognition in Practice* (Cambridge: Cambridge University Press, 1988).

142. Jean Lave, *Cognition in Practice* (Cambridge: Cambridge University Press, 1988).

143. See, for instance, Anthony P. Carnevale, Leila J. Gainer, and Ann S. Meltzer, *Workplace Basics: The Skills Employers Want* (Alexandria, Va.: American Society for Training and Development, n.d.).

144. M. Hass, "Cognition-in-Context: The Social Nature of the Transformation of Mathematical Knowledge in a Third Grade Classroom," Social Relations Graduate Program, University of California, Irvine (n.d.); Jean Lave, Steven Smith, and Michael Butler, "Problem Solving in Everyday Practice," in *Learning Mathematical Problem Solving,* Report No. IRL88–0006 (Palo Alto, Calif.: Institute for Research on Learning, 1988).

145. Sylvia Farnham-Diggory, *Schooling* (Cambridge: Harvard University Press, 1990).

146. Jean Lave, Steven Smith, and Michael Butler, "Problem Solving in Everyday Practice," in *Learning Mathematical Problem Solving,* Report No. IRL88–0006 (Palo Alto, Calif.: Institute for Research on Learning, 1988).

147. Senta A. Raizen, *Reforming Education for Work: A Cognitive Science Perspective* (Berkeley, Calif.: National Center for Research in Vocational Education, 1989); Barbara Y. White, "Sources of Difficulty in Understanding Newtonian Dynamics," *Cognitive Science* 7 (1983).

148. Roy D. Pea, *Socializing the Knowledge Transfer Problem,* Report No.

IRL89–0009 (Palo Alto, Calif.: Institute for Research on Learning, 1989); J. D. Bransford et al., "Three Approaches to Improving Thinking and Learning Skills," in S. F. Chipman, J. W. Segal, and R. Glaser, eds., *Thinking and Learning Skills*, vol. 1 (Hillsdale, N.J.: Erlbaum, 1985).

149. Gregory Bateson, *Steps to an Ecology of Mind* (New York: Ballantine, 1972).

150. Thomas Kuhn, *The Structure of Scientific Revolutions* (Chicago: University of Chicago Press, 1970).

151. Brigitte Jordan, *Modes of Teaching and Learning: Questions Raised by the Training of Traditional Birth Attendants*, Report No. IRL87–0004 (Palo Alto, Calif.: Institute for Research on Learning, 1987); Jean Lave, Steven Smith, and Michael Butler, "Problem Solving as an Everyday Practice," in *Learning Mathematical Problem Solving*, Report No. IRL88–0006 (Palo Alto, Calif.: Institute for Research on Learning, 1988); Jean Lave and Etienne Wenger, *Situated Learning: Legitimate Peripheral Participation*, IRL Report No. IRL90–0013 (Palo Alto, Calif.: Institute for Research on Learning, 1990).

152. Jean Lave and Etienne Wenger, *Situated Learning: Legitimate Peripheral Participation*, IRL Report No. IRL90–0013 (Palo Alto, Calif.: Institute for Research on Learning, 1990).

153. Employment and Training Administration, *Work-Based Learning: Training America's Workers* (Washington, D.C.: U.S. Dept. of Labor, 1989).

154. "Making a Mint on Mario," *The Washington Post* (Dec. 15, 1991).

155. U.S. Bureau of the Census, *Statistical Abstract of the United States 1991* (Washington, D.C.: Government Printing Office, 1991).

156. July 3, 1989; p. 54.

157. "The Ways We Learn," *The Washington Post* (Oct. 7, 1991).

158. Jean Lave, *Cognition in Practice* (Cambridge: Cambridge University Press, 1988).

159. T. N. Carraher, D. W. Carraher, and P. Duguid, "Situated Cognition and the Culture of Learning," *Educational Researcher* (Jan.-Feb. 1989).

160. Sylvia Scribner and E. Fahrmeir, "Practical and Theoretical Arithmetic: Some Preliminary Findings," Industrial Literacy Project, Working Paper No. 3 (New York: City University of New York, Graduate Center, 1982).

161. M. Mitchell Waldrop, "The Necessity of Knowledge," *Science* (Mar. 23, 1984).

162. Gregory Bateson, *Steps to an Ecology of Mind* (New York: Ballantine, 1972).

163. E. D. Hirsch, Jr., Joseph F. Kett, and James Trefil, *The Dictionary of Cultural Literacy* (Boston: Houghton Mifflin, 1991).

164. James Burke, *Connections* (Boston: Little, Brown, 1978).

165. Edward B. Fiske, *Smart Schools, Smart Kids: Why Do Some Schools Work?* (New York: Simon & Schuster, 1991).

166. Henry M. Levin and Gail Meister, "Is CAI Cost-Effective?" *Phi Delta Kappan* (June 1986).

167. "Scandal Over Cheating at M.I.T. Stirs Debate on Limits of Teamwork," *The New York Times* (May 22, 1991).

168. Nathan Keyfitz, "Putting Trained Labour Power to Work: The Dilemma of

Education and Employment," *Bulletin of Indonesian Economic Studies* (Dec. 1989).

169. Penelope Eckert, *Jocks & Burnouts* (New York: Teachers College Press, 1989).

170. Susan McGee Bailey, *How Schools Shortchange Girls,* report commissioned by the American Association of University Women (Wellesley: Wellesley College Center for Research on Women, 1992).

171. Penelope Eckert, *Adolescent Social Categories, Information, and Science Learning,* IRL Report No. IRL89–0012 (Palo Alto, Calif.: Institute for Research on Learning, 1989).

172. "Video Angst," *The Washington Post* (Dec. 10, 1990); "Mario's a Big Man on Campus," *The Washington Post* (Mar. 25, 1992).

173. Therese Margeau, "Teaching and Learning On-line," *Electronic Learning* (Nov.-Dec. 1990).

174. See James S. Coleman and Thomas Hoffer, *Public and Private High Schools: The Impact of Communities* (New York: Basic Books, 1987); James S. Coleman, Thomas Hoffer, and Sally Kilgore, *High School Achievement: Public, Catholic, and Private Schools Compared* (Basic Books, 1982). Also, John E. Chubb and Terry M. Moe, *Politics, Markets & America's Schools* (Washington, D.C.: Brookings Institution, 1990).

175. This chapter was based on extensive material contributed by Sue Berryman, director of the Institute for Education and the Economy at Columbia University. The material also benefited from the editorial assistance of Janet Topolsky.

176. See "How Infants See the World," *U.S. News & World Report* (Aug. 20, 1990).

177. Douglas J. Besharov, "Why Head Start Needs a Re-Start," *The Washington Post* (Feb. 2, 1992).

178. Gerald W. Bracey, "Why Can't They Be Like We Were," *Phi Delta Kappan* (Oct. 1991).

179. "Longer School Year Gains Majority Backing," *The Washington Post* (Aug. 23, 1991).

180. Gerald W. Bracey, "Why Can't They Be Like We Were," *Phi Delta Kappan* (Oct. 1991).

181. "Surprise! U.S. Sometimes Beats Japan in Understanding Science," *Science* (Mar. 1, 1991).

182. "Scientist Shortfall a Myth," *The Washington Post* (Apr. 9, 1992).

183. "They'd Rather Switch Than Fight," *Science* (Oct. 18, 1991).

184. "Engineer Shortfall Still Seen, Despite Industry Doldrums," *Aviation Week & Space Technology* (Mar. 4, 1991).

185. "Immigration Has Israel Awash in Scientists," *The Washington Post* (June 15, 1991).

186. "Skilled Chinese Quitting Hong Kong's Uncertainties for Canada," *The Washington Post* (Mar. 29, 1990).

187. Paul E. Barton and Irwin S. Kirsch, *Workplace Competencies: The Need*

to *Improve Literacy and Employment Readiness,* Policy Perspectives Series (Washington, D.C.: U.S. Dept. of Education, 1990).

188. Paul E. Barton, *Skills Employers Need: Time to Measure Them?* Policy Information Proposal (Princeton: Policy Information Center, Educational Testing Service, 1990).

189. "At High Schools, One in Five Students Carries a Weapon," *The Wall Street Journal* (Oct. 11, 1991).

190. "Are You Safe from Guns at School?" *The Washington Post* (Apr. 14, 1992).

191. "At High Schools, One in Five Students Carries a Weapon," *The Wall Street Journal* (Oct. 11, 1991).

192. "Violent Crime Said to Affect 2% of Students Age 12 to 19," *The Washington Post* (Sept. 30, 1991).

193. Table: "Coming Off High," *The Wall Street Journal* (Oct. 1, 1991), based on University of Michigan data.

194. "Fewer High School Seniors Use Drugs, Survey Finds," *The Washington Post* (Jan. 28, 1992).

195. Thomas A. Stewart, "GE Keeps Those Ideas Coming," *Fortune* (Aug. 12, 1991).

196. Notable exceptions are Chris Whittle, president of Whittle Communications, and Myron Lieberman, author of several works analyzing the need for privatization of educational institutions, including *Privatization and Educational Choice* (New York: St. Martin's, 1989).

197. Nathan Rosenberg and L. E. Birdzell, Jr., "Science, Technology and the Western Miracle," *Scientific American* (Nov. 1990); emphasis added.

198. John E. Chubb and Terry M. Moe, *Politics, Markets & America's Schools* (Washington, D.C.: Brookings Institution, 1990); viz. Tables 3–1 and 3–2. Also, the negative number for the lowest quartile "gain" does not necessarily mean that students "unlearned." Rather, it most likely reflects changes in the distribution of student scores.

199. Summarized in Chubb and Moe (1990), Table 5–8.

200. Personal communication, Jan. 31, 1992.

201. U.S. National Center for Education Statistics, *Digest of Education Statistics* (Washington, D.C.: Government Printing Office, 1990); data are for 1989.

202. Henry Kelly, *Technology and the American Economic Transition* (Washington, D.C.: Office of Technology Assessment, 1988).

203. News release of March 19, 1991.

204. John E. Chubb and Terry M. Moe, "The Private vs. Public School Debate," *The Wall Street Journal* (July 26, 1991).

205. Burton A. Weisbrod, "Rewarding Performance That Is Hard to Measure: The Private Nonprofit Sector," *Science* (May 5, 1989).

206. "Catholic School Cash Crisis," *The Washington Post* (May 14, 1991).

207. See James S. Coleman, Thomas Hoffer, and Sally Kilgore, *High School Achievement: Public, Catholic, and Private Schools Compared* (New York: Basic Books, 1982); James S. Coleman and Thomas Hoffer, *Public and Private High Schools: The Impact of Communities* (New York: Basic Books, 1987).

208. Michael Schrage, "Are Ideas Viruses of the Mind?" *The Washington Post* (Oct. 30, 1988).

209. See Financial Management Service, *From Paper to Plastic: The Electronic Benefit Transfer Revolution* and *Electronic Benefit Transfer: A Strategy for the Future* (Washington, D.C.: U.S. Dept. of the Treasury, 1990).

210. "Md. Brings Welfare Benefits into ATM Age," *The Washington Post* (May 13, 1991).

211. "Plastic Cards Approved to Replace Food Stamps," *The Washington Post* (Dec. 14, 1991).

212. "A New Trail Takes Oregon to High Tech," *The Washington Post* (Feb. 24, 1985).

213. *Heading for a Health Crisis: Eating Patterns of America's School Children* (Washington, D.C.: Public Voice for Food & Health Policy, 1991).

214. "Can Vouchers Hurdle Church-State Wall?" *The New York Times* (June 12, 1991).

215. Thomas A. Stewart, "Brainpower," *Fortune* (June 3, 1991).

216. Henry Kelly, *Technology and the American Economic Transition* (Washington, D.C.: Office of Technology Assessment, 1988).

217. Ithiel de Sola Pool, "Tracking the Flow of Information," *Science* (Aug. 12, 1983).

218. U.S. Department of Education budget data.

219. Estimate by Captain E. L. Lewis, U.S. Navy, commanding officer of Naval Training Systems Center, personal communication.

220. Estimates from Henry Kelly, *Technology and the American Economic Transition* (Washington, D.C.: Office of Technology Assessment, 1988).

221. Myron Lieberman, "'Research and the Renewal of Education': A Critical Review," *Education Week* (Sept. 19, 1991).

222. At the bottom of this group of thirty-three companies was a firm that invested *only* $790 per employee in R&D in the previous year. The composite (a weighted average) R&D spending per worker of the surveyed companies in this business was $18,428. Data from the latest (Oct. 25, 1991) version of the *Business Week* Scoreboard are qualitatively about the same, with absolute R&D spending per employee somewhat higher and R&D spending as a percentage of sales down slightly.

223. Data from the undated 1989 *Business Week* issue (entitled "Innovation in America") are used here for consistency with data from the 1988 OTA reports. The magazine surveyed companies reporting sales of at least $35 million and R&D expenses at least equal to $1 million or 1 percent of sales. So small firms or those making little investment in innovation are not included. But most academic enrollment is in school districts and public universities whose budgets would make them big businesses compared to companies on the magazine's list. And the point here is that educational organizations should be among the leaders in innovation. So the "Scoreboard" is a relevant yardstick of education's R&D gap.

224. Personal communication.

225. Linda G. Roberts, *Power On! New Tools for Teaching and Learning* (Washington, D.C.: Office of Technology Assessment, 1988).

226. U.S. Bureau of the Census, *Statistical Abstract of the United States 1991* (Washington, D.C.: Government Printing Office, 1991). Another survey cited found only one microcomputer for every 24.1 students in 1989.

227. For instance, see Cecil McDermott, *Assessment of Technology-Based Supplementary Instruction* (Cupertino, Calif.: Apple Computer, Inc., 1987).

228. "Computer Notes," *The Chronicle of Higher Education* (Oct. 17, 1990).

229. U.S. Bureau of the Census, *Statistical Abstract of the United States 1991* (Washington, D.C.: Government Printing Office, 1991).

230. Stuart Krasny, president, SK&A Research, quoted in Randy Ross, "Technology Tackles the Training Dilemma," *High Technology Business* (Sept. 1988).

231. For example, see "Computers in School: A Loser? Or a Lost Opportunity?" *Business Week* (July 17, 1989); and "Computers Make Slow Progress in Class," *Science* (May 26, 1989).

232. For diverse references on technology and instructional productivity, see Lewis J. Perelman, *Technology and Transformation of Schools* (Alexandria, Va.: National School Boards Association, 1986). Some specific studies of cost-effectiveness of automated instructional systems are: J. D. Fletcher, David E. Hawley, and Philip K. Piele, "Costs, Effects, and Utility of Microcomputer Assisted Instruction in the Classroom," *American Educational Research Journal* (Winter 1990); J. D. Fletcher, "Cost and Effectiveness of Computer Based Training," in *Proceedings of the 1987 IEEE Systems, Man, and Cybernetics Conference* (New York: Institute of Electrical and Electronic Engineers, Inc., 1987); Cecil McDermott, *Assessment of Technology-Based Supplementary Instruction* (Cupertino, Calif.: Apple Computer Inc., 1987); Jesse Orlansky, "The Cost-Effectiveness of Military Training," in *Proceedings of the Symposium on the Military Value and Cost-Effectiveness of Training* (Brussels: NATO, 1985).

233. *The Potential of Interactive Videodisc Technology for Defense Training and Education* (Alexandria, Va.: Institute for Defense Analyses, 1989).

234. Douglas Ellson, "Improving Productivity in Teaching," *Phi Delta Kappan* (October 1986).

235. See "France's Grand Computer Plan in Shambles," *The Washington Post* (Mar. 19, 1989); and "Soviets Launch Computer Literacy Drive," *Science* (Jan. 10, 1986).

236. "750,000 U.S. Children Receiving Stimulants," *The Washington Post* (Oct. 21, 1988).

237. Edward B. Roberts, "Managing Invention and Innovation," *Research-Technology Management* (Jan.-Feb. 1988).

238. W. C. Fernelius and W. H. Waldo, "Role of Basic Research in Industrial Innovation," *Research Management* (July 1980).

239. L. Tornatzky et al., *The Processes of Technological Innovation* (Lexington, Mass.: Lexington Books, 1990).

240. National Research Council, *Automotive Fuel Economy: How Far Should We*

Go? (Washington, D.C.: National Academy of Sciences, 1992); "Study: Sharp Boost in Gas Mileage Possible," *The Washington Post* (Apr. 8, 1992).

241. Walter S. Baer, Leland L. Johnson, and Edward W. Merrow, "Government-Sponsored Demonstrations of New Technologies," *Science* (May 27, 1977).

242. See: Tora K. Bikson, Barbara Gutek, and Don Mankin, *Factors in Successful Implementation of Computer-Based Office Information Systems: A Review of the Literature* (Santa Monica, Calif.: The Rand Corporation, 1983); Bonnie M. Johnson, *Innovation in Office Systems Implementation,* Report No. ISI 8110791 (Washington, D.C.: National Science Foundation, 1985); Dorothy Leonard-Barton and William A. Kraus, "Implementing new techology," *Harvard Business Review* (Nov.-Dec. 1985); Office of Technology Assessment, *Automation and the Workplace: Selected Labor, Education, and Training Issues* (Washington, D.C.: U.S. Congress, 1982); Paul A. Strassman, *Information Payoff: The Transformation of Work in the Electronic Age* (New York: Free Press, 1985).

243. Michael W. Kirst, "Toward a Focused Research Agenda," in *Voices from the Field: 30 Expert Opinions on "America 2000," The Bush Administration Strategy to "Reinvent" America's Schools* (Washington, D.C.: William T. Grant Foundation Commission on Work, Family and Citizenship; and Institute for Educational Leadership, 1991).

244. Peter F. Drucker, "Japan: New Strategies for a New Reality," *The Wall Street Journal* (Oct. 2, 1991).

245. Donald Schon, *Beyond the Stable State* (New York: Random House, 1971).

246. Alan C. Kay, "Computers, Networks and Education," *Scientific American* (Sept. 1991).

247. "Game-Maker Is Enlisted for Military Simulator," *The Wall Street Journal* (Feb. 9, 1989).

248. "Putting the Mind Under the Microscope," *Business Week* (Oct. 10, 1988).

249. *Educational Researcher* (Aug.-Sept. 1991), p. 35.

250. Committee on the Federal Role in Education Research, National Research Council, *Research and Education Reform* (Washington, D.C.: National Academy of Sciences, 1992).

251. Council for Aid to Education data.

252. "St. Paul District Touting Saturn School as Model for Technology in Education," *Education Week* (June 7, 1989).

253. "Projects to Measure the Effects of Computers on Campuses Make Major Advances, Leave Several Unsolved Problems," *The Chronicle of Higher Education* (June 21, 1989).

254. "The Good Principal: A Tradition Breaker," *The New York Times* (Feb. 21, 1990).

255. "Polish Copyright Pirates Peril U.S. Trade Ties," *The Washington Post* (Oct. 21, 1991).

256. "School daze: One year later, Bush education reform stalled," *Chicago Tribune* (Apr. 12, 1992); Pat S. Henry, "America 2000: No Friend to Public Schools," letter to the editor, *The Washington Post* (Apr. 29, 1992).

257. "A Call to Action on a Human Brain Project," *Science* (June 28, 1991).
258. Mark D. Hartwig, "Better Testing Key to Better Science Learning," *The Wall Street Journal* (Feb. 22, 1989).
259. James J. Kilpatrick, "Too Many Tests!" *The Washington Post* (June 25, 1990).
260. U.S. Dept. of Education, *America 2000* newsletter (Sept. 30, 1991).
261. "A First Step Toward National School Reform," *The Washington Post* (Sept. 29, 1989).
262. "What Was Lost Behind Ivied Walls," *Insight* (May 7, 1990).
263. John Huey, "America's Hottest Export: Pop Culture," *Fortune* (Dec. 31, 1990).
264. Cited in Sue E. Berryman, *Education and the Economy: A Diagnostic Review and Implications for the Federal Role,* Occasional Paper No. 1 (New York: Institute on Education and the Economy, Columbia University, 1988).
265. "Ailing College Treats Student as Customer, and Soon Is Thriving," *The Wall Street Journal* (July 17, 1991).
266. Secretary's Commission on Achieving Necessary Skills, *What Work Requires of Schools* (Washington, D.C.: U.S. Dept. of Labor, 1991).
267. "Cheaters in Schools May Not Be Students, But Their Teachers," *The Wall Street Journal* (Nov. 2, 1989).
268. "School Tests Closely Match Material in Commercial Practice Kits, Booklets," *The Wall Street Journal* (Nov. 2, 1989).
269. See Richard Moll, *Playing the Private College Admissions Game* (New York: Times Books, 1979); Allan Nairn and Ralph Nader, *The Reign of ETS: The Corporation That Makes Up Minds* (Washington, D.C.: Public Citizen, 1980); Warner Slack and Douglas Porter, "The Scholastic Aptitude Test: A Critical Appraisal," *Harvard Education Review* (May 1980); David Owen, *None of the Above* (Boston: Houghton Mifflin, 1985); James Crouse and Dale Trusheim, *The Case Against the SAT* (Chicago: University of Chicago Press, 1988).
270. Gerald W. Bracey, "The $150 Million Redundancy," *Phi Delta Kappan* (May 1989).
271. Peter F. Drucker, "Japan: New Strategies for a New Reality," *The Wall Street Journal* (Oct. 2, 1991).
272. "A Video Game That Tells If Employees Are Fit for Work," *Business Week* (June 3, 1991).
273. "Products to Watch," *Fortune* (June 17, 1991).
274. This is the Hollywood version. In the book, the wizard restuffed the scarecrow's head with bran ("bran-new brains") and needles and pins ("for sharpness").
275. "Academy Panel Joins the Fray Over Job Testing," *Science* (June 2, 1989).
276. "Academy Panel Joins the Fray Over Job Testing," *Science* (June 2, 1989).
277. Dinesh D'Souza, "Scoring America," *The Washington Post* (Aug. 25, 1991).
278. James J. Kilpatrick, "Civil Rights: Pass the Danforth Bill," *The Washington Post* (Aug. 13, 1991).

NOTES

279. G. A. Keyworth II and Bruce Abell, *Competitiveness & Telecommunications* (Indianapolis: Hudson Institute, 1990).
280. "The Baby Bells Learn a Nasty New Word: Competition," *Business Week* (Mar. 25, 1991).
281. "AT&T Seeks Pocket Phone Test Clearance," *The Wall Street Journal* (June 25, 1991).
282. "Private Education Firms Discovering a Lucrative Market in Public Schools," *Education Week* (June 7, 1989).
283. "Business Bulletin," *The Wall Street Journal* (Sept. 5, 1991).
284. "Reading the Market," *The Washington Post* (Feb. 3, 1992).
285. "Companies Team Up to Improve Quality of Their Employees' Child-Care Choices," *The Wall Street Journal* (Oct. 17, 1991).
286. "The Green in the Little Red Schoolhouse," *Business Week* (Oct. 14, 1991).
287. William Tucker, "Foot in the Door," *Forbes* (Feb. 3, 1992).
288. "A New Era of MECC Begins," *Ed Tech News,* Office of Educational Technology, Florida Dept. of Education (Jan.-Feb.-Mar. 1991).
289. "Low Marks for Channel One," *The Washington Post* (May 1, 1992).
290. See "The Global Rush to Privatize," special report, *Business Week* (Oct. 21, 1991).
291. See Jeremy Main, "When Public Services Go Private," *Fortune* (May 27, 1985).
292. "Factory's Downfall Symbolizes Problems of Polish Reforms," *The Washington Post* (Aug. 5, 1991).
293. David Lipton and Jeffrey Sachs, "Privatization in Eastern Europe: The Case of Poland," *Brookings Papers on Economic Activity,* no. 2 (1990).
294. "Toyota Expands Its U.S. Facilities for Research Work," *The Wall Street Journal* (June 3, 1991).
295. "The Brakes Go On in R&D," *Business Week* (July 1, 1991).
296. "When Medical High Tech Isn't Necessarily Better," *The Washington Post* (Oct 29, 1991).
297. Jessica Mathews, "Labs in Limbo," *The Washington Post* (Sept. 27, 1991).
298. "U.S. Funding of Small Firms' Research Yields Results," *The Wall Street Journal* (Oct. 2, 1991).
299. "Back-Yard Investing Yields Big Losses, Roils Kansas Pension System," *The Wall Street Journal* (Aug. 21, 1991).
300. "Britain Picks Wrong Way to Beat Japanese," *Science* (May 31, 1991).
301. Nan Stone, "Does Business Have Any Business in Education?" *Harvard Business Review* (Mar.-Apr. 1991).
302. See Jack E. Bowsher, *Educating America: Lessons Learned in the Nation's Corporations* (New York: John Wiley & Sons, 1989).
303. "Schooling Kids at Home," *Time* (Oct. 22, 1990).
304. James Fallows, *More Like Us: An American Plan for American Recovery* (Boston: Houghton Mifflin, 1989).
305. The French term *télématique* usefully represents the fusion of the technologies of telecommunications and computing.
306. European Round Table of Industrialists, *Education and European Competence* (Brussels: 1989).

INDEX

• • •

INDEX

INDEX

INDEX